MW00581960

DESERT KINGDOMS TO GLOBAL POWERS

This book has been donated by the
Lionel Gelber Foundation in partnership with the
Munk School of Global Affairs, University of
Toronto and **Foreign Policy Magazine**
committed to broadening awareness of the importance
of foreign affairs in our lives
2017

DESERT KINGDOMS TO GLOBAL POWERS

THE RISE OF THE ARAB GULF

RORY MILLER

YALE UNIVERSITY PRESS
NEW HAVEN AND LONDON

For information about this and other Yale University Press publications, please contact:
U.S. Office: sales.press@yale.edu yalebooks.com
Europe Office: sales@yaleup.co.uk yalebooks.co.uk

Typeset in Adobe Caslon Pro by IDSUK (DataConnection) Ltd
Printed in Great Britain by Gomer Press Ltd, Llandysul, Ceredigion, Wales

Library of Congress Cataloging-in-Publication Data

Names: Miller, Rory, 1971- author.
Title: Desert kingdoms to global powers : the rise of the Arab Gulf / Rory Miller.
Description: New Haven : Yale University Press, 2016. | Includes bibliographical references and index.
Identifiers: LCCN 2016024734 | ISBN 9780300192346 (c1 : alk. paper)
Subjects: LCSH: Persian Gulf Region—Economic conditions. | Persian Gulf Region—Politics and government. | Persian Gulf Region—Foreign relations.
Classification: LCC HC415.3 .M55 2016 | DDC 330.9536—dc23
LC record available at https://lccn.loc.gov/2016024734

A catalogue record for this book is available from the British Library.

10 9 8 7 6 5 4 3 2 1

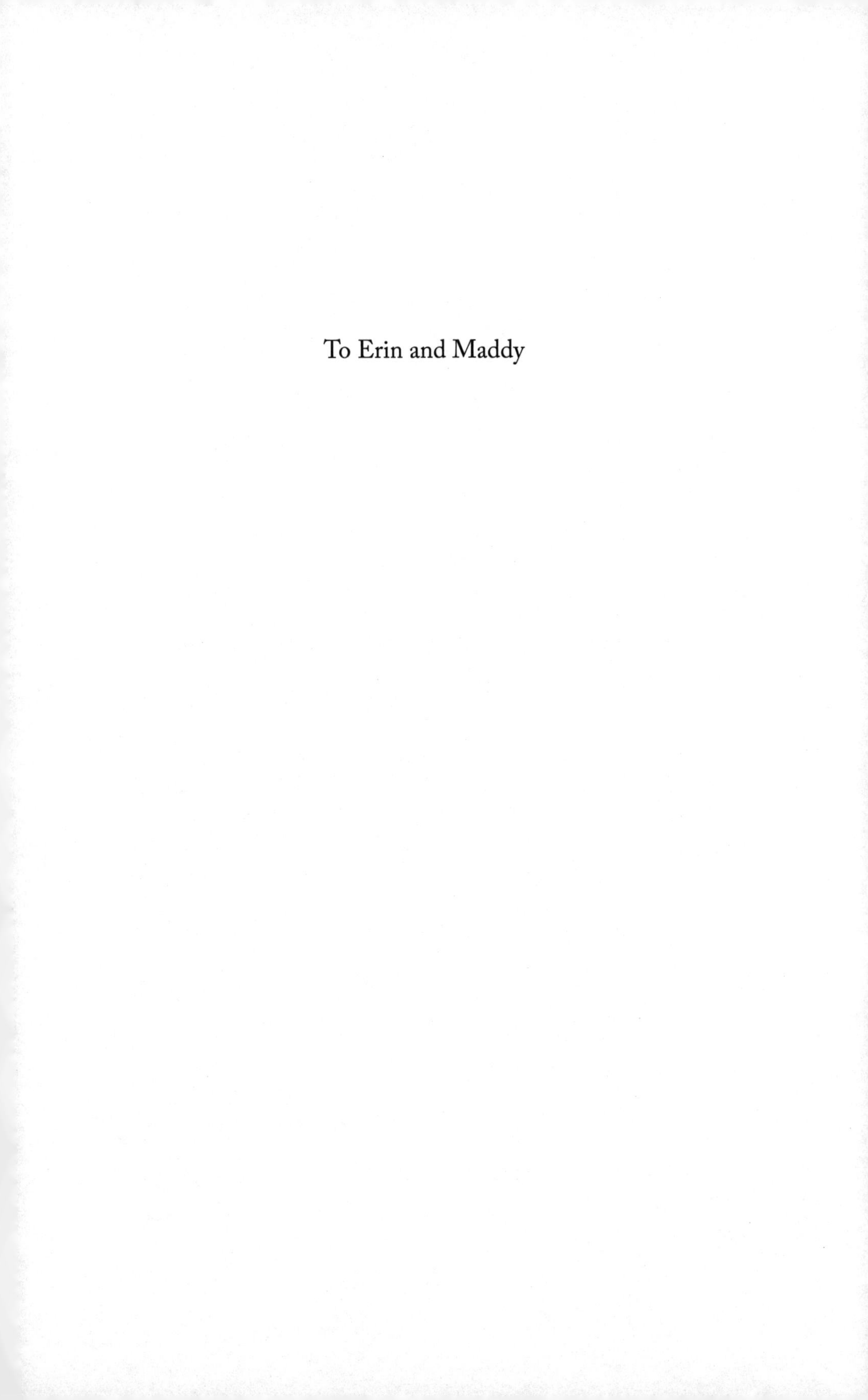

To Erin and Maddy

CONTENTS

ACKNOWLEDGEMENTS

The initial idea for this book was born out of conversations I had in 2012 with Phoebe Clapham, then a commissioning editor at Yale University Press, who had attended a talk I gave at the LSE a few months earlier on contemporary security challenges in the Arab Gulf. We believed that it could translate into a reader-friendly book on the region, aimed at a non-academic audience. In the years since then, I have been well served by my editors at Yale – Rachael Lonsdale, Heather McCallum and Melissa Bond. All have offered guidance, demonstrated great patience and, above all, been generous with their support and enthusiasm for this project throughout the entire process. I would also like to thank the various anonymous reviewers who provided feedback on the initial book proposal and on the final draft of the manuscript. The book has benefited greatly from their expert advice and recommendations.

Over the course of the project, the following former and current students have provided invaluable research assistance: Guiditta Fontana, Sarah Cardaun, Jihane Benamar, Yasmeen Hamad and Kareem Malas. I would also like to thank Rofaida Azzam, Haya Al-Romaihi and Jaber Al-Thani for their thoughts and feedback on many of the issues discussed here. My Georgetown colleagues Dan Stoll and Sonia Alonso gave detailed and invaluable comments on large parts of the manuscript. I'd also like to acknowledge the ongoing support of my colleagues and friends in academia in Doha, London and Dublin: especially Sohaira Siddiqui, Michael Kerr, Simon Waldman, Clive Jones, Amnon Aran, Eunan O'Halpin and Michael Kennedy.

On a personal note, Gus Nichols was kind enough to read some early chapters, and Alan Shaw has been a constant source of support over the last few years. I would also like to thank Dermot Brosnan, Jonny Orr, Stuart Fox, Andy McConnell, Richard Knatchbull, Rizwan Rahman, Mateen Qureshi, Mahveen Azzam, Louise O'Toole, Simon Meldrum, Jason Stuart and Cedric Heather for their continued friendship. I was an absentee friend while I worked on this book, but having them all there for me was always appreciated. My mother, Marion, my siblings, Lisa, Daniel and Emma, and their families have, as always, been hugely supportive. Finally, my wife, Michelle, and my daughters, Erin Ruby and Madeleine Rose, have had to endure me working on this project mornings, nights, weekends and holidays for much of the past few years. For that and for everything else, I am immensely grateful to all three. This book is for them.

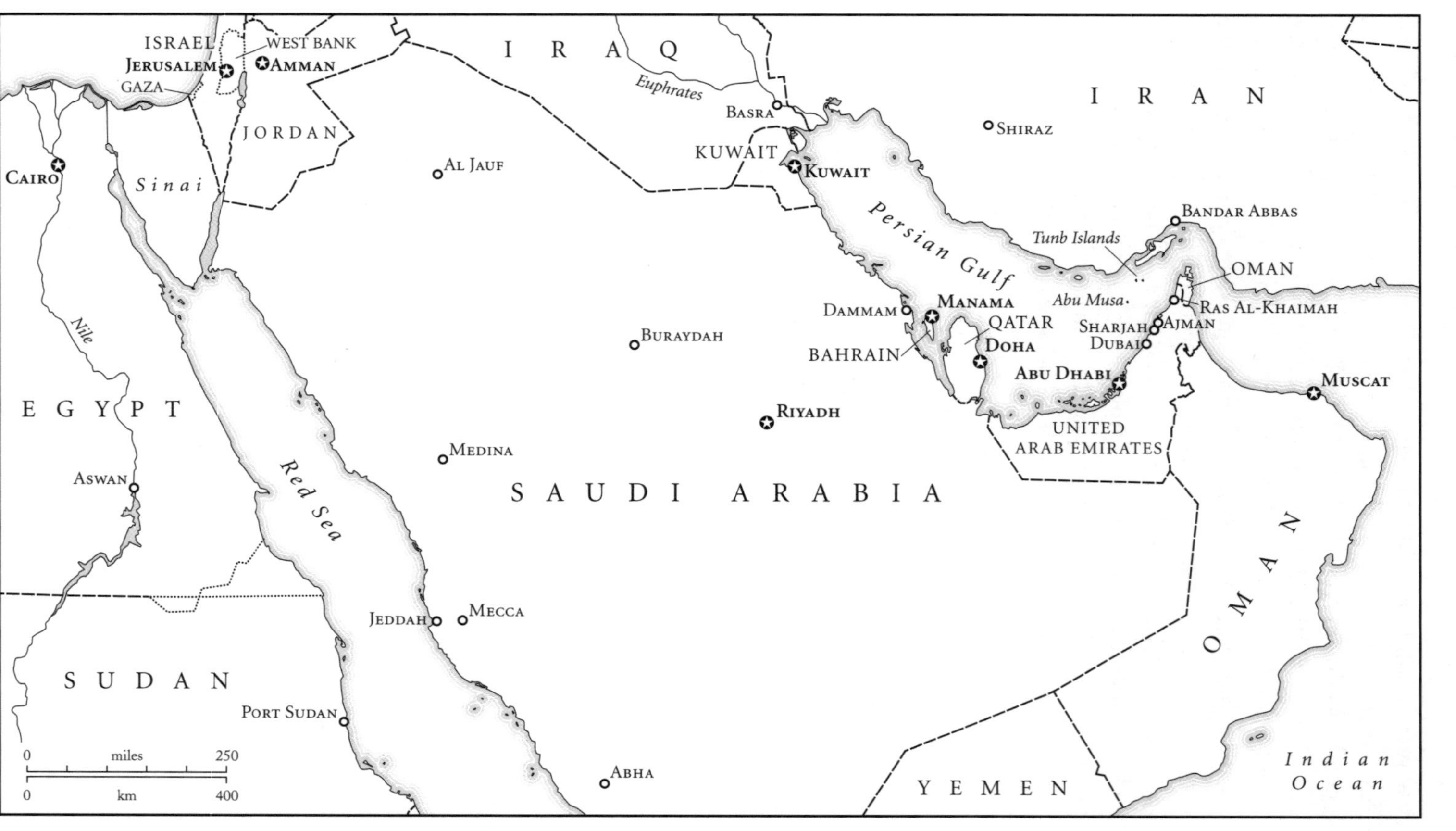

Map of the Arab Gulf States

INTRODUCTION

PARADISE FOUND

'Life isn't about finding yourself. Life is about creating yourself.'
– George Bernard Shaw

Money can't buy you love. But if you are an underdeveloped desert kingdom in a dangerous neighbourhood trying to catch up with the modern world and determined to protect your oil wells and gas fields you don't need love. You need stability at home and influence abroad. This book tells the remarkable story of how the oil- and gas-rich states of the Arab Gulf have found both, and how they have worked to hold on to them over the last four decades. It is not intended for the specialist reader. It is intended for those interested in history, politics and current affairs in general and the rise of this vibrant and turbulent region in particular.

The term Arab Gulf is common shorthand for the Persian Gulf and Arabian Peninsula when referring to the six Sunni Muslim Arab monarchies of Saudi Arabia, Oman, the United Arab Emirates (UAE), Qatar, Bahrain and Kuwait. Together they make up six of the region's eight countries, half of its entire territory, all of its western littoral and two-thirds of its northern area.[1] Long before any of these territories were nation states or important actors on the regional or world stage, travellers, writers, missionaries, diplomats and adventurers were enthralled by what the English poet Walter de la Mare fittingly described on the eve of the Great War as the 'spell of Arabia'. This long-time fascination with the history, natural beauty and people of the Arab Gulf remains as strong as ever today. On top of this, since their transition from 'pearls to petroleum, poverty to prosperity'[2] in the second half of the twentieth century, the time when this book begins, the Arab Gulf States have become increasingly important players in the regional and global economy. They are bustling centres of international commerce and finance and they aspire to turn their home region into a global hub between East and West. Nowhere in the world, except parts of coastal China, has undergone such a remarkable socio-economic transformation in recent years. All this makes the Arab Gulf a critical part of the global economy. Ambitious rulers have attempted to capitalize on this through extravagant marketing, advertising and sponsorship campaigns to build up their national brands and consolidate and extend their countries' standing at the heart of the globalized world. High-profile overseas purchases, the hosting of major international sporting events and massive investment in cutting-edge tourism, transport and cultural industries have similarly served to generate unprecedented interest in the region.

There are other explanations for the world's current preoccupation with the Arab Gulf. Simply put, what happens in the region matters and the stakes are high. The territories that this book deals with only cover about 4,000 kilometres in distance from the Shatt- Al-Arab inlet to the furthest tip of Oman. Yet they are home to more than half of the world's oil reserves and over a third of its natural gas. With the exception of Saudi Arabia, which was formed in 1932, and Kuwait, which gained its independence in 1961, all the Arab Gulf States achieved independence and entered the United Nations in the last few months of 1971. Since then they have been sovereign states responsible, ostensibly at least, for their own security. Despite spending hundreds of billions of dollars on arms in the ensuing years they have never been traditional military powers. They can't claim many successes in defending their territories from attack. They don't have much experience in fighting their foes outside of their borders.

Nonetheless, the petro-dollar revolution in international affairs that followed the Arab–Israeli war of 1973 redrew the power map of the Middle East. Suddenly, Gulf rulers controlled previously unimaginable riches and for the first time the world thought of oil, and with it the oil-producing states, in terms of political influence. As *The Economist* noted, this provided the Arab Gulf with a 'power almost unique in history'.[3]

Rule Britannia

Power in its most fundamental form is measured by the ability to influence outcomes and to provide institutional leadership. It also means being able to get others to act the way you want them to and to get them to take your interests into account before they act. It is fair to say that over the course of the last 100 years most Middle Eastern states have failed to acquire these types of power. All too often what has happened in the region has been defined by external interference and the economic and political dependence that comes with it. Historically, this was certainly the case for the smaller Arab Gulf States, though much less so for Saudi Arabia for reasons addressed later in this book. In 1798 the Sultan of Muscat signed a treaty with British officials. This marked the beginning of an informal British empire in the Arab Gulf that lasted from the 1820s until the beginning of the 1970s.

The British had three interconnected reasons for entering the region – to stamp out piracy and the slave trade, to keep out imperial rivals like the Ottomans and the French, and to protect vital trade routes and commercial interests. This final objective was of particular importance prior to the opening of the Suez Canal in 1869. Until then the waters of the Gulf played a key role in the communications lines to India, the jewel in the imperial crown. All this was achieved through a series of treaties with local rulers enforced by Royal Navy warships. Indeed, eight of the smaller Sheikhdoms in the south-east of the Gulf, including the six who would later come together to form the UAE, were known as the Trucial States in recognition of the treaties they signed with the British. These agreements gave the British the legal right to take charge of the foreign and defence policies of the Gulf Sheikhdoms. Initially, the famed East India Company, which controlled the profitable trade routes between India and Persia, was responsible for the formulation of Britain's Gulf policy and oversaw the earliest treaties in its role as Crown agent in the region. From the late 1850s onwards, the British administration in India took over, relying on political agents on the ground in Qatar, Bahrain, Dubai and Abu Dhabi to ensure that British interests were protected and that relations with the region's rulers ran smoothly.

In return for their deference on all matters of war and foreign policy, local leaders gained a British commitment to uphold their rule and where necessary, as in the case of the tiny Trucial States, provide military backing to help them deter all and any internal and external challenges to their rule. During the pre-oil era that lasted until the middle years of the twentieth century in Kuwait, Bahrain and Saudi Arabia and a decade later in Qatar and the Trucial Kingdoms, local rulers loyal to the Crown received rents in return for allowing British commercial and military interests use of their territories. These monies went directly to the ruler and played a very important role in consolidating power in the hands of specific individuals and their immediate families over future generations.

One can also see British influence in the way that rulers across the region chose to spend their rental revenues. Those under British protection and tutelage were more inclined to divide revenues up between major stakeholders in society. In Bahrain, for example, from the time the local Sheikh signed his first treaty with the British in 1820, he received roughly one-third of revenues, a third was paid out in government expenses and a final third was put aside for future needs. In Qatar, where the Sheikh of the Al-Thani tribe signed a treaty with the British in 1916, this policy had its own name, 'the rule of the four quarters', as revenues were divided four ways between the ruler, the large and growing Al-Thani family, savings and the rest of the population.[4] In contrast, in Saudi Arabia, where the British had much less influence and no direct say on spending policies, every single dollar went to the ruler, who had the absolute freedom to spend it any way he chose. For many, this total lack of accountability explains why Saudi Arabia still needed to borrow money during the 1960s even though revenues increased thirtyfold between 1955 and 1965.

In theory at least, and subject to 'constant advice and encouragement'[5] provided by their British interlocutors, local rulers possessed full autonomy in the areas of legislative, executive and judicial power, except where a matter was deemed by British officials to cross over into the realm of international relations. They were also free to determine their own matters of succession inside the ruling family, though it was customary for the British government to announce its recognition of the chosen candidate at an official ceremony during which the new ruler officially declared his willingness to honour treaties with and past commitments to the British.[6] In sum, the Arab Gulf was never colonized or ruled under a mandate like many British possessions in the Middle East and Africa. But the region was under de facto British control and the region's leaders cooperated closely on all matters of state with the East India Company, the India Office and, finally, from the middle of the twentieth century onwards, the Foreign Office.

End of the Affair

The 'policy of protectorates'[7] at the heart of the British informal empire helps us understand the evolving power structures in the Arab Gulf during more recent times. It also makes it impossible to ignore the colonial legacy in the region when thinking about power structures and relationships. At the same time, one cannot explain the evolution of the Arab Gulf, or any other part of the Arab world for that matter, only or even primarily in terms of outside British influence, malign or otherwise. Instead, as this book will show time and again, local suspicions, intense political rivalries, conflicting ideologies and opposing interests and ambitions have conspired to keep the region divided, unstable and weak. By the beginning of the 1960s, British governments no longer had the money, the political will or the popular support at home to continue to provide security and play a leading political role in the eleven Sheikhdoms of the Arab Gulf. The dissolution of the British protectorate of Kuwait in 1961 was an early indication of the future downward direction of British influence in the region.

Over the previous two decades the British had been worn down by rising anti-colonial nationalist sentiment, which had turned the British Empire into public enemy number one across the Arab and Muslim Middle East. One by one it had lost or abandoned its dominant influence or control in Palestine, Jordan, Iran, Iraq and Egypt. In these terms, it was hardly surprising that in January 1968 the British Labour government announced that it would withdraw all its forces from the Gulf by the end of 1971. At home the response to this decision to depart the region after 150 years was resignation. In the United States it had been expected, though that didn't stop US secretary of state Dean Rusk from deriding the move as the action of 'Little England' and reprimanding his British counterpart, foreign minister George Brown, 'For God's sake be British.'[8] Preoccupied as they were with regional security, Arab Gulf leaders had little desire to see the British pack up and leave. Bahrain's king harked back to the heyday of the empire and lamented how 'Britain could do with another Winston Churchill'.[9] Dubai's ruler, Sheikh Rashid bin Said Al-Maktoum, spoke for many at the time. 'The whole coast, people and rulers', admitted this influential figure, 'would all support the retaining of British forces in the Gulf even though ... they may not give a direct answer out of respect for the general Arab view'.[10] Though the ruling families of Saudi Arabia and Kuwait dissented, those of Bahrain, Qatar, Dubai and Abu Dhabi tried to convince British officials to stay by offering to meet the costs of remaining British troops. The Labour government had no intention of changing its mind and rejected the proposal out of hand, indignantly declaring that it was not in the 'white slaver' business.[11]

From Tribes to States

The tribal nature of Gulf society and its interaction with state formation has been a defining feature of the Gulf region over the last fifty years. Functioning states in the modern world share a number of common characteristics – a specific territory, legal authority, an effective financial system and a monopoly on legitimate violence. Beyond this, states are unique and are shaped by their individual circumstances as well as their formative experiences. In the case of the Gulf, the tribe has always played a crucial role in determining social, economic and political interactions. Even during the era of British rule, the concept of a nation state was largely irrelevant in a region where tribes had always spread out across what are today's national borders, and where families were, and continue to be, split between Saudi Arabia, Kuwait, Bahrain, the UAE and Qatar. Instead, tribalism was at the heart of society and characterized local identities. It also provided legitimacy for the local ruler, whose source of power traditionally came from his relationship with powerful tribes, as well as other factions within his own tribe. In the case of Saudi Arabia, the religious establishment was also crucial. In Kuwait it was the leading merchant families. In Qatar it was important families in the villages around Doha, who in the early 1960s led a strike in protest against the ruling family's monopoly on resources. Apart from these key constituencies, lesser groups including artisans, functionaries, smaller merchants, traders and fishermen received protection and rewards for their loyalty to the ruler.

This situation had little in common with the relationship between the citizen and the state in Western democracies, where legitimacy derives from the consent of the ruled. In the 1960s and 1970s, as rulers attempted to integrate the tribes into rapidly modernizing oil-rich states and as the idea of a nation state gained ground, the tribal structure was eroded somewhat. This evolving situation led many to argue that the rise of the oil-rich sovereign state resulted in the demise of the power of the tribe. Others have made the opposite claim, making the point that the historic unfamiliarity with the concept of the nation state made it impossible for the Gulf States to evolve into fully capable political entities in more recent times.

There is a third alternative. In her recent entertaining and informative work *Tribal Modern*,[12] Miriam Cooke addresses the question of modernity, nationalism and state in the contemporary Gulf. In it she shows how the state has consolidated its pivotal position in Gulf society in recent decades as its power has increased in all areas. Though this has led Gulf rulers to co-opt tribal legitimacy and nationalize tribal identity, it has also seen them emphasize the importance of the tribe as part of their ongoing quest for legitimacy through state-sponsored nationalism. In these terms, Cooke rejects claims that the modern Gulf State, with its ideas of sovereignty and nationalism, is on a collision course with the tribal structures that long underpinned society. They are, she believes, just as likely to complement each other as to clash. In defence of her thesis, she points to the evolution of national and cultural brands across the Gulf deeply rooted in the tribal past. As the logo of the Qatar Tourism Authority announces to travellers in the departures terminal of the new airport in Doha, the kingdom is 'timelessly traditional, distinctly modern'.

The 'Smallness' of Small States

Growing up in Ireland – a small, neutral island on the margins of Europe – I have always been fascinated by the role of small states in international affairs and well aware of the limits of small state influence beyond their shores. One of the aims of this book is to tell the story of the Arab Gulf in a way that takes into account the 'smallness' of its small states. In the decades after the Second World War, size played an important part in determining attitudes over whether a territorial unit was fit for statehood. So did military power and population size. There was a consensus in the literature for a long time that unless a country had more than ten million people, over 1 per cent of the world's total GNP, a large territory and a sizeable military capability it was small regardless of what other attributes it had or roles it played.

When Qatar, Oman, Bahrain and the UAE gained statehood at the beginning of the 1970s they were some of the smallest of the world's small states. Between them they could only claim a combined population of just over one million and no towns or cities with more than 15,000 people living in them. These new nations were so small that their entry into the United Nations engendered a passionate debate over whether the international organization would have more credibility if it refused entry to such tiny entities. As secretary general U Thant remarked, these 'micro-states' had raised a problem that was 'likely to become more acute in the years to come'.[13] Today, such concerns are no longer relevant. The great majority of the world's 200-plus legally sovereign states are small. This has required a major reassessment of what does and does not constitute a small state and, more importantly, what a small state can and cannot do.

In the decades covered in this book, the Arab Gulf States have consistently been at the forefront of challenging long-held notions of how small states use diplomacy to consolidate stability at home and influence abroad. Most notably, they have used their wealth and the political capital that comes with it to intervene diplomatically across the Arab and Muslim worlds. Such 'riyal politik',[14] as one leading regional expert has described it, has enabled them to become champions of conflict resolution in Yemen, Palestine and Lebanon and in the Western Sahara, Ethiopia and Darfur. On a regional level these interventions have been central to the Arab Gulf's rising power over recent decades. So has the capacity of the Arab Gulf

States to manipulate larger powers in order to protect and promote their own interests and to consolidate their external influence.

At the centre of the Arab Gulf sits Saudi Arabia. It has the largest population, economy and army, its longest involvement in international affairs, most of its oil and its most conservative rulers. Unlike its neighbours the kingdom, in territorial terms at least, has never been small. It is a massive country, the fourteenth largest in the world in terms of landmass, almost four times bigger than France, six times bigger than Japan and seven times larger than the next biggest Arab Gulf State, Oman. Though dwarfed by Saudi Arabia, Oman is still larger in size than Kuwait, Qatar, Bahrain and the UAE combined, a fact that goes some way to underscoring just how small those states are both in absolute terms and in comparison with the kingdom of Saudi Arabia.

So it's no surprise that over the years Saudi Arabia has been viewed with wariness and distrust by the rest of the Arab Gulf. In recent years, gas-rich Qatar has looked to knock Saudi Arabia from its perch atop Middle East diplomacy. The UAE has looked to do the same in the areas of trade and finance. Oman, for its part, has rejected repeated Saudi calls for political, economic or military union. Mutual tensions and differences in vision aside, all agree with the Saudi view that 'there is no life without stability',[15] as the kingdom's defence minister Sultan bin Abdulaziz put it many years ago. More recently, in 2004, Hamad bin Jassim Al-Thani, Qatar's then prime minister and foreign minister, made much the same point. 'Stability', explained one of the new millennium's most influential, high-profile and go-getting figures, 'is the basis for development and growth of our society and is the most strategic challenge facing the area.'[16]

Cooperation in Adversity

The scholarly definition of a region is a geographic unit made up of an interdependent cluster of states or territories that share a common space. In the Middle East, one can trace some form of informal order along these lines back to Ottoman times when almost the entire region except modern-day Iran were Turkish possessions and part of the largest land empire in history. After the demise of the Ottoman Empire in the early 1920s, those Arab states, colonies and mandates left behind struggled to promote cooperation on a regional level. In the wake of the ravages of the Second World War, regional groupings were established in many parts of the world including the Middle East, where seven former Arab possessions of the Ottoman Empire came together to establish the Arab League in

1945. Since then the idea of unity has played an important rhetorical function for an organization that can now boast twenty-two states and territories as members. Despite its growth over the years and its impressive achievements in some areas, the Arab League has always had a poor track record promoting cooperation on a regional level. The organization has been held back by a lack of community and cohesion, as well as persistent rivalries among members, not to mention the contested nature of the regional order and the oft-malign influence of external powers on inter-Arab politics. In short, Arab unity has been an elusive goal for the Arab League and on some levels it has even served to institutionalize divisions between Arab states rather than heal them.

In 1981 the Arab Gulf States, all members of the Arab League, came together at the sub-regional level to form the Gulf Cooperation Council (GCC). The initial hope was that this move would provide security in the wake of the recent revolution in Iran and at the start of a bitter war between Iran and Iraq that would ultimately go on for eight brutal and destructive years. From the outset the leaders of all six Arab Gulf countries of the GCC were full of optimism over the future prospects of this new body. Bahrain's king refitted the Sheraton Hotel in his capital to include a number of luxurious self-contained suites in oriental décor where he could accommodate and entertain his fellow GCC rulers in style. He hailed the GCC as 'a shining star in the sky of our region', as well as a river that would 'irrigate the path of the future where it meets with the streams of good and aspires to the coasts of glory'.[17] Other Gulf leaders made the same point in a more sober manner. 'We are thinking together, we are talking together, we are planning together, and we are seeing things together instead of individually,'[18] announced Qaboos bin Said Al-Said, the charismatic Sultan of Oman, who was only in his twenties when he took power in a bloodless British-backed coup against his father in 1970. Crown Prince Abdullah of Saudi Arabia came of age in a completely different time. Born in the 1920s, he was a son of Abdul Aziz Ibn Saud, the founder of modern Saudi Arabia. Abdullah had never even visited any other Gulf nation before the birth of the GCC. That didn't stop him from welcoming the new alliance as a 'great' idea that would have 'far reaching effects'.[19] His king and half-brother, Fahd, was just as positive. He hailed the GCC as the best example yet of regional cooperation and predicted that it would become a model for future cooperation in the Arab world.[20]

The establishment of the GCC was undoubtedly a monumental step towards regional integration. Yet, like the Arab League and all other regional blocs, including the European Union, its members have repeatedly grappled with the need to cede national sovereignty in order to achieve deeper regional integration. From the time of the GCC's launch, the one thing that has bound its members together despite this reluctance to give up independence for the benefit of all, is a shared belief that they are vulnerable to external actors who view them as rich and militarily weak states easily bullied, blackmailed or manipulated. This has engendered a deeply held belief among Gulf rulers that the safety of their kingdoms is more likely to be achieved by working together than by acting apart. For that reason the GCC has always been first and foremost a regional security grouping in which the main, if not the overriding, driver for cooperation is the never-ending pursuit of security in a volatile region. As this book will demonstrate, this explains why, at crucial moments, when their sovereignty has been threatened or the region has looked to be on the verge of the abyss the GCC states have closed ranks, put their grievances and national ambitions on hold, and chiselled out a united response in the political, economic and military realms. This was evident in the wake of the Iranian revolution in 1979 and during the Iran–Iraq war between 1980 and 1988. It was further underscored by the Arab Gulf's response to the Iraqi invasion of Kuwait in 1990 and by its prioritization of cooperation following the attacks on New York and Washington on 11 September 2001.

This preference for cooperation over confrontation at times of intense pressure was also very apparent following America's invasion of Iraq in 2003 and during the crucial months of the Arab Spring in the first half of 2011. As much of the region descended into chaos at that time, the Arab Gulf States kept their cool, cemented their status as the key Arab powerbrokers in a period of flux and quickly developed into a military and political force in defence of the regional status quo. Since then, they have had to deal with the fallout from instability in Egypt in the post-Mubarak era, the threat of a nuclear-capable Iran with hegemonic ambitions, a post-war Iraq divided on sectarian lines, as well as civil wars in Syria and Yemen and an Islamic State threat that knows no borders. All these and other security concerns not only preoccupy the Arab Gulf but also top the security agenda of the international community, ensuring that the region remains at the centre of the global security system well into the twenty-first century.

Despite sharing many of the same security challenges the Arab Gulf States do not always share the same national interests or priorities in foreign affairs. Like the member states of the European Union, they regularly compete against each other. They have also engaged in numerous squabbles and political stand-offs over oil, borders, Iran, Israel and much else besides. On occasion, tensions have led to clashes and the loss of life. In fact, for such diplomatic trailblazers they have been pretty poor in settling, if not defusing, their own intra-Gulf disputes, particularly on matters of territorial rights. This has cast a long shadow over relations across the Gulf. In particular, it has hampered the development of the bonds needed for the GCC member states to trust each other fully with their own strategic security. On the other hand, according to the scholarly literature, bordering states that harbour some kind of territorial dispute are forty times more likely than other countries to be involved in war. By that measure alone the Gulf States have done a remarkable job in never having militarized their differences with each other beyond localized and irregular clashes.

One explanation as to why such major differences have never boiled over into all-out conflict is that all the Arab Gulf States share much more than a belief in the benefits of collective security. They also share the same language, religion and monarchical political structures, as well as similar identities, customs and values and, to varying degrees, the same source of revenue – oil.

Little Big Spenders

Oil is a key consideration in social, political and economic structures in the Gulf. The Arab Gulf States are central players in the global financial system and world economy because of oil. Oil wealth enabled them to navigate the recent credit crunch and global financial and economic crises better than any other regional grouping. Their sovereign wealth funds (SWFs), state-owned investment vehicles, played a key role in responding to those same crises. In the process, they created what has been aptly termed an 'aristocracy of liquidity', whose influence stretches across the world. In the West, these funds, many only founded in the early 2000s, have taken substantial stakes in big-name companies, top financial institutions and luxury brands through high-profile purchases. They have bought up some of the world's prime real estate and have financed the construction of some of the most noted new buildings. In the process the city skylines of some of the world's great cities are increasingly coming to be defined by the iconic, innovative reminders of the Gulf's presence and influence.

Throughout the Middle East and in key emerging markets like China and India, the GCC states are now also leading investors in tourism, finance, energy, construction and agriculture, playing a key role in shaping urban and rural landscapes for decades to come. The decision by Saudi Arabia's King Abdullah to make his first ever state visits outside the Middle East to China and India in 2006 highlighted this evolving axis of power. So did the launch of the China–GCC Strategic Dialogue in 2010. What is true for China is also true for India. Speaking recently, the country's foreign minister was categorical. The Gulf region, explained Sushma Swaraj, is 'pivotal to our national development goals and ... crucial to our national interests in myriad ways'.[21]

The Gulf's capacity to spend hundreds of billions of dollars of oil and gas revenues at home and abroad on cutting-edge projects and high-profile assets should not obscure the fact that though the Gulf States are rich, they are small rich. In the early 2000s, for example, after almost two decades of low oil prices, Americans spent the same on tobacco in a year as Saudi Arabia received in oil revenues. To take another example, Washington spent US$89 billion in Iraq in its first full year occupying the country in 2004. The same year Kuwait's annual GDP was about half that at US$45 billion. To use another, more recent example, in the middle of 2015, it was announced that Apple, America's biggest company measured by market capitalization, was worth more than Saudi Arabia's annual GDP. The point being that amid the newspaper stories of wealth, excess and grandeur one shouldn't forget that, oil and gas aside, in purely economic terms the Arab Gulf States have never been able to compete with the world's economic powerhouses. Even when one takes into account the region's unprecedented global spending spree over the last decade, the GCC states still only hold 1 per cent of the world's assets between them and still rank outside the top ten biggest economies when measured in terms of nominal GDP.

This has not stopped them from looking to lead the Arab world into new relationships with much bigger traditional and emerging powers including but not limited to China and India. Nor has it stopped outsiders from viewing them in the same way they view much larger emerging markets. 'The real economic action in the world', explained then British foreign secretary William Hague in 2010, 'has been taking place in Brazil and India and China and the Gulf States, and that is where ... we now have to connect ourselves much more strongly.'[22] Many, though not all, Gulf citizens share a sense of pride with their leaders over being compared to such major economies and they also support the vision of the region as a global trading and financial hub that brings together East and West. Apart from their excellent location, the Gulf economies are certainly well positioned to undertake this highly ambitious project. They are the most globalized nations in the Arab world. They export goods and services at twice the percentage of GDP as other Arab states. Their markets are far more open and they attract far more foreign investment than other Arab economies. Some now even estimate that by 2030 the combined GCC economies will be challenging for a place in the top five economic blocs in the world, members of an exclusive club of economic giants that currently includes the European Union, the United States, Japan and China.

Across the region ambitious rulers have looked to develop their kingdoms into popular holiday destinations that they hope will one day lure and dazzle the world's visitors. With this in mind they have invested heavily in urban spaces to turn them into attractive destinations for the more refined traveller. This 'instant urbanization',[23] as it has been called, has taken place alongside an aggressive campaign to attract major sporting and cultural events to their new cities. Qatar's success in being awarded the world's most popular sporting event, the FIFA Football World Cup, is the most obvious example of this. But not a week goes by without a major sporting event taking place in some part of the Gulf. The region is also home to branches of world-renowned museums and galleries like the Louvre and the Guggenheim. There are also several home-grown symphony orchestras, a thriving art and theatre scene, and thanks to the Sultan of Oman's love of music, Muscat now boasts one of the world's largest and most ornate opera houses.

The Arab Gulf is only home to 10 per cent of Arabs but Arabic is the fastest-growing language on the web, in no small part because Internet use in the GCC grew by more than 2,000 per cent between 2000 and 2012. The region's young are now three times more likely to be connected to the Internet than other Arabs and this has sped up the integration of the Gulf's young into global society. Saudi Arabia alone boasts more than ten million Internet users, more than one-third of the total population and up from only 500,000 a decade ago. The kingdom also has more Facebook users than all other Arab countries combined except much larger Egypt. Members include top royals who joined the site during the Arab Spring to demonstrate, somewhat feebly, their commitment to modernity. Saudi Arabia also has the highest number of YouTube views in the world per Internet user at ninety million per day and, along with the UAE, has more smartphones per capita than any other country in the world. The UAE is also only one of three less-developed status countries (the others are Israel and Slovenia) in the top twenty globally for broadband penetration.

Balancing Act

This leap into the technological age took place before the Gulf experienced the social and cultural evolution that usually accompanies this kind of progress. This has meant that modernization in the Arab Gulf and, in particular, the shift from tribal to urban society has taken place within the traditional confines of the tribal and monarchical order. In 1974, Mana Al-Otaiba, the UAE's energy minister during the first oil boom, summed up a concern that this engendered even then. 'I like to live in the desert, far from complication. We can try to keep our good traditions, but I can't promise we'll succeed.'[24] Almost half a century later, such sentiments are still commonly held by Gulf citizens and are a constant preoccupation for Gulf policymakers. This makes politics, as well as modernization, a complicated affair.

The same families have ruled continuously for generations. Even when there have been coups they have been bloodless intra-family affairs, and transition has been smooth. The socio-economic contract between ruler and ruled has allowed the state to maintain legitimacy without ceding political power to the people. With the exception of Bahrain, there have been surprisingly few protest movements and citizens have shown little appetite for revolution. GCC member states can boast an impressive record of internal stability at home. Crime rates are low and the standard of living is high. On average, Gulf citizens have incomes at least five times higher than those of their fellow Arabs. A recent study found that Kuwait had the fourth highest number of millionaires in the world as a proportion of population; Qatar and the UAE came fifth and sixth in the rankings.

The mid-1990s saw important progress on the political front. In 1997, in a speech before a packed auditorium of students, professors and Gulf watchers at Georgetown University in Washington, DC, the then emir of Qatar, who had come to power the previous year, was frank. 'Unrest', Hamad bin Khalifa Al-Thani told those assembled before him, was the result of 'a lack of democracy'. At the same time, he also justified a cautious approach to implementing full political reform on the grounds that his country was 'not yet ready', and because 'I want everything to go smoothly, and non-stop'.[25] Up to the mid-2000s political reform in GCC states was hardly smooth but it was gradual and consistent. There were municipal elections in Qatar and Saudi Arabia and elections to a national council in the UAE. Female suffrage was introduced in Kuwait and universal suffrage in Oman. Qatar launched a new constitution, Bahrain opened a new constitutional and bicameral assembly and the consultative assemblies of Saudi Arabia and Kuwait were enlarged.

Since then political reform has not simply ground to a halt; in many cases it has been reversed. During the Arab Spring, Gulf leaders rolled back some of the real political progress of the past. Censorship of anti-regime sentiment increased and in some cases this has been accompanied by the introduction of draconian laws. To ensure stability and prop up the status quo, during the Arab Spring citizens also received pay-offs, adding up to hundreds of billions of dollars in cash handouts, higher wages and better pensions. Yet the events of the Arab Spring underscored very clearly that buying loyalty and cracking down on free speech does not guarantee stability or regime survival in the longer term. To make things more complicated, the Internet-savvy young know what is happening in the rest of the world and see the lack of freedom and opportunity at home as a generational as well as a political issue. Nor do they only look at political participation in terms of voting rights or constitutional developments. No less important to this younger generation are practical reforms like freedom of the press, institutional transparency and human rights. None of these have been priorities for Gulf governments in recent years. Instead, they have preferred to cling to the status quo and let oil money do the talking.

Early on in his reign, Saudi Arabia's founder and one of the most successful rulers in the history of the Arab Gulf, Abdul Aziz ibn Saud, explained that his goal was 'modernization, not secularization'. Even now his words serve an important purpose in reminding us that Islam is central to Gulf Arab identity, and serves as a powerful force that overlaps with and regularly finds itself in conflict with the modern state system. In an interview published in the French paper *Le Monde* in 1979, Sheikh Zayed bin Sultan Al-Nahyan of Abu Dhabi, the visionary founder of the UAE, was clear: 'We have devoted everything and all our wealth to increasing the standard of living of our nation and to its progress and prosperity. If we felt for an instant that this was opposed to the teaching of our religion, we would not have done so.'[26] In the same year, Crown Prince Abdullah, a future Saudi king, made a similar point when he promised that money and oil would be 'utilized and directed by the Islamic spirit'.[27]

Saudi Arabia's ruling family has always worked on the assumption that religion plays a positive political role, not least in consolidating its own dominant position at the centre of Saudi society. For many believers, the king of Saudi Arabia is *Khadim Al-Haramayn*, guardian of the Holy Places, and leader of the world's Muslims. The Saudi city of Mecca is the 'mother of all cities'. It is the birthplace of the Prophet Mohammed and home to the most sacred shrine in Islam. Five times a day devout Muslims across the world turn in its direction to pray and every year millions flock there for the annual hajj pilgrimage. This places the Gulf region in general and Saudi Arabia in particular at the heart of Islam, giving the kingdom a global relevance in a world where religion remains a significant factor in all walks of life.

It is an enormous task to build a modern economic system in a society in which some citizens see their loyalty as owing more to religious or tribal structures than to the nation state. This explains why the efforts of home-grown religious conservatives to block social reform are often so successful. It also explains why leaders have looked to keep a lid on Islamists while they attempt, at the same time, to provide an effective and realistic forum for political participation that complements the Islamic make-up of society. This tension is often evident in everyday political life. In Kuwait, the emir has intervened in the past to stop the influential Islamist bloc in parliament from amending the penal code to allow the death penalty or life imprisonment for anyone who 'mocks God, the prophets and messengers'. On other occasions he has not, as in the case of the young Kuwaiti jailed in 2012 for allegedly posting blasphemous comments about the Prophet Mohammed on Twitter.

That said, it would be wrong to overestimate Islam's role in the everyday evolution of the contemporary Gulf. Across the region as a whole, in recent decades religion has not monopolized either economic or political debate to the exclusion of other considerations. Even in Saudi Arabia, often held up as a beacon of backwardness by GCC partners looking to highlight their own progressive credentials, religion has not stood in the way of modernization and international engagement.

Complex Contradictions

Gulf rulers face complex and at times contradictory challenges from stakeholders at home and key players abroad. At home they have to navigate a middle way between those who embrace globalization and 'Western values' as the price that must be paid to achieve sustainable development and those who fear that such progress is not worth the loss of local culture, religious identity and traditional values. As well as playing a delicate balancing game between these two opposing forces, the ruling class also has to find ways to accommodate the growing army of privileged but increasingly disaffected and frustrated youth. Half the region's population will soon be under fifteen years of age. In its most extreme form this is bringing about a real disconnect between rulers and ruled. In Saudi Arabia, a country where 60 per cent of the population is under twenty years of age, most top decision makers have been in their seventies or eighties. King Salman ascended to the throne in early 2015 at seventy-nine years of age amid rumours that he already suffered from dementia. In private, other GCC leaders joked that what the Saudis really need more than anything else is a retirement system.

It is true that Salman soon appointed the fifty-something Mohammed bin Nayef as crown prince and heir apparent and put the thirty-one-year-old Prince Mohammed bin Salman in charge of defence and the economy. It is also true that across the rest of the GCC the age of rulers is not so much the problem. Qatar's current emir was only thirty-three when he came to power in June 2013. Three years later he appointed a foreign minister who was also in his mid-thirties. Abu Dhabi's crown prince acceded to that position in his mid-forties. Yet, even those countries with younger leaders or leaders in waiting face similar challenges to Saudi Arabia in terms of dealing with the youth issue. The Arab Gulf's young people, male and female, are the most literate and best educated in the Arab world. Many are bright, ambitious, engaged, open minded. They are preoccupied with looking for ways to help their countries find new, more equitable, sustainable and inclusive ways to achieve socio-economic progress. There are, however, few opportunities for the young to demonstrate their talents outside of a bloated public sector. The private sector is tiny and foreigners take most of the white-collar and high-skilled jobs that are available. There are few financial incentives to take the plunge and join the fledgling entrepreneurial class by setting up your own business, while there is a social stigma attached to locals, even undereducated ones, taking jobs in the service industries or on building sites, despite high demand. A few years back, a Saudi twenty-something even made the front page of a local newspaper for becoming the first citizen to take a job as a waiter in a local hotel.

The massive infusion of oil wealth from the 1960s onwards and the ambitious attempts to rapidly modernize societies with only small pools of citizen labour explain the huge rise in the number of foreign workers entering the Gulf from the Arab and the non-Arab worlds in recent decades. Some of these arrivals provided the cheap labour needed to build and staff new airports, hotels, hospitals, schools, universities and communication networks. Others brought the skills needed to manage those institutions and networks once they were up and running.[28]

On average expatriates now account for between 80 and 90 per cent of local workforces and between 60 and 90 per cent of total populations. This has created a three-tiered society. Privileged, mostly Western, expats live beside local citizens who lead lives of privilege but have few opportunities or incentives to develop careers that interest them. Across town, but inhabiting a whole different planet, is an underclass of mostly south Asian workers doing the jobs nobody else wants. This has pushed the issues of migration, citizenship, identity and human rights to the top of the agenda. In the longer term this situation is economically unsustainable. It also reduces the opportunities for indigenous development and threatens the fabric of local culture and society. On top of this, Gulf leaders need to find a new role and place in society for women. Female GCC citizens are at least as well educated as men. They have higher literacy rates and make up a larger proportion of recent university graduates. Yet, they only make up around 10 per cent of the workforce. If the GCC is to meet the predictions of many and become a top-five trading bloc in the next decade, then it is vital for a well-educated female population to be fully integrated into the knowledge economy.

These are just some of the challenges that the Arab Gulf States currently face in building their nations. Outside their borders they also have to deal with and plan for profound changes in the energy market, as well as the ongoing turmoil caused by the crises in Syria, Iraq and Yemen, not to mention the threat posed by Iran, Islamic State and other increasingly influential non-state actors, all of whom have thrived in the post-Cold War and post-9/11 environment. The Gulf region is also experiencing societal uncertainty as traditionalists and modernizers, conservatives and moderates battle to decide the basis of its engagement with the outside world. All this is being played out in the context of divisions among Arab Gulf States themselves over the economic and political direction of their region going forward as alignments and alliances shift between local and global powers, most notably Iran, Turkey, Israel and Egypt, China, Russia, Europe and the United States.

This book begins in the early 1970s at a time when the long-time British role in the Arab Gulf had just ended and the Royal Navy was no longer responsible for ensuring the survival of local leaders. Since then the Arab Gulf States have successfully moved beyond the subordinate status that had been the norm in the region for a century and a half. In the process, as I hope to show in this book, they have become increasingly influential in regional and international politics, economics and finance. They have very skilfully projected power in the service of their own interests when dealing with each other, the wider Arab world, and the local non-Arab powers and major global players, all mentioned above.

This book is in part about that journey. I started writing it while living and working in London. I completed it in Doha, Qatar, where I have lived and worked at the branch campus of Georgetown University's famed School of Foreign Service since 2014. Teaching international politics since then in the heart of the Arab Gulf to students from across the entire Middle East, as well Asia, Africa, Europe and North America, has given me a ringside seat to observe the complexities and contrasts in the Gulf region in the years since the Arab Spring. This has inspired me to try to understand how these former desert kingdoms, their leaders and their peoples have arrived at this point and to think about what their futures hold.

CHAPTER 1

OVER A BARREL

> 'I think the entire industrialized world faces a clear and present danger of economic destruction by the Arab oil cartel.'
>
> – Senator Henry 'Scoop' Jackson

Chatham House can claim an illustrious history. Located in St James's in the heart of London's West End, this listed building has been home to three British prime ministers. Since the 1920s it has housed London's most distinguished think tank, the Royal Institute of International Affairs, and can boast a long list of big-name speakers, from economist John Maynard Keynes to Indian patriot Mahatma Gandhi to Britain's very own Winston Churchill. None pulled a bigger crowd than the guest of honour on a windy and rain-swept mid-September day in 1974. The largest audience in the institute's fifty-year history piled into the main theatre and overflow space to hear one of the most recognizable public figures on the planet, Sheikh Ahmed Zaki Al-Yamani, Saudi Arabia's oil minister.

Yamani had been the face of Saudi oil for years. He had overseen the country's rise to become the world's number-one exporter and number-two producer of black gold. The world's press had devoted vast amounts of column space to the Harvard-educated Yamani's impeccable style, rhetorical brilliance and unrivalled negotiating tactics. The *New York Times* crowned him the 'mastermind of Arab oil strategy', going so far as to compare him to Talleyrand, Napoleon's influential diplomatic troubleshooter.[1] Henry Kissinger, Washington's key foreign policy player in these years, knew all about diplomacy in the age of Napoleon. Before becoming a legendary statesman himself he had written his PhD thesis on the subject. Perhaps this explains why he held a less romantic view of Yamani than most did. Kissinger acknowledged that the Saudi oil minister was charismatic, 'extraordinarily intelligent' and a first-class technical expert. But Kissinger was under no illusions as to Yamani's place in the pecking order of Saudi power politics. He would later recall that the oil minister was rarely invited to his own meetings with King Faisal. On the odd occasion that he did make an appearance, nobody sought his opinion. The sardonic Kissinger dryly noted that this was fortunate because Yamani was invariably seated so far away from the action that he would not have been heard even if he had spoken up.[2]

Yamani may have been a technocrat who served at the pleasure of his king, but he was an exceptional one. To outsiders this royal messenger was a powerful, as well as a flamboyant, functionary. His packed-out Chatham House audience of business, political and diplomatic leaders hung on his every word. They had, after all, come to hear him speak on the subject that had preoccupied the world's policymakers to the exclusion of almost all else for the previous year – the price and politics of oil. Less than one year earlier, on 6 October 1973, the armies of Syria and Egypt had launched a surprise attack on Israel on Yom Kippur, the holiest day of the Jewish calendar. Taken by surprise, Israel was at first unable to stop the Arab offensive. Facing what seemed to be a real threat to its survival only a quarter of a century after its birth, Israeli leaders looked for political and military support from the West. After some high-level debate and low-level bickering, the Nixon administration in Washington agreed to provide a massive arms airlift to Israel. Resupplied with American hardware, Israel regrouped, rolled back Arab advances and threatened total victory in one of the great counter-offensives in modern military history.

On 17 October 1973, eleven days into that eighteen-day war, the oil ministers of the seven Arab member states of OPEC, the oil-producing cartel,[3] made an unprecedented and monumental move. In the smoke-filled conference rooms of the Kuwait Sheraton Hotel, Yamani along with his counterparts from Kuwait, Iraq, Abu Dhabi, Qatar, Libya and Algeria launched the oil weapon against the West. The goal was simple: force an oil-deprived world to compel Israel to withdraw from occupied Arab territories and to restore Palestinian rights. The decision to use the oil weapon demonstrated an impressive display of Arab unity few expected or even thought possible. In 1960, the year of OPEC's birth, US president Dwight D. Eisenhower spoke for many when he dismissed the capacity of oil producers to mount a united front. 'Anyone could break up the Organization', the soldier turned statesman told a meeting of the US National Security Council, 'by offering five cents more per barrel for the oil.' As late as 1971, a US National Intelligence Estimate was no less certain. 'We do not believe', it advised, 'that cooperation among the producing states would soon reach a point where they would consent to withhold oil for an extended period.'[4]

Little more than two years later, in a move that dispelled the belief that the Arab oil producers were cheaply bought and easily divided, these same states agreed to place a total oil embargo on the United States, the Netherlands and Portugal for their practical and moral support for Israel during the war. A small group of 'friends', including France, Spain, the United Kingdom, India and Pakistan, continued to get oil at September 1973 levels. All other states saw a 5 per cent reduction in their oil imports every month. Kuwait and Saudi Arabia went further and threatened an immediate reduction of 10 per cent. Neither the limited embargo nor the more widely applied reduction in supply resulted in a real shortage of petroleum on the international market. A number of non-Arab oil-producing countries, including the Arab Gulf's neighbour Iran, refused to join the boycott and instead increased production and supply. Such moves did little to stem global panic. Fear drives the price of oil as much as supply and demand. As fear started to spread, eight leading American economists, including all four living US Nobel prize winners in economics, held a press conference at Harvard University to plead with politicians and the public to stay calm. The world, they insisted, was experiencing 'energy difficulties' rather than a 'crisis'.

The Arab states had planned to use the embargo to 'modify' Washington's Middle East policy, as senior Saudi officials explained once oil supplies were halted. It quickly became apparent that Europe was far more vulnerable than the US to a reduction in Arab oil exports. In a frank exchange with Kissinger at the height of the crisis, French president Georges Pompidou explained the entirely different predicaments that Europe and the United States faced on this matter: 'You only rely on the Arabs for about a tenth of your consumption. We are entirely dependent upon them.'[5] Pompidou was actually overestimating American reliance on Arab oil at this time.

In the previous decade America had started to import more oil than ever but the Arab world still supplied less than 5 per cent of US oil imports by 1973. Demand for oil across Europe had increased by about 10 per cent per year during the 1960s. Much of this rising demand was satisfied by Arab Gulf suppliers who now hoped that an oil-dependent Europe could be pressured into exerting influence on future US policy in the Middle East. As one Baghdad newspaper explained in May 1975, a key Arab objective was to make Europe 'use pressure on the USA to stop helping the Zionist entity'.[6] If that did not work, the hope was that Europe would be forced to break with Washington, isolate the US and place it in an untenable position among the Western states. Either way, the plan was for 'Europe [to] ease the way for the Americans in due course',[7] as Farouk Kaddoumi, a senior figure in the Palestinian liberation movement, diplomatically explained to British officials in the mid-1970s.

Even in energy-dependent Europe, the situation in late 1973 and early 1974 was not desperate. Political posturing and public fears aside, even at the height of the crisis there was plenty of available oil for sale and there was no need to tap European reserves and stockpiles to meet needs. The Dutch, the main European targets of the embargo, could still get significant amounts of oil from outside the Arab world; Italy even managed to buy more oil during the crisis than it had before it started.[8] Supply levels did not matter nearly as much as price. A day before they announced their embargo, the Arab oil producers meeting in Kuwait City increased the price of crude oil. This was the first time in their history that they had acted unilaterally without bothering to consult with Western oil companies, their traditionally dominant partners. This move resulted in an immediate and massive jump in the price of a barrel of oil from US$3 to over US$5 a barrel. By the end of the year it had doubled to more than US$11.

As a result the bill for an international community dependent on oil skyrocketed. In 1974, the four biggest consumers – the United States, Canada, Europe and Japan – had to find an extra US$40 billion a year just to pay for the same amount of oil. This situation triggered the worst recession in the developed world since the 1930s. As US treasury secretary William E. Simon made clear, 'High oil prices are central to all our problems.'[9] Everywhere oil-importing countries, no matter how small, had to deal with enormous balance of payments deficits. Industrial output shrank, tax revenues plummeted, jobs were slashed and consumer confidence was shattered. In Europe voters expressed their anger at the ballot box. Between November 1973 and March 1974 governments fell in Britain, France, Italy, West Germany and Belgium. The European Community, barely a decade old, showed itself completely incapable of acting in a united manner. The Euro-American partnership, the fundamental pillar of the Western Cold War alliance, came under severe strain. Japan's miraculous economic growth since the late 1940s had been fuelled by cheap oil. When the 1973 crisis started it fell into recession for the first time since the end of the Second World War. Without the strategic oil reserves that provided a cushion of sorts in Europe, the country experienced an even greater, and far more practical, shock than that caused by President Nixon's surprise visit to China the previous year, when Washington provided Tokyo with just one day's notice of the historic trip.

In the 1930s the introduction of cheap factory-produced Japanese cultured pearls was responsible for ruining the Arab Gulf's hugely important natural pearl industry. In an ironic twist, now the tables were turned. The small Sheikhdoms of the Arab Gulf were not the only Arab oil producers to benefit from the rising price. Iraq, Algeria, Libya and even Egypt all produced significant quantities of oil for export. But the Arab Gulf States, home to only one million of the Arab world's 100 million citizens, received 80 per cent of Arab oil revenues. This made them the biggest beneficiaries of the doubling and then redoubling of oil prices in the last three months of 1973. The sums involved were astronomical. At the beginning of 1973 the combined monetary reserves of the Arab Gulf States were US$13.1 billion. By the end of 1974 they neared US$50 billion. On a per capita basis at least, the smaller Gulf kingdoms had been rich before the 1973 crisis – in 1970 Kuwait and Abu Dhabi had the first and second highest GDP per capita in the world. But the rising oil price of the mid-1970s resulted in one of fastest and largest transfers of wealth in history. 'We found ourselves in a tidal wave, awash with money,' recalled one Abu Dhabi official. His oil minister made a similar point. The whole Gulf was covered in 'heaps of paper money',[10] explained the precocious Mana Al-Otaiba, only twenty-seven years of age at the time.

Until the 1920s oil explorers and geologists agreed that there was little oil to be found on the Arab side of the Gulf. This was soon shown to be a major mistake as international oil companies hit rich seams across the region over the following two decades. By 1960 the world's top oil companies, a consortium known as the Seven Sisters,[11] controlled most of these oilfields, as well as production levels and price. They were also the biggest beneficiaries by far of the doubling of oil demand from ten million to twenty million barrels per day during the 1950s. OPEC was founded in 1960 with the objective of rebalancing power between oil-producing countries and the international oil companies. It failed to do so dismally during its first decade. The oil companies continued to hold most of the power in the industry and used their advantage to make sure that their priorities – high levels of production and a low price – prevailed over the producing nations' preference of higher prices. The upshot was that oil prices continued to fall during the 1960s. By the time of the Arab–Israeli war in 1967, a barrel of oil cost just US$1.80, even less than when OPEC was founded at the beginning of the decade.

The kingdom of Saudi Arabia was home to the largest oil reserves in the region. Its founder, Abdul Aziz Ibn Saud, had a special interest in the Palestine Question. In early 1945, the matter had topped the agenda of his historic meeting with US president Franklin D. Roosevelt. This was the Saudi king's first trip outside of his kingdom and he met Roosevelt on board the USS *Quincy* on the Suez Canal. The talks lasted several days. Few details of what they discussed or agreed ever became public and Roosevelt died less than two months later. It was, however, widely rumoured that the Saudi king had received guarantees over Palestinian Arab rights from the president. Yet, as long as oil companies controlled both the supply and price of oil, Abdul Aziz ibn Saud opposed the use of oil as a political weapon in the fight for Palestine. In September 1947, as the diplomatic and military battle over Palestine reached its climax, a representative of the Saudi king spoke forcefully on this issue at a special session of the Arab League's political committee held in Lebanon. Oil sanctions would be divisive, he argued, and worse, the oil-producing countries would end up the biggest losers in such a move.[12]

Two decades later, in May 1967, Middle East war appeared to be inevitable once more. The Arab countries warned that the flow of oil would be interrupted in the event of a new conflict. Following Israel's pre-emptive military attack on Egypt on 5 June, oil ministers met in Baghdad. As the extent of Israel's decisive victory on the battlefield became clear over the next few days, Kuwait and Saudi Arabia stopped providing oil for British and US tankers as a token expression of displeasure at Western support for Israel in the war. It was also a symbolic demonstration of their support for Egypt's president Gamal Abd Al-Nasser, the charismatic local champion of pan-Arabism. Despite the scale of the Israeli victory – it captured the Gaza Strip and Sinai Peninsula from Egypt, the West Bank and East Jerusalem from Jordan and the Golan Heights from Syria – Saudi Arabia, backed by Kuwait and pre-revolutionary Libya, rejected the calls from Syria, Egypt and Iraq to stop all Arab oil production.[13] King Faisal, who had come to power in Saudi Arabia in 1964 following a long spell as the country's foreign minister, was as adamant at this time as his father had been in the 1940s that 'oil and politics should not be mixed'.[14]

In 1968 the Arab Gulf oil producers established OAPEC – the Organization of Arab Petroleum Exporting Countries. The original idea for establishing this body came from Yamani. It had two functions. The first was to address the lack of Arab oil power, something made abundantly clear by the outcome of the previous year's war with Israel. The second was to provide a forum that insulated the oil business from the business of politics in which Arab oil producers could meet to talk to each other free from the interference of Arab countries with no oil.[15] Like OPEC before it, OAPEC was slow to make its mark. America's paper of record, the *New*

York Times, only mentioned it twice in the two years following its establishment. This Western indifference did not reflect emerging realities on the ground. Two in particular – one political and one economic – made the oil weapon an increasingly viable and politically necessary option for the Arab Gulf States. On the political level, the humiliation of the Arab armies in 1967 had increased the credibility of Palestinian guerrilla warfare against Israel. Seizing on this, the Palestine Liberation Organization (PLO), founded in 1964 under Egyptian control, now became an important player in its own right for the first time. Since the 1950s Fatah, Yasser Arafat's power base in the Palestinian movement, had presented itself as part of the same anti-colonial movement as the Front de Libération Nationale (FLN) in Algeria and the Viet Cong in Vietnam. In 1969, Fatah gained control of the PLO, in what the celebrated Palestinian–American academic Edward Said termed the 'year of legitimacy'[16] for the Palestinians. Fatah's rise to power inside the PLO led to an upsurge in Palestinian attacks on high-profile international targets – including airliners and oil tankers – in order to arouse the consciousness of the world's policymakers and awaken global public opinion. 'Suddenly', as Fawaz Turki eloquently recalled, 'Palestine became the Palestinians, the Palestinians became the PLO, and the PLO became in an age that looked romantically at such things, a national liberation movement.'[17]

At the same time as the Palestinian cause was becoming increasingly hard to ignore, especially in places with large Palestinian communities like the Arab Gulf, a revolution in the oil industry was under way. In 1971 and 1972, after a hard-fought battle with the international oil companies, oil-producing nations successfully negotiated new agreements on price setting and production levels. This gave them participation – partial ownership – in the previously dominant oil companies, as well as a much greater share of oil revenues than ever before. It also meant that the oil majors could no longer unilaterally decide the price of crude oil. As a Central Intelligence Agency (CIA) memorandum of the time explained, the Arab oil producers rather than Western oilmen were now in 'the driving seat for the first time'. Top oil executives were less matter of fact. The deal, complained the chairman of British Petroleum, had turned the oil majors into little more than 'tax-collecting agencies'.[18] In particular, Saudi Arabia, the number-one Arab oil producer, quickly emerged as a 'potential money power in global finance'.[19]

With these new agreements in place, Arab Gulf producers started to think much more about using their oil power to help the Palestinian cause against Israel. In 1972, and in the first part of 1973, officials from across the

Arab oil-producing states made fifteen separate threats to use the oil weapon against their 'enemies' in the future. Kuwait's emir was even more explicit. His kingdom's support for the Palestinians was 'unlimited' and oil would be a vital weapon in the battle for their rights when the right moment arrived.[20] This growing tendency to link oil to Palestine was notable. So was the fact that none of these threats came from King Faisal of Saudi Arabia, the single most important figure in the energy business following the oil agreements of the early 1970s. Faisal had been involved in the Palestine problem from the very beginning. He was the chief Saudi delegate at the United Nations in 1947 when members voted to partition Palestine and establish the state of Israel.

From that time onwards Faisal's worldview was defined by a deeply held conviction that Zionism and Israel, along with communism, were the 'cause of all evil in the world', as US secretary of state William Rogers reported back to President Nixon after a brief stay with Faisal in mid-1971. Nicholas G. Teacher, the US ambassador in the Saudi capital of Riyadh at the time of Rogers's visit, eloquently expounded on this matter in reports home. The king's 'renowned theory' on the links between Zionism and communism, he noted, was 'a framework in his own mind to which he accretes wherever he can find them such facts as may tend to strengthen his hypothesis'. Even the deeply paranoid Richard Nixon was taken aback at how Faisal 'saw Zionist and Communist conspiracies everywhere'.[21]

James E. Akins, the American ambassador in Riyadh during the 1973 war and the subsequent oil crisis, recalled that he had huge difficulty even getting Faisal to meet secretary of state Henry Kissinger because the king viewed him as a Jew and a Zionist. Kissinger would eventually visit the king on several occasions. Every time they met, Kissinger had to listen to Faisal's 'standard speech' on how Jews and communists were undermining civilization and trying to take over America. As Kissinger later recounted in a private conversation with President Gerald Ford, 'The first time I went, his speech to me was that all Jews are bad. They are cowards, who are mentioned unfavourably in the Quran. The second time I went, he pointed out he recognized the difference between Jews and Zionists. The third time, [he] said he didn't consider me a Jew but a human being.'[22]

Kissinger viewed Faisal as a 'shrewd cookie' as well as a 'kook'. Ever the pragmatist, he also appreciated the fact that Faisal's growing stature meant that 'all Arabs come to him'.[23] Faisal was also a pragmatist. He had an instinctive preference for moderation in international affairs and knew that close ties to the US were vital for the safety of his oilfields and for stability across the wider region. Combined with his innate conservatism, this had served to keep his visceral opposition to Washington's Palestine policy under control for decades. Until the late summer of 1972, Faisal insisted that Saudi Arabia had a moral, as well as a financial, commitment to sell its oil to consumer countries and would never resort to the oil weapon. The following month Yamani, on Faisal's orders, offered the Nixon administration a deal that seemed to back this up. Saudi Arabia, he proposed, would make a massive investment in the US energy sector in return for preferential treatment for Saudi oil in the US market.

At the same time, according to US intelligence reports, Faisal's long-held belief that American support was a 'cornerstone' of Saudi stability had been eroded since the 1967 Arab–Israeli war. More and more, the Saudi king now viewed Washington's Middle East policy as the cause of, rather than the antidote to, the radicalism and instability that he so feared. By the beginning of 1973, Faisal's top officials were expressing a new willingness to link oil to the Palestine issue in private meetings with Western oil executives and policymakers. Yamani travelled to Washington in April to tell the Nixon administration that Saudi Arabia would not increase oil production unless the US began working for an Israeli withdrawal from the territories occupied during the 1967 war. The following August, Prince Saud Al-Faisal, Yamani's number two at the oil ministry, told a Beirut-based magazine that Arab oil and petro-dollars would soon be used as political weapons in the Arab–Israeli conflict.

Later that month, King Faisal, who had long been regarded as the most discreet, as well as the least radical and most pro-Western, of all Arab leaders, went public with his concerns. In an interview with NBC Television he did not pull his punches. 'We are now under attack from the Arabs themselves', he told viewers, 'because of our friendship with the US, and we are accused of being in collusion with Zionism and American imperialism against the Arabs.' He followed this up with an interview in *Newsweek* magazine where he set out the new rules of the game. From now on a 'suitable political atmosphere' that took into account 'Zionist expansionist ambitions' would be a condition of a smooth oil supply.[24] Faisal's new willingness to unleash the oil weapon if needed after decades of rejecting this option did not come easy. He was instinctively cautious and, according to Kissinger, this decision was 'taken with a bleeding heart'. American diplomats on the ground in Riyadh were even more melodramatic, noting how the usually poker-faced Faisal had warned them of what was coming 'with tears in his eyes'.[25]

The majority of Western officials, oilmen and experts watching this drama unfold remained convinced that Arab producers were incapable of manipulating the oil supply for political goals. They found it incomprehensible that

Faisal, despite his increasingly tough rhetoric and emotional outbursts, would follow through on his threats. Even Yamani's eloquent warnings could not convince Western policymakers to change their minds. He would later describe his April 1973 meetings with then national security adviser Kissinger, secretary of state William Rogers and treasury secretary George Shultz, as a 'dialogue of the deaf'.[26]

Between 1945 and 1964, eleven out of the nineteen giant oilfields discovered across the world were located in the Middle East. By the end of the 1960s it was widely accepted that at least 300 billion of the world's 500 billion proven barrels of oil were also to be found there, with the heaviest concentration by far in Iran and the Arab Gulf States. This explains the commonly held view that producers could not tolerate, never mind provoke, an interruption in the oil supply. Any refusal to pump or sell oil would be, in the words of one American intelligence assessment, 'too painful' for them to bear. It would greatly reduce Gulf Arab income, put a halt to their domestic development programmes, and limit their ability to service their massive debt. President Nixon summed up this thinking in a meeting of his intelligence chiefs in June 1970. Arab oil producers, he opined, 'could not drink their oil and must have a market'. Nixon would later admit that he, like so many others, had been wrong on this point. The 'oil producing countries', he would recall, 'had leverage, and they were using it'.[27]

As the war against Israel got under way in early October 1973 the Arab Gulf States provided between US$500 million and US$700 million in hard currency to pay for Russian arms shipments to Egypt and Syria. By the middle of the month, as Israel reversed early Arab successes, Gulf leaders came under intense pressure to do more for the Arab cause than hand over cash. These demands came from the PLO, the frontline Arab states involved in the war and the more radical oil producers – Algeria, Libya and Iraq. Radio Baghdad, for example, repeatedly charged Gulf leaders with treason for their inaction up to that point. The idea of the Gulf States taking a more proactive role in the struggle against Israel also had widespread popular support among Gulf citizens and local Palestinian populations who lived and worked in large numbers in all Arab Gulf States except Oman and Bahrain. In this environment the leaders of Kuwait, Qatar and the UAE knew that they had to act, but the decision to do so did not come any easier to them than it did to the Saudi king. The stakes were high for all. Oil and oil money were the lifeblood of their nations and they did not like to gamble with either. This reality influenced greatly the nature of their response. None had any desire to implement a massive and immediate cutback in production and supply. Nor were they willing to agree to the proposal put forward by Libya and Iraq to nationalize US oil interests across the Arab world and cut off financial and diplomatic relations with Washington. Instead, Gulf leaders argued for a moderate and gradual approach that, in the words of Yamani, would 'make a political point and hopefully effect political change'.[28] This is often forgotten in the fog of war, panic and profound shifts in the oil business and global economy that occurred during the last months of 1973. The divide between Gulf States on the one side and the more radical oil producers and frontline Arab states on the other resulted in bitterly contested negotiations in Kuwait City in the middle of October over how, and to what end, the oil weapon should be used.

The decision ultimately taken in Kuwait City to raise the oil price and reduce production were a gamble and there were understandable concerns that it might backfire. It was very possible that Western sceptics would be proved right about the inability of the Arab oil producers to work together or that their actions might soon hurt them more than the countries that were being denied their oil. None of these possible scenarios played out. Instead, the Gulf States scored a major victory, which had economic, geo-strategic and political ramifications in the Arab world and beyond long after the oil embargo ended in March 1974.

Until the early 1970s, the Arab Gulf States played almost no important role outside the Arabian Peninsula. They were militarily weak, commanded little political influence in the Arab world and depended on the British to provide security. Even before the oil crisis, the British withdrawal from the region had forced the fragile Gulf States to do more to contribute to regional stability and to project power internationally. In 1972, Faisal undertook a state visit to France, the first by a Saudi king. Soon after, he hosted British defence minister Lord Carrington in Riyadh. In the same year, he also led his country's delegation to the conference of Non-Aligned Nations in Algeria. His foreign minister Omar Saqqaf visited Africa, South America and the Far East in the same period. By the summer of 1973 Saudi Arabia's rising diplomatic influence, as well as the country's evolving role as the 'power behind the scenes in the Arab World',[29] was starting to make headlines.

The oil crisis that followed later on in that year underscored the new political and economic status of the Saudi-led Arab Gulf. This translated quickly into a growing Gulf role in inter-Arab political and diplomatic affairs. In 1976, the Saudis and Kuwaitis summoned the leaders of Egypt, Syria, Lebanon and the PLO to an emergency summit in Riyadh to discuss the civil war then raging in Lebanon. This meeting did not achieve peace and fighting between the warring factions continued until 1990. But it was a notable event that gained the full backing of other Arab leaders and signalled the new regional role of Saudi Arabia, the richest, largest and most powerful of the Gulf oil states. On the back of this, Crown Prince Fahd travelled to north Africa to try to resolve the Western Sahara war that had been raging between Morocco and local rebels since the withdrawal of Spain from the Spanish Sahara in 1975. Saudi Arabia also provided financial aid to Sultan Qaboos of Oman in his war against rebels in Dhofar; at the same time Riyadh bought off South Yemen's support for Omani insurgents. This financial diplomacy was the order of the day. With hands 'dripping with oil . . . not blood',[30] as one Iraqi intellectual of the time put it, Gulf money now also funded Assad's Syria, Arafat's PLO and King Hussein of Jordan.

The Gulf's new-found 'sense of responsibility and leadership',[31] as the Saudi Arabian ambassador in Washington termed it, had an impact beyond the Middle East. The oil crisis and its aftermath put paid to the commonly held view until then that in the overall scheme of things oil politics and oil producers, though a presence on the world stage, were of secondary significance. Over the next few years it became impossible to think of oil matters separately from political matters. As one Saudi policymaker candidly informed the *New York Times*, 'We no longer think of oil in terms of money alone.'[32] Oil prices and production issues became matters that threatened the independence and sovereignty of nations. Even those who could not find Saudi Arabia on a map and who had never heard of Qatar or Abu Dhabi were now aware of the potential of Arab oil producers to affect their day-to-day lives.

Henry Kissinger, for one, had no doubt that the events of 1973 had 'made possible a revolution in world affairs', which had, in turn, brought about an 'upheaval in world balance of power'.[33] The stakes involved went 'beyond oil prices and economics, and involve the whole framework of future political relations', he told a September 1974 meeting in Washington attended by the foreign and finance ministers of Great Britain, France, West Germany and Japan. In particular, Kissinger expressed a real fear that oil producers would 'attain huge political power' if nothing was done to contain their rising wealth and influence. The top officials from the major industrial nations listening to Kissinger's pessimistic briefing all agreed with his assessment. West German foreign minister Hans-Dietrich Genscher weighed in with the view that there was 'a great shift in political power under way' and that the entire world faced a threat of 'considerable danger'.[34]

Such discussions underscored just how quickly the Arab Gulf States had risen to the top of the international agenda. As the British Foreign Office acknowledged somewhat resignedly, going forward 'equality and interdependence'[35] would be the order of the day in the West's relationship with the Arab world. Gulf officials suddenly had unfettered access to the West's most senior politicians and policymakers. During their late 1973 tour of European capitals, Yamani and Beleid Abdul Sallam, the Algerian minister of industry and energy, met a succession of leaders who begged them to convince their governments to refrain from further destabilizing Europe. In turn, the two Arab oil ministers pressured their hosts to take a firmer stand against Washington's Middle East policy if they wanted to protect their oil supply and promote other strategic interests in the future. In state visits to Saudi Arabia in 1976 and 1977 Chancellor Helmut Schmidt of West Germany and President Valéry Giscard d'Estaing of France both publicly described Saudi Arabia as a world power for the first time. A few years later François Mitterrand, Giscard d'Estaing's successor, chose Saudi Arabia as the destination of his first presidential visit outside Europe.[36] In the same year China reinstituted the hajj for Chinese Muslims in a gesture that demonstrated clearly Beijing's new appreciation for Saudi Arabia's rising international standing.

This new global centrality of the Saudi-led Arab Gulf was first and foremost a function of financial power. Until the beginning of the 1970s money had been tight in the region. After the end of the 1967 Arab–Israeli war the Kuwaiti media criticized its own government's commitment of millions of dollars to Egypt and Jordan on the grounds that the country could not afford such lavish support at a time of economic stagnation. Soon afterwards, Saudi leaders complained to American officials that they could 'not afford' to carry out much-needed domestic development.[37] The rise in oil revenues that followed the OPEC agreements of 1971 and 1972 and the huge increase in the oil price in 1973–4 put an end to such worries. By the time of Faisal's death in 1975 Saudi earnings from oil royalties stood at over US$50 billion, forty-five times higher in real purchasing power terms than they had been in 1958 when he became king.[38] Saudi Arabia pumped four times more oil than Kuwait, the second-biggest oil producer in the Arab Gulf. But Kuwait still controlled 10 per cent of the world's oil reserves. It had become rich before the other Gulf States but apart from a few brick palaces, the majority of houses in Kuwait in the 1950s had been made from mud. G. N. Jackson, the country's second British ambassador, reported home how they were inclined to fall apart after a week of rain.[39] The situation had changed greatly by the time Sheikh Sabah Al-Salem Al-Sabah died in late 1977. He left behind a kingdom of 1.2 million people with one of the most developed welfare states anywhere, as well as the highest per capita income in the world.

At the time of Saudi Arabia's birth in 1932, the Al-Saud family had ruled an impoverished desert territory dependent on revenues from the annual hajj pilgrimage to survive.[40] Into the 1950s, the main towns in Saudi Arabia, the capital Riyadh and the Red Sea resort of Jeddah, later the summer destination of the Saudi elites, were little more than mud-brick townships. Saudi Arabia's Eastern Province, soon to be the oil capital of the world, was poor even by the standards of the day. Even after Saudi Arabia had established itself as a leading player in the energy markets, it faced major challenges in harnessing its new oil wealth for development. As a US National Security Council briefing paper of the time put it, 'There are two basic facts about Saudi Arabia that stand above all others – its wealth and its backwardness.'[41]

In acknowledgement of his new international role and standing, King Faisal was named *Time* magazine's 'Man of the Year' for 1974. At home, he introduced a plan to invest almost US$150 billion by the end of the decade to build a massive industrial economy in the heart of the desert. Saudi planning minister Hisham Nazer clarified what this meant. His government, he explained, would reshape the nation and, in the process, 'serve as a model for the entire Middle East'.[42] Like Saudi Arabia, the smaller Arab Gulf oil producers also used their growing wealth to move beyond reliance on the sale of crude oil. They entered the petrochemical sector, built refineries and petrochemical plants and developed a transportation business so they could ship their own products to customers. The precedent had been established in Kuwait in the early 1960s when a royal decree had established the Petrochemicals Industry Company, the first chemical manufacturing business in the Gulf. A decade later Qatar established QAPCO, the national petrochemical company. Even Bahrain, a relatively minor energy producer whose oil exports were not great enough to qualify it for OPEC membership, looked to invest in a refinery and an aluminium smelter. With the support of its Gulf partners, Bahrain also built the world's biggest dry dock to house and service the Gulf's newly purchased fleet of supertankers. A few years later the governments of Bahrain, Kuwait and Saudi Arabia established the Gulf Petrochemical Industries Company in 1979 as a joint venture for the manufacture of fertilizers and petrochemicals.

Though they had less ambitious goals in terms of non-petroleum-related industrial development, Saudi Arabia's neighbours also looked to pour vast amounts of money into basic infrastructure like roads, sewerage, air and sea communications, and urban development. During the 1970s, there was a forty-two-fold increase in spending on construction across the six Gulf States. There was also heavy investment in the healthcare sector and in the provision of primary and secondary education. The UAE's education budget for 1974 was double that of the previous year. When Sultan Qaboos overthrew his father in a palace coup in Oman in 1970, his citizens earned little more on average than US$400 a year and over 90 per cent of the population relied on agriculture and fisheries for their livings. He also inherited a country of almost one million people with no hospitals, only three schools and 10 kilometres of asphalted roads. By 1976, the sultanate had over 70,000 pupils in primary and secondary schools, as well as thirteen hospitals and 1,800 kilometres of asphalted roads. In the same year Oman introduced its first five-year plan. This channelled rising oil revenues into ports, an airport, government buildings, power stations and communication centres as well as more roads, schools and hospitals.

The pace of this development across the region from the mid-1970s onwards can be illustrated by one anecdote. Until the end of the 1960s, the territories on the southern shore of the Persian Gulf that would soon become the UAE were almost entirely desert and could only be crossed by camel or four-wheel-drive vehicles. In 1970, after a series of visits to the region, a British company set out to develop a new type of vehicle able to deal with the lack of properly surfaced roads across the Trucial coast. After spending the next few years building and refining a prototype, its salesmen returned to the region in the mid-1970s, confident that orders for new fleets would flood in. Instead they found a country that was the proud home to an extensive, high-quality asphalt road network with no need for their now obsolete vehicle.[43]

Apocryphal or not, this story points to the profound and rapid change that the relatively primitive states of the Arab Gulf underwent in the years immediately following the oil crisis. Taken in its entirety this was part of a massive effort by local rulers to drag the region into the modern world. Nor was oil the only factor driving this development. The kingdom of Bahrain, located twenty-five miles off the coast of Saudi Arabia, had been the first state on the Arabian side of the Gulf to strike oil. But it only ever found small quantities. This meant that its transition 'from pearls to riches', as the tagline in its tourism adverts in the 1970s went, was not achieved by relying on oil revenues. Instead it capitalized on its strategic location, as well as its more advanced social development compared to its neighbours. Most notably, Bahrain took advantage of its relatively highly educated population to establish itself as a centre of regional communications, commerce, finance and banking prior to the oil boom and long before the rest of the Gulf.

Ambitious modernization projects from Bahrain to Saudi Arabia and Oman to Qatar brought great advances in everything from water and electricity to communications networks and residential and commercial infrastructure. UAE oil chief Mana Al-Otaiba summed up the thinking behind all these moves. 'The time when our lands were a farm of raw materials is now over,' he explained, before calling for a future emphasis on the production of high-value products, which would promote economic development and improve the overall standard of living across the region.[44] The scale of development needed to transform the Gulf States from traditional rural societies into modern economies in quick time required technology and training. 'We have abundant capital, cheap energy and the suitable territorial locations', Yamani explained in 1974, 'but we lack the necessary technology. We therefore stretch out our hands to the industrialized countries in quest of their technical know-how, which is indispensable.'[45] In subsequent years, Saudi leaders and their counterparts across the region would sporadically declare that they were making impressive headway in overcoming this problem. In a 1983 interview in the Kuwaiti press, Crown Prince Abdullah announced somewhat triumphantly that 'modern technology has placed us at the centre of the world, moreover it has made the world the centre of Saudi Arabia.'[46] His proclamation was premature. Gaining access to foreign expertise and technology remained an ongoing challenge that impeded development for many years.

Apart from technology transfers, industrialization on the scale and at the pace under way also demanded a much larger workforce than was available in the sparsely populated Gulf kingdoms. Even prior to the first oil boom, the lack of home-grown workers meant that restrictions on immigration caused economic damage. When the Kuwaiti government imposed limits on hiring foreign labour during the 1960s, the kingdom suffered a mini-recession and real estate prices crashed. This lesson was well learnt and when the massive development plans got under way following the oil crisis of 1973 there was an influx of foreign labourers. They needed somewhere to live, which contributed further to the rapid growth in the size and population of cities. It also made social upheaval inevitable and it brought with it a gradual erosion of traditional values. In the late 1970s this phenomenon was viewed to be a much less problematic aspect of domestic development than it is today. It was still widely believed that infrastructural projects would soon be finished, removing the need for foreign labour, and newly educated citizens would be ready to replace expatriate workers in more skilled jobs.

A much bigger obstacle at the time was viewed to be the limited capacity of the Gulf States to absorb the vast amounts of money they had to spend. Despite its impressive and costly development plans, Saudi Arabia had a combined petro-dollar surplus for 1975 and 1976 of US$45 billion. Over the next five years, until 1981, Arab Gulf States along with Iran and Libya accounted for 90 per cent of the US$450 billion total cash surplus accumulated by OPEC members. With development programmes at home running at full capacity, the Arab Gulf States started to pay more attention to the best ways to use their vast holdings of dollars, sterling and francs, all sitting in banks on New York's Wall Street, in the City of London and on the Paradeplatz on Zurich's Bahnhofstrasse. The first option was to invest in the developing world. Much of Africa and parts of Asia, as well as the non-oil-producing Arab world, had been hurt badly by the rising oil price and the global recession that followed the 1973 crisis. In the wake of the oil crisis the total foreign debts of over 100 developing countries tripled in size. Johan Witteveen, a top figure at the International Monetary Fund (IMF), warned that the international monetary system was facing its 'most difficult' time since the devastating depression of the 1930s. For once it seemed that both the world's rich and poor were in agreement about what needed to be done. France's President Giscard d'Estaing spoke for many in the industrial countries when he called for the oil-rich Gulf to demonstrate global responsibility by pumping money into the third world. The Organization of African Unity (OAU) spoke for some of the world's poorest nations. It echoed Giscard d'Estaing's call, and expressed the hope that the Arab Gulf would support struggling nations on a scale big enough to make a real difference. Others spoke of an 'Arab Marshall Plan', along the lines of the American aid programme to Europe after the Second World War. Failing that, the Gulf should play the role of a modern-day 'Robin Hood', redistributing the petro-dollars taken from the rich industrial nations to the most needy in the developing world.

Not everyone agreed. Prior to the oil crisis, 80 per cent of Gulf development aid went to other Arab countries. Since the early 1960s, the Kuwait Fund for Arab Economic Development had led the way in providing substantial loans to a dozen other Arab states. Speaking in early 1974, Kuwait's finance minister, Abdel Rahman Sale Al-Atiki, asked why this should change and 'why everybody expects us to be the Godfather?' before adding that Arabs and Muslims would continue to be the 'major beneficiaries' of rising oil wealth.[47] Al-Atiki's worldview did not win the day, even at home. Within a year, Kuwait began to lend hundreds of millions of dollars for special assistance to non-Arab nations in Asia and Africa for the first time. Saudi Arabia, and to a lesser extent the UAE, also established themselves among the world's top aid donors in both absolute and per capita terms as they provided significant sums to help poorer nations deal with the rising cost of oil and imported goods. In 1977, at the Afro-Arab

Conference in Cairo, the four richest Arab Gulf States – Kuwait, Qatar, the UAE and Saudi Arabia – committed to invest US$1.35 billion in African development projects over the next five years.

The growing involvement and influence of Arab Gulf States in the World Bank and the IMF also reflected their new centrality to international development. World Bank president Robert McNamara appealed to the oil-rich Gulf for support to help it in its task of providing financial and technical assistance to developing countries. By the late 1970s it was estimated that about a quarter of the bank's total funds came from the Arab world. As the only nation in the world to spend consistently more than 1 per cent of national income on foreign aid, Kuwait established itself as one of the top four backers of the organization. Saudi Arabia was also a major donor to the World Bank, and the second largest subscriber to the IMF, the international organization based in Washington, DC, mandated to improve financial stability, facilitate international trade and reduce global poverty. In 1978 Saudi Arabia was invited to join the IMF's executive board. In the same year the IMF substituted the Saudi (and Iranian) currencies for the South African rand and the Danish crown in the 'basket' of sixteen world currencies used to determine the value of the Fund's Special Drawing Rights (SDRs).

In 1974 Yamani had explained that the Gulf's rulers wanted most of their oil revenues to go towards domestic development. This is one reason why they had not developed coherent national strategies for investing their petro-dollars in the international economy in the wake of the oil crisis. They did have one thing in common. They were, in the words of the *New York Times*, as 'conservative [as] Irish bishops'.[48] This predisposed them to spend their money on prime real estate, government securities and stakes in blue chip companies in the United States, Western Europe and Japan. These were the most stable and secure economies in the world and the only ones with capital markets big enough to absorb and recycle the vast sums of money involved.

In 1976 Kuwait, the UAE and Saudi Arabia between them received over 40 per cent of all OPEC revenues. The following year the US Treasury estimated that the external assets of the Gulf countries had risen from US$7 billion in 1972 to around US$110 billion five years later. By the end of the decade Saudi Arabia's external assets alone were valued at about US$75 billion, with over US$30 billion invested in the US. Kuwait, the UAE and Qatar also had substantial holdings in hotels, office blocks and publicly quoted companies in the US and Europe. In 1974, for example, Kuwait made a major investment in Daimler-Benz and bought properties along the landmark Champs-Elysées in central Paris that, according to some reports, covered 1.2 hectares of the French capital. The Arab Gulf States invested heavily in state-owned industries across Europe, including the troubled gas and coal sectors in the United Kingdom. They also made sizeable loans to cash-poor European governments. In 1976 Saudi Arabia financed a US$1 billion loan to Italy and US$300 million loan to Ireland.[49] Initially, Western governments and businessmen welcomed this extensive Gulf financial interest in public and private assets across a wide range of economic sectors. They were cheered on by influential opinion makers as they competed to attract more and more Gulf money. In one notable example, one of the most important opinion makers in American business and finance – the editorial page of the *Wall Street Journal* – called on the Nixon administration to embrace the opportunities of Arab petro-dollar spending.

Such positivity was short lived. The CIA had been warning policy-makers in Washington since the beginning of the decade that rising Arab oil revenues might end up 'causing havoc in international financial markets'.[50] Once the scale of Gulf petro-dollar wealth became apparent, these fears began to resonate more widely. In the summer of 1974, Otto Miller, a former chairman of Standard Oil of California, warned a Senate committee that it was vital to have 'friendly relations' with the Arab oil producers because the West was 'completely at their mercy'. Public statements like this by informed observers like Miller resulted in a forceful response from the political class.

As the unofficial watchdogs of the global economy, US leaders were particularly sensitive to the negative economic implications of the rising oil price during the second half of the 1970s. In his September 1974 Chatham House speech, Yamani had pleaded with his audience to avoid 'mischievous and irresponsible accusations'[51] when discussing Arab oil wealth. Few politicians in either major American political party honoured this request. In the same month as Yamani's London appearance, Senator Henry 'Scoop' Jackson, the long-serving chairman of the influential Senate Committee that oversaw energy issues, told an audience in New York that the 'entire industrialized world faces a clear and present danger of economic destruction by the Arab oil cartel'. President Gerald Ford, who succeeded Richard Nixon in the White House in mid-1974, warned that 'exorbitant' oil prices threatened 'worldwide depression and ... the breakdown of world order and safety'.[52]

Kissinger had continued on in his role as secretary of state after Nixon left the White House in disgrace following the Watergate scandal. He was deeply concerned over the problems posed by massive Arab oil revenues.

They were not, he told a group of visiting Western officials, 'merely entries in bank accounts'. 'Sooner or later', he feared, they would 'be converted into command over resources, and thus into political power'. Producers would then have control over consumer economies. This would weaken the West's 'unity' and 'resilience' in the face of the Soviet threat. It could even 'provoke a major political and economic crisis in the Western world'. In short, according to Kissinger, Arab oil revenues threatened to 'become a threat to global and regional peace'. Other Western leaders agreed. 'We should never assume that the Arabs will react . . . rationally,'[53] British chancellor of the Exchequer Denis Healey warned in the same meeting.

The media gave widespread coverage to such concerns. Kissinger's very blunt public attack on the 'strangulation of the industrial states'[54] by Arab oil producers was originally published in *US News & World Report*. It quickly became front-page news around the world. Less widely reported, though potentially more significant, was the arrival of the American aircraft carrier USS *Constellation* in Gulf waters for the first time. This coincided with a warning by US secretary of defence James Schlesinger that Washington reserved the right to take military action if the oil weapon crippled the industrial world. The press took to reporting business deals involving Arab Gulf money as major world news stories, even running them as front-page headlines. In July 1976, for example, the British media led the campaign over news that a group of Arab investors wanted to buy the Dorchester Hotel in London's Park Lane. Cartoonists filled newspapers with drawings of camels hitched to parking meters and of harems being set up in the luxurious surroundings of the hotel's famous ballroom. J. B. Kelly, the outspoken Gulf scholar and commentator, lamented the fortunes of the citizens of Paris, London and other great Western capitals, whose cities were being turned into 'Middle Eastern Caravanserais, bazaars, and bagnios'. It was, he wrote at the time, both absurd and humiliating that the West's 'very financial survival depends in grotesquely disproportionate degree upon the condescending indulgence of a handful of desert Sheikhs'.[55]

James Abourezk openly challenged those who attacked Arabs for the high oil price and their petro-dollar investments. The son of Lebanese immigrants to the US, Abourezk was an up and coming Democratic senator from South Dakota and one of *Time* magazine's '200 faces of the future'. 'I find it strange', he wrote in early 1977, three years before setting up the American–Arab Anti-Discrimination Committee, 'that stories continually pop up in the press that Arabs are buying all the banks, or property . . . the upshot of this kind of reporting is to encourage further a highly unfavorable image of the Arabs'.[56] Conservative Gulf leaders were horrified over this state of affairs. They insisted that they had no desire or intention to take over the world's financial markets. Nor, they explained, were they plotting to wreck the world economy. Always sensitive to Western opinion, Yamani used the opportunity provided by his numerous media interviews, press conferences and speeches to promise that the Arab oil producers would act responsibly and would not misuse petro-dollars. He stressed time and again that the majority of Gulf spending and investment took place at home in the Gulf and in the Arab and Muslim world rather than in the West. He also rejected claims that the global balance of power was shifting away from the industrial world towards the oil-producing nations on the grounds that 'raw materials are not the main source of power – technology is'.[57] Some of Yamani's fellow countrymen were less diplomatic. Farouk Al-Akhdar, a senior technocrat working on the kingdom's industrialization programme, asked rhetorically, 'Do they want investments or do they not want investments?' Suliman Olayan, a successful Saudi businessman, mocked the popular pastime of bashing oil producers. 'If it wasn't for them', he sarcastically argued, 'life would be easy and we can all go for a holiday at the seaside'.[58]

The truth was that the petro-dollars invested in the industrialized oil-importing nations made it possible for recipient countries to better manage their enormous balance of trade deficits and protect their monetary reserves. Gulf money also created jobs. By 1977 it was estimated that more than half a million American jobs depended directly on the Saudi connection and two to three times that number were employed indirectly. On top of this, far from spending to undermine the status quo, by investing so much in the West, Gulf leaders had more reason than ever to work closely with their Western partners to prevent instability in the markets or economic downturn. Kuwait's commitment to the British economy can be traced back to the early 1950s when it opened up the Kuwait Investment Office (KIO) in the City of London. A quarter of a century later, as Kuwaiti oil money poured into the British economy, the kingdom's finance minister reassured the prime minister, James Callaghan, that a British economic recovery was in their joint interest because his country had invested so much of its reserves in British assets. Similarly, Western fears, expressed most forcefully by Kissinger, that petro-dollar investments could result in the exploitation of vulnerable nations and lead to the rise of radical forces, were totally misplaced. Saudi Arabia's huge loan to Italy in 1976 was not driven by economic opportunism or political intrigue but by a desire to underpin the status quo. It was hoped that this massive infusion of money would help prevent the collapse of the Italian economy, thus reducing the chance of communist takeover, with all the potential that such an eventuality had for social, political and economic meltdown across Europe.

Critics of the Arab Gulf's rising influence also tended to ignore the limits of Gulf financial power. As noted in the introduction to this book, the Arab Gulf is rich but it is small rich. That was true even in the heyday of the mid-1970s. In the months and years after the oil crisis had begun there was widespread speculation that power centres of the financial world would soon shift from London, Zurich and New York to the capitals of the Gulf. Kuwait, Dubai, Abu Dhabi and Bahrain all developed into credible regional financial and banking centres in subsequent years. This was not only due to the rising oil economy. It was also due to the demise of Beirut as the number-one Arab banking hub following the outbreak of the Lebanese civil war in 1975. At no point during the years after the oil crisis did any Gulf financial centre come close to challenging any of the long-established Western centres of finance, all of which had access to, and control over, funds that dwarfed those available to Gulf States.

Total global oil revenues between 1973 and 1981, including those earned in the Gulf, only accounted for around 1.5 per cent of the world's GDP. Petro-dollar reserves, though impressive in size and rising all the time over the same years, were tiny compared to the value of major Western financial entities like the multi-trillion-dollar US stock exchange. Such disparities meant that if the Arab Gulf countries were truly motivated in their investment decisions by a desire to achieve political or economic influence in recipient countries then they would have pumped their petro-dollars into other Arab countries rather than much larger Western economies. For example, if Kuwait had carried out its mid-1979 threat to withdraw more than US$1 billion held on deposit in Egyptian banks, it could have devastated the Egyptian financial sector and economy in a way that was unthinkable if it had acted similarly in the West.

Those holding the Arab Gulf responsible for inflating the oil price also rarely took into account the role of Saudi Arabia, sometimes assisted and occasionally hindered by its Gulf neighbours, in ensuring a stable and affordable supply of oil in the second part of the 1970s. During meetings with Kissinger in October 1974, Saudi foreign minister Omar Saqqaf passed on assurances from King Faisal that his country would do all it could to keep the oil price at reasonable levels. After King Faisal was assassinated by a deranged nephew in 1975, his half-brother and successor, King Khalid, continued to resist attempts by other OPEC members to increase the price of oil significantly or to move away from the dollar as the standard currency for oil pricing.

King Khalid stuck with Yamani as his point man in this endeavour. During an OPEC meeting in Vienna in September 1975 in the full glare of the world's media, the Saudi oil minister abruptly abandoned the discussions and flew to London to speak with his new king by phone. This was a piece of theatre typical of Yamani. It was intended to demonstrate very publicly just how dedicated his king was to keeping the price of oil low even when he had little support from other OPEC members. The next year in Doha, Yamani threatened to undercut the oil price by flooding the market with cheap oil if the rest of OPEC insisted on pushing up the price by more than Saudi Arabia's preferred 5 per cent level. This was no idle threat. Saudi Arabia was the only oil producer able to increase or reduce production by millions of barrels a day without damaging its own finances. On the eve of Jimmy Carter's presidential victory over the incumbent Gerald Ford in late 1976, the influential Egyptian paper *Al Ahram* noted that Saudi Arabia, sometimes in the company of Abu Dhabi and other Gulf States, decided its oil price on the basis of political considerations. The paper even speculated that Riyadh would increase oil production following the election to ensure that the next US president – whether Ford or Carter – would not have to face an energy crisis immediately on taking office.[59]

Once in office, Carter welcomed the Saudi role in keeping down the OPEC oil price but he denied that this influenced his administration's policies in any way. True or not, few doubted that Saudi dominance of the oil market gave the kingdom real standing in Washington in the final years of the 1970s. In early 1978, following a personal request from King Khalid to President Carter, the US intervened on a dramatic scale to support the falling dollar and to restore order to the financial markets. This was important for Riyadh because oil payments were made in dollars, which meant that the weak dollar cost the oil-exporting Gulf countries, first and foremost Saudi Arabia, billions in lost revenues. By the end of the 1970s, such mutually beneficial cooperation led some commentators to argue that Gulf oil and investment strategies, and even political choices, were being made on a 'decision by decision' basis in line with American interests. Others went so far as to describe the Washington–Riyadh axis as the 'central truth' in international politics.[60] Though both claims were exaggerated, they gained even more currency following the Islamic revolution in Iran in February 1979 and the overthrow of the country's pro-Western ruler, Shah Mohammad Rezā Shāh Pahlavī.

Iran under the shah was the world's second largest oil producer after Saudi Arabia, as well as Washington's number-one strategic partner in the region. The shah's fall from power triggered a second energy crisis, a rising oil price, further balance of payments deficits and recession around the world. Saudi Arabia controlled around one-third of OPEC's oil reserves at the time of the revolution in Iran. It attempted to relieve the strain on the industrial economies by increasing oil production by one million barrels a day. Significant as this move was, the revolution in Iran occurred at a time when Saudi leaders were becoming more and more reluctant to fight to keep the oil price down inside OPEC. In February 1979, following a visit to the Gulf, Britain's foreign secretary reported back to the cabinet that he had 'not been able to detect any sign of Saudi determination to resist an increase in the oil price'.[61] In part, this was due to the zealous determination of the new revolutionary leaders in Tehran to challenge Riyadh wherever it could, including inside the oil cartel. It was also a consequence of growing Saudi disillusionment over the actual benefits they had reaped from acting as a moderate element inside OPEC in the years since the oil crisis of 1973.

Yamani always stressed that he found the term 'oil weapon' distasteful and preferred the term 'political instrument' because a 'weapon is used to hurt people'.[62] In the years after 1973 he did, however, call repeatedly on Western partners to 'appreciate'[63] the Saudi role in contributing to global stability by keeping the price of oil at reasonable levels. And he acknowledged that this had a price. Such help, he explained, required the West to demonstrate a real commitment to finding a 'comprehensive, overall solution for the Middle East crisis, which must, first and foremost, mean a solution for the increasingly desperate Palestinian people'.[64] Crown Prince Fahd made a similar point. His country, he argued, had fought hard to keep oil prices down and had done so to 'safeguard the integrity of the world economy'. However, this commitment, Fahd added, was also intended to 'encourage the friendly countries to have a moderate attitude towards our Arab cause in such a way as to achieve peace'.[65]

In a speech broadcast live on Italian television during a 1979 meeting of Arab and European leaders in Rimini, Mana Al-Otaiba, the UAE's oil minister and then OPEC president, was even more explicit. There could be no effective dialogue between the West and the oil-producing countries unless the PLO was recognized as the only legitimate representative of the Palestinian people. Dismissing the accusation that such talk constituted 'oil blackmail', he countered that it was simply a matter of rights. 'Hungry for justice, frustrated in their decades old national aspirations,' he pointedly warned, 'the Palestinians may one day set fire to the wells. If the oil catches fire, there will be none either for [us] or you'.[66] Such dramatic statements undoubtedly reflected the deep commitment of Gulf Arab leaders towards the Palestinian cause in the years after the 1973 crisis. At the same time, this rhetoric also served as a substitute for the oil weapon, which by the end of the 1970s was an increasingly obsolete political instrument. Quota busting by OPEC members and rising production by non-OPEC oil producers, including the United States, Mexico and the United Kingdom, made it harder and harder for the Arab Gulf to control either the oil price or production levels from the late 1970s onwards. Falling global demand for oil also took its toll. By this time a number of major oil-consuming countries had also started to reap the benefits of earlier investments in alternative energy programmes, like civilian nuclear power in the case of France, as a way of reducing dependence on foreign oil.

At the start of the 1970s there had been considerable sympathy in the Western world for the attempts of less developed oil-producing states, including those in the Arab Gulf, to wrest control of their own oil resources from international companies. As one 1971 editorial in a business magazine argued, a victory for the oil producers over the oil majors would serve as an 'important blow in gaining major economic benefits for poorer countries and in showing the rich countries that the latter cannot go on living affluent lives at the expense of the poorer nations'.[67] A decade later, after years of high oil prices that had resulted in major economic problems for consumer countries, there was a lot less sympathy for producers choosing to use their oil resources for political ends. Even those in positions of power who sympathized with the Palestinian cause, like British foreign secretary Lord Carrington, now spoke out about the dangers of playing politics with oil. Oil, lamented Carrington in 1979, had become 'a major cause, not a symptom, of international tension, instability and distress'.[68] The message was clear – further Arab attempts to manipulate the oil price were unacceptable. In 1980, Yamani acknowledged this emerging reality when he dramatically declared that the era of the oil weapon was over, even though Israel was still in control of occupied Arab land, the PLO was still denied widespread acceptance and the issues of Palestinian self-determination and statehood remained unresolved.

The oil weapon may not have achieved its primary objectives but it was not a total failure. Most notably, it had been instrumental in forcing Europe to address the Palestine issue in a much more serious manner and to give far greater weight to Palestinian claims than it had done prior to the oil crisis. In the first week of November 1973, the European Economic Community, the forerunner of the European Union, issued a declaration that called for the 'legitimate rights of the Palestinians' to be taken into account and stressed the need for Israel to 'end territorial occupation' of land gained in 1967. This was the first time since 1967 that European leaders had collectively placed the Palestinian issue at the centre of the political debate. Just weeks into his new job as US secretary of state, Henry Kissinger took a dim view of this European move, which he had only heard about while on a visit to Cairo. Israeli leaders reacted even more negatively. Foreign minister Abba Eban claimed that it had more to do with 'oil for Europe . . . than peace for the Middle East'. His successor in the foreign ministry, Yigal Allon, was even more damning. 'The European countries', he argued, 'have behaved in an un-European way. They bowed to pressure. They bowed to blackmail.'[69] At the time, European officials rejected such accusations as 'nonsense',[70] but Allon had a point. The declaration had been published just two days after eight of OAPEC's ten member states agreed to consider possible future reductions of up to 25 per cent in oil supplies to Europe. Subsequently, British prime minister Edward Heath would have no reservations in acknowledging the link, at least in his mind, between the November declaration and growing oil pressure, noting that 'in recognition . . . we were treated, along with France, as a "friendly" nation'.[71] It was also later confirmed by senior OPEC officials that the French and British governments, among others, provided guarantees, including support for the Dutch boycott, in return for keeping their places on the 'friendly' nations list.

For the rest of the decade Europe's overriding economic and political priority was to ensure stable energy supplies at affordable prices. To achieve this, European leaders looked for ways 'to make the Arabs think twice, if not three times, before taking discriminatory action against us',[72] as one British diplomat explained it. Arab governments working with the PLO took advantage of these vulnerabilities to push for greater political support for the Palestinian cause across Europe from Spain, Greece and Portugal, to France, Italy and the United Kingdom. By 1979, the *New York Times* was even speculating as to which European countries would normalize relations with the PLO first. Following a visit to Europe in the same year, a State Department official reported back that it was 'amazing'[73] how much progress the Palestinian cause had made on the political as well as the popular level since his last visit to the continent earlier in the decade.

In Europe at least, the achievements of the oil weapon, though limited, were hard to ignore. It was even harder to ignore the rising financial power of the Arab Gulf. In 1979, the monetary reserves of Saudi Arabia, Qatar, Kuwait and Abu Dhabi were estimated to be worth more than the entire monetary reserves of the world at the start of 1974. 'Never before', Henry Kissinger would later recall, 'had nations so weak militarily – and in some cases politically – been able to impose such strains on the international system'.[74] The well-known Arab economist Yusif A. Sayigh urged the Gulf States to take advantage of this unprecedented good fortune to formulate a comprehensive oil strategy that found a balance between self-interest and international responsibility.[75] Others more intimately involved with high politics believed that this was already happening. 'Yesterday we spoke English, now we speak Arabic,' pronounced OPEC chairman Mana Al-Otaiba at the end of the decade.[76] This was a novel way of saying that the balance of power between the West and the Gulf Arab oil producers was already tilting in favour of the latter.

It was too soon to know if Al-Oteia was correct. What was not in doubt was that since the oil crisis the Arab Gulf States had established themselves as regional political powers and global economic powers of the first rank. In the words of veteran British Arabist Elizabeth Monroe, they had transformed themselves in the few short years from 'desert obscurity to world status'.[77] Neither their rising profile nor wealth changed the fact that they were still, in the words of the outspoken American senator William Fulbright, 'militarily insignificant gazelles . . . in a world of lions'.[78]

As the rollercoaster decade of the 1970s came to an end it remained to be seen which of these two contradicting characteristics – new-found riches or traditional political and military weakness – would dictate the future fortunes of the Arab Gulf States. Would they be able to further expand their power? Or would the significant, and in some ways unprecedented, geo-political developments taking place in the wider region conspire to prevent them from consolidating stability at home and extending influence abroad in the coming years?

CHAPTER 2

NEIGHBOURHOOD WATCH

'You can change friends but not neighbours.'

– Atal Bihari Vajpayee

Shortly after the start of the Iranian revolution in early 1979, the PLO's diplomatic troubleshooter, Farouk Kaddoumi, visited Saudi Arabia for a series of high-level meetings. As a young man, Kaddoumi had worked for Aramco, the giant Saudi oil company, before founding the Palestinian revolutionary group Fatah, alongside Yasser Arafat, and rising to the rank of de facto foreign minister of the PLO. Now he was in the kingdom to warn his Saudi counterpart, foreign minister Saud Al-Faisal, that in any regional war between Iran and the Arabs, the kingdom's oilfields and the holy places in Mecca and Medina would be top targets. Kaddoumi's words carried some weight. As soon as they came to power the revolutionary leaders in Iran had embraced the PLO and promised to champion the Palestinian cause. Yet Saud, the son of the late King Faisal, responded calmly to Kaddoumi's unwelcome news. 'The holy places are protected by God', he told him. 'As for the oil fields, they are protected by man.'[1]

Such composure served him well over more than three decades as foreign minister in a career that stretched from the time of the Iranian revolution to beyond the Arab Spring. He only left his post in April 2015, a couple of months before he died at the age of seventy-five. Less senior Gulf officials displayed similar calmness in the face of upheaval next door in Iran. 'We've got nothing to worry about,' a Kuwaiti delegate reassured those gathered around him at the opening drinks reception at the opulent Palais Pallavicini in Vienna at one of the last OPEC meetings of the 1970s. 'Don't be so worried . . . it will all come right in the end,' added a Saudi colleague.[2] Such confidence, that events in Iran would not threaten stability at home or influence abroad, was understandable.

The oil price rose by over 1,500 per cent between 1971 and 1981. This brought the Arab Gulf States vast wealth that provided them with the means to make huge progress at home. By the end of the 1970s, the region's cities were increasingly important centres of trade and finance and among the most highly developed in the Arab world. Until the middle of the twentieth century, Abu Dhabi on the eastern horn of the peninsula was a fishing village made up of narrow streets and tin huts. It came into its available oil wealth relatively late compared to Saudi Arabia and Kuwait and until the beginning of the 1970s only spent a tiny amount of its oil revenues on domestic development. This made its transformation over the rest of that decade all the more impressive. One British diplomat who had lived there for many years noted that an aerial photograph of Abu Dhabi in the 1950s would have shown nothing but 'a bare sandbank'. By 1980 he was delighted to report that a similar picture taken from above would have recorded a 'mini Manhattan . . . and the whole island covered by building, roads and gardens'. A Saudi diplomat made a similar point about his own kingdom. His fellow countryman, he noted with pride, 'used to go to Cairo and stand baffled in the face of what he saw there. Now the Egyptian would go to Riyadh and not believe what he saw at the airport'.[3]

Beyond their borders and across the wider Middle East, the Gulf States had successfully navigated the fallout from the 1973 Arab–Israeli war and subsequent oil crisis, civil war in Lebanon and rebellion in Oman to reposition themselves as increasingly influential players in inter-Arab politics. As the flow of oil continued uninterrupted they emerged as a major factor in the global financial system, as well as significant backers of international institutions like the IMF, the World Bank and the United Nations. Speaking in 1980, one very informed regional commentator expressed doubt that there had ever been a time in the history of mankind that such a group of 'intrinsically insignificant polities, at a comparatively primitive stage, has possessed such enormous financial power'.[4] But the events of 1979 – the overthrow of the shah of Iran, the US-backed peace deal between Israel and Egypt, and the Soviet invasion of Afghanistan – provided a stark reminder to the Gulf Arabs that despite their previously unimagined wealth they still faced upheaval and potential calamity on their doorstep, across the Arab world, and at the hands of the two superpowers.

The revolution in Iran was the first of these direct and open challenges to the Gulf. Long before the shah had lost power, the Gulf Arabs had resented his megalomania. This self-proclaimed 'King of Kings' was only the second member of his family to become shah, but his modest lineage did not stop him from hosting one of the largest, most expensive and most extravagant gatherings of royals and presidents ever held to celebrate 2,500 years of the Persian Empire in 1971. Within a decade he was gone and Gulf Arab leaders shed few tears over his demise. He 'insulted Islam. He tyrannized his people. What can you expect?'[5] eulogized one senior UAE official soon after he lost power. Following the shah's downfall, Saudi officials enjoyed recounting a story from the late 1960s when the shah had taken it upon himself to send King Faisal a series of letters in which he advised the Saudi leader to modernize, open up the country and Westernize lest the royal family be overthrown. King Faisal, so the story goes, wrote back to his neighbour to thank him for his concern and advised him to remember that he was not the shah of France sitting in the Elysée Palace in Paris but the ruler of a nation with a huge Muslim majority and he should act accordingly. This anecdote would end with the Saudi storyteller pointing out that the shah had ignored these wise words and within a decade he had been removed by Islamic revolutionaries.

Before that happened, the shah and his state-controlled media revelled in proclaiming Iran the 'real power' in the region, and promised his Arab neighbours, somewhat patronizingly, that he would ensure their 'peace, freedom and co-existence'.[6] Over the centuries ambitious Iranian rulers had attempted to dominate the Gulf. They had been prevented from doing so during the twentieth century by the powerful British presence that provided protection for the Arab Sheikhdoms. Following the British withdrawal from the region in 1971, the shah quickly seized the islands of Abu Musa and the two Tunbs, situated near the Strait of Hormuz in the lower Gulf. This aggressive action against territory owned by the tiny Gulf emirates of Sharjah and Ras Al Khaimah placed a spotlight on the shah's evolving regional ambitions. His public statements did little to help the situation. He made no secret of the fact that he disdained his Arab neighbours, telling a French interviewer in the mid-1970s that they had 'no value and are worthless'.[7]

His refusal to join the oil embargo of 1973, and his decision to increase production to meet consumer demand, was viewed as evidence of his opportunism. His military build-up, the biggest anywhere in the world since the American deployment in Vietnam during the 1960s, also provided evidence of the real threat he posed. This mighty military machine included a sophisticated domestic defence industry that was part of his vastly ambitious industrialization and modernization programme – his plan for a 'Great Civilization', as he liked to call it. What he could not make he bought, spending almost US$12 billion on American military hardware in the first half of the 1970s alone.[8] This was all paid for by rapidly rising oil revenues that shot up from under US$1 billion in 1971 to almost US$18 billion in 1975. As his military capability grew along with his ego, the shah liked to boast that his armed forces were ten to twenty times larger than Britain's. This was a gross exaggeration, though by the time he lost power his army and air force were both larger than their British equivalents. The only Arab state in the region able to match Iran's air force was Iraq on its eastern border. The Iranian navy, still half built, dwarfed those of the Arab Gulf States. Its standing army of around 300,000 men was only about 6,000 less than the combined totals of Saudi Arabia, Iraq and Kuwait.

There was another side to the Arab Gulf's relationship with Iran. Between 1954 and 1979, the shah worked hand in hand with the Americans and British to prevent an anti-Western coup in Iran and to keep the country at the heart of the anti-Soviet regional defence alliance. In the process Iran had become the 'cornerstone'[9] of Western security policy in the Gulf. Both Washington and London considered the pro-Western, pro-modernization and anti-communist shah as the natural defender of the small, for the most part pro-Western, and virulently anti-communist, Gulf kingdoms. Before withdrawing from the region, British officials even reassured Gulf leaders that the shah would come to their aid in any future crisis.[10] Despite their major differences with the shah, the Gulf Arabs shared his profound distaste of Islamic radicals, social revolutionaries and Arab nationalists.

During the 1970s, the Gulf Arabs did benefit from this common cause. The shah had never hidden his dislike of Iraqi rulers, whom he once described as 'crazy, blood-thirsty savages', and he blocked any Iraqi threat to the Arab Gulf States, in particular Kuwait. Though he had refused to join the oil embargo in 1973, later in the decade he put aside his rivalry with Saudi Arabia inside OPEC in the interests of keeping more radical oil producers at bay. He even sent 3,000 troops to Dhofar, Oman's largest province, to help the forward-thinking young Sultan Qaboos put down a rebellion backed by South Yemen, Moscow's closest ally in the region.

In the immediate wake of the 1979 revolution, the short-lived interim government that had taken power in Tehran set out to reassure its Arab neighbours that it had much more in common with them, and posed much less of a threat to their interests, than the former shah. In an interview with an Abu Dhabi paper in March 1979, Abbas Amir Entezam, Iran's interim deputy prime minister, explained that he wanted to build good relations with Gulf countries. His foreign minister went further. The Islamic Republic of Iran, Ebrahim Yazdi promised, would never act as the policeman in the region and his government's short-term goal was to convince its neighbours of its peaceful intentions and its opposition to exporting revolution to other countries. Mehdi Bazargan, who headed up the interim government and served as Iran's first prime minister after the revolution, was clear that his country would no longer serve as America's policeman in the Gulf, but it would develop relations with local states on the basis of respect and equality.[11]

Gulf leaders welcomed these conciliatory words. In public they expressed their respect for the choice of the Iranian people and made it clear that they had no intention of meddling in their neighbour's internal affairs as long as, in the words of Prince Saud, Iran also refrained from 'foreign interference, which might tilt the balance of power in the area'.[12] In private they had several major concerns. As a point of principle they viewed the overthrow of the shah, who was also one of the world's longest-serving monarchs, as an unwelcome and ill-boding precedent that undermined the status quo in the neighbourhood. As a British diplomat stationed in Jeddah reported back to London at the time, there was no getting away from the fact that 'a monarchy backed by the strongest and best equipped forces in the Middle East was overthrown by an elderly religious leader backed by the people'.[13]

The elderly religious leader in question was Ayatollah Sayyid Ruhollah Khomeini. Since the early 1960s, when Khomeini was first arrested by the shah's secret police, he had been the symbol of Islamic opposition to the prevailing regional order. Following his exile in 1964, he continued to urge his followers in Iran to depose the pro-Western shah during fourteen years living in Turkey, the Iraqi city of Najaf and then suburban Paris. Two weeks after the shah fled the country, the seventy-seven-year-old Khomeini returned triumphantly to Iran. In November 1979, revolutionary students loyal to Khomeini stormed the US embassy in the Iranian capital. This resulted in a 370-day hostage siege that defined and haunted US–Iranian relations over subsequent decades. More immediately, it served notice to the world that radical factions were gaining the upper hand inside Iran. Bazargan resigned his post as prime minister once the embassy siege began. As one perceptive chronicler of the revolution noted soon afterwards, he was a 'moderate who found himself heading a revolutionary movement'.[14] His withdrawal from office at the start of the hostage crisis demolished any lingering hopes that Iran's new rulers had any interest in normalizing relations with the US, never mind remaining at the centre of the pro-Western alliance in the region.

In case anyone was still unclear about this new reality, Khomeini drove the point home. Iran was the region's major military power and the world's second largest oil exporter and it would no longer serve as Washington's key ally. Nor would it follow in the shah's footsteps and serve as the unofficial protector of the Arab Gulf. Khomeini also showed no interest in following the condition set out by Gulf leaders that his new regime refrained from promoting its revolutionary ideas outside its borders. As he explained in a speech published in a collection of his writing in 1981, 'The Iranian revolution is not exclusively that of Iran, because Islam does not belong to any particular people ... we will export our revolution throughout the world because it is an Islamic revolution.'[15] This sort of talk was anathema to Gulf Arab leaders. They were further angered by the Iranian clerical leadership's disapproval of their conspicuous consumption and growing Westernization and by the Iranian tendency to question their Islamic credentials and thus their legitimacy. In television and radio broadcasts Khomeini himself attacked the Saudi royals as 'pleasure-seeking mercenaries' and asked, 'How long must Satan rule the House of God?' This threatening reference to Mecca and Medina gave credibility to Kaddoumi's warning to Saud over the fate of the holy cities in any regional conflict.[16]

Senior Iranian clerics focused their attacks on another long-time preoccupation of Iranian leaders – Bahrain. In 1957 the shah proclaimed this small island kingdom off the coast of Saudi Arabia to be Iran's fourteenth province. Over the next thirteen years the British navy stood in the way of any plans he had to make this a reality. In 1970, under international pressure, the shah renounced this claim. When the revolution started, the government in Bahrain attempted in vain to prevent news of what was happening from reaching the island's majority Shia population in fear they might look to foment a revolution of their own. Pro-Iranian demonstrations broke out almost immediately on news of the shah's overthrow. Most notably, Ayatollah Sadeq Rohani attacked the kingdom's ruling family and called for the country's annexation to Iran. Senior Bahraini officials denounced these attacks as 'irresponsible' and made hollow threats that they would take a tough stand in response to further Iranian-inspired disturbances. In an attempt to play down the affair, Iran's interim foreign minister, Ebrahim Yazdi, rebuked Rohani. Iran's ambassador in Kuwait went further, describing him as a 'nonentity' who carried little influence.[17]

Rohani held no official role in the new government and he had an uneasy relationship with the revolutionary leadership in Tehran. It would later place him under house arrest for fifteen years for criticizing its religious decisions. But as a senior cleric with a large following and a long record of opposition to the shah, he had some influence in the early days of the revolution. At exactly the same time as Ayatollah Rohani demanded the annexation of Bahrain, Hadi Al-Modarresi, an Iraqi cleric of Iranian origin and the representative of Ayatollah Khomeini in Bahrain, organized a series of anti-regime demonstrations. In addition, graffiti appeared across the island that accused the royal family of working for Savak, the shah's despised security service, and called for the 'Khomeini of Bahrain' to take power.[18]

The internal and external challenges that Bahrain faced were held up across the Gulf as evidence that the new Iranian leadership was reviving the shah's territorial claims to the island kingdom. As one Kuwaiti newspaper put it, the Islamic leadership in Tehran should 'discard the dreams of expansion and the nonsense of the shahs and emperors since Darius'.[19] The fact that Khomeini himself never publicly disavowed Rohani's statements fuelled such views. Hadi Al-Modarresi's move to Tehran, where he was rumoured to have found a job at the newly established and forebodingly named Office of the Liberation Movements, also aroused suspicion. In his new role, Al-Modarresi broadcast what British officials at the time classed as 'absurdly inflammatory' propaganda against the status quo in Bahrain.[20] This and similar state-sponsored provocations were a constant reminder of the dangers that the revolution in Iran posed to the precarious sectarian balance between Sunni and Shia Muslims across the region.

Adherents of Shia Islam follow Mohammed's son-in-law and cousin Ali, whom they hold to be Mohammed's rightful successor. The second-largest branch in Islam and a minority across the Arab world, by the time of the revolution Shia made up over 90 per cent of Iran's population and over 70 per cent of Bahrain's population. They also accounted for smaller but not insignificant numbers across the Arab Gulf States, including around 10 per cent of Saudi Arabia's citizens. These communities had closely followed Khomeini's sermons and statements during his long years of exile. At the beginning of 1979, in the early days of the revolution, British diplomats reported home that Gulf Arab leaders were 'alive to the new significance of their minorities', but did not feel that they were 'at any immediate risk of being toppled'.[21] This customary British understatement ignored the fact that for a long time Arab Gulf leaders had been deeply concerned that the religious identity of their Shia communities inspired more loyalty than their national identity. The Iranian revolution had made these suspicions even more acute. Oman's tiny Shia community had much closer ties to India and Pakistan than Iran. Yet following the revolution, the authorities in Muscat confiscated religious literature coming into the country and a Shia bookstore in the Omani capital was briefly shut down.[22] Kuwait and Bahrain experienced pro-Khomeini demonstrations following his rise to power that fuelled concerns that these communities might turn into fifth columns working for Tehran. There was much more serious rioting by the Shia population of Saudi Arabia, the majority of whom lived in the oil-rich, and thus critically important, Eastern Province of the country.

In November 1979, about 90,000 members of Saudi Arabia's Shia community defied the official ban on the commemoration of Ashura, an important Shia holiday that commemorates the martyrdom of Hussein. The violence that followed between protestors and thousands of members of the Saudi National Guard left several dead on both sides. Three months later, on the first anniversary of the Islamic revolution in Iran, Saudi Shia staged a second demonstration, which saw more riots and a further deployment of the National Guard. At the same time as the authorities in Saudi Arabia, as well as Bahrain and Kuwait, were dealing with potentially devastating sectarian discord at home, Egypt and Israel did something that would have been unimaginable only a few years earlier. In late March 1979, on the north lawn of the White House, under the watchful eye of a nervous American president Jimmy Carter, they signed a peace deal.

This unprecedented agreement was a blow to the Arab Gulf. Since the oil crisis of 1973, Riyadh had built up close ties with Cairo at the centre of the pro-Western axis in the Arab world. Between 1973 and 1976 Saudi Arabia gave Egypt US$2 billion, including most of the money needed to finance a US$350 million pipeline from the Red Sea port of Suez to the Mediterranean. Along with Qatar and the UAE, Saudi Arabia also joined Egypt in investing US$1 billion to establish the Arab Military Industries Organization (AMIO). Even though the whole Arab world had condemned Egyptian president Anwar Sadat's unilateral peace negotiations with Israel at the expense of the Palestinian cause, the Gulf Arabs were opposed to the total isolation of Egypt. They feared that if they abandoned Sadat, Egypt might fall prey to radical forces and that this would destabilize the entire Arab world. This explains why Saudi Arabia provided Egypt with a US$1.5 billion loan in response to food riots on the streets of Cairo in January 1977, even though Israeli–Egyptian talks were already under way. Two years later, on the eve of the March 1979 peace deal, Gulf finance ministers promised to honour past commitments of multilateral aid to Egypt, while Kuwait never followed through on its threat to punish Egypt for its peace deal by withdrawing around US$1 billion of its money held on deposit in the country's banks.

Though they were not willing to abandon Egypt totally, the Gulf Arabs could not ignore the damage that Sadat had done to their attempts since the 1973 oil crisis to promote the Palestinian cause. William Quandt, a Middle East expert close to the Carter administration, noted at the time how Sadat's peace moves made it impossible for the Palestinians to achieve substantive political concessions. An Arab commentator put it more bluntly. Sadat's unilateral initiative 'demolished'[23] any chance of a comprehensive peace and with it much of the Arab Gulf's influence on the matter. For Arab Gulf rulers, the peace deal also raised another major concern. They now worried that Egypt would become increasingly reluctant to work closely with them, instead preferring to focus its efforts on building up strategic ties with the United States and Israel.

The Soviet invasion of Afghanistan in December 1979 added to Arab Gulf woes. With the exception of Kuwait, all the Arab Gulf kingdoms were vehemently anti-Soviet during these years. The reality of vast numbers of Soviet troops stationed next door to Iran and only a short distance from the Straits of Hormuz raised the spectre of a Soviet invasion of the oil-rich Gulf. US war planners and local leaders had anticipated and dreaded this since the 1950s due to their shared belief that the Soviets would move south against the Gulf oilfields prior to launching an all-out invasion of Western Europe. If all this was not bad enough, in September 1980 Islamist Iran and Ba'athist Iraq went to war. On top of everything else, this required that the Gulf Arabs deal with the outbreak of regional conflict between the two largest local powers, both of whom they distrusted and feared.

Long before Saddam Hussein became president of Iraq in 1979 he had established himself as the dominant force in the country. During his rise through Ba'athist ranks he had exhibited three traits that would define his years in power – ambition, brutality and paranoia. He saw enemies and competitors everywhere and he had long desired to stamp his authority on Iran, his only real competitor in the region. In 1975 he had repudiated an agreement with Iran on the Shatt-al-Arab waterway along their shared border. Like his far less powerful Arab neighbours in the Gulf, Saddam viewed the rise of the revolutionary regime in Tehran as a force for instability in the region and a grave threat to his rule. He was particularly concerned that it would lead to a concerted attempt by his country's large and long-persecuted Shia population located around the holy cities of Najaf and Karbala to rise up against him.

To ensure that none of this would happen, Saddam took pre-emptive action. In September 1980 his army invaded Iran. In a coordinated operation, infantry and tanks crossed over a number of points on the shared 480-kilometre border. Iraqi warplanes targeted Iranian airfields and strategic sites, while artillery pounded towns within reach. This was not a declaration of all-out war. It was intended to be a limited military operation that sent a message to the new regime in Tehran to stay out of Iraq's internal affairs and to defer to its external ambitions. The moment was well chosen. The Iranian army had been purged of suspected royalists following the revolution and the country was preoccupied with insurgencies by Marxist rebels, Kurds and other ethnic groups. The new government also had to deal with a faltering economy and a Western economic embargo, as well as an increasingly bitter confrontation with the US. For all these reasons Saddam was convinced that Iran would not be able to counter his invasion. He was so sure of this that when the Iranian air force retaliated against his initial attacks by launching bombing missions he assumed it was Israel attacking Iraq.

Saddam's strategic miscalculation over the Iranian capacity to fight back resulted in a hugely destructive eight-year war that profoundly shaped the future course of the Middle East. In the more immediate term this titanic regional clash over ideology and power politics posed the Gulf States with a real dilemma – how to respond to the conflict. A week after the Iraqi invasion one senior Gulf royal speaking anonymously summed up the prevailing mood – 'God help us if one of them wins.'[24] For many in the Gulf, an Iranian victory would speed up Tehran's attempts to export revolution and consolidate its power in the region. On the other hand, the Gulf Arabs had lived in fear of Iraq for decades. They did not want Saddam, boosted by a victory over Iran, turning his attention their way. This was particularly true for Kuwait. As far back as the early 1930s Iraqi leaders had been calling for the integration of Kuwait into their country. Abd Al-Karim Qasim, the nationalist general who overthrew the monarchy and seized power in 1958, described Kuwait as a district of Iraq and vowed that it was his 'sacred mission' to recapture the territory. Under his leadership Iraq was the only Arab League country not to endorse Kuwaiti independence in 1961. In the same year, his troops even crossed the border into Kuwait, only to withdraw in the face of intense British pressure and the dispatch of a Royal Navy warship.

Qasim lost power to a Ba'athist coup in 1963, known as the Ramadan revolution, which resulted in his trial and execution. His successors, adherents of a heady mix of secularism, Arab nationalism and socialism, disavowed his territorial claim. Instead, they labelled the pro-Western Sheikhdoms of the Gulf as 'reactionary and pro-imperialist regimes'[25] and looked to undermine them by providing clandestine assistance and military aid to home-grown subversives. Following the Iranian revolution, Saddam made a conscious effort to improve ties with the Gulf States. He agreed to participate along with Kuwait, Qatar, the UAE and Saudi Arabia in a joint arms industry based in the UAE. In the summer of 1980 he also became the first Iraqi ruler since 1958 to visit Saudi Arabia when he met King Khalid at the summer resort of Ta'if.

Once his war with Iran began, Saddam presented his army as the only thing standing between the Arab Gulf and the revolutionaries in Tehran. As one Arab diplomat perceptively noted at the time, 'There is a curious reversal of roles here. Now it is Iran which is raising the banner of revolution, while [Iraqi] president Saddam Hussein is assuming the shah's mantle as guarantor of the status quo in the Gulf.'[26] Saddam worked hard to develop and entrench this perception. A hotline was set up connecting Baghdad to Riyadh and he regularly sent his emissaries to brief other Gulf leaders on the war's progress. His PR offensive was made easier by the stream of Arabic broadcasts emanating from Tehran threatening the Gulf Arabs in the name of the Islamic Revolution Organization in the Arabian Peninsula.

By the end of 1981, with the war in full flow, concerns over the threat posed by Saddam quickly evaporated as the full horror of the implications of an Iranian victory sank in. Prince Bandar, a grandson of Saudi Arabia's founder Abdul Aziz Ibn Saud, served his country as ambassador in Washington for twenty-two years between 1983 and 2005. He was a consummate networker, a political pragmatist and a shrewd strategist. Bandar would later explain Gulf Arab thinking in the early days of the Iran–Iraq war. The message of Islamic revolution, he recalled, combined with the anti-Arab content of the sermons and statements of Iran's new leaders, led the Gulf States to support Saddam. 'It was in our interest to stop Iran on the Iraqi borders, rather than fight them at our borders,' he explained, before adding that Saddam was 'a very bad man, but Khomeini was worse', which left the Gulf Arabs with 'a choice between bad and worse'.[27] In later years, some senior Iranian officials did acknowledge, at least in part, the truth behind Bandar's statement. After he became president in 1989, Akbar Hashemi Rafsanjani even speculated that if his country had shown a little more consideration for the interests and feelings of the Gulf Arabs they might not have been so supportive of Iraq during the war.[28]

The Arab Gulf States demonstrated their support for Iraq in numerous ways. They deported Iranians suspected of subversion and censored newspapers that drew attention to Iraqi setbacks on the battlefield. They stepped in to supply Baghdad's oil customers and provided the main overland route for weapons and civilian supplies entering into war-torn Iraq. They passed on valuable intelligence on Iran and allowed Iraqi planes returning from missions in Iran to refuel on their territory. They even flooded the oil market and forced down the price of oil in order to reduce the amount of money Iran had available to pay for its war. Most importantly, the Gulf States became Saddam's bankers, justifying the vast amounts of money they pumped into his war chest on the tenuous grounds that mutual assistance agreements that predated the war, such as the Arab Joint Defense Pact, required them to come to his aid. Many years later, a former Iranian official claimed that the GCC had 'fully supported the invasion' with over US$100 billion in financial support. More realistic estimates range from between US$22 and US$35 billion in the first five years of the war, rising to US$40 billion in total by the end of the conflict.[29]

The extent of this financial support – most of it provided by Kuwait and Saudi Arabia – was all the more impressive given that it came at a time of falling global demand for oil and rising production from non-OPEC producers like the United Kingdom and Mexico. This reduced oil revenues, resulting in rising budget deficits and higher levels of borrowing across the Gulf. Despite these financial pressures, Gulf leaders were convinced that their investment in Saddam's war was money well spent if it staved off an Iranian victory, and contributed to a military stalemate that kept both Iran and Iraq preoccupied with each other instead of the Arab Gulf. Bankrolling Saddam's war also allowed Gulf leaders to squeeze concessions out of Iraq on outstanding diplomatic and territorial disputes. In return for their largesse, for example, the Saudis got Saddam to sign an agreement ending a nearly sixty-year-old border dispute. Yet, the Iran–Iraq war clearly demonstrated to the Gulf Arabs that their quest for stability at home and influence abroad in the post-1973 era would prove to be extremely difficult, not to say costly, if they could not keep the ambitions of their bigger neighbours in check. A shared understanding of this unpleasant reality brought the Arab Gulf States closer together.

Since the 1973 oil crisis, and in some cases even before then, officials from the six Gulf States had cooperated in areas of common concern such as aviation, fisheries, agriculture, communications and education. There even existed some inter-Gulf institutions such as the Gulf News Agency, the Gulf University and Gulf Air, a joint venture between Abu Dhabi, Bahrain, Oman and Qatar. What had never existed until the Iran–Iraq war was the political will required to establish a formal regional grouping. Two months into the war, in November 1980, the Amman summit of Arab leaders approved a Kuwaiti document calling for a union of Gulf countries. After further discussions, in early February 1981 at a meeting in Riyadh, the foreign ministers of the six Arab Gulf States agreed to establish the Gulf Cooperation Council (GCC). This was followed by a signing ceremony in March in Muscat and a launch meeting in late May in Abu Dhabi, attended by the rulers of the six prospective members.

Kuwait always claimed credit for the birth of the GCC. Following the death of Sheikh Jaber Al-Ahmed Al-Sabah in 2006, obituaries of the

Kuwaiti leader, who had ruled the kingdom at the time of the GCC's founding, recalled how the organization had been his brainchild. Kuwait had hosted the first meeting of the six that paved the way for the formation of the GCC in early February 1981. It had won the right to appoint the first secretary general of the new organization from its stable of senior diplomats. In every other way Saudi Arabia was the source of the idea and the key to its establishment. Even before the British left the Gulf in 1971 the Saudis had been pushing for some form of Gulf federation. They argued that a formal pact would improve regional security. The other Arab Gulf States also wanted enhanced security. But they were unwilling to abandon their own national interests or to formalize Saudi, Iranian or Iraqi economic, demographic and military dominance in order to develop a collective security framework in the Gulf. This explains why those few formal attempts to institutionalize security coordination prior to the creation of the GCC had failed dismally. At a meeting of Gulf foreign ministers in Jeddah in July 1975, the big three – Iran, Iraq and Saudi Arabia – all supported the convening of a regional security summit. A six-point draft agenda was drawn up and preparations got under way. The summit never took place, following a Kuwaiti veto at a time of rising tensions with Iraq over border disagreements. The Iranian revolution and the Iran–Iraq war did not mark the end of deeply embedded historic rivalries and suspicions, or concerns over territorial integrity and national independence. Nor did they neutralize the worries of smaller Arab Gulf States over potential Saudi dominance. Both events did, however, create a situation in which immediate security took precedence for the first time. This was underscored by the fact that vocal Iraqi and Iranian opposition to the founding of the GCC was framed in terms of concerns over the birth of a military and security alliance on their borders.

As Abdullah Bisharah, the straight-talking first secretary general of the GCC, acknowledged at the time, 'Without security we cannot do anything'. He followed this up with the claim that there was 'complete accord' among member states on the 'basic principles of collective security'.[30] Bisharah was a skilled negotiator who remained in the post for ten years, despite the official limit of two three-year terms. But even he could not overcome the fact that consensus, in principle, on the need for coordination on security matters did not translate into agreement on how joint action should express itself in practical terms. Only Oman's sultan publicly called for security to be the GCC's 'principal and fundamental role'.[31] He pushed hard for this for historic, geographic and strategic reasons. The second largest GCC state, Oman is located on the vulnerable south-east tip of the Arabian

Peninsula. Its nearly 2,000-kilometre coastline straddles strategic sea-lanes and looks away from the Gulf towards east Africa and the Indian subcontinent, cut off from much of the rest of the Arab world. A story doing the rounds for decades even told of a meeting of the Arab League in the 1950s being adjourned so that those attending could consult a map. The name of an obscure Arab country called 'Oman' had come up and nobody present knew were it was located.[32] The Omani desire for the GCC to address security issues was due to its unique strategic situation as well as its geography, which isolated it somewhat. It had experienced civil war in Dhofar in previous decades and it was also a frontline state in the global Cold War, a status underscored in the summer of 1981 when Oman's neighbour South Yemen entered into a Soviet-backed pact with Libya and Ethiopia. Both of these challenges explain why the nascent GCC appealed more to Oman than its Gulf partners for its potential as a security organization.

Despite Omani lobbying and the efforts of secretary general Bisharah to gain backing for his conviction that there could be 'no economic progress without stability',[33] there was little support among the other member states for turning the GCC into an overarching security organization after its launch. From the time of the first GCC summit in Abu Dhabi in May 1981 onwards, Gulf rulers openly grappled with each other over how such security could be achieved within the GCC framework. On every occasion national security trumped regional security and official GCC pronouncements reflected this position. The GCC's launch document, known as the Riyadh Communiqué, and issued by foreign ministers attending a meeting in the Saudi capital in February, did not refer to security or defence arrangements explicitly, only addressing these issues briefly under a section headed 'Other Fields'.[34] The body's charter, published on 25 May 1981, did not mention security or defence at all. Instead, early GCC documents and meetings focused on cultural and social issues, as well as political integration and, most importantly, economic cooperation.

There was agreement on one point at least, that Gulf stability required the major global Cold War powers – the United States and the Soviet Union – to stay out of the region. The Arab Gulf States inhabited a bipolar Cold War world dominated by the Americans and Soviets. Though they would never had admitted it in public, if forced to take sides they would all have lined up behind Washington. Kuwait was the only GCC state with diplomatic relations with Moscow at the time, and these had been initiated after independence as a way of gaining extra insurance against Iraqi claims to annex its territory. Despite this lack of official relations between the Gulf and the Soviet Union on the eve of the founding of the GCC, Bisharah was dispatched from New York, where he was still serving as Kuwait's UN ambassador, to Moscow to reassure Soviet leaders of the GCC's neutrality.

In sum, local Gulf actors had no desire to be dragged into superpower conflicts and proxy battles. Speaking in May 1981, the same month as the GCC Charter was unveiled, the UAE's president Sheikh Zayed bin Sultan Al-Nahyan summed up this thinking. 'Our conception of Gulf security', this astute and visionary leader told journalists, 'is one in which the countries of the Gulf are allowed to live peacefully and securely without interference from foreign powers, and without great powers trying to determine the area's fate'.[35] One important explanation as to why all Gulf leaders wanted to distance themselves from the machinations of the superpowers was to avoid being viewed as 'stooges of the Great Satan', as officials in the revolutionary regime in Tehran liked to label them.[36] During their war with Iraq, the Iranians also explained Saudi support for Saddam Hussein as 'natural' on the grounds that it was an 'American war', and that the Gulf States and Iraq were puppets of the US.[37] Gulf leaders were deeply concerned over such accusations. They believed that they had the potential to antagonize their own citizens, and engender anti-Gulf feeling in the rest of the Arab world, which was increasingly hostile to American policies in the Middle East.

According to conventional wisdom, Washington has carefully orchestrated its dominance of the Middle East for generations in the interests of oil, Israel and the military-industrial complex. In doing so, it excluded its competitors and allies from the region and sacrificed the region's peoples to the whims of a pro-Western elite. There was some truth in all these claims. Oil, for example, had undoubtedly been the key determinant of American involvement in the Gulf for decades. At the same time, there has been much soul searching and internal debate among American policymakers before the US has engaged in or taken the lead Western role anywhere in the Middle East. When it has done so it has looked, with some notable exceptions, such as the US invasion of Iraq in 2003, to cooperate with its Western allies in defence of global interests. The origins of this cautious and considered approach can be found in the First World War. As a western hemisphere power with few political or military interests in the region, American leaders recoiled from involvement in a Middle East war that was, in their opinion, both morally distasteful and strategically unnecessary. On this basis, the US refused to declare war on Turkey or to join negotiations over a post-war settlement for the region when hostilities ended. This allowed the British Empire to add Transjordan, Palestine, Iraq and the Hejaz to its pre-war possessions of Egypt and Cyprus. In the process,

Britain established itself as the paramount power in the region in the inter-war era. At the same time, American interests were limited to protecting and developing cultural and economic ties and engaging in humanitarian causes, as evidenced by the leading role taken by US ambassador Henry Morgenthau in overseeing the Turkish–Bulgarian population exchanges with Greece in the early 1920s. The ramifications of America's self-imposed absence from the Middle East during the 1920s and 1930s became obvious during the Second World War. On a diplomatic level the US entered the war woefully underrepresented in the region. In 1943, for example, during the great-power conference in Tehran, President Roosevelt was housed, to the consternation of British prime minister Winston Churchill, at the residence of the Soviet ambassador because the US had no representation of its own in the Iranian capital.

The US experience of supplying the Soviet war effort against Germany on the eastern front from its Persian Gulf Command in Tehran highlighted the strategic value of the region. So did the increased importance of oil to US war and post-war planning. American companies entered oil exploration in the Gulf for the first time in Bahrain in 1930. By the end of that decade they had established themselves in Saudi Arabia and Kuwait. But prior to the war, oil was viewed as a commercial rather than a strategic issue. In 1939, for example, secretary of state Cordell Hull expressed the view that US interests did 'not warrant representatives' in the Persian Gulf. By 1943 the attitudes of American policymakers on this issue had shifted profoundly: the Joint Chiefs of Staff informed the administration that in the absence of short-term energy self-sufficiency, the US would require external sources of oil for its future strategic needs. Soon afterwards, President Roosevelt was in no doubt what this meant. 'The defense of Saudi Arabia', explained America's wartime leader, 'is vital to the defense of the United States'.[38]

During the Cold War it was just as important for the United States to deny the Soviets control of the resources of the oil-rich Gulf as it was to secure the region's supply for their own or their allies' energy needs. Thus began almost half a century during which successive American administrations viewed the Middle East primarily in terms of the global clash with the Soviet Union. Numerous plans were drawn up to prevent the Soviets from ever taking control of the Gulf. One called for moving explosives to the Gulf so that the oilfields could be blown up and plugged before the Soviets got to them. Another recommended deploying 'radiological' weapons in the region in the event of a Soviet breakthrough as a way of denying their enemy local oilfields. The CIA rejected this proposal on the grounds that the Soviets might use 'expendable' Arabs to man the oil wells, regardless of the risks they faced of exposure to high levels of radiation.

By the early 1950s, it was an article of faith among US war planners that any Soviet attempt to engage the West in a global military conflict would be preceded by a move into the oil-rich Arab Gulf via Iran and Afghanistan. Named the Northern Tier states because of their location on the southern borders of the Soviet Union, both of these nations had looked to Britain for diplomatic and military backing in the decades before the Second World War. As British power faded in the wake of the war, they now turned to the US for protection. Washington was initially reluctant to undertake this new responsibility. As late as 1950, it signed a tripartite agreement with France and Britain that restated that America's role in the region would be primarily economic and diplomatic rather than military or strategic. Ultimately, however, Washington's view of Soviet hostile intentions and its evolving Cold War philosophy of containment seemed to offer little alternative to integrating these strategically sensitive states into the US-led anti-Soviet alliance.

It was not an easy task. As secretary of state John Foster Dulles noted after a visit to the region in 1953, local priorities were just that – local. The Arab states, as Dulles had discovered for himself, were almost totally focused on domestic and regional concerns. The US, on the other hand, viewed the Middle East almost entirely through the global Cold War prism. Regardless, the US felt that it had little choice but to proceed in establishing itself as the dominant Western actor in the region because, as noted previously, Britain was increasingly incapable of fulfilling this task. This became eminently clear in the Gulf context, following the British withdrawal from the region in 1971. Left to pick up the pieces, the US now found itself as the key Western power in the Gulf and responsible for providing security for an area that at the time supplied 32 per cent of the free world's oil and contained 58 per cent of its proven reserves. To meet this burden, Washington adopted a strategy that was 'selective, low key and somewhat detached'.[39] Under the Nixon Doctrine of the early 1970s, the administration offered to build up the pro-Western twin pillars of Saudi Arabia and Iran as local powers committed to leading regional efforts to prevent the spread of Soviet influence.

Like Nixon before him, on taking power in January 1977 President Jimmy Carter aggressively courted the shah of Iran, describing him publicly as his best friend after only two meetings. This made his administration's failure to prevent or even predict the shah's overthrow all the more shocking. Worse, in August 1978, six months before the US-backed shah fled Iran, the CIA infamously concluded, 'Iran is not in a revolutionary or even a pre-revolutionary situation'.[40] Washington's impotence in responding to the Tehran embassy siege and its unwillingness to respond to the Soviet invasion of Afghanistan at the end of 1979 also undermined American standing in the Middle East and across the entire globe. In a desperate attempt to regain some credibility, senior policymakers in Carter's White House reassured the Arab Gulf nations that neither the events in Iran nor in Afghanistan had altered the US commitment to stand by them in the face of attack. In January 1980, President Carter used the State of the Union address, the biggest speech of the presidential year, to drive this point home: 'Let our position be absolutely clear: an attempt by any outside force to gain control of the Persian Gulf region will be regarded as an assault on the vital interests of the United States of America, and such an assault will be repelled by any means necessary, including military force'.[41]

The Carter Doctrine, as this policy became known, was nothing less than a promise that the US would use military force to defend its vital interests across the Persian Gulf and Arabian Peninsula if need be. It led to the establishment of a Rapid Deployment Joint Task Force (RDJTF) of 15,000 men based in North America, on constant alert to respond to crises in the region. Carter's doctrine was explicitly designed to reassure pro-Western regimes in the region of America's commitment to the Gulf's security and stability. It was also intended to take into account the real worries that existed in the region over the problems caused on the 'Arab Street' by an obvious US military presence on the ground in the Gulf.

Although the GCC was a pro-Western alliance from the start, its leaders were keen to avoid being perceived as Washington's puppets in the Arab or Muslim world. This was harder for some Gulf Arab leaders to achieve than others. For example, Bahrain's rulers, like their GCC partners, opposed superpower intervention in the region. Yet, they had allowed the US to set up a Naval Task Force on the kingdom's coast in 1971. In 1975, they had also approved the upgrading of this facility so that it had operational responsibility for the Gulf, the Arabian Sea and the Red Sea. Other Arab Gulf States also looked to Washington for practical, if more discreet, support. As one Saudi official explained on condition of anonymity at the time, 'Everyone wants the Americans here, but no one wants to be the first to say so'.[42] During the early 1960s, in the face of mounting criticism from Arab nationalists in the wider region who appealed directly to citizens of the kingdom, Saudi Arabia had stopped the US Air Force from using the airbase at Dahran in the oil-rich Eastern Province, which they had been operating out of since the end of the Second World War. Despite this move, in subsequent years US officials remained confident that Riyadh still wanted Washington to serve as its 'powerful protector'.[43] Successive American administrations were content to play this role from afar as long as the Saudis worked to keep the price of oil down and spent billions of dollars on American weapons.

With revolutionaries in control in Iran and the Soviets engaged in a full-scale war in Afghanistan, leaders in Riyadh privately believed that US backing was more vital than ever by the end of the 1970s. Publicly, however, the Dahran base closure set a precedent for how they responded to anything that resembled an obvious American presence on their territory. In January 1980, looking to pre-empt adverse local opinion, Saudi Arabia's Crown Prince Fahd stated explicitly that his country would not agree to the establishment of military bases on its territory by the US or anyone else.[44] This preference among Gulf leaders for the US to remain 'over the horizon', which for many meant outside the Straits of Hormuz, was also born out of a fear that the superpower rivalry in the region could lead to an East–West showdown in their own backyard.

Immediately after the fall of the shah, senior US figures, such as Carter's special adviser Clark Clifford, warned that any Soviet move towards the Gulf 'means war'.[45] The Soviet Union's main ally in the region was Iraq. The two nations had signed a maritime agreement in 1974 that gave the Russian navy unlimited access to the Gulf. Soviet and East German advisers and technicians, as well as Cuban troops, also played an important role in the southern part of the Arabian Peninsula, while Soviet ships tasked with shadowing the local American fleet were based at Aden. Despite this Soviet presence, only Oman, located next to Aden on the strategically vulnerable entrance of the oil-rich Gulf, showed any enthusiasm among the GCC states for a formal and public US military role in the region. During a 1975 visit to Washington, Sultan Qaboos agreed in principle to accept President Gerald Ford's offer to provide his kingdom with American arms. In return, Oman allowed US forces occasional access to the British-built base facilities on Masira Island off Oman's south-east coast, a vital strategic point for the defence of the Straits of Hormuz.

In October 1979 Oman, having abandoned its traditional isolation from the Arab world, went further. It called for the establishment of a Gulf security force made up of oil producers and consumers, in which the US military would have a central role. This proposal was rejected out of hand by other Arab Gulf States. They feared that it would anger and alienate revolutionary Iran and the wider Arab world, still reeling from Washington's sponsorship of Egyptian–Israeli peace. Unperturbed, Oman allowed the

United States to use its territory in its failed Tehran hostage rescue attempt in 1980. In the same year it signed an agreement with the US that gave Washington the right to use certain Omani military installations in exchange for hundreds of millions of dollars of aid. This led the Soviets to describe Oman as a 'bridgehead'[46] for US penetration into the Gulf. Sultan Qaboos also faced criticism from his soon-to-be GCC partners over this move. Subsequently, he dismissed these reactions as 'overblown' and a 'big hullabaloo'. The agreement with the US, he explained, was limited to the temporary use of air and naval facilities on terms that had long been acceptable to the majority of pro-Western Arab states.[47]

Ronald Reagan became American president in January 1981. After the overthrow of the shah, the Tehran hostage crisis and the invasion of Afghanistan, Reagan was determined to restore his country's standing in the world by re-establishing American credibility in international affairs. This required reasserting American influence in the Gulf, and included a very clear commitment to prevent what Reagan described as 'Soviet meddling' in the region. This was, the new president insisted, 'something the United States would not tolerate'.[48] But the fall of the shah had left Washington with a power vacuum, as well as a credibility issue in the Middle East. In response, the Reagan administration immediately moved to strengthen relations with America's two most significant remaining regional allies – Israel and Saudi Arabia. To bolster and expand ties with Riyadh, Washington offered to station a squadron of American F-15 fighter planes in the kingdom. This offer required the presence of US military personnel on Saudi territory and was very publicly rejected by the leadership in Riyadh for exactly that reason. Washington's next proposal was much more warmly received. The Reagan administration offered Saudi Arabia the opportunity to purchase state-of-the-art airborne warning and control system (AWACS) technology.

Israel's supporters in the US Congress were outraged by the prospect of the AWACS deal. They were committed to ensuring Israel's qualitative technological advantage over its Arab enemies. This, they argued, would inevitably be eroded by the sale of such sophisticated radar technology to Saudi Arabia. In the ensuing heated debate in Congress and the media, the breadth and depth of US–Saudi ties became a matter of public record. This turned the spotlight on a history of bilateral security and military cooperation that Saudi officials, who valued discretion above all else, would have preferred to remain secret. As one anonymous Washington lawyer with close ties to Riyadh put it at the time, the Americans 'wanted to make love in public but Saudis are saying "let's have a private affair"'.[49] Such differences aside, the US refusal to bow to pro-Israel pressure on the AWACS issue highlighted very clearly the importance of Saudi Arabia to American Cold War interests by the early 1980s. It also underscored the limits of influence of the powerful Israel lobby when perceived to be opposing vital US strategic interests. President Carter would recall that the AWACS affair was a 'political hot potato' but one that was worth the battle. President Reagan agreed. He would subsequently sum up what motivated him on this matter: 'I didn't want Saudi Arabia to become another Iran.'[50] His administration was convinced that the overthrow of Saudi Arabia's ruling family would, in the words of an American intelligence report, result in the fall of the Saudis and the rise of a regime in Riyadh that was 'radical, militantly anti-Israel, and markedly anti-American'. This prospect was absolutely unacceptable to the US. Aware of this, Saudi decision makers displayed growing confidence, as one senior official in Riyadh put it, that the Americans would 'maintain us in power, whatever we do'.[51] This perceived open-ended and unconditional support from Washington may have provided Saudi Arabia and its Gulf Arab partners some comfort but it did not address the specific threats that they faced at the start of the 1980s.

The Iran–Iraq war, like the Iranian revolution before it, raised the spectre of Shia communities, backed by Tehran, acting as potential fifth columns across the Arab Gulf. In the final weeks of 1981 there was an abortive coup in Bahrain. Arab Gulf leaders immediately blamed Iran and convened the first ever extraordinary meeting of the GCC ministerial council. On its conclusion, a statement was read out that offered 'full support' for Bahrain and condemned in the strongest terms Iranian 'acts of sabotage'.[52] In the summer of 1982, Iran claimed its first major battlefield successes since the early days of the war and planned another major counter-offensive to keep up the momentum. The situation looked bleak for the Gulf Arabs. Iraq was on the defensive. Shia communities in Kuwait and the UAE openly celebrated Iran's military victories. Khomeini and other top officials in Tehran warned the Gulf Arabs to 'repent and return to Islam', and even questioned whether the Saudis were 'qualified'[53] to administer the holy cities of Mecca and Medina.

These developments were so worrying that an emergency meeting of GCC foreign ministers was convened solely to discuss the consequences of an upcoming Iranian victory in the war. Even in this environment top officials in GCC member states still refused to acknowledge openly that the Iranian threat was their main security challenge. The UAE backed Iraq in the war but was very concerned not to take too tough a stand against Tehran.

Two of the seven emirates in particular – Dubai and Sharjah – were Iran's access points to the Arab Gulf. They had large Iranian populations and, along with the five other emirates, they also had highly profitable trade links with wartime Iran. There wasn't even any consensus inside the GCC over the role the Arab Gulf States played in the war. Secretary General Bisharah was adamant that GCC member states had taken a 'side' in the conflict and could not be classed as observers. His fellow countryman, Kuwait's foreign minister, Sheikh Sabah Al-Ahmed Al-Jaber Al-Sabah, disagreed. 'We are not partners in this war,' he told the media, 'we will never be partners in it'.[54] The reluctance of GCC member states to commit explicitly to an anti-Iranian military alliance did little to reduce the vocal attacks they faced from Iran. Speeches by senior officials in Tehran, government statements, and sermons in mosques during Friday prayers all regularly threatened to export revolution to the Arab Gulf. Iranian television, radio stations and the newspapers were full of similar content. In the weeks and months after the revolution Tehran's Arabic Service had castigated the shah for his 'imperialist conspiracies' against the Gulf Arabs.[55] Only a few years later, in the midst of the war, the same station attacked its Arab neighbours in the same terms as part of its harsh criticism of their backing of Iraq.

On a visit to Washington in mid-1984, Kuwait's defence minister downplayed the possibility that his country would come under attack. His kingdom, he argued, had good relations with both of the warring parties. Such statements did not reflect reality by this time. During the mid-1980s, a Kuwaiti airliner was hijacked and landed in Tehran. Popular cafés in Kuwait City were bombed. There was even a failed attempt on the life of the emir as he travelled by motorcade through his kingdom. The Kuwaiti government blamed Iran for these attacks and the kingdom's foreign minister, Sheikh Sabah Al-Ahmed Al-Jaber Al-Sabah, reminded Tehran that it had 'no right to wreak vengeance on states which are not parties to the Iraq–Iranian conflict'.

In 1982, at a time of Iranian military gains, GCC army chiefs were ordered to speed up discussions on the formation of a joint fighting force. Over the next two years they developed a strategy around the establishment of a joint GCC command and a Gulf rapid deployment force drawn from the six member state armies. This had become necessary by the middle of the decade because, in the words of Bisharah, 'There can be no ideological or economic development unless the security aspect is assured.'[56] Others at the highest levels agreed. Sheikh Zayed of the UAE lamented the 'extremely sensitive and difficult circumstances'. Bahrain's king spoke of the 'enormous challenges' caused by the ongoing war. His foreign minister even described the conflict as the 'biggest crisis' the region had faced in modern times.[57] These alarming statements by GCC leaders were an indirect admission of their failure to resolve the conflict or at least to insulate themselves from its fallout. Sultan Qaboos put this down to the GCC's 'Arab affiliation', and thus Iranian suspicion that the Arab Gulf States were automatically pro-Iraqi on ethnic and religious grounds. Iran's ambassador in Kuwait during the war did not agree. The GCC's impotence, argued Ali Shams Ardenkani, had nothing to do with sectarian differences. It was purely a matter of power or, as he put it, 'When a lion and tiger are fighting, sheep cannot stop them.'[58]

Such dismissive views should not hide the fact that the GCC states spent over US$50 billion between them on military facilities and equipment in the first half of the 1980s in order to build a deterrent capability. Oman had always been the most hawkish of the six GCC member states on security matters. Yet even Sultan Qaboos was acutely aware of the limits of GCC military power from the outset. 'Let us be frank,' he explained after he had led the first ever GCC joint military manoeuvres in 1983. 'We do not possess the military capability needed to confront the other side . . . We do not have the army that can defend the security of the Gulf'.[59] According to the sultan, one of the main reasons why he had signed a security agreement with Washington in the early 1980s was because his 'GCC brothers'[60] had refused his various requests for funds to upgrade his country's defensive military capabilities. As the security situation in the region deteriorated rapidly in the mid-1980s, the sultanate received US$2 billion from GCC coffers to develop its radar and air defence capabilities so that it could monitor and secure the Straits of Hormuz in case of Iranian attempts to block its use. This signalled a new GCC seriousness of purpose in promoting defence and security cooperation at a time of profound uncertainty.

Its limits were encapsulated by the difficulty that the GCC experienced when it launched a joint GCC military unit, the Peninsula Shield force. It was established at the third GCC summit in Manama in 1982. From that point onwards, competition and suspicion, as well as diverging national interests, conspired to reduce the value and effectiveness of this outfit. During the initial negotiations on the establishment of the unit, Saudi Arabia proposed that it be divided into two sections, one located in the north-east and one in the south-west of the Gulf. This was rejected by Oman out of fear that such a move might provoke Iran. Kuwait, Oman and the UAE also refused Riyadh's offer to host the Peninsula Shield's command and control headquarters. It took three years of tough negotiations before Riyadh's partners agreed to the Saudi demand that the 5,000-strong Shield force be headquartered in the kingdom's oil-rich Eastern Province. Even after the matter of its location was resolved, the more sensitive matter of when it would be activated continued to sow division inside the GCC. Oman and the UAE blocked Kuwait's request that the Peninsula Shield force be used to defend the Bubiyan Islands against Iranian threats. In total, the Peninsula Shield was only deployed in its first decade in response to a couple of Iranian offensives during the latter part of the Iran–Iraq war. Its most significant achievement was providing a focal point for joint military exercises between the GCC states, the first of which, codenamed Peninsula Shield I, was held in the UAE desert in October 1983.

In an interview with the Saudi daily *Al-Riyad* following the completion of these military exercises, Bisharah spoke honestly. 'Our ambitions are enormous,' he reflected, 'but our capabilities are not. We know our resources, hence we have to be realistic'.[61] Nevertheless, improved defence cooperation, combined with high military spending, served a political as well as a security function. It was intended to flag up the gradual, if stilted, move towards a viable GCC security community that minimized the pretext for the superpowers to intervene in the region to restore stability. Despite its practical limitations, this strategy paid dividends. Washington supported this ambitious commitment to collective security as a positive development. Some US officials even speculated that over time a GCC military force might become strong enough to create a three-way balance of power in the region between Iraq, Iran and the Gulf States. In reality, neither the rousing statements emanating from the Gulf nor the massive investment in military hardware did anything to change the regional balance of power during the 1980s. The Arab Gulf remained at the mercy of Iran and Iraq. Both could act with impunity, as Saddam Hussein proved in 1986 when he ordered his air force to bomb two UAE-owned oil rigs to convey his disappointment over what he felt was a dropping off of GCC support for his war effort at this time.

Since its launch, the GCC had assumed that it could deal with regional threats through a combination of traditional diplomacy, money, its own military capabilities and support from larger, more powerful, Arab states like Egypt. As the all-out war between the Iranian 'lion' and the Iraqi 'tiger' intensified in the second part of the 1980s, it became obvious that none of these options could provide the Arab Gulf the security it craved. In acknowledgement of this, in November 1986, at the seventh GCC summit, there was a move to play down the concept of self-reliance and drop the emphasis on joint military arrangements. The GCC 'sheep' needed a shepherd capable of guiding it safely through the final, desperate, stages of the war. The only candidate for this job, whether they liked it or not, was the United States. During the early years of the Reagan presidency, Washington spent US$10–15 billion building up its military presence from Egypt to Somalia and across the Indian Ocean. This culminated in the establishment of Central Command (CENTCOM), which replaced Carter's Rapid Deployment Force. CENTCOM was a fully fledged regional command modelled on US commands in other parts of the world.

Despite upgrading its Gulf-specific military capability, the Reagan administration was adamant that there were only two possible scenarios under which American troops would intervene in the Gulf. The first was in response to an invitation from local leaders concerned that their oilfields were about to be seized by home-grown opponents or foreign enemies. The second was in response to massive price hikes or embargos that undermined the economic health of the Western world and threatened the Cold War balance of power. For all its destruction and devastation, the Iran–Iraq war did not meet either criterion for intervention and Washington saw no advantage in explicitly taking sides in the conflict. In the middle years of the war the Reagan administration did open up an arms supply channel to Iran in a bid to get the release of American hostages held in Beirut by pro-Iranian militias. Washington also provided Tehran with intelligence on both Iraq and the Soviets and sent National Security Adviser Robert McFarlane and other officials to Tehran to open up a dialogue.

During the 1970s, the Soviet state-run Arabic radio service ruminated extensively on the need for the Arab Gulf to wake up to the 'danger' of US military intervention in the region.[62] At the end of the decade, Soviet leader Leonid Brezhnev put forward a five-point plan that offered non-intervention in the Gulf region in exchange for local states setting out a clear policy of non-alignment in the Cold War. This determination to keep the American military out of the Gulf explains why Moscow was no more enthusiastic than Washington over Saddam's subsequent decision to invade Iran in 1980. Like their American counterparts, Soviet leaders also had a somewhat ambivalent approach to arms transfers, allowing Syria and Libya to provide Iran with Soviet weapons at the same time as they encouraged members of the Warsaw Pact to supply Iraq.

Saddam started targeting Iranian oil tankers in the Gulf in the spring of 1983 precisely because he was frustrated by the unwillingness of either Moscow or Washington to become more actively involved in the war. His plan was to force both to take a more hands-on approach to the conflict by extending the war into the much-prized oil sector. The Iranian blockade of Iraqi ports was already in place when Saddam started his campaign against commercial shipping. This left the Iranian navy with few opportunities to retaliate against Iraqi shipping. Instead, it started to target ships going in and out of Arab Gulf ports. Soon Saudi and Kuwaiti tankers were coming under Iranian fire. The official US position was slow to change. As Reagan explained, local parties could look after themselves and there was still only a 'very slight' chance of US intervention to protect Gulf shipping.[63] In reality, Gulf navies lacked minesweeping capabilities and the shipboard defences required to deal with Iranian air attacks. This became increasingly obvious as the decade continued. The number of GCC ships damaged by acts of war rose from five in 1980 to fifty in 1985 to over 100 in 1986, with twenty-six attacks alone in the December of that year. Things were getting desperate. As Bahrain's oil minister, Tariq Almoayed, put it: 'Twenty years ago we were in the Middle Ages. Oil wealth has brought us progress, education, modernity. Now all is threatened by the fighting among our neighbors. It is a dangerous time'.[64] As the tanker war continued, Kuwait became the main target of Iranian operations, as part of an attempt to convince the kingdom's leaders to distance themselves from Saddam and stop allowing their territory from being used as a transit point for equipment and material bound for Iraq.

In an attempt to put an end to this intolerable situation, Kuwaiti officials first called on the UN Security Council to guarantee the security of its tankers. When this achieved little, they approached both Moscow and Washington with the same request in late 1986. Unable to provide their own military or diplomatic solution, other Gulf Arab leaders warily endorsed the unprecedented Kuwaiti request at a GCC summit in the Saudi city of Ta'if in early 1987. The Russians eagerly accepted. Washington reluctantly agreed to place half of Kuwait's twenty-strong tanker fleet under the protection of the American flag. In a nationally televised broadcast, President Reagan pulled no punches in accounting for the new US willingness to get involved. 'In a word,' he explained, 'if we don't do the job, the Soviets will and that will jeopardize our security and that of our allies'.[65]

On reflection, at the end of the war, US officials would describe this unprecedented move as an 'unusual step in an unusual situation'. Their Kuwaiti counterparts were adamant that their initial request was motivated solely by a desire to keep oil flowing to customers and that they had no interest 'playing the big powers off against each other'.[66] In reality, the original request to Moscow had been intended to draw Washington into the conflict as a way of resolving the stalemate. Soon after Kuwait had made its request, Saudi Arabia asked the US, Britain and France to provide security for its own oil tankers and to conduct minesweeping operations on its behalf. On one level this move by the GCC states to draw the superpowers into the region made perfect sense. In a bipolar world where two dominant states compete with each other globally, weaker local actors will always have the opportunity to use this competition to their own advantage to pursue their own interests. On this occasion the GCC states, led by Kuwait, deftly manipulated the Cold War vulnerabilities of the superpowers to play the US and its Western allies off against the Soviets.

This was a high-stakes game that required the Gulf States to place themselves squarely in the middle of superpower rivalries without turning the region into a frontline in the Cold War. The Iranian leadership disparaged this gamble. Prime Minister Hoseyn Musavi told a visiting Omani minister that 'superpower flags cannot ensure the security of the Persian Gulf'. President Ali Khamenei described the decision of Arab Gulf States to sail their ships under foreign flags and hide behind Western navies as a 'disgrace'. Hashemi Rafsanjani, then speaker of the parliament, called it 'childish'. Subsequently, he accused the Gulf States of being 'weak and spineless' and compared them to Israel, which he described as another puppet of Washington.[67] For years the Gulf Arabs had worked hard to minimize risk. On the other hand, they had always been firmly in the American camp and were committed to maintaining the balance of power in the region in line with Western interests. As Secretary General Bisharah explained, the main GCC goals were 'to keep the region at a distance from the Iran–Iraq war . . . to preserve the status quo and to maintain the prevailing balance of forces'.[68]

After six years of war between Iran and Iraq these key priorities were becoming increasingly difficult to achieve. As one senior Bahraini official explained, 'We reached the stage where the aggression from Iran was going to be at our shores instead of just out there in the sea.'[69] The UAE, Oman and Qatar are located much nearer to Iran than Bahrain, Kuwait and Saudi Arabia. This has always made them much more careful not to antagonize Iran than their GCC partners, and explains their reluctance to support openly the Western naval intervention under way at the time. 'After the war ends we don't want to have an enemy,' explained one Qatari official.[70] Nevertheless, even these countries, which had carefully managed relations with Iran over the course of the conflict, found it increasingly difficult to find points of common ground with Tehran.

It was inevitable that the conservative Gulf Arabs and the revolutionaries in Iran would eventually split. Their interests differed on many issues, including the need for stability. As the introduction made clear, the Arab Gulf has always placed a premium on stability. Policymakers in Iran after the revolution, especially in the wake of the unprovoked Iraqi invasion, believed that their interests were best served by destabilizing the wider region. These conflicting tendencies came to a head in the summer of 1987. The Iranian revolutionary government had always viewed the annual hajj pilgrimage to Mecca as a political event and a propaganda opportunity. During that year's hajj hundreds of Iranian pilgrims and Saudi soldiers died in clashes and demonstrations. Soon after, the Saudi embassy in Tehran was ransacked. Over the next six months the situation got worse. Kuwait expelled most of the Iranian diplomats stationed there after three missiles landed in the kingdom. Saudi fighter jets scrambled in response to Iranian speedboats moving towards Kafji, the Saudi offshore oilfield in the northern Gulf.

In mid-1988, following almost a year of uninterrupted mutual hostility, Riyadh broke diplomatic ties with Iran and rejected an OPEC proposal to cut production and raise the oil price. The Iranians were furious. Hashemi Rafsanjani charged Saudi Arabia with the one crime that it had worked hard to avoid being accused of for decades – 'flagrant treachery that serves the interests of the United States'.[71] The situation was spiralling out of control. The UAE and Oman tried to restore calm by opening up discussions with Iran. There were rumours that they had offered Iran a deal – if Tehran promised to leave the Gulf States alone they would convince their GCC partners to ask Western navies to leave the region. Even as Western warships and mine cruisers patrolled Gulf waters it seemed that the Arab Gulf States wanted American protection free of the political baggage that came with it. This was becoming harder and harder to achieve.

In August 1988 Iran and Iraq agreed to a ceasefire that ended eight years of war. In the same month, a confidential State Department memorandum was circulated among policymakers in Washington. America's future role in the Gulf, it argued, had to reflect its 'national interests' and required a military capability 'commensurate' with regional threats.[72] This signalled a growing consensus in American foreign policy circles over the rising importance of the Gulf in America's list of strategic priorities. As a senior administration official explained in evidence before a congressional committee in the final months of the war, the US had 'major – yes, vital – interests' in the region. As the next chapter will show, the threats posed to those interests were about to increase greatly as Iraq turned its sights on its Kuwaiti neighbour. This act of war totally destabilized the Arab Gulf as the region once more occupied the policy considerations and news coverage of the entire world.

CHAPTER 3

TAX AMERICANA

'A small nation can disappear, and it knows it.'

– Milan Kundera

Just months before taking office in January 1969, US President-elect Richard Nixon had a brief visit from Kuwait's ruler, Sheikh Sabah Al-Salem Al-Sabah. In Washington on official business, the emir wanted to pay his respects to the world's most powerful man in waiting. Introductions and pleasantries over, he asked Nixon two questions of substance. What plans did his administration have for Gulf security and what would America do if Kuwait was ever attacked by Iraq, its much larger northern neighbour?[1] Expecting a courtesy call rather than substantive policy discussions, Nixon had not been briefed on these issues and he brushed them off. At 5 a.m. on 2 August 1990, President George H.W. Bush received news he could not brush off. Iraqi president Saddam Hussein had sent 100,000 troops and 700 tanks into Kuwait. At the same time the Baghdad government falsely informed the world that it had acted in response to a request from the 'Democratic Government of Kuwait', which it claimed had overthrown the ruling Al-Sabah royal family.

President Bush later recalled that the following few days were his 'most hectic 48 hours' since becoming president. Amid the chaos of those early days of crisis, Bush's mind turned to the people of the Gulf, writing in his diary that they must be 'quaking in their boots'.[2] He was wrong. Shock and denial, not fear, were the initial feelings across the region. Saddam's move was so incomprehensible that for the first few days after the invasion Gulf radio and television broadcasts made almost no mention of what had happened. It was left to the BBC and CNN to report the story to the world. As one Arab journalist admitted a week after Saddam's tanks rolled across the Kuwaiti border, 'We are only now beginning to believe that Saddam really did this.'[3]

Saddam Hussein met nobody's definition of a good neighbour, but the idea that he would plunder Kuwait's wealth and brutally occupy its people seemed absurd. The concept of a single Arab nation had evolved in the late nineteenth century as a response to both the Ottoman policy of Turkification and the flow of Western political ideas into the region. A century later it was little more than a romantic ideal based on past Arab glory rather than on a sober assessment of recent history. Nonetheless, it was a romantic ideal that was still treated as a guiding principle of Arab political life. Not even President Anwar Sadat's decision in the late 1970s to choose a deal with Israel and the return of his prized Sinai Peninsula over support for a Palestinian state had killed off the belief in pan-Arab solidarity as a pillar of inter-Arab affairs.

'They are Arabs like us and we know them',[4] was how one Gulf official downplayed Iraqi threats to Kuwait during a period of heightened tension in the mid-1970s. Iraq's war against non-Arab Iran during the 1980s fuelled such sentiments further. As Saudi Arabia's long-serving minister of the interior, Prince Nayef Abdul Aziz Al-Saud, explained at the time, Iraq was not only fighting Iran to defend itself but 'also to protect the entire Arab nation'.[5] In 1985, at the height of the Iran–Iraq war, Oman's sultan noted that one of the dynamics at work in the conflict, and not always a good one, was that 'Arab duty dictates that we should support it [Iraq] without reservation and regardless of any consequences'.[6] Even the Kuwaitis, who had lived with Iraqi threats for decades, got into the act. In the bleak, middle years of the war, the Kuwait National Assembly, a vibrant political institution whose various factions almost never agreed on anything, unanimously passed a resolution applauding how 'Kuwaitis and our Arab people in Iraq are bound by a common fate and destiny'.[7] Soon afterwards, the Kuwaiti government expressed its support for Iraq joining the GCC once the war with Iran was over. Saddam himself took advantage of such sentiments in the run-up to his invasion of Kuwait. 'We are Arabs,' he told the US ambassador in Baghdad in 1990. 'It is enough for us that someone says "I am sorry. I made a mistake", then we carry on.'[8]

The GCC had been established in response to the revolution in Iran and the Iran–Iraq war. During the 1980s, the organization proved itself to be adaptable and flexible in responding to the threats it faced. Its member states made gradual progress building regional institutions in a far from stable environment. They even managed to lay the foundations for future economic integration in these turbulent years. Prior to the launch of the GCC, traditional tensions between Arab Gulf States had prevented proper cooperation and effective coordination in almost every important area of economic endeavour. Oil was the key driver of the economy and oil, as one Kuwaiti expert explained at the time, was a jealously guarded priority of 'national policy'.[9] Infrastructural projects had also been viewed primarily in terms of national interest rather than regional cooperation. In 1974, for example, when the Arab Gulf oil producers chose Bahrain as the site of a planned supertanker dry dock, Dubai's ruler Sheikh Rashid bin Said Al-Maktoum ignored this decision and went ahead with his own plans to build a dry dock in Dubai despite the cost and the very obvious lack of business sense of locating two identical facilities so near to each other.

In November 1981, GCC members signed up to a Unified Economic Agreement. From the outset the intention was that this document would provide the framework for the gradual, not rapid, economic integration of the Arab Gulf States. This explains why some of its early provisions were technical in nature and attempted to build confidence rather than a true economic union in the short term. The establishment in 1982 of uniform weights and measures across the six GCC member states under the watchful eye of the Gulf Standards Organization was one example of this. So was the decision by GCC members the following year to jointly negotiate lower prices on the bulk purchase of rice.

In the words of Secretary General Bisharah, the 1981 agreement was a 'giant turning point for the Gulf',[10] precisely because it was intended to overcome long-time obstacles to economic cooperation and to lay the foundations for joint action in all areas of economic activity. It also hinted at much more ambitious longer-term plans. Included among its proposals was the setting up of joint infrastructure projects and the possible coordination of oil prices, industrial activities and import and export policies and regulations. There were also provisions for the free movement of labour and capital, the dismantling of tariffs and other barriers as a prelude to a common market and later, when conditions were right, the establishment of a single economic entity. Other clauses offered the prospect of coordination of financial and monetary policies, possibly even leading, at some future unspecified point, to a common GCC currency. When this agreement came into effect on 1 March 1983 it provided official acknowledgement that the six Arab Gulf members of the GCC had for the first time established the legal basis for conducting business and trade in a similar manner to the European Community's founding document, the 1958 Treaty of Rome. This was an encouraging start and the prospects for future economic cooperation between the fourteen million people of the Arab Gulf appeared to be promising.

In 1986, one informed regional observer assessed the GCC's achievements in its first five years. It was home, he declared, to the most stable group of states in the developing world and its achievements up to that point, particularly in the economic sphere, compared favourably with those of the European Community in its early years.[11] This did not alter the fact that the GCC was forged in the midst of one of the twentieth century's most brutal and destructive conflicts. Once the Iran–Iraq war ended it remained unclear whether the organization would be able to hold itself together in peacetime. Even if it could, there was no guarantee that it would be able to move ahead with its ambitious, if somewhat stilted, quest for deeper economic, political and military cooperation.

The post-war period coincided with the final years of the Cold War. In December 1989 at an impromptu summit meeting in Malta, Soviet leader Mikhail Gorbachev and US president George H.W. Bush agreed to put an end to the fifty-year conflict between East and West. Over the following two years the Soviet Union disintegrated and was formally dissolved on 26 December 1991. While it had lasted, the bipolar international order had provided some comfort to small and weak states like those in the Arab Gulf because it offered, in theory if not always in practice, some political certainty. The end of the Cold War removed the fear of a Soviet invasion. Apart from that, it did not radically alter the domestic or external priorities of the Gulf States. They still needed to cooperate with each other as much as possible to keep Iranian revolutionaries out and Arab radicals down, while ensuring the continued flow of oil through the sea-lanes of the Gulf to customers across the world. In order to achieve these objectives, serious regional threats would now be bought off or held in check by a massive US deterrent. If this failed to keep the peace then it would be up to other Arab states, or in the last resort, the Gulf States themselves, to uphold the status quo.

In principle this all seemed to make sense. In practice, however, it failed to take into account one key factor – the plans of a bloodied but unbowed post-war Iraq. Saddam had always taken pride in the fact that his relatively small country had one of the largest armies in the world. In the wake of his war with Iran he spent billions rebuilding Iraq's depleted military capability. His army quadrupled to nearly one million men and his air force grew by more than one-third. This posed a significant challenge to the Gulf States as it made regional strategic balance and thus regional stability much more difficult to achieve. For the duration of the Iran–Iraq war, Iraqi officials were under orders to build up positive relations with the Gulf

Arabs. At war's end they reverted to norm and once more began to claim ownership of Kuwaiti territory, in particular the strategically located islands of Bubiyan and Warba. Baghdad also requested a US$10 billion loan from Kuwait, needed to help with post-war reconstruction, estimated to require between US$400 and US$450 billion to complete. This was followed by further territorial claims, the occasional trespass by Iraqi troops over the Kuwaiti border, and vocal attacks on Kuwait's long-time policy of exceeding OPEC production quotas.

This quota busting kept the oil price down and made it harder for Iraq to earn the foreign currency it needed to pay for its post-war reconstruction and arms build-up. For Saddam such actions were intolerable at a time when Iraqi war debts amounted to US$40 billion, inflation levels were at nearly 50 per cent and the country only had three months of cash reserves left in the bank. In the middle of July 1990, in an outburst aimed directly at Kuwait and its GCC partners, Saddam accused 'certain Arab rulers' of having 'thrust their poisoned dagger into our back'.[12] He then threatened to punish those traitors who conspired to keep the oil price low. In a subsequent letter to the Arab League's secretary general, Iraqi foreign minister Tariq Aziz went even further. Aziz claimed that Kuwait had not only refused to write off wartime loans made to Iraq but that it had stolen US$2.4 billion worth of Iraqi oil. As tensions rose during the first half of 1990, Kuwaiti leaders dismissed Iraq's territorial claims. They also refused to cut oil production and rejected demands for billions of dollars in new loans. In the months leading up to the invasion, top Kuwaiti officials who met Saddam had no idea the price they would soon pay for their refusal to bow to the Iraqi demands. In May 1990, during a meeting with Kuwait's emir in Baghdad, Saddam promised his guest that their border dispute would soon be settled for good. Completely misreading this ominous prediction the Kuwaiti ruler returned home relieved.

Other GCC leaders also demonstrated little anxiety, in public at least, that Saddam was gearing up for war. At an early summer meeting of GCC leaders in the city of Ta'if, the Saudi hosts pressured Kuwait to look for a compromise with Iraq. Those present agreed that the best way forward was to ignore Saddam's threatening rhetoric and to 'cool things down'. They also decided to try to defuse the situation by playing down upcoming joint military exercises with the US, which they now characterized as a routine training mission that had nothing to do with the tensions between Iraq and Kuwait.[13]

Not long after the Kuwait crisis ended in the middle of 1991, a Saudi diplomat who had worked for many years with Prince Bandar in Washington wrote that his ambassadorial colleague had achieved a 'degree of political effectiveness' in the American capital that not even Israeli officials could claim.[14] In the run-up to the Iraqi invasion this access to top American policymakers actually worked against Saudi interests. Instead of stirring his powerful Washington friends to action, including his racquetball partner, the US army chief Colin Powell, the well-connected Bandar – known to many as 'Bandar Bush' – spent his time reassuring them that an Iraqi attack on Kuwait 'wouldn't happen'. Neither the increasingly tough threats emanating from Baghdad nor the US satellite imagery showing a major Iraqi military build-up on the border with Kuwait changed his mind. On 31 July, two days before the invasion, Bandar departed Washington on his annual holidays, confident that little would happen over the next few weeks that might require him to return to his post. He could not have been more wrong. Within days he was back in Washington trying to get to grips with the crisis. 'What happened to Kuwait', he lamented, 'is unique – so blatant, so arrogant, so violent, so deceiving that it makes pause to question the whole Arab situation in a way I have never questioned before.'[15] Abdullah Bisharah made a similar point. 'We in the Gulf and the people of Kuwait', he explained in 1993 a year after he resigned as secretary general of the GCC, 'have paid the price of fixed emotional positions and our basing of policy on so-called solidarity.' He then counselled that future inter-Arab relations should avoid 'emotional theories'.[16]

The 'vicious Iraqi invasion of the sisterly state of Kuwait',[17] as the emir of Qatar described it at the time, demolished any lingering illusions that pan-Arabism was a relevant factor in regional affairs. For many, the Iraqi invasion even ranked alongside the establishment of Israel in 1948, and the devastating Israeli victory over the Arab armies in 1967, as one of the worst disasters to befall the Arab world in modern times. The 'sadness and anger' caused by Saddam's invasion of Kuwait was, according to Arab-American intellectual Edward Said, 'equal to and in some aspects worse' than what the Arab world had experienced in 1967.[18]

Saddam used the period of dazed uncertainty following the invasion to try to reassure the rest of the GCC and the international community that Kuwait was a 'special case'[19] and that Iraq would not follow up its intervention there with other attacks anywhere else in the Arab Gulf. Few in the region believed him. There were reports that Iraqi forces had crossed the Saudi border in the first few days after the invasion of Kuwait. King Fahd rejected assurances from a top Iraqi emissary that these incursions had been 'mistakes'.[20] He also told US officials that he believed that once Saddam had achieved his objectives in Kuwait he would attack the oil-rich Eastern

Province of Saudi Arabia before moving on to the rest of the GCC member states. Prince Bandar used evocative language to sum up this fear in the American media. 'He who eats Kuwait for breakfast', he explained, 'is likely to ask for something else for lunch.'[21] Bandar's Iraqi counterpart in the US capital privately reassured US officials that there was 'not one iota of truth'[22] in these claims. Nor did coalition forces in Kuwait find any evidence pointing to such plans among the hundreds of thousands of documents they confiscated during the ground war phase of the crisis in early 1991.

Nevertheless, in the early weeks of August 1990, as the world grappled to come to terms with what had happened, it seemed highly improbable to many that Saddam would settle with the conquest and occupation of Kuwait. He had already misled the Gulf States and other Arab leaders, notably an enraged and unforgiving Hosni Mubarak of Egypt, about his intentions regarding Kuwait. There was no reason to believe he would not do it again. Even if he had no immediate plans to extend his aggressive actions, the move against Kuwait still left other Gulf kingdoms very vulnerable because it established the precedent of a direct Iraqi attack on a GCC member state sometime in the future, perhaps once America and its coalition partners had withdrawn from the region.

No less intolerable, from the perspective of Gulf rulers, was a scenario in which Iraq emerged from the crisis as the strongest Arab economic and military power, in full control of Kuwait's oil, wealth and territory. This raised the appalling prospect of Saddam, the brutal Iraqi strongman, establishing himself as the 'Knight of Arabism' and the 'Second Saladin', idolized by millions of ordinary citizens across the Arab world for having taken on the modern-day crusaders and their puppets in the Gulf. All of this meant that the Gulf Arabs interpreted the invasion of Kuwait as part of a larger Iraqi 'bid for regional hegemony', as Saudi Arabia's top soldier, General Prince Khalid bin Sultan, explained it. Bahrain's ruler, Sheikh Hamad bin Isa Al-Khalifa, presented the threat in less strategic terms. 'Peace would never work with Saddam', he told US secretary of state James Baker, because 'a rabid dog bites anyone who comes his way'.[23] It was inevitable, Baker later recalled, that if Saddam had gone unchallenged, the Gulf kingdoms would have been his 'next dominoes'. British prime minister Margaret Thatcher made a similar point. 'If you didn't stop him and didn't turn him back', she would later explain, 'he would have gone over the border to Saudi Arabia, over to Bahrain, to Dubai . . . and right down the west side of the Gulf.'[24]

From the outset of the crisis, such arguments in favour of intervention by Western leaders like Thatcher were presented in the media as purely a function of the Gulf's vital position in the energy markets. 'Cold War Ends,

Oil War Begins',[25] ran a representative headline in the *Christian Science Monitor*. Lawrence Corb, a former US government adviser and well-known figure in foreign policy circles, encapsulated a view held by many: 'If Kuwait grew carrots we wouldn't give a damn'. This sentiment was widely expressed, especially among those opposed to any war. Writing in the British press, Robert Fisk, a trenchant critic of America's Middle East policy, argued that if Saudi Arabia had no oil and its people lived in poverty, 'not a single soldier would be deployed'.[26]

Far from denying or countering such arguments, both the Thatcher and Bush governments acknowledged that oil and close strategic ties with Saudi Arabia were key considerations in their responses to the crisis. 'You can't separate Kuwait from Saudi Arabia,'[27] the straight-talking Baker repeatedly argued in these early days. In a meeting with his Canadian counterpart in November 1990, he spelt out exactly why America needed to take a stand. If Saddam retained Kuwait's oilfields in his possession it would lead to a recession and the loss of millions of American jobs.[28] During their discussions with the Saudis over how best to respond to Saddam, US officials also pointed out a direct corollary to this. Iraqi forces in Kuwait, they repeatedly stressed, were only forty kilometres from Saudi oilfields and could be in the kingdom in half a day.

With the exception of Oman, whose troops had fought against Dhofar rebels during the 1970s, the armies of the Arab Gulf had almost no experience of modern warfare. Yet over the previous decade Gulf officials, with Kuwaitis most vocal among them, had made numerous claims that they could 'repulse any aggression'[29] they faced. The ease with which Iraqi forces entered and occupied Kuwait demolished this belief. Kuwaiti army units located in the area around the emir's palace did manage to hold off invading Iraqi troops for a couple of hours after they had arrived in the capital city. The Kuwaiti air force remained operational for twenty-four hours. Other than that, Saddam's troops faced little resistance as they overran the country.

Small, weak and vulnerable states typically look to find security by entering into bilateral alliances with major powers or by joining multilateral alliances like NATO that are dominated by major military powers. Other options they have for improving their security include non-alignment, neutrality or banding together with other small states to form an alliance that can balance the threat posed by stronger regional neighbours.[30] When they came together to form the GCC a decade earlier, the Arab Gulf States chose this final option. They hoped that this strategy would provide them with more security than if they pursued security independently from one other. As the Iran–Iraq war raged on during the 1980s it further fuelled the hope in some Gulf quarters that effective military cooperation could be achieved in the future. Though strong bonds of interdependence developed among Gulf Arabs during the tumultuous years of the 1980s, the difficulties they had in fully developing collective security structures like the Peninsula Shield did demonstrate the pervasiveness of mutual distrust, and deep rivalries among Gulf partners.

The GCC states spent billions of dollars on arms in the decade prior to Saddam's invasion of Kuwait. By 1990 Qatar had the highest per capita military expenditure of any country in the world. Oman ranked fourth, Kuwait sixth and the UAE eleventh. Even Bahrain, with the lowest per capita military spending of any GCC state, ranked relatively high in twenty-seventh place globally. However, this massive military shopping spree took place without any focused purchasing strategy. For example, the Kuwaiti air force had more fighter planes than trained pilots. Nor had the Gulf States made any concrete progress in coordinating their military defences under the GCC umbrella by this time. These factors made it difficult for the GCC to develop into an effective 'security community' prior to the invasion of Kuwait. The upshot was that when Saddam struck, Kuwait did not have a chance. Within three hours of the start of the invasion Kuwait's leaders appealed to the US embassy for military help.[31] They did not even bother to make a similar request of their GCC partners, whom they knew to be also woefully outmatched by Saddam's war machine. At the time of the invasion, Iraq had four times the number of combat aircraft as the combined GCC military forces, as well as eight times more regular troops and artillery pieces, and ten times more tanks. As Saudi army chief General Khalid bin Sultan sombrely admitted later, faced with this stark reality the GCC's system of defence was 'absolutely incapable of coping with Saddam's aggression'.[32]

After the debacle in Kuwait, the GCC states could no longer deny this and had little choice but to fundamentally reassess their strategic and security priorities. Five days after the invasion began, an emergency meeting of GCC leaders agreed to capitalize on their wealth and their global strategic importance as oil producers in a vital region to ensure that they did not face the same fate as Kuwait and fall victim to Saddam's ambitions. Their first move was to unite behind the now exiled Kuwaiti royal family. Their second was to convince, cajole, bribe and beg until the international community agreed to eject Saddam from Kuwait and defend the rest of the region from his aggressive intentions. This strategy required the GCC states to rethink their relationship with international allies, in particular the only remaining global superpower, the United States. One consequence of the collapse of the Soviet Union was that it ended the bipolar international order that had driven US involvement in the Middle East since the 1940s. Another was that it led to widespread speculation as to whether the US, having defeated its Soviet foe, would have the political will, the domestic support, or the strategic need to continue to play the lead external role in the new Middle East.

Saddam would later accuse the US of having tricked the Arabs into a war against him so that it could control the region and benefit Israel following its defeat of the Soviet Union. The reality was somewhat different. In the days and weeks after Saddam invaded Kuwait the overriding fear among Gulf Arab leaders was not that Washington would use the crisis to impose itself on the region. Rather, the fear was that the US would be unwilling to act decisively to counter the threat they faced. This had been the case at the time of the Iranian revolution and the Soviet invasion of Afghanistan little more than a decade earlier. There was also concern that even if the Bush administration did agree to act militarily in defence of Kuwait and its GCC partners, once American casualties started to mount it would quickly lose its nerve and withdraw before the job was done, as had occurred after the bombing of the US marine barracks in Lebanon in 1983.

These were legitimate concerns. A poll carried out in the US in early January 1991, prior to the start of the military campaign to liberate Kuwait, showed that public support for the war stood at 63 per cent. Support dropped to under 50 per cent among those polled if 1,000 American troops lost their lives. It fell to around 30 per cent if 10,000 troops died on active duty. Saddam was so convinced that Washington did not have the political stomach to go to war, and that even if it did it would not be able to suffer heavy casualties, that this thinking shaped his military strategy. The Iraqi plan for defeating a US-led coalition focused on drawing US troops into a ground war early on and inflicting heavy casualties on them. This, it was hoped, would mobilize that anti-war movement in Europe and North America, which up to that point had failed to gain political or popular support for its 'no blood for oil' campaign. In turn, this would force the Bush administration to accept a deal that would leave Iraq in control of much of Kuwait's wealth. This thinking explained Iraq's SCUD missile strikes against Israel and Saudi Arabia, as well as the decision to pump oil into the Gulf and to set fire to oilfields. All made sense as part of Saddam's strategy of trying to pull US ground troops into combat at an early stage in the military conflict. Aware of this plan, the US-led coalition refused to engage Saddam's troops in a premature ground war. Instead, it focused its efforts on a sustained air campaign that degraded the Iraqi military capability as a way of minimizing coalition casualties when the ground offensive actually began.

In the early days of the crisis President Bush had moved rapidly to reassure Gulf leaders that America was committed to the liberation of Kuwait and their defence. 'If you ask for help from the United States, we will go all the way with you,' he told the Saudi king.[33] Private commitments like this one were accompanied by public statements to the American people, in which the president promised that American forces would defend the 'kingdom of Saudi Arabia, and other friends in the Persian Gulf'.[34] Such expressions of support reassured Gulf leaders and helped to reduce concerns over America's seriousness of purpose. So did the decision of a previously divided US Congress to vote in favour of military action against Saddam in the second week of January 1991. Yet Gulf leaders still remained wary that the Bush administration might embrace one of the proposals put forward by Arab and other intermediaries that avoided war and left Saddam with substantive gains. Included on this list of unacceptable outcomes was any deal that saw Saddam agree to a troop withdrawal in exchange for concessions from Kuwait. 'Not a single inch' of Kuwaiti territory was up for negotiations, explained the kingdom's ambassador in Washington. An even worse outcome for Kuwait and its Gulf partners was a deal that forced the Kuwaiti royal family to give up power in return for a peaceful end to the crisis. This was a worst-case scenario that would have set a precedent for the future overthrow of other ruling families across the region.

For all these reasons, the Gulf States continually urged the Bush administration and its coalition partners to cease their search for compromise solutions. All it did, Prince Bandar told top US officials, was encourage Saddam to think they were all 'chicken'.[35] An organization known as Citizens for a Free Kuwait was set up in Washington to rally American public opinion to the anti-Saddam cause. It spent millions of dollars on PR firms and it championed stories that showed the Iraqi occupation of Kuwait in the worst light possible. One story claimed that Iraqi soldiers had emptied babies out of incubators in Kuwaiti hospitals and left them to die. The US Congress and the UN Security Council both launched investigations. It was later discovered that the testimonies of 'eye-witnesses' who gave evidence at both the UN and congressional hearings had been fabricated and that the entire story was false. The resort to such desperate propaganda underscores just how worried pro-Kuwait advocates were that without public and political backing at home the Bush administration might renege on its commitment to save Kuwait and protect the rest of the region.

At the same time, the existential threat posed by Saddam demanded that Gulf leaders, for the first time ever and with the whole world watching, publicly admitted their strategic dependence on the United States. On 9 August 1990, the UN Security Council unanimously adopted Resolution 662, which declared that Iraq's annexation of Kuwait was null and void. On the same day King Fahd addressed the Saudi people. Wearing his customary tinted glasses, looking down at a prepared script and speaking slowly, he warned his citizens that the 'painful and regrettable events' in Kuwait directly threatened their nation. He then addressed the most sensitive issue of all – the role of foreign troops. He explained that the need to protect Saudi Arabia from 'huge' Iraqi forces in Kuwait demanded the support of 'fraternal Arab forces and other friendly forces'.[36] His speech only lasted for ten minutes but it was unprecedented. Never before had a senior Gulf royal so openly acknowledged such reliance on outside support. This was a necessary move at this point in time in order to prepare public opinion in Saudi Arabia and across the region for the arrival of over 650,000 troops and several thousand tanks, combat aircraft and warships from thirty-six countries. Saudi Arabia soon became home to over half a million of these troops, the majority American. It also hosted thousands of planes, and an impressive assortment of tanks, artillery and ammunition. Qatar, Bahrain and the UAE were located further away from Iraq than Saudi Arabia and were not directly in Saddam's firing line. Nevertheless, while the massive deployment was under way in Saudi Arabia, these other GCC states also committed troops, allowed foreign access to bases, and provided logistical support to coalition forces. These important contributions, as the final report to Congress on the war would later recall, were 'often attended by direct risks of Iraqi reprisals'.[37]

There was no little irony in the fact that this massive US-led military intervention was undertaken to liberate Kuwait. More than any other Gulf country Kuwait had always insisted that regional security was a matter for Gulf nations alone. Kuwait refused to join its neighbours in offering to pay the British to remain as the main security guarantor in the Gulf at the beginning of the 1970s. Instead, the kingdom's foreign minister reassured neighbours, somewhat incredulously, that his country would defend the region when the British departed. During the early years of the Iran–Iraq war, Kuwait was equally emphatic in its opposition to outside involvement in the region. The 'protection and security of this area', foreign minister Sabah Al-Ahmad Al-Jaber Al-Sabah made clear, 'is mainly the responsibility of its countries alone without any foreign intervention'. He also criticized talk emanating from Washington on the need to get access to local bases in the case of an emergency as 'some kind of intrigue'.[38]

Kuwait's official ties with the Soviet Union had begun in the early 1960s. By the mid-1980s, the desire to keep the US at arm's length was so great that some senior Kuwaiti officials favoured moving closer to Moscow in order to limit Washington's influence in the area. As part of this strategy Kuwait bought hundreds of millions of dollars of arms from Moscow and invited Russian leaders to visit the kingdom. During the last phase of the Iran–Iraq war, at the same time as its own tankers were sailing under the US flag, Kuwait leased three Soviet tankers to retain its perceived balance and neutrality. It also refused to allow US warships to enter its own territorial waters and blocked US planes and helicopters from landing on its territory. These moves irked many American observers, including the outspoken *New York Times* columnist William Crystal, who accused the kingdom of 'jerking the US around'. Even after Saddam's troops invaded the country in August 1990, Kuwaiti leaders were reluctant to abandon past habits, asking the US to keep secret the initial request for military support on the first day of the attack. Washington's response to Iraqi aggression profoundly changed the Kuwaiti position. There was a huge outpouring of warmth for America. During a meeting with President Bush in the Saudi city of Jeddah three months after he had fled his kingdom and at the same time as hundreds of thousands of US troops prepared to take on Saddam, the ousted Kuwaiti emir lavished praise on his visitor, describing America as a 'shelter for all who love freedom'.[39]

Ultimately the US-led coalition of over half a million troops was tasked with blocking Saddam's regional ambitions and liberating Kuwait from its Iraqi occupiers. The American contingent was twice as large as the rest of the force combined, and twelve times larger than the next biggest single contributor, the United Kingdom. All five of Kuwait's GCC partners contributed troops. So did the Arab countries of Syria, Egypt, Morocco and the Muslim nations of Pakistan, Bangladesh and Senegal. All were under the command of the Saudi chief of staff, General Prince Khalid bin Sultan. Arab troops were deployed closest to the Kuwaiti frontier. They were ordered to block Iraqi lines of communication north of Kuwait City to prevent the reinforcement of Iraqi troops. Arab Gulf air forces also undertook a number of bombing raids during the war.

The military phase of the Kuwait crisis, known as Operation Desert Storm, was launched in mid-January 1991. A few weeks later, as Saddam's SCUD missiles rained down on Saudi Arabia, GCC forces clashed with Iraqi troops in the border town of Ra's al-Khafji on the coastal road leading south from Kuwait into Saudi Arabia's oil-rich Eastern Province. The following month, as the conflict drew to a close, Arab forces also had the honour of leading coalition troops in the recapture of Kuwait City. The troops participating in this operation were drawn from all the Arab countries in the coalition. The intention behind this decision, as General Khalid bin Sultan later explained, was to ensure that credit was shared so that 'no one country could later claim to have done the job alone'.

From the American perspective, this and other Arab contributions to the war effort had symbolic and political significance but they were of negligible value in terms of their importance to the overall success of the military campaign. As CIA chief Robert Gates frankly explained, with the exception of the British and the French, 'most coalition partners were more trouble than they were worth in terms of actual military effectiveness'. After the crisis had ended, General Khalid bin Sultan expressed significant frustration with the tendency of senior American officials, in particular his American co-commander in the military campaign, General H. Norman Schwarzkopf, to overplay the US role by 'running down just about everyone else'.[40]

Saudi Arabia's top general may have had a point in relation to some specific cases or on a tactical level but the reality was that from its start the entire Gulf campaign demonstrated one reality beyond all others – American military dominance in the immediate post-Cold War era. By late February 1991, the US-led coalition, working with the Kuwaiti Resistance, controlled Kuwait City and the retreating Iraqi occupation army came under intense fire from coalition airpower, though half of Saddam's crack Republican Guard made it back over the border unscathed. In southern Iraq, allied armoured forces stood at the Euphrates River near Basra, and internal rebellions broke out against Saddam's regime. On 26 February, just three days after the start of the massive US-led ground offensive, the Soviets informed the UN Security Council of a message from Saddam Hussein to President Gorbachev. The Iraqi leader agreed to comply with UN Security Council Resolution 660 (1990) and promised to withdraw all troops from Kuwait immediately. The next day President Bush ordered a ceasefire and the surviving Iraqi troops were allowed to escape back into southern Iraq. Two days later the US president announced that the war was over. Finally, on 3 March 1991, Iraq accepted the terms of the ceasefire and the fighting ended. In only 100 hours of ground combat, coalition forces had liberated Kuwait. Iraqi TV weathermen still referred to the kingdom as the country's nineteenth province, but Operation Desert Storm had put an end to Iraq and Kuwait's 'eternal and inseparable merger', as Saddam's officials had prematurely described the August invasion.

In the wake of the crisis, some experts and commentators argued that the international anti-Saddam coalition proved that collective action and a multinational approach to security issues was possible following the end of the Cold War. Some even predicted that it had opened the way for secondary actors during the Cold War to play a more active role in Gulf security and to have far greater influence in regional affairs going forward. Europe, explained one noted Washington foreign policy expert, would soon have 'more influence ... a more sustained and durable political, economic and cultural presence ... than either the United States or the Soviet Union'.[41] The opposite happened. The crisis established Washington as the undisputed post-Cold War power in a region that held 65 per cent of the world's proven oil reserves and controlled 45 per cent of its net oil exports. This consolidated America's global dominance. At the same time it very clearly highlighted the political and military weakness of Europe, even after German reunification had further enhanced its economic power. Few failed to notice that while the Bush administration had successfully assembled an unprecedented international coalition under its command to free Kuwait, Europe failed to build a common diplomatic front even among its own members. Speaking in London less than a week after the end of hostilities in Kuwait, European Commission president Jacques Delors admitted as much. The Gulf crisis, he acknowledged, 'provided an object lesson ... on the limitations of the European Community'. The noted US political commentator Charles Krauthammer went further. Europe's 'disjointed national responses' to the Gulf crisis, he argued, showed that it was a 'materialist illusion' to think that economic power 'inevitably translates into geopolitical influence'.[42]

The Soviets were no more capable than Europe of offering a viable military or security alternative to the US. With the exception of Kuwait, the Arab Gulf States had been vehemently anti-communist for much of the Cold War. At the time of the Soviet Union's invasion of Afghanistan, Sheikh Yamani told a group of businessmen in Davos, Switzerland, that if Moscow 'marches to the oilfields, this will be a third world war'.[43] Saudi Arabia then became the first country to boycott the 1980 Summer Olympics in Moscow in protest over Moscow's Afghan intervention. Relations gradually improved over the course of the decade. The UAE established diplomatic relations with Moscow in 1984 in order to emphasize the federation's 'nonaligned [and] neutral policy',[44] its foreign minister explained. The following year Oman did the same and Qatar initiated diplomatic relations with Moscow in 1988.

Mikhail Gorbachev's accession to power in 1985 was one important explanation for these improving relations. On becoming Soviet leader he introduced a policy of 'New Thinking' in foreign affairs based on positive diplomacy and economic relations. This culminated in his March 1990 call for the Warsaw Pact to be transformed from a military alliance into a political organization. In line with this revolution in Soviet strategic thinking, top Russian officials initially joined Washington in condemning the Iraqi invasion of Kuwait. Soviet diplomats at the United Nations also voted in favour of Security Council resolutions demanding the restoration of Kuwait's sovereignty.

This support for the US-led coalition against Saddam, a long-time Moscow ally, highlighted the profoundly weakened state of the former superpower. In an attempt to demonstrate some last remnants of global relevance, Soviet foreign minister Eduard Shevardnadze and his envoy Yevgeny Primakov worked hard in late 1990 and early 1991 to find any alternative to war that would allow Saddam to leave Kuwait with his dignity and military power intact. Gulf Arab leaders took a dim view of these last-ditch Soviet attempts to rescue Saddam. They dismissed Primakov's failed November 1990 visit to Baghdad to mediate the crisis as a complete 'fiasco'.[45] They were no less critical of the two subsequent Soviet attempts to push for a deal – on the eve of the air war in mid-January 1991 and in mid-February, just before the start of ground operations.

During a March 1991 victory tour of the Middle East, US secretary of state James Baker expressed the hope that Desert Storm might be the 'last great battle in the region'.[46] Few believed that this would be the enduring outcome of the Kuwait crisis. What was not in dispute was that it had demonstrated clearly just how vulnerable a united, never mind divided, Arab Gulf was to sudden attacks and how dependent it was on outside military support for its protection. Speaking in December 1990 at the first GCC leaders' summit following Saddam's invasion and occupation of Kuwait, Khalifa bin Hamad Al-Thani, the emir of Qatar, told the assembled kings and princes that the Iraqi action had 'upset all the realities and standards which we had taken for granted regarding the basis of inter-Arab relations, the concept of Gulf security, and Arab security'.[47] Something needed to change and Kuwait's UN ambassador, Muhammad Abu Al-Hassan, believed he had the answer. The GCC, he explained shortly after the liberation of his country, had to start to 'take security seriously'.

Grand statements by Gulf leaders about their military self-sufficiency, the norm during the previous decade, were no longer enough. It was time, as the Saudi diplomat, poet and commentator Ghazi Algosaibi urged, for the people of the Gulf to 'liberate themselves from any "delusions of grandeur"'.[48] It was still possible to take some positives away from the Kuwait crisis. In the summer months before the invasion, Saddam's incessant Kuwait-bashing became a pastime of sorts for some in the region, as well as many in the wider Arab world, who had long resented the oil wealth of the tiny Gulf kingdoms. Once the invasion took place few, inside the GCC at least, continued to see the joke. They even sympathized with the Kuwaiti official who threw plates at a delegation from Iraq at an Arab League meeting in Amman, Jordan, soon after the August 1990 invasion of his country.

On this basis, all the GCC member states worked closely with each other in support of Kuwait. As one American diplomat stationed in the region reported home, those disagreements that did arise were 'amazingly few and generally of a marginal nature'.[49] The Saudi leadership in particular demonstrated its commitment to the people and rulers of Kuwait. Thousands of the occupied kingdom's homeless citizens were welcomed in and quickly settled into their new lives as a 'nation living in hotels', in the words of King Fahd. Kuwait's government-in-exile received sanctuary in the city of Ta'if, and Kuwait's emir, who had fled across the border in an armour-plated Mercedes, became the honoured guest of the Saudi royals.

Such unconditional support engendered a real sense of optimism that the 'spirit of war', as one local official described it, would translate itself into improved cooperation and coordination on defence and security issues in the aftermath of the conflict. The most radical plan put forward was the 'Damascus Declaration'. Announced after a meeting in the Syrian capital in March 1991 it attempted to provide an Arab solution to the problem of Gulf insecurity. It called for Egypt and Syria to station up to 50,000 of their own troops on GCC territory as the first step towards a long-term Gulf security partnership between the GCC member states and their allies in the wider Arab world. Opposed by Tehran and backed by Washington, it never got off the ground. In the final account, the Gulf States were just too uncomfortable with the implications of hosting non-GCC Arab soldiers on their territory. Saudi leaders in particular quickly went off the idea when they started to think about the negative impact such a move might have on domestic stability and the kingdom's standing beyond its borders.

After rejecting the vision of a pan-Arab security strategy for the Gulf embodied in the 'Damascus Declaration', GCC leaders pushed ahead with finding other ways to enhance their security. Sultan Qaboos of Oman, a long-time champion of collective security in the Gulf, was appointed to head up a new GCC Supreme Committee on Security tasked with finding a 'GCC Plus' security framework acceptable to all member state governments. This committee put forward a number of ambitious proposals. It recommended that member states increase their logistical and financial support for GCC departments dealing with military and security matters.

At the time of the Kuwait crisis, thirty times more GCC officials worked on economic and social issues than on defence and security.[50] The sultan's committee also proposed enlarging the Peninsula Shield force from 15,000 to 100,000 men; adding to the GCC's existing early warning capabilities; and deepening GCC member state cooperation in military planning, command and control and training. Some of these proposals made headway. The GCC partners signed up to an open-ended commitment to provide troops to protect Saudi Arabia and Kuwait from any future Iraqi threats. They also agreed to integrate further GCC-wide early warning systems and to develop a more coordinated arms-purchasing strategy before spending dozens of billions of dollars on any new weapons systems.

Ongoing fears of Saudi hegemony, unresolved border disputes and deeply held local resentments all stalled attempts to build on the above proposals to develop a more extensive collective security framework following the Kuwait crisis. Throughout the 1980s, concerns over Saudi influence had prevented deeper military cooperation beyond the problems of the Peninsula Shield. Kuwait blocked any GCC security agreement that allowed Saudi personnel to enter Kuwaiti territory without permission. Even in early 1991, on the eve of the ground war in Kuwait, Qatar rejected a Saudi request for permission to deploy its forces on its territory. Deeply suspicious of Saudi intentions, Qatar quickly constructed observation posts on its border to monitor the movements of Saudi forces stationed nearby. Subsequent clashes between Saudi and Qatari troops left two dead. In protest, Qatar withdrew from GCC military exercises and refused to attend a November 1994 GCC summit. The following year Qatar and Kuwait refused to sign a comprehensive GCC security agreement dealing with the exchange of intelligence information proposed by Saudi Arabia. King Fahd was so angry over this snub that he considered boycotting the annual GCC summit in Muscat scheduled for December 1995, though in the end he did not attend the summit because he suffered a stroke.

This clash between Qatar and Saudi Arabia was a stark reminder of the failure of the GCC member states to put aside their differences in the interests of improved defence and security cooperation even while Saddam, still in power in Baghdad, continued to pose a real threat. Nor were the Arab Gulf States able to agree unanimously on how to deal with Iraq after Saddam's forces were defeated in February 1991. Kuwait was adamant that there should be no normalization of ties with Baghdad. Oman and the UAE wanted an immediate return to normal relations. Their reasoning was cold and calculating. Iraq, they argued, should be allowed to retain enough power to be able to play its traditional role of balancing the Iranian threat.

In the early 1990s there was less disagreement among GCC member states on the need to back the sanctions imposed on Iraq by the international community at the start of the Kuwait crisis. These restrictions on oil, weapons and a variety of manufactured goods were defended as a necessary evil needed to contain Saddam's threat. Over subsequent months and years, as it became less and less likely that Saddam's opponents inside Iraq had the strength to oust him from power, Gulf officials became distinctly uneasy over supporting, or even discussing, sanctions in public. When Gulf leaders did raise the issue they expressed open hostility to the sanctions policy. Crown Prince Abdullah of Saudi Arabia bemoaned the disturbing fact that those worst affected were not Saddam's closest and most loyal supporters but the average Iraqi citizen, regardless of age or gender. The UAE's president, Zayed Al-Nahyan, made the same point and called for the US to ease restrictions for the benefit of the Iraqi people. In 1996 the government in Baghdad agreed to participate in the UN-sponsored Oil-for-Food scheme. This plan allowed for two-thirds of the oil revenues generated by Iraq every six months to be used to buy humanitarian goods. The hope in the Arab Gulf was that this would go some way towards improving the situation. Instead, it further entrenched Saddam's grip on power and his refusal to compromise with the international community.

In order to contain the threat posed by Saddam during this period, the Gulf Arabs relied on the US security guarantee. Even before he returned home from his Saudi refuge, Kuwait's emir made clear his desire for US forces to remain in his kingdom indefinitely. Other GCC leaders also abandoned past opposition to a visible American military presence in the region and embraced American protection as the main pillar of their security doctrine. The Gulf States entered into a number of cooperation and arms-purchasing agreements with foreign powers other than the United States in the 1990s. Kuwait, for example, signed defence and security pacts with Britain and France in 1992. The following year it signed an agreement with Russia, which provided the formal framework through which Kuwait became the first country to buy Russia's Smerch multiple rocket launchers. In 1994 Qatar and France signed a defence agreement worth US$1.4 billion and they followed this up with a bilateral defence treaty in 1998. In between, in 1995, Qatar and the United Kingdom signed a US$500 million arms deal. The UAE signed mutual defence treaties with France in 1995, Britain in 1996 and Turkey in 1997.

None of these matched the post-crisis defence cooperation agreements Washington signed with Kuwait, Bahrain, Oman, Qatar and the UAE. Together they formalized the GCC's status as home to thousands of US troops, as well as hundreds of tanks, squadrons of warplanes and enough pre-positioned heavy equipment to fight, or at least start a war, at short notice. To complement these land-based forces, the US maintained about 10,000 military personnel aboard ships in the region at any given time. The emir of Bahrain, who had recently confided in James Baker that he wanted the US navy to stay in his kingdom for another fifty years, granted Washington permission to extend its naval base in his kingdom. By 1995, the entire Bahrain operation was home to fifteen US naval vessels, including an aircraft carrier, and had been upgraded to fleet status as the Fifth Fleet.

Saudi Arabia was the only Gulf monarchy not to sign a defence agreement with the US following the Kuwait crisis. This absence of a formal arrangement did not block greater US–Saudi military cooperation in the face of the ongoing Iraqi threat. Even after it was routed in Kuwait, Saddam's army was still five times larger than its Saudi counterpart. Though Riyadh turned down Washington's post-war request to establish a new airbase in the kingdom, it did grant permission for 10,000 US troops to remain in the country. The US air force was also allowed use the Dahran base they had built forty years earlier and to patrol the southern no-fly zone in Iraq (Operation Southern Watch) from Saudi territory.

After the boom of the 1970s, the Arab Gulf experienced economic slowdown during much of the next decade. Global demand for oil fell at the same time as non-OPEC exporters increased production. By the mid-1980s combined annual GCC oil revenues were down by more than US$100 billion on earlier years. The costs associated with funding the Iraqi war effort against Iran, as well as ongoing expensive domestic development projects, all led to severe financial pressures across the region. For the first time since the late 1960s Gulf governments had to deal with dwindling cash reserves that required them to borrow heavily, cut public spending and implement pay freezes. The oil price dropped again towards the end of the 1980s, leading to further spending cuts at home and the unprecedented sell-off of overseas assets.

The Arab Gulf's economic troubles did not stop the US from making it clear from the start of the Kuwait crisis that local countries should cover most of the cost of neutralizing the Iraqi threat. Only a few years after the Gulf States had funded Iraq's war against Iran, they had to pick up a large part of the bill for the cost of operations Desert Shield and Desert Storm. Estimates of the actual cost of war differ – even inside the US bureaucracy. The Defense Department puts it at US$70 billion, the Office of Management & Budget puts it at US$61 billion and the General Accounting Office comes in lower at US$50 billion. Between them the three biggest Arab Gulf donors – Saudi Arabia, Kuwait and the UAE – pledged around US$40 billion in cash and various payments in kind towards the cost of allied operations.[51] This included monthly payments running into the billions to cover the costs of transporting US forces to the Gulf, as well as the cost of fuel, water, construction and in-country transportation for allied troops once they got there.

At Washington's request the GCC also provided the Soviets with US$4 billion worth of credit through the winter of 1991 as a pay-off for their agreement not to block the anti-Saddam coalition; and they gave just under US$1 billion to the east European nations who had been hit badly by the rising oil price only months after they had broken free from almost half a century of Soviet control. Saudi Arabia, Qatar and the UAE also sat on the Gulf Crisis Financial Coordination Group, established under American leadership to coordinate the transfer of billions of dollars in financial aid to pro-Western states whose economies had been worst affected by the higher oil price, lost trade revenues and UN sanctions. Turkey, Egypt and Jordan topped the list of recipients of this money, the majority of which was provided by the Arab Gulf. According to the World Bank, Turkey's financial shortfall for 1991 alone was US$6–7 billion. It was estimated that Egypt and Jordan each lost between US$2–4 billion in the same year. During their annual meeting in December 1990, GCC leaders also set up their own fund worth US$10 billion over ten years to support economic development in those Arab states that had supported them during the crisis. On a bilateral level, the GCC states also provided funds to, and signed new economic, trade and technical agreements with, a number of Arab states that had loyally backed them in their time of need.

All of this placed further financial pressure on the Arab Gulf after years of tough economic conditions. On the other hand, the oil price rose sharply as a consequence of the crisis. By some estimates this had the potential to bring in extra annual oil revenues to Saudi Arabia of US$25–$50 billion depending on the price and the level of production. It also seemed that austerity meant something different in the Gulf than elsewhere. A senior Kuwaiti minister suggested that citizens could economize in the post-crisis era by hiring no more than two maids when they returned to their homes.[52] This is not to minimize the enormity of the bill that Gulf rulers had to cover to liberate Kuwait. Nor did the costs associated with Saddam's invasion and occupation end with the Iraqi defeat. The cost of rebuilding Kuwait was estimated at over US$50 billion.

On coming to power in 1993 President Bill Clinton embraced a strategy of 'dual containment' to deal with Iran and Iraq. This aggressive strategy was hugely expensive. It necessitated the deployment of unprecedented numbers of US troops and combat planes across the Gulf. In a series of intense discussions during 1994, US secretary of state Warren Christopher got the GCC foreign ministers to agree grudgingly to share the cost of this US deployment on the grounds that its main task was to counter ongoing Iraqi threats to Kuwait. It is estimated that total GCC contributions towards the cost of ousting Saddam from Kuwait in 1990–91 and then policing him in subsequent years, as well as payments to other Arab states and Turkey for their economic losses, was well over US$50 billion.

The GCC states also played a crucial role in stabilizing, as well as subsidizing, the oil price during the crisis. The cost of a barrel of oil doubled from US$19 to US$40 between August and December 1990, in part because Iraqi occupiers had damaged beyond use more than 800 of Kuwait's 1,100 oil wells. In response, Qatar, Saudi Arabia, Kuwait and the UAE made up a bloc within OPEC to oppose higher oil prices. This move succeeded, thanks mainly to a Saudi decision to increase production to over eight million barrels a day. By the time that Iraqi forces retreated from Kuwait in February 1991, the price of oil had dropped from US$40 a barrel to below US$20 a barrel. By 1995 it stood at US$16.

The Kuwait crisis also illuminated the difficulties that regional organizations face in pushing ahead with economic and institutional integration in an unstable security environment. The Arab Cooperation Council, established in 1989 by Egypt, Iraq, Jordan and North Yemen, fell apart as a result of the Kuwait crisis. So did the Arab Maghreb Union of five north African Arab states. The GCC was a much more developed entity than either of these endeavours and its members embraced cooperation with unprecedented enthusiasm once Saddam's assault on Kuwaiti sovereignty came to an end. In the economic sphere this was most evident in their renewed willingness to prioritize the establishment of a customs union, a free trade area with a common external tariff that is an important, if early, step toward economic and monetary union.

On the political level the Arab Gulf States also moved closer together after the war ended to deal with Palestinian leader Yasser Arafat, the PLO and the Palestinian people. In order to justify the invasion and occupation of his much smaller and much richer neighbour, Saddam Hussein had presented his action in Kuwait as the first step in his plan to achieve 'the liberation of Jerusalem'.[53] GCC leaders, like the majority of those in the rest of the Arab world, were outraged by this move. They rejected Saddam's attempt to link the hopes of the Palestinian people to the dismemberment of Kuwait. Instead they argued that this was a cynical attempt by the Iraqi leader to hide his true motives – greed, power and survival.

The Gulf Arabs had resorted to the oil weapon in 1973 because Egypt and Syria had failed to find a solution to the Arab–Israeli problem on the battlefield. Over the rest of the 1970s, the oil-producing Gulf then leveraged its influence in Europe in the interests of the Palestinian cause. In other parts of the world, and at multilateral organizations like the United Nations, they also promoted Palestinian interests and attempted to use their new-found international standing to influence and educate the international community on Palestinian rights. Speaking in 1980, Mohammad bin Mubarak Al-Khalifa, Bahrain's then foreign minister, expressed a view held across the entire Arab Gulf at the time, even in places like Bahrain with small Palestinian populations. 'We want to be with the West', he explained, 'but it is very hard to throw in our lot with the US while it preserves an attitude to Israel as if it were the one country with which it shares its interests.'[54]

Despite loudly championing self-determination for Palestine on the international stage, Gulf citizens and rulers suspected the loyalties of their Palestinian guest communities. Both before and after the 1973 crisis there existed a widely held fear that Palestinian frustration might spill over into radical politics, including Marxism and Ba'athism. There were fears that the Palestinians in the Gulf might even turn to post-revolutionary Iran. In order to pre-empt any of these possible eventualities Gulf governments marginalized local Palestinian populations. Saudi Arabia's Aramco provided one notable example of this. By the late 1970s, over 60 per cent of the oil giant's total workforce was made up of either Palestinians or Palestinian-born Jordanians, without whom it could not have functioned. Nonetheless, whenever possible Palestinians were excluded from jobs in sensitive oil installations such as the Ras Tanura refinery and tanker-loading terminal.

These underlying tensions caused resentment across Palestinian society in the Gulf and at the highest levels of the Palestinian leadership. Yet few imagined that the Palestinian movement would turn against the Gulf Arabs when Saddam invaded Kuwait. Ultimately, Yasser Arafat could not resist the opportunity occasioned by the crisis to coopt Saddam's pro-Palestinian rhetoric. The PLO leader hailed Saddam as the champion of the Palestinian people and predicted that Saddam's actions would bring 'glory' to the Palestinian cause. He also acknowledged Saddam as the leader of the Arab world and warned that 'anyone responsible for shedding the blood of Iraqis will be punished'.[55] The PLO's influential de facto foreign minister Farouk Kaddoumi weighed in behind Arafat. 'We stand with Iraq 100 per cent,' he explained. This backing for Iraq was also evident in Palestinian intellectual circles. One well-known poet expressed a commonly held view of the time that 'a thousand George Bushes wouldn't be worth a pair of Saddam's shoes'. The vast majority of Palestinian inhabitants of the towns and refugee camps of Jordan, and the occupied West Bank and Gaza Strip, also backed Saddam. They considered him to be a hero who had stood up to America, Israel and all those Arab leaders – in Rabat, Damascus and Cairo – who had repeatedly betrayed the Palestinian cause. Those in the Palestinian movement who argued that this strategy would eventually backfire were ignored. Ultimately, as one PLO official explained at the time, when it came to choosing sides on Kuwait, 'bitterness prevailed over loyalty'.[56]

At war's end the Arab Gulf States immediately responded to this lack of loyalty by cutting funding to the PLO, which had amounted to over US$10 billion during the 1980s alone. They also took revenge on the large Palestinian communities living in their kingdoms. According to one NGO, Middle East Watch, 6,000 Palestinians who lived in Kuwait were detained following the liberation. Thousands more were summarily expelled, in many cases leaving behind jobs, homes and families. Those who remained faced reprisals from vigilantes whose plans for revenge were only thwarted when senior royals threatened to hand out harsh punishments to the perpetrators of such attacks.

This significant deterioration in relations between the GCC governments, the PLO and local Palestinian populations took place alongside a gradual improvement in GCC–Israeli relations. In the final months of 1991, the Arab Gulf States sent representatives to the US-sponsored Arab–Israeli peace conference held in Madrid. Just under two years later, in September 1993, they welcomed the launch of the Oslo peace process as the 'first step toward reaching a just, lasting and comprehensive settlement'. The following year the GCC also agreed to end the blacklisting of foreign companies who traded with Israel and also placed a proposal before the Arab League that linked a total end of the fifty-year economic boycott of Israel to 'progress' in the peace process. The Arab League rejected this idea and even refused to put the boycott issue on the agenda of their discussions, a move which highlighted how much more open the GCC states were to improving ties to Israel than many other Arab countries. The Gulf Arabs also began to allow visitors with Israeli travel stamps in their passports to enter their countries and they opened up their ports and airspace to aeroplanes and foreign-flagged ships that had stopped at Israeli airports and ports.

During the early Oslo years, senior GCC leaders met their Israeli counterparts for talks at the UN headquarters in New York and other, less public, venues. They also attended some of the official signing ceremonies marking key moments in the phased peace deal between Israel and the Palestinians. In 1994 Sultan Qaboos invited Israeli government representatives to a conference on water desalinization. Soon after, he welcomed Israeli prime minister Yitzhak Rabin to Muscat. This was the first public visit by an Israeli leader to a GCC member state. In 1996, following Rabin's assassination at the hands of a right-wing extremist opposed to peace, Oslo's architect, Shimon Peres, visited Qatar to mark the opening of an Israeli trade office in Doha. This made Qatar the first GCC state – and only the fourth Arab nation after Morocco, Mauritania and Tunisia – to have a representative office in Tel Aviv or an equivalent Israeli office in its own capital. Soon after Oman approved the opening of an Israeli office in Muscat. Together Oman and Qatar set a precedent for the rest of the Arab Gulf of using trade ties as a way of fostering much more positive relations with Israel short of de jure recognition.

A working paper published in May 1981, in the earliest days of the GCC's existence, expressed the hope that some day the organization would 'jointly have a say in the international and regional fields, which will express its respected and feared place in the world economy'.[57] The commitment made by almost forty nations to free Kuwait and to defend Saudi Arabia and the rest of the GCC from Saddam's nefarious intentions demonstrated just how important the oil-rich region's stability and security was for the rest of the world. Likewise, the US decision to leave troops in the region in unprecedented numbers in the wake of the crisis served to highlight the centrality of the region in the emerging post-Cold War order. This was not a universally popular decision in the United States. From the start of the crisis there was extensive public comment on the lack of appreciation the Gulf Arabs had shown for the American-led rescue operation. 'Not so much as a Thanks for Western Forces', ran one representative *New York Times* headline. Reports that Gulf diplomats disparaged American and other coalition troops in private, and labelled them hired mercenaries and 'white slaves', generated even more distaste.[58]

After the liberation of their country, the entire Kuwaiti population from the royal family down expressed hugely positive feelings towards the post-war security role of the United States in the region. In other parts of the Gulf there was much less enthusiasm for the ongoing presence of US troops following Saddam's defeat. Many were not amused by the joke of the hour – that the US should now join the Arab League because it was going to be in the region for a long time. Two groups in particular – Arab nationalists and Islamists – were upset over this course of events. For nationalists, the entire Kuwait crisis had been a catastrophe that only served to reinforce existing views of the US as an 'imperial-enemy',[59] just one more in a long line of foreign powers who had penetrated the region in order to impose their own interests on local populations. Within weeks of Saddam's invasion of Kuwait in early August 1990, rumours circulated across the Gulf that the US was using the crisis to establish a permanent military presence in the region. Conspiracy theories about US plots to enslave and colonize the Gulf resonated deeply with many ordinary people and were expressed widely in café conversations and across the media. Statements made by figures in the US administration further fuelled speculation. In off-the-record briefings and in testimony before congressional committees they argued that Saddam's invasion of Kuwait made it necessary to establish an effective 'regional security structure'[60] in the Gulf.

For Islamists, the highly visible US military presence on holy Muslim land was a lightning rod for anti-regime opposition. As Hasan Al-Turabi, the Western-educated Sudanese Islamist politician, put it at the time, the American military presence in the region 'provides a means for the Islamic movement'.[61] This was especially true in Saudi Arabia. Long before hundreds of thousands of US troops had arrived in the second half of 1990, pro-American sympathies in the kingdom had been confined to the royal family and its inner circle of advisers, the military and security services and the government-controlled media. All took care to handle the complex, contentious and often covert relationship with Washington with extreme care. The Saudi authorities went to great lengths to hide the depth of anti-American feeling among some influential domestic constituencies and played down demands by ordinary citizens for political rights and freedoms. They also endeavoured to prevent US officials from coming into contact with critics of the regime. It was even reported that during the late 1980s, Saudi officials had requested that Washington withdraw its ambassador in Riyadh, Hume Horan, because he spoke fluent Arabic and could interact with opponents of the ruling family in their native language.

During the war for Kuwait, King Fahd had earned the praise of Western leaders for convincingly linking the deployment of foreign troops in his kingdom to the security and well-being of his citizens. The Saudi people grudgingly accepted that trade-off as a necessary evil in the period of intense uncertainty and fear that immediately followed Saddam's invasion of Kuwait. For decades, Westerners working in Saudi Arabia's oil sector and other industries had been kept away from the local population wherever possible. In a similar move, once the military deployment began, the Saudi authorities kept contact between citizens and foreign soldiers at a minimum. Most American troops were based in the Eastern Province, the heartland of the oil business, where the local population was more used to interacting with foreigners. The movements of troops were strictly controlled and they were kept out of cities like Riyadh. One US commander on the ground would later recall, 'They wanted us to be kind of low-key, low profile, and [told us] don't upset the population.'[62]

These tactics worked well while the crisis continued. There were only a handful of isolated incidents in which Western soldiers came under attack from local populations anywhere in the Gulf. In Saudi Arabia, a truck carrying US servicemen was fired on but those inside escaped unharmed. In Bahrain, a local citizen with mental health issues stabbed a British soldier, while an Italian soldier was also stabbed in Dubai. Once Kuwait was liberated King Fahd reduced the price of grain for farmers and livestock owners and cancelled two years of debt repayments for everyone in the kingdom as a way of ensuring the loyalty of his population despite the ongoing presence of US troops on Saudi soil. In order to reduce tensions further, almost half a million US troops left Saudi Arabia over the next ten months, leaving behind a force of less than 40,000 by the start of 1992. Within six months, this number was down to 10,000.

For religious conservatives in Saudi society, this rapid reduction of American troops stationed in the kingdom mattered little more than the ruling of 350 top Saudi clerics that it was permissible to allow non-Muslims to help in a holy war. What mattered was that the US had used the Kuwait crisis to establish a massive military presence in Saudi Arabia, home to Mecca and Medina, the two holiest shrines in Islam. Worse, Washington had taken advantage of the end of hostilities to expand its power across the Gulf and to interfere in Muslim domestic affairs. To some degree, these concerns, as well as similar claims made by conservatives in other GCC states, were warranted. Liberal political ideas of sorts started to find backing at the highest levels across the Arab Gulf in the wake of the conflict. Sultan Qaboos increased the powers of the consultative council in Oman, for the first time turning it into a quasi-elected representative body. The Kuwaiti National Assembly had been dissolved in the 1980s due to disagreements between the government and the opposition. After Iraqi troops invaded the kingdom, rulers promised that they would re-establish the Assembly once Saddam's forces had been expelled. Following the liberation, they kept their promise and agreed to new elections in the autumn of 1992. For his part, in November 1990, the Saudi king announced that once the crisis next door was over he would initiate a process that would lead to the establishment of a consultative council. He also made several other public declarations of his intention to initiate a wide-ranging review of society as a whole.

Moves like these greatly alarmed more conservative elements across Saudi society. In March 1991, 400 religious figures, including members of the Saudi *ulama*, the legal and religious establishment, sent a 'Letter of Demands' to King Fahd. Among other things, this letter denounced the presence of non-Muslim troops on Muslim territory. The following year, in 1992, a group of clerics issued what came to be known as the 'Memorandum of Advice'. This had two key demands: stricter observance of Islamic (shariah) law and the end of close ties with the West. Many important clerics, including Sheikh Abd Al-Aziz Ibn Al-Baz, a powerful figure, appointed the kingdom's Grand Mufti in 1993, backed the royal family on these matters, most notably providing religious legitimacy to the invitation to foreign troops to enter the kingdom in 1990.

Other senior clerics refused to do so and were dismissed from their posts. In 1994, the Saudi government overhauled the religious establishment. The Ministry of Islamic Affairs was given responsibility for the appointment and actions of imams and other communal religious leaders. Political content during sermons at Friday prayers was also censored. Moves like this achieved their goal. The mainstream Saudi *ulama* was successfully coopted by the ruling elite and tasked with legitimizing the leadership's position on sensitive issues, including the ongoing American presence in Saudi Arabia in particular, and the region in general.

There were, however, other sources of dissent. The 'Awakening Movement' attracted much support for their advocacy of a literal interpretation of the Quran, their call to arms against heresy in the Muslim world and their criticism of the ruling family's relationship with the West. This movement emerged from Islamic networks linked to the Muslim Brotherhood, which had gained influence in Saudi Arabia's educational system. The tape recordings of the sermons and teachings of the movement's leaders, including Salman Al-Awada and Safar Al-Hawali, were popular among academics, religious scholars and other members of the elite and overall its supporters were inclined to be more university educated than lower class. At the same time, its ideology also resonated among less prosperous segments of society who had been the biggest losers in the rapid programme of modernization, urbanization and domestic development since the mid-1970s. Unlike the new generation of increasingly wealthy middle-class citizens, members of this struggling group had benefited little from decades of oil wealth. They had no experience of Western education and rejected the Western consumerism now increasingly evident in some sectors of society. Most worrying for the authorities, they blamed their own socio-economic misfortune on the failings of a pro-Western elite, indifferent and out of touch. For this dissatisfied class, the provocative slogans used by radical preachers to delegitimize the ruling establishment, including the accusation 'America has become your God',[63] struck a particular chord.

Hassan Ali Al-Ebraheem, a well-known Kuwaiti historian, once counselled his fellow Gulf citizens never to forget that they lived 'in a bad neighborhood'.[64] Saddam Hussein's invasion and brutal occupation of Kuwait had shown the wisdom of his words. In these terms, the US presence in Saudi Arabia following the end of the Kuwait crisis did provide GCC member states with the physical security that comes with the protection of the world's only military superpower. This ensured stability in the short term but it was never a viable strategy for ensuring either long-term domestic stability or regional security. The Clinton administration in Washington knew this. In the mid-1990s, it vetoed a proposal put forward by senior intelligence officials to initiate a detailed study of Saudi stability because it rightly worried that the findings would be too politically sensitive to handle. If the study had been allowed to go ahead it would have shown that the US presence in Saudi Arabia had served to further radicalize Islamist opponents of the pro-Western ruling family, though Saudi royals continued to insist that there was nothing to worry about. Such institutionalized denial in both Washington and Riyadh set in motion a chain of events that led to the September 2011 attacks on New York and Washington, and the subsequent US invasion of Iraq in 2003. To their consternation and regret the Gulf Arabs found themselves at the centre of these epoch-changing events, both of which made it more difficult than ever for them to further consolidate stability at home and influence abroad at a time of profound regional and global upheaval.

CHAPTER 4

THY BROTHER'S KEEPER

'Am I my brother's keeper? Yes I am.'

– Nino Brown, *New Jack City*

On the morning of 11 September 2001, nineteen hijackers killed 2,996 people from ninety countries when they crashed four passenger jets into targets across the United States. They also caused an estimated US$10 billion of property and infrastructure damage, including the total destruction of the Twin Towers of the World Trade Center, two of the world's tallest buildings that had dominated New York's skyline for decades. The attacks were unprecedented in conception, execution and death toll and sent shock waves through the entire world. They resulted in the launch of the war on terror as well as the US invasions of Afghanistan and Iraq. In the Gulf they threatened to completely overturn the status quo as they brought to the surface the very real tensions in the long-time strategic relationship between Saudi Arabia and the United States. They also required Gulf Arab leaders to face up to the threat of home-grown radical Islamists in a way, and to an extent, that they had never had to do before. In short, the 9/11 attacks made it harder than ever for the Arab Gulf States to achieve stability at home and influence abroad.

The man ostensibly responsible for all this was Osama bin Laden. He was a member of an extremely wealthy Saudi family with close business ties to the country's ruling elite. The nineteen perpetrators of the attacks on the United States had been his followers, disciples and members of Al-Qaeda, the radical Islamist group that he had founded at the end of the 1980s. Like him, they were driven by a belief that the religious duty of a proper Muslim was to undertake jihad against secular Muslim regimes and non-Muslim occupiers of Muslim lands. 'This war is fundamentally religious,' bin Laden explained in a statement broadcast by Qatar's Al-Jazeera television news network in the wake of the 9/11 attacks. The belief that Islam had embarked on a 'decisive [battle] . . . between infidelity and faith', as a subsequent Al-Qaeda statement explained, provided the legitimization for the mass killing of innocents on a scale previously unknown.

Saudi leaders were no strangers to bin Laden. He had first made his reputation in the 1980s during the mujahideen's war against the Soviet Union in Afghanistan. Shortly after Saddam had invaded Kuwait in 1990, bin Laden made a proposal to his country's top officials. He would raise an army of 100,000 fighters to defend Saudi borders from the threat posed by Saddam, thus removing the need to rely on the American military to do the job. This offer was rejected out of hand as both impractical and undesirable. From this point on bin Laden turned his sights on the Saudi royals. These supposed protectors of the Holy Places, he argued, were responsible for a 'calamity'.[1] They had invited infidel invaders on to holy Muslim land and then allowed them to stay on indefinitely after the war against Saddam had ended.

By 1992 bin Laden had left the country of his birth for the last time, never to return. He admired the 'Awakening Movement' and echoed their demands that Saudi rulers expel the US military and adopt proper Islamic laws. He then went much further. He accused the royal family of criminal negligence and called for its overthrow. In 1994, the Saudi leadership stripped bin Laden of his passport and citizenship. They despised him but they also underestimated him before 9/11. After the attacks, one senior royal, a younger son of the founder of Saudi Arabia, told the media that on the rare occasions he had encountered bin Laden in the early 1990s he found him to be a 'simple man'. 'We just thought he was a nuisance,' explained Prince Bandar in a similar recollection. 'I thought he couldn't lead eight ducks across the street.'[2]

The 9/11 attacks altered dramatically the Saudi elite's view of bin Laden. That did not make it easier for them to come to terms with the reality of what he had done. As soon as the attacks occurred, senior Saudi royals condemned them as 'regrettable and inhuman'.[3] Over the next few days, as the body count rose and the smouldering remains of New York's World Trade Center and Washington's Pentagon building continued to burn, Crown Prince Abdullah and foreign minister Saud Al-Faisal visited Washington. They met with President Bush three days after the attacks to pay their respects to an ally. The United States had guaranteed Saudi security for generations, most visibly with troops on the ground since the

Kuwait crisis a decade earlier. They were also there on business. Even in these early days, it seemed likely that the attacks had been planned, funded and undertaken by bin Laden and his supporters. A statement published a week after the attack in the name of King Fahd seemed to acknowledge this, if only implicitly. Saudi Arabia, it stated, 'rejects being associated with any person whose name is linked to terrorism'.[4]

Crown Prince Abdullah, the fifth son of the founder of Saudi Arabia, had been de facto ruler of the kingdom since King Fahd suffered a stroke in November 1995. He had a reputation for being more willing to challenge America's Middle East policy than his half-brother had been before his illness had incapacitated him. This was one reason why Abdullah had strong support across all sectors of Saudi society including tribal groups and religious conservatives. While in Washington Abdullah urged President Bush to avoid rushing to conclusions about who carried out the attacks and warned against blaming Arabs and Muslims in general. So did Prince Nayef Abdul Aziz Al-Saud, the kingdom's influential interior minister, who had been responsible for ensuring Saudi internal security since the mid-1970s. Within a few years of 9/11, Nayef would oversee the Saudi crackdown on Al-Qaeda in the kingdom, but in the first few weeks after the attacks he repeatedly rejected any links between Saudi Arabia, bin Laden and the events of 9/11.[5] He only acknowledged these connections in late October after the US authorities officially named bin Laden as the mastermind behind the operation and announced that fifteen of the nineteen hijackers were Saudi nationals.

In Washington, Prince Bandar did not try to deny Saudi links to the events of 9/11, which were becoming increasingly obvious with every passing day. Instead, he blamed them, indirectly at least, on Iran. If Iran had not targeted Gulf tankers during its war with Iraq in the 1980s, he argued, America would never have entered the region to protect Gulf shipping. There would have been no precedent for America's military presence in the Gulf in the 1990s, which in turn would have removed a main cause of the radicalization that bred bin Laden and his supporters.[6] Such denial, diversionary tactics and tortuous arguments pointed to the sheer magnitude of the crisis that the 9/11 attacks, bin Laden and Al-Qaeda represented for the Saudi elite.

Over the entire course of the twentieth century, fewer than twenty terror attacks killed 100 people or more. Groups like the IRA in Northern Ireland, Spain's Basque separatist ETA, the Kurdish PKK in Turkey and numerous Palestinian factions randomly targeted civilians and often killed in cold blood. Yet all these traditional terror groups viewed violence primarily as a means of pressuring opponents, and the international community at large, to make political concessions. This strategy necessitated achieving a balance between using violence to gain publicity and political leverage and avoiding the mass killing of civilians for fear of discrediting the cause, and reducing public sympathy, even among loyal supporters. Groups like the IRA and ETA sought limited political objectives and though responsible for much suffering, often placed limits on the execution of their terror tactics. It is inconceivable – in terms of scale, objectives and casualties – that any of the numerous groups that practised international terrorism in the late twentieth century would have undertaken an operation like the one carried out by Al-Qaeda on 9/11 or its affiliated groups since then. To take one example, the 199 commuters killed in the March 2004 Islamist attack on the Madrid rail system far exceeded the number of victims of any single ETA operation up to that point and claimed ninety more lives than ETA was responsible for in the whole of 1980, its bloodiest year of terror.

The upper echelons of the Saudi military and the state security apparatus, as well as members of the royal court (*diwan*) and consultative assembly (*Majlis al-Shura*), had never had any sympathy for bin Laden. As the reality of what he had done became harder to avoid, the public utterances of much of the Saudi elite turned to anger and soul searching. Prince Bandar called bin Laden 'evil'; Ghazi Algosaibi, the Saudi ambassador in London, described him as a 'human monster'. Prince Turki Al-Faisal, who in his role as head of Saudi intelligence from 1979 until just ten days before 9/11, arguably knew more about bin Laden than most people, asked rhetorically, 'Who are we?' and wondered, 'How could such a thing happen after years of development and contacts with the outside world?'[7] There was more support for bin Laden's views, if not always his violent methods and revolutionary goals, across other parts of Saudi society. He was most popular in academia, among the merchants of Jeddah, the city of his youth, and among radical imams and their followers located outside the mainstream religious community. His wider message, particularly as it related to the crisis in the Muslim world in general, and Saudi society in particular, also found support among members of the struggling middle and working classes who had sympathized with the 'Awakening Movement'. Many in this constituency agreed with bin Laden's argument that Saudi rulers had sold them out to American interests, squandered the country's oil wealth, mishandled its economic development and tolerated corruption on a phenomenal scale.

In the aftermath of the 9/11 attacks, outside observers wanted Saudi Arabia to answer some questions of their own. Why, for example, had the

Saudi authorities been the number-one source of funds for thousands of radical madrassas and charitable organizations established in Arab and Muslim communities across the world in previous decades? Why had they done little to prevent an estimated 25,000 of their citizens from receiving military training abroad so they could go off to fight in the name of Islam in Afghanistan, Chechnya, Bosnia and Kosovo? Why had they shown little willingness to cooperate with earlier investigations into the role of bin Laden and other Saudi citizens in terror attacks during the 1990s? These questions, and numerous other allegations of Saudi impropriety, were raised repeatedly in the international media. The London-based *Sunday Times*, for example, claimed that the Saudi government had paid hundreds of millions of dollars to Al-Qaeda in the late 1990s as 'protection money' to stop the group targeting the kingdom. The *New York Times* was just as uncompromising in a series of editorials that described Saudi behaviour as 'malignant' and condemned the kingdom's 'tolerance for terrorism'.[8] A controversial briefing by a policy fellow at the Rand think tank in front of a committee of senior advisers to the Pentagon claimed that the Saudis were 'active at every level of the terror chain, from planners to financiers, from cadre to foot-soldier, from ideologist to cheerleader'.[9] This also gained widespread media attention and led one conservative American columnist to advise 'Team Bush' to 'confront the Saudi dictatorship' and to 'stop pretending that Saudi Arabia is Holland with sand dunes'.[10] Aware that the court of international opinion was judging his kingdom harshly, Crown Prince Abdullah claimed that Saudi–American bilateral relations had been bin Laden's top target in September 2001. Over subsequent years, other senior Saudi royals would repeat this argument, sometimes explaining that bin Laden had specifically recruited Saudi citizens as hijackers to destroy the special relationship between Riyadh and Washington.

The 9/11 attacks and subsequent events did profoundly test the durability of the Saudi–American strategic relationship. On a practical level, the US government responded immediately to the attacks by introducing tough new visa and banking regulations for Saudi citizens, and major American firms reconsidered their involvement in the kingdom. Most notably, Citigroup, one of the first global financial institutions to enter the Saudi market, sold its holdings in the kingdom in 2004 in a move that many put down to tensions in the US–Saudi relationship since the 9/11 attacks. There were demands to freeze Saudi assets in the US, which led Saudi investors to withdraw US$100–US$200 billion from the country. Bilateral trade relations also suffered. In 2000 about 20 per cent of Saudi annual imports came from the US. After 9/11, this figure dropped significantly and did not recover for the rest of the decade.

The US–Saudi relationship had never only been about commercial ties. First and foremost it was about the security of the kingdom and the free flow of oil. America's key role in guaranteeing both was made more difficult after 9/11 by the increasingly negative views of Saudi Arabia in the United States. Many blamed the kingdom for bin Laden, Al-Qaeda and the horrific attacks that had taken place in 2001. Many others were convinced that the country's leaders, their protestations aside, disdained America and its interests and continued to fund radicals. Trillions of dollars of lawsuits were filed against the kingdom by relatives of the 9/11 victims on the grounds that major Saudi institutions, as well as senior members of the royal family, funded terrorism.[11] There was also anger over reports that the Bush administration had given the green light to the emergency extraction of almost 150 Saudi nationals including members of the bin Laden family from the US in the days after 9/11. For their part, politicians from across the political divide publicly questioned the value of the long-time strategic relationship with Riyadh. Senator Joseph R. Biden, chairman of the Senate Foreign Relations Committee, accused Saudi Arabia of 'funding hatred', and argued that Washington's 'love affair' with the kingdom had 'gone overboard'. Senator Carl Levin of the Senate Armed Services Committee admitted that America needed a regional base but called for it to be located in a 'more hospitable' place. It was time, he argued, to correct the apparent Saudi belief that 'somehow they are doing us a favor by having us there helping defend them'.[12]

Speaking on Saudi state television, Crown Prince Abdullah accused the US media of conspiring to damage Saudi Arabia's international reputation. Ambassador Bandar in Washington dismissed reports that Riyadh had funded, or continued to fund, organizations connected to 9/11 as 'malicious and blatantly false'. Other senior Saudi officials played down the deep and underlying tensions with Washington that had been brought to the surface by 9/11. Foreign minister Saud Al-Faisal was adamant that the 'special relationship [was] not damaged'. He would only admit, publicly at least, that it was going through a 'rough patch'. These statements were part of a carefully orchestrated Saudi strategy to clear its name in the wake of 9/11. In November 2001 the Saudi government spent millions of dollars on a twelve-page advertisement in praise of contemporary Saudi Arabia and its king, published in major media outlets including the *New York Times*, the *Washington Post*, the *Wall Street Journal*, *Newsweek* and *The Economist*. In an unprecedented move early in the next year, the six GCC member states jointly took out a full-page advert in the *New York Times*. It condemned the 'false accusations' made against Saudi Arabia and described any claim of links between the Saudi government and those involved in 9/11 as 'unjust, unfair, and wrong'.

The Saudis found little comfort in the findings of the impressive report of the independent and bipartisan 9/11 Commission. Published in mid-2004, following a speedy and comprehensive investigation, it found that the kingdom had not furnished material support to Al-Qaeda, though a twenty-eight-page section of the report that alleged that senior Saudi officials had funded charities and other institutions that may have supported the 9/11 attacks was removed from the declassified version.[13] Instead of holding up the 9/11 report as a vindication of its position, foreign minister Saud bemoaned the fact that 'everyone is having a field day casting aspersions about Saudi Arabia', and the Saudi media dismissed the report as a 'charter for Saudi-bashing' prepared by 'anti-Saudis'.[14]

A statement published in the name of King Fahd less than a week after 9/11 was clear – Saudi Arabia would support the US 'in combating terrorism wherever it is'.[15] In reality, Saudi backing for the US-led war on terror was reluctant and contradictory from the outset. The authorities in Riyadh broke off all practical and moral support for the Taliban, bin Laden's Afghan protectors. Yet this decision, they explained, was made because the group had 'hurt Islam and ... distorted the reputation of Muslims throughout the world', not because of its role in facilitating the Al-Qaeda terror attacks. They agreed to share their files on bin Laden and Al-Qaeda with US intelligence agencies but refused a request to provide passenger lists of flights to the US prior to the attacks.

This reluctance to cooperate fully on this critical matter caused significant American frustration. 'They won't give us information, won't help track people down, and won't let us use bases,' an exasperated former senior US official told the media.[16] For many years the Saudi elite had been, in the words of one former American ambassador in Riyadh, 'prickly about their sovereignty and their public identification with the United States'. They had long worried that the intimate and multi-layered relationship with Washington would ultimately cause more damage that it was worth. As Crown Prince Abdullah put it in the mid-1990s, the US was like a guard dog hired to protect the sheep that turned out to be a wolf in disguise. In the wake of 9/11, Saudi leaders, including Abdullah, became increasingly concerned over US plans for the region. They were also distrustful from the outset over the evolving war on terror. Soon after the 9/11 attacks had taken place, a Congressional Joint Resolution was passed that authorized

President Bush to use 'all necessary and appropriate force' against the perpetrators of 9/11 and their backers. This provided the Bush administration with the legal authority to go to war in Afghanistan. When the war against Al-Qaeda and the Taliban in Afghanistan began in the first week of October 2001, top Saudi policymakers warned the country's 28,000 mosques not to engage in 'excessive' criticism of America. They also allowed the US military to access its airspace and its command centre in the kingdom during that war. But they swore that they would 'never allow' the US to use Saudi-based forces to participate in any military operations. For good measure, they also refused to join the eighty-nation US-led coalition that pledged support for the war in Afghanistan.

Saudi leaders also tried to cancel a visit to Riyadh by British prime minister Tony Blair at the start of the Afghan campaign at a time of some of the heaviest Anglo-American bombing of the Taliban in their Kandahar stronghold. This visit to the kingdom by Washington's most outspoken and supportive ally had been planned long before 9/11 and it eventually went ahead but it was hard work, even for the usually charming Blair. Throughout his trip he had to contend with Saudi officials preoccupied with their role and standing in the Arab and Islamic world and obsessed with distancing themselves from the fighting in Afghanistan and the war on terror. Indeed, a government statement issued after a meeting of the Saudi cabinet during Blair's visit did not even mention the situation in Afghanistan. A BBC correspondent who accompanied Blair on his visit noted that the prime minister's entire time in Saudi Arabia was 'intensely difficult and at times embarrassing'.[17] Tony Blair came away from this ill-timed and awkward October visit convinced that the West needed to win over 'hearts and minds' in the Arab and Muslim world. Some Gulf residents sympathized with bin Laden's rhetoric. Some saw him as a hero for standing up to the West. Others were just confused. 'We are in a Catch-22 situation', explained one Westernized Bahraini, a former airline pilot who had worked in the US. 'We condemn what happened, anybody with a little bit of brains would condemn it, but the Taliban and bin Laden are trying to mobilize Arabs by telling them Americans are on a new crusade against Islam, and some Muslims believe it.'[18]

GCC leaders reflected on many of the same issues and concerns during an emergency session in the Saudi port city of Jeddah in the last week of September 2001. They left that meeting united in their staunch opposition to any attempt to link Islam to what they described as 'heinous terrorist acts'.[19] Soon after, GCC interior ministers drew up the 'Muscat Declaration on Combating Terrorism', a document that recognized the importance of addressing the root causes of terrorism, as well as the need to act militarily to neutralize specific terror threats on the ground. The following December, only two weeks after the end of the military phase of the Afghan war, Gulf leaders came together once more, this time in Oman. As well as discussing the situation in Afghanistan, they also addressed the toll that the 9/11 attacks and the global war on terror had taken on the image of Arabs and Muslims across the world. They did not agree to any official GCC commitment to participate actively on the side of the US in that war against Islamist terror. Early in the next year the GCC ran a full-page advert in the *New York Times*. This summarized the findings of the Oman summit, which was presented as a historic meeting in the organization's history, and restated the positive contribution of the GCC's member states to international affairs. It was, however, vague in addressing the organization's role in prosecuting the war on terror.

Such reticence at the GCC level did not reflect the full extent of the Arab Gulf's contribution to the war on terror. As noted above, despite profound apprehension over the fallout from American policies after 9/11, Saudi Arabia continued to serve as home to the US air force command in the region. Other GCC states also played increasingly important roles in support of the US-led war on terror. Between 2001 and 2003, the emir of Qatar, Hamad bin Khalifa Al-Thani, served as chairman of the Organization of Islamic Cooperation (OIC), the international body that at the time represented 1.2 billion Muslims from fifty-seven Islamic countries. The Qatari ruler condemned the 9/11 attacks as 'unprecedented, and almost beyond our imagining',[20] but he also publicly called for the US to act cautiously in response. In particular, during an official visit to Washington in early October 2001, he called on the US to provide 'definitive proof' before unleashing its military capabilities on Afghanistan. At the same time, he played an important role at the head of the OIC in lobbying Muslim countries not to oppose US military action against the Taliban and he chaired an emergency meeting of the Islamic organization that, much to the relief of the Bush administration, agreed on a deliberately vague statement that did not condemn the US operation in Afghanistan.[21] Like his emir, Qatar's influential foreign minister and prime minister, Hamad bin Jassim Al-Thani, was adamant that his country would not serve as a base for the US to bomb Afghanistan. He was less willing to be drawn on what this meant in practice. For example, he called for the US to provide 'strategy' and 'leadership' and acknowledged, somewhat elusively, that any future Qatari decisions would depend on past agreements with allies as much as personal preferences.[22]

Kuwait was the only Gulf state that actually owed its existence to US military and diplomatic intervention. Since their liberation from Saddam, the kingdom's people had struggled to come to terms with their experience of occupation. Several studies carried out during the 1990s recorded extremely high levels of post-traumatic stress disorder across all socio-economic and age groups. Nightmares and outbursts of violence against teachers, co-workers and employers became increasingly common. Past trauma was made worse by the knowledge that Saddam Hussein, though weakened and contained, was still in power next door. Youssef Abdel-Moati of the Center for Research and Studies on Kuwait gave voice to these feelings. 'As long as Saddam Hussein's regime is there', the well-known commentator explained, 'there is something threatening us. We've been told, "Turn the page, forget it and go on." We cannot, and we should not.'[23]

After the liberation in 1991, Kuwaiti citizens had returned to their homes chanting 'God bless Kuwait; God bless the USA'. A decade on, such gratitude was still evident. Hundreds lined up in the late summer heat of Kuwait City to donate blood following the 9/11 attacks. Others laid flowers and lit candles at the American embassy in memory of those who had lost their lives. Kuwait's Red Crescent Society donated US$500,000 to the victims of the tragedy and a delegation of Kuwaiti citizens also visited the US to pay their respects.[24] Kuwait's foreign minister Sheikh Sabah Al-Ahmad Al-Jaber Al-Sabah described the events of 9/11 as 'hideous'. In an interview on Kuwaiti television he reflected on the attacks and promised to provide the US 'complete' support, 'both politically and in every way the United States requests', before adding that America was his kingdom's 'ally, and we in Kuwait do not forget our ally'.[25] For the same reason, a couple of years later, Kuwait made the largest donation of any country in the world to the reconstruction of New Orleans when it pledged US$500 million in response to Hurricane Katrina.

Unlike Kuwait, Bahrain had never relied on the United States to save it from a neighbour's aggression. That did not stop the kingdom's emir from being extremely supportive in the wake of the attacks. Labelling Al-Qaeda and the Taliban 'lunatics who call themselves Muslims', Sheikh Hamad bin Isa Al-Khalifa made no secret of where his loyalties lay in the war on terror: 'I am so happy America and Britain are going into Afghanistan . . . saving it from this evil Taliban will only be good for women, men and children. It is a very good war of liberation.' To back up this verbal support he also offered the use of his territory as a staging post to bomb the Taliban and he committed the kingdom's only frigate to participate in coalition maritime surveillance and interception operations. He also admitted publicly that he would consider sending Bahraini troops to join the US coalition in the right circumstances. He even accused those Arab states unwilling to make a practical contribution to the war on terror as having 'lost their mind'.[26]

Two UAE citizens had been among the perpetrators of the 9/11 attacks. In response, the UAE joined Saudi Arabia in cutting off diplomatic ties with the Taliban. Top officials also gave assurances to Washington that they would cooperate fully in the fight against terrorism.[27] Over the next few years, the UAE deployed more than 200 special forces operatives in Afghanistan, making it the largest Arab troop contributor to the American-led campaign. At home in the Gulf, this support expressed itself in a new agreement to expand Al-Dhafra airbase near Abu Dhabi, home to a US air force refuelling squadron since the early 1990s. Under the new deal, Al-Dhafra would house reconnaissance aircraft operating in Afghanistan. The UAE also became one of the most proactive Arab countries in supporting Washington's terror financing and anti-money-laundering efforts. It provided information relevant to hundreds of anti-terror-financing investigations. Suspected Islamist terrorists and their financiers also had their bank accounts frozen and the government passed laws imposing stiff penalties, including jail time, for money laundering.

In the immediate wake of the 9/11 attacks, Oman's Sultan Qaboos made it clear to senior Western visitors including Tony Blair and Donald Rumsfeld that the perpetrators of the massacre and their Taliban patrons in Afghanistan were a 'perversion of the true teachings of the Islamic faith'. He called on Muslim states to stand up to the Islamist terror threat and gave the green light for British troops to conduct a long-planned military exercise in the sultanate. This was the biggest UK military deployment in the Middle East since the 1991 Gulf war. More than twenty naval vessels and over 20,000 troops participated in what many saw as a trial run for British involvement in the war on terror in the region. Once operations in Afghanistan began, Oman also agreed to host port calls by coalition navies, allowed US war material to be pre-positioned on its territory and opened up its military and airbases at the mouth of the Persian Gulf to combat and transport aircraft involved in the fight against the Taliban and Al-Qaeda.

By the middle of 2002 the American military had air force, army and naval command posts in Saudi Arabia, Kuwait and Bahrain respectively, and one of its biggest pre-positioning supply bases in Qatar. This provided the United States and its anti-terror coalition with valuable military facilities in the heart of the Arab world. Much more importantly, the Gulf States played a pivotal role in providing political credibility and cover for the US-led war on terror. This was especially true in the case of Saudi Arabia.

The kingdom was not only a key Arab economic and political player; it was also the birthplace of bin Laden and its king was custodian of the Two Holy Mosques, protector of the holiest sites in Islam. Any public Saudi condemnation of the war on terror would have caused problems across much of the Sunni Muslim world. The other Arab Gulf States also served an important political function in speaking out against Al-Qaeda, bin Laden and Islamist terror and played a valuable role convincing other Arab and Muslim countries to refrain from publicly opposing Washington, just as Qatar had done during its chairmanship of the OIC at the start of the Afghan war.

Top US officials did everything they could to ensure that nothing got in the way of this vital support. In an attempt to counter anti-Saudi political and public opinion at home, the Bush administration constantly presented Saudi policies in the best possible light. According to one PR consultant hired by the Saudis to improve their image in the US, this thankless task only had one thing going for it – the White House had 'placed the Saudis off limits from criticism'.[28] More than that, the White House press machine repeatedly denied claims that the president was unhappy with the Saudi role. Instead, George Bush's spokesman made it very clear that 'the president is very pleased with [their] contributions'.[29] Senior members of the administration also pitched in to defend the Saudis. In a widely publicized op-ed in the *New York Times* in the last weeks of September 2001, secretary of defence Donald Rumsfeld singled out Saudi Arabia (and the UAE) for praise for breaking ties with the Taliban. Importantly, as far as relations with Saudi Arabia were concerned, he also defended the fact that some countries whom 'we consider our friends may help with certain efforts or be silent on others'. During a visit to Saudi Arabia a few days later he expounded on this point: 'We do not expect every nation on the face of the earth to be publicly engaged in every single activity the United States is.'[30] In acknowledgement of this support, Crown Prince Abdullah told journalists that President Bush had spoken to him on the telephone to reassure him that the criticisms his kingdom faced did not reflect the views of his administration or the majority of the American people.[31]

The Palestine problem was one constant political factor that had overshadowed US–Gulf relations since the early 1970s. It had, after all, been the cause of the initial oil crisis in 1973. It became an increasingly important consideration in the wake of 9/11 as Washington attempted to consolidate Arab Gulf support for the war on terror. As noted in the previous chapter, the PLO's backing of Saddam Hussein during the Kuwait crisis had alienated the GCC member states from the Palestinian cause during the 1990s. The Oslo peace process had led to a dramatic though gradual improvement in Gulf–Israeli relations until mid-1996 when Benjamin Netanyahu's Likud party, which was staunchly opposed to the Oslo process, won the Israeli national elections.

At a meeting of GCC foreign ministers in Riyadh in early 1997 it was agreed that the new Israeli government's anti-Oslo stance made it impossible to continue on the path of normalization. As the peace process gradually ground to a halt over the next few years, the Arab Gulf States became increasingly disillusioned. There was, however, no unanimity inside the GCC on how best to demonstrate their displeasure. In mid-November 1997, Qatar refused to rescind an invitation to Israel to send a delegation to the fourth Middle East and North Africa economic summit in Doha. Organized by the Geneva-based World Economic Forum (WEF), this annual meeting was intended to bring together Arab and Israeli business and political leaders to discuss regional economic cooperation. A number of Arab countries, including some of its GCC partners, had called on Qatar to disinvite Israel from the conference. Doha refused. In response Saudi Arabia, the UAE and Bahrain, along with Egypt and Syria, boycotted the meeting. Kuwait and Oman agreed to attend but sent much lower-level delegations than had originally been planned.[32] Such differences within the GCC over how to respond to Israel evaporated following the collapse of the Oslo process and the outbreak of the Al-Aqsa intifada in September 2000. Over the next three years the conflict between Israel and the Palestinians descended into unprecedented levels of violence and loss. There were over 16,000 attacks against Israeli targets by various Palestinian groups that left over 700 dead.[33] Over the same period of time the Palestinian Authority estimated in excess of 3,000 Palestinian dead and 34,000 wounded.

Sultan Qaboos was a long-time advocate of improved relations between Israel and the Arabs. Unlike other Gulf leaders, he had refused to condemn the Egyptian–Israeli peace agreement of the late 1970s. Instead, he had expressed the hope that it had 'opened the doors to peace in the region'.[34] In 2000, as Israeli–Palestinian fighting raged, the sultan shut down Oman's trade office in Tel Aviv and ceased official contact and dialogue with Israel. Soon after, Qatar officially announced that it had ordered the Israeli trade office in Doha to shut in preparation for the upcoming Organization of Islamic Cooperation (OIC) summit in the city in November.[35]

In August 2001, just weeks before the 9/11 attacks, Crown Prince Abdullah of Saudi Arabia wrote to President Bush to warn the American leader that unless he actively intervened to resolve the Palestinian issue, the kingdom would review its relations with the United States. To demonstrate that he was not bluffing, he followed up this ultimatum with an order to his officials to withdraw from high-level military talks planned for Washington. At an emergency meeting held two weeks after 9/11, GCC leaders called on Israel to end its 'terror acts' against the Palestinians and urged Washington not to use the Al-Qaeda attacks as a pretext 'to ignore what is happening to the Palestinian people at the hands of the Israeli government'.[36] In regular meetings with American counterparts, Gulf officials repeatedly blamed Israel for the support bin Laden's movement could claim across the Muslim world. This argument reflected the thinking of many Gulf citizens. As one Omani merchant told a journalist a few weeks after the 9/11 attacks had taken place, if the West did not address Palestinian grievances, 'then there will be many more people like bin Laden to follow'. Though Palestine was the major cause of resentment, such was the 'Arab Street's' distrust of the US by this time that, as one Gulf businessman explained, 'No matter the issue these days, if the US is on one side, everyone else wants to be on the other.'[37]

In October 2001, the Qatari chairmanship of the OIC called on the UN Security Council to convene a meeting to discuss the escalating crisis faced by the Palestinians. The following month, once more speaking in his capacity as OIC chair before the UN General Assembly in New York, Qatar's emir insisted that 9/11 should not be used as a pretext to condemn legitimate national liberation struggles. 'We need to have a clear definition of terrorism,' he argued in an implicit but obvious reference to the Palestinian struggle, in order to 'distinguish between this phenomenon, which is based on criminal practices and attacks against civilians and innocent people, and legitimate struggles to get rid of the yoke of illegitimate occupation and subjugation'.[38]

Though sincerely held, statements like the above also served the valuable function of demonstrating very publicly to the rest of the Arab and Muslim world that the Arab Gulf States had not forgotten the Palestinian cause and that they would exert a price from Washington for supporting its war on terror. As one Saudi daily paper put it, President Bush could not 'kick Arabs in the teeth' over the Palestine issue and then demand that they fall in line on the war on terror at the same time. For its part, the Bush administration was concerned that the Palestine issue was becoming an obstacle to its successful execution of the war on terror. 'The people that we expect to work with closely in combating terrorism are interested in the Israel–Palestinian situation,' a State Department official explained diplomatically in a briefing document. He then acknowledged that there was a direct link between the attitudes of Arab allies to the war on terror and America's commitment to Israeli–Palestinian peace.[39]

Such arguments, at least at this stage, cut little ice with more senior US officials. In his January 2002 State of the Union address, President Bush accused Yasser Arafat of 'enhancing terror'. From that point onwards he categorically refused to deal with the Palestinian leader. Soon afterwards, in an interview in the *New York Times*, Saudi Arabia's Crown Prince Abdullah set out a peace plan known as the Arab Peace Initiative (API).[40] This called for full Israeli withdrawal from the West Bank, Gaza and part of Jerusalem, in return for Israeli sovereignty over Jerusalem's Jewish Quarter and Arab recognition of Israel. European leaders welcomed the proposal. EU foreign policy chief Javier Solana described it as an 'opportunity that has to be taken' and President Jacques Chirac of France hailed it as 'strong and courageous'. Initially, the US response was far more cautious. The White House press spokesman only described it as a 'note of hope'.[41] Secretary of state Colin Powell was no more enthusiastic, describing it as one of the 'minor developments we might be able to work with'. Eventually President Bush telephoned Prince Abdullah to welcome the proposal and sent two of his top officials to Riyadh to follow up. Yet, Washington's underwhelming response to Abdullah's plan so infuriated the Saudis that they threatened to deny US access to airbases in the country if Washington did not rein in Israel's military operations in the Palestinian territories. For the first time since the 1973 oil crisis the Palestine issue threatened to derail the bilateral strategic relationship between Riyadh and Washington.

Relations improved following Crown Prince Abdullah's visit to the presidential ranch in Crawford, Texas, in April 2002. Though President Bush remained steadfast in his refusal to deal with Arafat, in mid-2003 he announced a 'vision' of 'two states [Israel and Palestine] living side by side in peace and security'.[42] This was the first statement by a US president to provide explicit support for the establishment of a Palestinian state. It appeared that the Arab Gulf States, again led by Saudi Arabia, had once more managed to leverage their crucial involvement on a key regional issue – the war on terror rather than oil on this occasion – on behalf of the Palestinian cause. No doubt aware of the parallels, Saudi officials were careful to emphasize that unlike in the 1970s, Gulf oil producers would not resort to using oil power to force progress on the issue. 'Oil is not a weapon,' explained Ambassador Bandar in Washington. 'Oil is not a tank. You cannot fire oil.'[43]

Senior figures inside the Bush administration had supported extending the military operations from Afghanistan to Iraq since the beginning of the war on terror in late 2001. Their justification for doing so was the Bush doctrine of pre-emptive action, the intellectual blueprint for American foreign policy action after the 9/11 attacks. It was based on a number of core assumptions. The first was that authoritarian, brutal and corrupt regimes at home were more likely to behave badly outside their borders. Bad dictators, so the argument went, would sponsor terrorism, attack their neighbours and threaten US interests. The second was that imposing democracy through regime change would often be beneficial even if it caused short-term instability, because overthrowing bad regimes and replacing them with democracies would deter aggressors, reduce the threat of terror, and spread peace and stability. The third was that the United States had a responsibility and a duty to stop rogue states before they could threaten or use weapons of mass destruction against America or its allies, especially when unbalanced dictators like Saddam might secretly provide such weapons to terrorist allies.

The Iraq issue was particularly sensitive for the Gulf States because of the devastation wrought on the country's civilian population by the most wide-ranging economic sanctions ever instituted by the UN over the previous decade. In 1998, two years into the Oil-for-Food programme, Iraq stopped all cooperation with weapons inspectors. In response, in mid-December the US and British governments ordered a series of air strikes. The Gulf States were reluctant to be involved in any way in Operation Desert Fox, as this military action was known. The UAE, for example, made it clear that it did not support this move and refused to serve as a base for US aircraft participating in the mission. This did not stop Saddam from publicly blaming the GCC states for these attacks or for using them as a pretext to call on the people of the Arab world to rise up and overthrow their 'charlatan leaders'. Tensions rose further when Iraq directly threatened Saudi Arabia and Kuwait in 1999. The official Saudi response to this was unflinching. The Saudi Press Agency called for the overthrow of the 'tyrant of Baghdad'.[44]

In this hostile environment Saudi and other Gulf leaders were still committed to keeping Saddam's regime militarily weak. At the same time, they were increasingly sensitive to accusations that they had the blood of innocent Iraqi civilians on their hands for providing a base for coalition operations.[45] And they were no longer willing to be associated with a sanctions regime that kept the Iraqi people on their knees. This engendered a growing consensus inside the GCC states that they had to become more proactive in searching for a way to normalize the situation in Iraq. There were only two possible alternatives. The first was to find a way to end sanctions that was acceptable to all the relevant parties, most importantly Iraq, the US and the rest of the Arab world. The second option was to end

Saddam's reign of terror in Iraq by some means short of all-out war. Neither was easy to achieve.

In early 2002, as tensions between Baghdad and Washington escalated, Crown Prince Abdullah refused to allow his kingdom to be used for planned air strikes against Iraq. Later in the year it was reported that Qatar's prime minister had met privately with Saddam to convince the Iraqi leader to go into exile.[46] Other GCC leaders also looked to find alternative compromise solutions in an effort to avert a war. Saudi Arabia quietly enquired in Washington and other key capitals whether there was any support for a coup in Iraq by top regime officials who would then replace Saddam in power. But by the end of 2002 those inside the Bush administration backing war had won the argument in Washington.

On Christmas Day 2002, GCC leaders met in Doha for their annual summit. Iraq topped the agenda. There was general agreement on four points. Saddam was as dangerous as ever. The US was determined to go to war with him. Any US invasion would further strain GCC–US relations; and it would also threaten to destabilize the entire Gulf region. Though publicly top Gulf officials repeatedly protested that war was not inevitable, in private they were under no such illusions. 'Narrowing to slim' was the Qatari foreign minister's assessment of the chances of avoiding war by this time.[47] Over the next few weeks, representatives from all of the six member states met secretly to consider how the GCC could improve security coordination, including the exchange of intelligence, and to examine the role of the GCC in Iraq after Saddam was inevitably toppled. A new high-level joint defence committee was established to deal with this inevitability. Its members included GCC foreign and defence ministers and it met for the first time in Saudi Arabia in early 2003. The opening item on the agenda of its inaugural meeting was the military and political implications for the GCC of the burgeoning crisis over Iraq.

By the early 2000s, the Peninsula Shield force was on its last legs. It had been reduced to one brigade of 5,000 men under Saudi leadership with no naval or air capacity. The likelihood of war in Iraq once more forced the Gulf Arabs to work together to develop what one Qatari official described as a GCC-wide 'concerted and well considered approach' to collective security.[48] One important practical, as well as symbolic, consequence of this was the unanimous agreement by GCC member states to deploy 8,000 troops, tanks, attack helicopters and warships to defend Kuwait from any reprisal attacks by Saddam following a US invasion. This show of solidarity, described as a 'sacred duty' by Bahrain's defence minister, did not succeed in reassuring Kuwait's civilian population. In the run-up to the American invasion, 300,000 of them fled their homes to avoid the fallout from any war.

At a tense and much-anticipated Arab League summit of early March 2003, Gulf leaders faced the scorn of Muammar Gaddafi. In front of banks of television cameras broadcasting live coverage across the Arab world, the Libyan leader attacked Saudi Arabia for having formed 'an alliance with the devil' when it opened its territory to American troops in 1990. An angry Crown Prince Abdullah rejected these accusations, and dismissed Gaddafi as 'an agent for colonizers'.[49] During the meeting itself, the UAE openly called for Saddam Hussein to step down in order to save the region from war. The plan was laid out in a letter from UAE president Sheikh Zayed Al-Nahyan to all Arab heads of state. It offered Saddam immunity from prosecution in return for agreeing to give up power. Following his departure, the Arab League and the UN would take control of Iraq until the country returned to 'its normal situation'. Kuwait and Bahrain endorsed this proposal at a follow-up GCC meeting in Doha. According to senior Kuwaiti officials, the plan put forward by the UAE was the 'last chance for a peaceful solution'.[50] Other GCC proposals intended to avert a war followed. The GCC's secretary general, the Qatari diplomat Abdul Rahman bin Hamad Al-Attiyah, and the Kuwaiti National Assembly both put forward plans that, like the UAE proposal, required Saddam to give up power.[51] Just hours before the expiry of the US deadline for Saddam Hussein and his two sons to leave Iraq or face war, Bahrain's King Hamad bin Isa Al-Khalifa offered the Iraqi leader sanctuary if he stepped down.

Iraq was dismissive of these neighbourly attempts at conflict prevention. The country's foreign minister dismissed the UAE proposal as a Zionist plot, while the daily paper *Babil*, run by Saddam's son Uday, accused Sheikh Zayed of having 'chosen to side with the devil' in order to divide the Arab world.[52] The people of the Gulf had lived with Saddam's threat for decades. They paid little attention to the accusations his regime now made against their rulers. At the same time many ordinary citizens of the Gulf opposed unilateral American military intervention in Iraq and hoped that their leaders would refrain from working with Washington in any war against Saddam. 'Don't ignore local wishes,' warned an editorial in the English-language Dubai-based *Gulf News* entitled 'Listen to the People'.

In the run-up to the war most of the people did their protesting behind closed doors. There were only a few public demonstrations across the region. They were peaceful, well organized and limited to small groups of educated protestors. This was completely different to the much larger and more populist anti-war marches that took place in cities all over the

Western world. They were also smaller than the demonstrations against Israeli policies towards the Palestinians held across the Gulf in 2000 and 2002. In Bahrain, for example, only a few protests took place outside the US and British embassies and they were much smaller and caused much less damage than the anti-Israel protests in the spring months of 2002 at the height of the Al-Aqsa intifada, when angry crowds attacked the US embassy and set fire to official US vehicles. In the UAE emirate of Ras Al Khaimah, a few dozen students expressed their opposition to any upcoming war by making a 30-metre-long 'peace banner' that they planned to mail to the White House. An even smaller group of students at the American University of Sharjah welcomed the US ambassador to their campus with pictures of dead and injured Iraqi and Palestinian civilians. Another small group of female protestors marked the same visit by holding up candles in a silent vigil.

These low-key public expressions of anti-war sentiment did little to allay the worries of Gulf leaders over the possible consequences of an American invasion of Iraq. 'We are living in the region. We will suffer the consequences of any military action', said the Saudi foreign minister. Their first concern was that any unilateral US action, especially if it was not concluded in a swift and comprehensive fashion, would further alienate the rest of the Arab and Muslim world from the US and its Gulf partners. Their second was that a US invasion would trigger chaos and a civil war in Iraq that empowered the country's Shia majority and opened the way for Iranian influence and even military intervention. It was also feared that having initiated a conflict in Iraq, the Bush administration would get cold feet and withdraw before finishing the job. Recalling the American refusal to topple Saddam in 1991 after the liberation of his country, one member of a Kuwaiti delegation visiting Washington in 2002 reminded his hosts, 'You came, you bombed, and you left.'[53] Gulf policymakers were also concerned that a US invasion would result in domestic unrest in GCC states or even lead to terror attacks. In the run-up to the invasion a bomb maker in a residential compound in Riyadh blew himself up. In the wreckage the security services found an assortment of weapons and explosives including AK47 rifles, hand grenades and explosives.

In June 2002, US defence secretary Donald Rumsfeld visited Qatar, Bahrain and Kuwait. During his visit he denied he was 'soliciting allies' for an invasion of Iraq. Instead, Rumsfeld insisted that the reason for his visit was to thank his hosts for their support in Afghanistan. In another visit to the region the following December, he publicly insisted that his ongoing discussions on military matters including the upgrading of US military bases was 'not connected to Iraq'.[54] By the time that Rumsfeld travelled to Saudi Arabia, Qatar and Kuwait in March 2003, such denials were pointless. His visit was expressly intended to discuss preparations for the upcoming war and to reassure his allies that their support for US action would not come back to haunt them. Rumsfeld received the same message from senior officials in all the Gulf States on his regular visits to the region. The war was a mistake, they told him, before adding that if it was inevitable then the US had to ensure stability in Iraq after Saddam had been defeated. This required that the existing administrative structures and security forces remain in place in order to hold the country together. They further advised that once this had been accomplished the next priority had to be the rapid establishment of a locally run administration in an undivided Iraq. Other senior US officials visiting the region received identical advice on numerous occasions.

The Gulf States were particularly troubled that the Bush administration viewed the invasion of Iraq as a test case for reshaping the region into a bastion of pro-American liberal democracy. They viewed this as naïve and dangerous and worried that it would distract Washington from what needed to be done in Iraq once Saddam had been toppled; they were no less concerned that the Bush administration's apparent obsession with democratization might challenge their own interests some day. This made them increasingly reluctant to be seen as Washington's allies in the Arab world. The one exception was Kuwait. A report written for Congress in the weeks leading up to the start of the war speculated that Kuwait, with its first-hand experience of suffering at the hands of Saddam and its unique debt of gratitude to America, was likely to be the only GCC member state willing to provide open support for a US military action in the absence of a further UN Security Council resolution specifically authorizing the use of force against Iraq.[55] Sure enough, just days before the war, in the middle of March 2003, Washington published a list of forty nations it claimed had signed up to the coalition to topple Saddam. Kuwait was the only GCC or Arab country named on this list of allies. Though loyal to the US and desperate to get rid of Saddam, Kuwaiti leaders shared the same profound reservations over the coming war and its consequences as their GCC counterparts. Nor were they more inclined to publicize their backing for the US mission in Iraq any more than was necessary. For all these reasons, an envoy was dispatched on a tour of Arab capitals to explain that Kuwait had 'nothing to do with war'.[56]

The Turkish refusal to allow the US to deploy forces on its territory made GCC support even more crucial and placed even more political pressure on Gulf leaders to cooperate with Washington. Ultimately they all did agree to provide America with extensive support despite the objections of their people and widespread criticism in the local media that they lacked the 'willpower and ... dignity'[57] to stand up to US demands. They did so because they feared risking a breach with their top military and political ally at a time of potential flux in the region. The upshot was an impressive level of Gulf backing for the American operation in Iraq from the time of the invasion and throughout the first years of occupation. The UAE agreed to host dozens of American combat aircraft and over a thousand military personnel. In 2002, Bahrain, home to the US Navy's Fifth Fleet, become the first Gulf State and only the third Arab state to be designated a major non-NATO ally of the US. Within a year, and despite opposition in the media and in parliament, Bahrain backed Washington on Iraq. Soon after, Bahrain became the first Arab state to host a permanent CENTCOM command headquarters, responsible for directing naval operations in the Arabian Gulf, Arabian Sea and Gulf of Aden.

After living so long under the shadow of Saddam, Kuwaitis saw the US invasion of Iraq as a long-anticipated opportunity to play a role in the overthrow of their tormentor. In pursuit of this cause, the government put its entire territory at the disposal of the US military. It gave permission for the construction of three new airbases and the world's largest heliport. Kuwait also served as one of the main launch pads for the invasion when it began. In total, the US government estimated that between late 2002 and late 2003 Kuwait provided over US$2 billion worth of support, including US$100 million a month in fuel assistance, to the US campaign against Saddam.

On taking power in 1995 and bristling from Saudi support for his recently deposed father, Qatar's new emir, Hamad bin Khalifa Al-Thani, initiated an independent approach to regional diplomacy. This challenged Saudi Arabia's long-time position as the Arab Gulf's unrivalled foreign policy player and it placed Doha on the path of direct confrontation with Riyadh. Following Washington's launch of the war on terror, Qatar took advantage of its status as home to a major US airbase, as well as one of the largest overseas American military pre-positioning bases, to capitalize on the unprecedented strains in the US–Saudi relationship. By the beginning of 2002 the media was reporting that American officials had started to consider seriously a military withdrawal from Saudi Arabia and the establishment of a new base in the region. Top Qatari officials remained adamant over the second half of 2002 that the US military build-up had nothing to do with Iraq. They also stated categorically that they would never permit their territory to be used to wage war on Iraq. At the same time, the US media reported that the Bush administration had received assurances from Qatari leaders that they would not place limits on US operations from bases located in their country.

In the last few months of 2002, hundreds of staff, about one-quarter of the entire operational command, moved from Central Command (CENTCOM) headquarters in Tampa, Florida, to Qatar to participate in military exercises. This was the first forward deployment of Central Command staff since preparation for war against Saddam in Kuwait got under way in 1991. The practical implications of this move were widely understood. It seemed that Qatar was increasingly becoming Washington's preferred location for its command and control headquarters in any war in Iraq. By January 2003 CNN was running news segments titled 'Qatar 101', and the network's anchor Wolf Blitzer was speculating over how the tiny kingdom 'could be vital if the United States brings military action against Iraq'.[58] Not long after, an estimated 6,000 CENTCOM and other US staff officers, as well as 120 fighter planes, relocated to various bases on the outskirts of Doha.

On the first day of the invasion of Iraq, the Saudi government issued a forceful statement on the operation. It strongly rejected 'any blow to Iraq's unity, independence and security', and was adamant that it would 'not participate' in the war. Saudi officials then followed up with a public call for the US, to 'stop the war, sit down, and have a breather'. This option was rejected out of hand and instead, exactly one month after the American campaign in Iraq began, the Bush administration announced that it was relocating its regional air operations centre from Prince Sultan Air Base near Riyadh in Saudi Arabia to Al-Udeid Air Base in Qatar. Loyal to their long-time, if troubled, relationship with their Saudi ally, American officials diplomatically attempted to justify this move on practical grounds. The end of the military phase of the Iraq campaign, they briefed reporters, made it sensible to relocate to a smaller headquarters. Others looked to downplay the move by hinting that it could only have occurred with Riyadh's blessing.[59] Neither of these explanations obscured the fact that Washington's decision to relocate this strategic facility from Riyadh to Doha at a crucial time represented a changing power dynamic inside the GCC, and between the GCC partners and their most important external partner, the United States.

This shifting dynamic was clear for all to see during a visit by Qatar's emir to the American capital in the middle of 2003. In front of the media at a meeting in the Oval Office, President Bush publicly thanked his Qatari counterpart. 'You made some promise to America', Bush told the emir, 'and you kept your promise.'[60] Coming as it did in the wake of a very positive *60 Minutes* profile on Qatar's ruler that portrayed him as the visionary embodiment of a new generation of leaders in the Arab world, the president's praise served to consolidate the public perception of Qatar as a moderate, reliable and vital ally for the twenty-first century. The contrast with Saudi Arabia, with its reputation at an all-time low in American political and popular opinion, could not have been more obvious. In response, the Saudis criticized Qatar extensively through the stable of mostly London-based Arabic newspapers they financed and controlled.[61] Washington's love-in with Qatar did not irk only Saudi leaders. Kuwait had loyally provided the US with extensive financial and political backing both before and after the invasion of Iraq. The kingdom's top officials were extremely irritated by the unmerited tendency, as they saw it, of American leaders to give Qatar too much credit.[62]

Despite such festering resentments, GCC governments kept in constant communication with each other following the launch of Operation Iraqi Freedom on 19 March 2003. Officials attended regular meetings to discuss Gulf security and defence needs, as well as the deteriorating situation on the ground. There was unanimous agreement that the GCC's priorities had to be internal security, economic reconstruction and regional stability. There was even discussion over the possible participation of GCC troops in any post-conflict peacekeeping force. From the time that Baghdad fell and US forces took effective control of Iraq in the first weeks of April, GCC leaders also repeatedly stressed, as they had before the invasion, that it was essential that Washington maintain Iraq's territorial integrity as a priority. Qatar's foreign minister spoke for all during a speech in Abu Dhabi when he made clear that a divided Iraq would not be acceptable to the GCC.[63] This required the US occupying authorities to prevent any attempts by Kurdish or Shia citizens or neighbouring Iran to destabilize the country. It also required them to engage with tribes, clans and other key stakeholders to find a workable solution that held post-Saddam Iraq together. The Americans also had to find a way, Gulf leaders pointed out, to make it clear to the Arab world that independent Iraqis rather than American protégés would take control of the country's future at the appropriate time. As Gulf leaders told American officials in their regular meetings, any new Iraqi government – interim or permanent – imposed on the people by Washington would lack credibility in the Arab world and would ultimately fail. For all these reasons, Gulf leaders also opposed the de-Ba'athification of Iraqi power structures as a massive mistake that would lead to a vacuum that would split Iraq. If this resulted in pro-Iranian Shi'ite groups consolidating their control over the country it would also bring an end to Iraq's traditional role as a strategic counterweight to Iran in the region.

For their part, Gulf citizens, as opposed to the top-level policymakers, expressed most concern over the illegitimacy of the war and the prospective colonization of Iraq, as well as the whereabouts of Saddam Hussein and his alleged weapons of mass destruction. One American journalist who spent a week in Saudi Arabia in April 2003, not long after the initial invasion, recalled how every single one of the dozens of businessmen, shopkeepers, public intellectuals, newspaper editors and students, as well as government officials, she interviewed were highly critical of the US in the region.[64] An estimated 10,000 people participated in a peaceful anti-war demonstration near the American embassy in Doha in April 2003. Among the crowd were well-known local figures including the famous Egyptian cleric Sheikh Yusef Al-Qaradawi, a resident of Doha and one of Al-Jazeera's most popular hosts. The Doha march was by far the largest public demonstration against the war in the Gulf. It reflected the depth of popular opposition to the US invasion. This resentment was further fuelled by graphic images of civilian casualties. Broadcast on Al-Jazeera, and other networks across the Gulf, including Abu Dhabi Television, MBC and Al-Arabiya, this coverage appeared to provide evidence of indiscriminate bombing and large-scale loss of life.

The same was true for the print media. 'The least we can say is it is a clear aggression on an Arab independent state. The Americans, British and all those who took part in the war will pay a heavy price for this adventure,' argued an editorial in one Saudi paper. Another Saudi daily asked rhetorically, 'How can we know that the Anglo-American war against Iraq is not a new crusade?' As the war continued, the Gulf media became increasingly sceptical over American motives and demanded answers. A Qatari paper had its own explanation of what had just happened: 'The USA has declared war on Islam.'[65] Rising anti-American feeling peaked following revelations by Amnesty International and the Associated Press of the torture of prisoners at Abu Ghraib prison in 2003. As another Gulf paper put it, in Iraq the 'American mask fell off, democracy and human rights fell off, and before that the US credibility was lost'.[66]

Gulf leaders had been concerned that the destabilization of post-invasion Iraq would increase the likelihood of Islamist terror inside the GCC. The run-up to the war coincided with the activation of terror networks and cells across the Gulf belonging to Al-Qaeda in the Arabian Peninsula (AQAP). In May 2003, Al-Jazeera aired an audiotape attributed to top Al-Qaeda figure Ayman Al-Zawahiri, in which he condemned Arab countries for providing the US with support in Iraq, singling out Saudi Arabia, Kuwait, Qatar and Bahrain.[67] In the same month, AQAP claimed responsibility for the simultaneous suicide bombings of three Western housing compounds in Riyadh, which left twenty-nine dead and injured almost 200. Following these attacks, Saudi interior minister Prince Nayef Abdul Aziz Al-Saud warned the population that radicals wanted to destabilize the state and bring about its collapse. Crown Prince Abdullah, who became king in 2005, described AQAP as a 'deviant' group and a 'scourge' that would inevitably be crushed.[68] An effective crackdown took place but this did not prevent another attack on a residential compound in the capital the following November that claimed the lives of seventeen people.

In response to the attacks in Saudi Arabia, GCC leaders once again agreed on the need to prioritize security cooperation in order to defeat terrorism. The foreign ministers of the six met in the Red Sea port city of Jeddah under the chairmanship of Kuwait's foreign minister. 'The terrorist acts in brotherly Saudi Arabia', explained Mohammed Sabah Al-Salem Al-Sabah following this meeting, 'continue to represent a real danger to the whole world.' That being the case, he argued, it was incumbent on the Gulf Arab partners to 'deploy all efforts and cooperate with the international community to fight this epidemic'. GCC interior ministers then followed this up by signing a major counter-terror agreement, described by the GCC's secretary general, Abdul Rahman bin Hamad Al-Attiyah, as the most important demonstration of cooperation between member states since the birth of the organization.

Less than two weeks later, GCC leaders vowed to prioritize anti-terror efforts in a one-day meeting in Jeddah. Counter-terrorism also topped the agenda at the GCC leaders' summit in Kuwait in December 2003. During this meeting Gulf leaders agreed that all member states would join the international convention on combating terror and would look to enter into an anti-terror pact at some unspecified future date. This was followed by the launch of a wide-ranging counter-terror strategy across the GCC. The authorities rounded up suspected extremists, shut down suspected money-laundering operations and drew up new plans to ready themselves for attacks on ports and airports, oil infrastructure and critical water and power facilities. Saudi security forces were especially proactive in looking to stamp out Al-Qaeda in the kingdom. In 2004 alone, they either captured or killed nineteen out of the twenty-six suspects on their most wanted terror list.

The Saudi government also started to educate the public about Islamist extremism and the dangers and moral corruption of terrorism as part of a strategy of trying to delegitimize radical Islamist ideologies. In June 2004, the kingdom's Grand Mufti, Sheikh Abd Al-Aziz Al-Sheikh, issued a fatwa that called on Saudi citizens to report suspected militant activity to the authorities. They also invested heavily in a wide range of programmes that looked to steer young men away from terror groups. These included sports and academic programmes and programmes for rehabilitation, retraining and after-care counselling for convicted radicals and thousands of radical clerics who were given the option of enrolling or losing their jobs. These far-reaching responses to terror were so unprecedented that religious conservatives in the kingdom started to think the unthinkable. That in their determination to stamp out terror the royal family might move to reduce the power of the religious elite in society.

At their end-of-year summit in Bahrain, in the last week of December 2004, GCC leaders expressed solidarity with the ongoing Saudi campaign to eliminate what they called the 'perverted group' responsible for terrorism in the kingdom.[69] The US authorities also acknowledged for the first time that they were now receiving real substantive cooperation from Saudi Arabia. In early 2004, Cofer Black, the Bush administration's coordinator for counter-terrorism, spoke frankly on the matter. 'The Saudis are a key ally in the global war on terror,' he told a congressional committee. There was also, he continued, 'clear evidence' that they were addressing the terror challenge they faced with an unprecedented seriousness of purpose.[70] The State Department reported a similar view. According to its assessment, the Saudi authorities had recently begun to apply 'concerted pressure' on the militants and had made great strides in a number of areas that they had previously ignored. Most notably, they had greatly increased their cooperation in the crucial area of terror financing and had instituted an impressive array of new institutional, legal and regulatory changes including restrictive measures related to charitable donations. Saudi banks also started to implement stricter rules to ensure the transparency of all account holders.

There were still some concerns. In his congressional testimony Black noted that the Saudis still needed to improve their effectiveness in some areas of counter-terror and that they had 'a large task before them'. Privately, there also remained some scepticism in Washington and across the GCC over the true effectiveness of the Saudi crackdown on extremists in the absence of a willingness at the highest levels to institute a profound overhaul of the underlying problems in society that bred radicalism. In a 2004 article in *Al-Watan*, a frustrated Prince Bandar touched on this when he urged his fellow countrymen to take responsibility for the rising terror in the kingdom and to stop 'blaming others when the reason lies within our own ranks'.[71]

Riyadh's improved cooperation with Washington on counter-terrorism from 2004 onwards was replicated across the entire Arab Gulf. All the GCC member states received high marks for their counter-terror efforts and their cooperation with the US in the State Department's annual reports on international terrorism. Bahrain, home of the Middle East and North Africa Financial Action Task Force, regularly gained special mention. The UAE was praised for organizing a series of meetings on how to monitor the flow of funds to terrorists outside of the formal banking sector. Kuwait gained recognition for acting pre-emptively to disrupt terror operations in the planning stage. For example, the authorities thwarted a number of planned attacks, on one occasion apprehending a GCC citizen carrying instructions for using surface-to-air missiles along with maps of locations, presumed to be potential targets, in Kuwait and other GCC countries.[72]

Despite these achievements and the threats they faced, the Gulf States did not succeed in establishing a comprehensive region-wide counter-terror strategy in the wake of the invasion of Iraq. There remained an ongoing reluctance to coordinate resources and share intelligence capabilities with one another. For example, Saudi Arabia and the UAE refused to provide information about their citizens to their GCC partners. This made it very difficult to track suspected extremists from either country as they travelled around the region. There were ongoing attempts to address this problem, including the proposal for the establishment of a permanent GCC anti-terrorism committee, as well as the launch of a virtual counter-terror 'operations room', to serve as a mechanism for top GCC officials to regularly discuss major terror challenges. But both proposals failed to develop significantly beyond the planning stage. Yet real progress in GCC intelligence and security cooperation was achieved in the early years of the 2000s. This was the unavoidable, and perhaps even the inevitable, consequence of the destabilization of the Gulf that followed the rise of Al-Qaeda, the 9/11 attacks and the invasion and occupation of Iraq. All these factors also precipitated another important development in the same years – a significant and long-term rise in the price of oil. As the next chapter will show, this resulted in the Gulf oil producers earning unprecedented energy revenues that, despite the dangers of the times, provided them with the means to consolidate stability at home and extend influence abroad as they looked to project almost unrivalled financial power on the global stage.

CHAPTER 5

BLOC PARTY

> 'The politics of energy . . . has given extraordinary power to some states that are using that power in not very good ways for the international system.'
>
> – Condoleezza Rice

Wadi Al-Ayoun, a character in Abdul Rahman Munif's classic work *Cities of Salt*, observes how the 'words *rich* and *gold* hung in the air like smoke', before asking rhetorically, 'Had they come to stay?' Many real-life figures in the Gulf and far beyond have wondered the same since the oil boom of the mid-1970s. Born in a period of conflict and instability in the early 1980s, the rationale for the establishment of the GCC was from the outset economic, even if the original motive was to fend off the threats of dangerous neighbours. As the GCC's first secretary general, Abdullah Bisharah, explained, the plan was to 'convert six chambers in a big house into a big house without barriers'.[1]

This did not mean that GCC member states had signed up to deep integration in the short term. Instead, the agreed plan was for them to capitalize on the 'rich and gold' that the oil boom of the previous decade had brought in order to build up the organization as a regional economic bloc. The steady, considered, and at times flawed, efforts at economic cooperation and development in the 1980s took place during an era of easy money, government subsidies, massive development projects and rampant speculation. It was also a time of growing economic pressure across the Arab Gulf as it counted the cost of war between regional giants Iran and Iraq, and saw its own military spending and populations rise rapidly. These pressures were compounded greatly by the psychological and financial 'hangover'[2] wrought by Saddam's invasion and occupation of Kuwait in 1990–91. This situation was made worse by low oil prices for much of the 1990s. In some GCC countries, oil revenues during these years were smaller than returns from overseas investments. Saudi Arabia, the world's number-one oil producer, was hit particularly hard. The kingdom's GDP per capita, a key measure of prosperity, fell from more than US$28,000 at the beginning of the 1980s to less than US$7,000 by the end of the 1990s.

The year 1995 brought particular highs and lows for the global economy. Mexico almost went broke, forcing the US to pump US$20 billion into the country just to keep it afloat. Baring's Bank, the oldest investment bank in England, was not so lucky. It collapsed after one of its brokers lost more than US$1billion on the Tokyo Stock Exchange. The Dow Jones Industrial Average, the stock market index measuring the performance of the thirty biggest publicly owned companies in America, soared above 4,000 points for the first time ever in February. In November it broke the 5,000-point barrier. In comparison, the launch of the World Trade Organization (WTO) in January 1995, after eight years of painstaking negotiations, seemed a little dull. The main function of this Geneva-based body was to ensure the free and smooth flow of global trade. To facilitate this, the WTO had the unenviable task of finding consensus among trading nations on the best and fairest ways to open markets and lower trade barriers. Yet its potential impact on the long-term fortune of the world economy was huge. It was of particular importance for developing nations and emerging economies with global ambitions, like those of the Arab Gulf.

Six months after the WTO's birth, the World Bank's top official for the Middle East delivered a blunt speech to businessmen, policymakers and academics in Muscat, Oman. In his talk, Caio Koch-Wester spoke of the perils posed, as well as the opportunities offered, by the new trade regime. As the only forum dealing with the rules of trade between nations, the WTO, he explained, heralded a new era for globalization and rapid trade liberalization. The problem, he then warned, was that this would only lead to increased prosperity if all members of the international trading system, including the Arab Gulf, followed the new rules. Going forward they would have to open up their economies and embrace economic integration. If the GCC states failed to meet these demanding challenges they would, he predicted, soon be 'marginalized'[3] and would fall even further behind the developed economies.

The likelihood of this happening was increased by the outbreak, in 1997, of a crippling financial crisis in Asia, Russia and Latin America that plunged many millions into poverty in all three regions and hit global demand. The related decision by OPEC to approve an increase in oil production precipitated a drop in the price of a barrel of oil to around US$10 and led to a massive drop in oil revenues, down to US$80 billion from a peak of US$150 billion a year in 1980. At a summit of GCC leaders at the end of 1998, Saudi Arabia's Crown Prince Abdullah, speaking on behalf of an ill king, addressed the challenge of falling oil revenues, the sharp decline in growth and the drop in lender and investor confidence across the Gulf. 'The age of abundance is over,' he informed an audience of the region's royals.[4] Taking advantage of the evolving situation across the Gulf and, in particular, Saudi Arabia's weakened state, both Venezuela and Russia attempted to challenge the kingdom's status as the number-one oil economy. Unwilling to cede this position Riyadh fought back. The ensuing battle led to a further drop in the price of oil, which in turn resulted in a further drop in oil revenues. This threatened to derail regional plans for domestic development, and was viewed by many to be unsustainable.

By the start of the new millennium Saudi Arabia was in particular trouble. One of the kingdom's most successful investors and businessmen, Prince Al-Waleed bin Talal bin Abdul Aziz Al-Saud, predicted a 'nightmare scenario'[5] if there was no stabilization in the oil price. Cash reserves had dropped by about US$100 billion, the country had endured two decades of budget deficits, and debt had reached 100 per cent of GDP and cost a massive US$10 billion a year to service.[6] By one estimate Americans now spent the same on cigarettes in a year as Saudi Arabia earned in oil revenues. Some observers doubted whether Saudi Arabia would even be able to pay its bills, never mind find the money for the ambitious infrastructural projects it planned in coming years. This unhealthy state of economic affairs prompted several petitions to the king that called for major socio-economic change, including better long-term economic planning to achieve diversification, a crackdown on corruption, and more stringent controls on public spending and levels of national debt.

The 9/11 attacks on New York and Washington and the subsequent launch of the war on terror led to two more years of economic stagnation. The Gulf's tourism trade, an important source of foreign income in places like Oman and Dubai, was hit particularly hard. As hotel occupancy rates plummeted across the region, Dubai's government-owned Emirates Airlines launched a massive PR campaign under the 'Fly and Try Dubai' tag to convince people that the region was safe from Al-Qaeda plots. Stock markets dropped in value, productivity fell and economies contracted. By 2003, returns on overseas investments, the second most important source of income after oil, were at their lowest levels for over a decade as Gulf investment portfolios took a multi-billion-dollar hit. Despite the multitude of pressures they faced, the Gulf States still had major financial commitments to meet. Expensive weapons systems and massive debt repayments topped the list of costly outgoings. Foreign worker remittances also drained money from the region. In Saudi Arabia alone this amounted to an estimated 30 per cent of oil income. Since the oil boom of the mid-1970s, the Gulf States had also emerged as the major aid donors and financial patrons of poorer Arab and Muslim countries. From Palestine to Pakistan, across north Africa and in the heartland of the Arab world – in Lebanon, Syria and Egypt – Gulf money built vital infrastructure, supported refugees and provided a financial safety net for governments who could not meet the needs of their people. On top of these long-time commitments there were also more recent burdens to meet. Following the American invasion of Afghanistan in late 2001, Gulf State contributions to rebuilding the war-torn country amounted to hundreds of millions of dollars.

These budgetary pressures and demands resulted in serious cash-flow problems across the Gulf. Governments had to make tough choices on spending priorities. Cutting back public spending was an obvious but unappealing choice. Over the previous two decades the region's citizens had become used to a high standard of living and they continued to expect their leaders to provide for their every need. At the same time, the cost of basic services like housing, healthcare and education shot up as the citizen, expatriate and foreign worker populations all continued to grow rapidly. This bleak financial situation was made worse by a lack of available credit on the financial markets at a time when it was estimated that only fifteen international banks conducted business across the entire Middle East and North Africa (MENA) region. This left the Gulf States with little choice but to delay some existing and planned infrastructural and industrial projects, even though there were concerns that doing so might send a negative signal to existing foreign lenders and potential future investors. In order to minimize the downside of this, wherever possible those GCC countries that could afford it provided grants and loans to their less wealthy partners for priority projects in certain areas. In 2002, to take one example, the UAE provided Oman with almost US$400 million to extend its road network and complete other vital development projects.

The low oil price, the instability caused by 9/11 and the war on terror, the slump in the financial sector and the slowdown in domestic development all posed real challenges for the Gulf States. They responded by going on the offensive in order to demonstrate to the world that they were not only open for business but were attractive partners and preferable destinations for funds. This explains Qatar's hosting of delegations from 142 countries at the World Trade Organization (WTO) ministerial meeting in mid-November 2001, only shortly after the 9/11 attacks. This summit ran smoothly without any incident at a time of high alert across the international community. Its success provided Qatar with massive global exposure. The subsequent rounds of trade negotiations that followed the meeting, dubbed the Doha Round, continued to shine a positive spotlight on the kingdom.

The incomparable rise of Dubai over the same years also reflected well on the Gulf as a whole. Following the British withdrawal from the region in 1971, Dubai's ruler, Sheikh Rashid Al-Maktoum, had joined forces with Abu Dhabi's Sheikh Zayed Al-Nahyan to establish the UAE. Bahrain and Qatar were invited to join this novel federation but declined, preferring instead to go it alone as independent states. Over the next few years, five far smaller emirates – Sharjah, Ajman, Ras Al Khaimah, Fujairah and Umm Al Quwain – did sign up. Between them, this 'collection of leftovers',[7] as one commentator unkindly described them, had combined total revenues of only US$500,000. They now looked to Abu Dhabi and Dubai to provide economic security and political leadership. From the beginning of the UAE, Abu Dhabi accounted for most of the federation's territory, wealth and military power. Unlike Abu Dhabi, which possessed around 10 per cent of the world's proven oil reserves and had the fourth largest reserves of natural gas, Dubai lacked energy resources. As a tongue-in-cheek advert for a Dubai chicken restaurant liked to advertise, 'Our neighbours are rich in oil. Not us.'[8]

Despite its lack of resources, Dubai was the most populous and dynamic of the UAE's seven emirates. Historically, it was also an important commercial centre and home to many local and foreign businesses. This laid the groundwork for the transition to a market economy. With few resources in a regional economy dominated and driven by oil, Dubai chose to rely on promoting entrepreneurialism and private-sector growth. By the mid-1970s the emirate had already gained a reputation among foreign diplomats as the 'Monaco of the Gulf', as well as an 'extraordinary merchant city state' under the 'financial wizardry' of the ruling Maktoum family.[9] In 1985, Dubai established the region's first and largest free zone, Jebel Ali. The free zone concept, replicated widely across the region in later years, championed the idea of attracting foreign businesses and investment by offering 100 per cent foreign ownership, full repatriation of profits, and excellent infrastructure and services in a tax-free environment. By the mid-1990s, Dubai had started to complement its free zone strategy with a massive investment in the luxury tourism and real estate sectors, both of which defined Dubai's economic model going forward. By the early 2000s Dubai was the undisputed regional economic success story. It was booming under its de facto ruler, the pro-business Crown Prince Sheikh Mohammed bin Rashid Al-Maktoum. 'Open-minded, open-hearted and wide open for business',[10] was how *The Economist* described Dubai under his leadership. By the time Crown Prince Mohammed succeeded his elder brother in 2006, his achievements, ambitions and leadership had become legendary. When he attended the World Economic Forum in Davos in 2004 he was surrounded by crowds of admirers in scenes usually reserved for the visits of rock stars like U2 lead singer Bono, a regular attendee at the annual event.

Under his leadership Dubai built up its reputation as one of the world's 'most dynamic and diverse' economies.[11] The crown prince's mantra was that 'everything must be world class'.[12] Sultan bin Sulayem, one of the emirate's top businessmen and chair of the Free Zone Authority, laid out the principles behind the Dubai model. 'Our philosophy is simple,' he explained to one of the many authors writing on the Dubai 'miracle' in the mid-2000s. 'We build world-class infrastructure, we cut out the red tape, we offer a business-friendly environment, and we encourage productive investment and productive human capital. We also prize innovation and talent.'[13] The ministry of labour estimated that people from 202 nations worked and lived within Dubai's city limits by the 2000s, along with 95 per cent of the emirate's entire population. All participated in some way or another in the visionary economic experiment under way. Hugely ambitions construction projects and property ventures covered the landscape. These included one of the world's largest airports and Jebel Ali, one of the top ten ports in the world. Dubai was also home to some of the world's most luxurious and ambitious holiday resorts, including the Palm Islands – two 6-kilometre-long artificial luxury residential peninsulas in the shape of palm trees designed to stretch out along the Dubai shoreline – and 'The World', a archipelago of 300 artificial islands shaped to replicate a map of the globe.

In the rest of the Gulf and across the wider Arab world 'Dubai envy' became an increasingly common phenomenon. Businessmen visiting the emirate expressed the wish that their own leaders were as dynamic as Dubai's. Kuwaiti parliamentarians debated how Dubai's economy, even without oil, was doing better than their own.[14] In turn, Dubai's leaders embraced their growing reputation and worked to consolidate it whenever possible. It was reported that Sheikh Mohammed wanted to be known as the emirate's CEO, not its hereditary ruler. His best-selling book *My Vision* made the case for Dubai Inc. as a model for the Arab world and there appeared to be no limits to what he believed Dubai, under his leadership, could achieve. In a 2006 meeting with former US secretary of state Colin Powell, he explained that each year less and less of his vision for Dubai was being achieved compared to previous years because his vision for Dubai was 'always growing'. Or, as he put it on an earlier occasion, 'In the race to excellence, there is no finish line.'[15]

For many in the Arab world, Dubai symbolized much more than entrepreneurial ambition and economic success. It was also important because it challenged the perception that the region was unable to develop into a global economic leader or move beyond its colonial past. Others welcomed Dubai's success as evidence that the security problems that plagued the region, from Al-Qaeda and Islamist terror to the seemingly insoluble Israel–Palestine conflict, did not have to mean that success in other areas was unachievable. For those who thought along these lines, the fact that Dubai was not a major energy power whose success had been funded by its oil money made its achievements all the more satisfying.

No less impressive was the story of risk taking, vision and ingenuity behind Qatar's journey to gas superstardom from the 1990s onwards. This move from oil to gas was an important regional, as well as national, development. Though never a major oil player, regularly coming near the bottom of OPEC rankings on production, Qatar's economy, like those of many of its GCC partners, had been dependent on oil revenues for decades. During the 1990s, oil accounted for more than a third of the kingdom's annual GDP. To put this into perspective the financial, property, industrial and manufacturing sectors combined only accounted for around one-fifth of GDP. The decision to use existing and future oil revenues to build up the country's underdeveloped gas sector was both very costly and very risky. It is much more expensive to extract gas than to drill for oil. This was particularly true in the Qatari case because much of its gas was located in the deep waters off its northern coast, in particular the North Field, the largest natural gas field in the world. Another obstacle at this time was the lack of existing pipelines needed to ship gas to some key target markets like India. Other potential markets in Asia, notably Japan and South Korea, had existing pipeline access but were already buying gas from major producers such as Indonesia and Malaysia. Europe, one of the most lucrative markets, already had sufficient pipelines pumping gas from Algeria, Russia and the North Sea.

The low oil price during the 1990s also meant that Qatar had less available surplus revenues to spend on the huge setting-up costs associated with gas projects. Extracting gas was only one major expense. It also cost billions of dollars to dredge a port in the shallow coastal waters of the Gulf that was fit for purpose and to build suitable port facilities and infrastructure at Ras Laffan, which by the late 1990s would be transformed into one of the largest gas-exporting hubs in the world. Due to a lack of readily available pipelines, Qatar also had to purchase a very expensive fleet of state-of-the-art specialist tankers fitted to transport their gas to customers. The risks attached to this investment were especially high as a number of the key potential buyers of Qatari gas did not have the technology in place at this time to handle such sophisticated gas tankers.

To finance its ambitious gas plans, Qatar borrowed heavily on the international financial markets. The kingdom also showed an impressive willingness to enter into innovative and mutually beneficial production and sharing deals with external partners. As far back as 1984 a joint-venture agreement was signed between Qatar, British Petroleum and Chimie de France (CdF, subsequently renamed Total, currently France's largest company, in which Qatar has a small shareholding). This officially established Qatar Liquefied Gas Company (Qatargas) with the function of managing, operating, marketing and exporting liquefied natural gas (LNG) from the North Field. In 1991, the Qatar Europe LNG Company was formed as a partnership between Qatar and the Italian conglomerate ENI's Snamprogetti, with shareholdings of 65 and 30 per cent respectively. Over the rest of the decade, joint ventures and production-sharing agreements (PSAs) with American, Italian, Dutch, British, Danish and French energy companies proliferated, with ExxonMobil, Total and Royal Dutch Shell in particular undertaking further major investments in projects across the rapidly expanding gas sector. Though US giant ExxonMobil is now the largest foreign investor in Qatar, Shell can claim the single largest investment in the country at the Pearl Gas to Liquids (GTL) plant at Ras Laffan. This is also the company's largest investment anywhere in the world.

This kind of cooperation provided Qatar with cutting-edge technology, experience and know-how, as well as further investment to complement funds borrowed from banks. It also set them apart from other major Gulf energy producers. Kuwait always carefully maintained stringent regulations blocking foreign investment in its energy industry. In the early 2000s, Saudi Arabia launched a new and unprecedented initiative, intended to attract significant investment by international oil companies in the kingdom's gas industry. Through an inability to agree terms, the plans failed to materialize, preventing the launch of a gas partnership along the lines of that so successfully implemented in Qatar. Qatar also embraced an innovative approach to winning new clients in the face of stiff competition by agreeing to invest in the gas infrastructure of recipient countries in return for gas contracts. Qatari leaders also demonstrated impressive business sense and pragmatism by walking away from high-profile projects when they began to look like bad investments. On one notable occasion, Qatar's state energy company agreed with its partner ExxonMobil to abandon a hugely costly project to produce clean-burning diesel from natural gas. This only seemed to strengthen relations. By 2003, ExxonMobil senior management lauded Qatar's 'unique position' as a politically stable partner with a great vision for its gas future and even described its joint agreements with the country as central to its own gas business.

As outlined above, Qatar's gas strategy demonstrated the country's willingness to take risks and its ambition to become a global as well as regional economic force. By 2004 it was the fastest-growing economy in the Middle East. This was fuelled by rising oil prices and the diversification of the energy sector away from oil and towards natural gas. It was also driven by massive government investment in the tourism, educational and hospitality sectors that resulted in a boom in construction and real estate development. In 2004, foreign direct investment into Qatar reached record levels, increasing by more than 1,500 per cent over the previous year.[16] In that same year Qatar announced its intention to invest US$25 billion over the next six years to quadruple its gas export capacity in order to become the first country to sell gas to Europe, Asia and North America at the same time. This was on top of the estimated US$70 billion in foreign investment that the kingdom's gas industry would absorb by the mid-2000s. Soon afterwards, Qatar announced its intention to become the world's number-one exporter of LNG by 2011. In December 2010, the same month it was awarded the 2022 FIFA World Cup, and one year ahead of its target date, Qatar's high-risk, high-cost strategy paid off when it became the world's top exporter of LNG.

In the early months of 2003, as the US prepared for war in Iraq and the Gulf States braced themselves for the fallout of this inevitable conflict, the price of oil rose sharply. As it had done so many times since the mid-1970s, Saudi Arabia once again attempted to keep the oil price down by pumping millions of extra barrels to meet demand. This time the strategy failed and the oil price continued to rise. On one level this was bad for Saudi Arabia as it underscored very clearly the kingdom's reduced ability to single-handedly use production to control the oil price. The upside was that Saudi Arabia and the other oil-producing members of the GCC benefited from the surging oil price, which by the end of 2004 was at its highest level in two decades. By 2005 the oil price was twice what it had been prior to the invasion of Iraq and annual oil revenues had jumped sevenfold compared to 1999 levels. An estimated US$600 million a day filled Gulf coffers and vast sums of cash moved from oil-consuming to oil-producing countries. This resulted in budget surpluses that even dwarfed those being achieved by China in the same years. With so much money available, financial sectors across the Gulf expanded rapidly, real estate prices shot up and stock markets boomed. The Qatari stock exchange, known as the Doha Securities Market, grew by 70 per cent over the course of 2005 alone. In the same year the Saudi stock market was one of the world's top performers, and its market value for the year was about twice as large as the country's oil revenues.

In the first decade of the 2000s the GCC economy tripled in size due to the high oil price.[17] One unexpected consequence of this rising wealth was a renewed willingness to pay for the expensive business of regional integration. The benefits of deeper integration are widely accepted. It increases the level of trade between the parties involved and provides them with a much larger domestic market. It also generates opportunities to take advantage of economies of scale and to become more competitive. Along with domestic liberalization and stable monetary and fiscal policies, this makes a region a more appealing destination for foreign investment. The Middle East and North Africa (MENA) had always been one of the lowest-ranking regions in terms of integration. It had been plagued by cumbersome administrative procedures, trade protectionism and political rivalries that all played themselves out in the economic field. A particular block to intra-regional trade had always been the fact that many local countries produced the same goods, resources and services so that there was very little that they wanted to buy off each other. All of these obstacles also existed in the Gulf region, but despite differences in outlook, policies and interests, intra-Gulf trade rose rapidly from the 1990s, tripling in value to over US$65 billion in the first decade of the 2000s. The more Gulf Arabs worked together to open up the regional economy, the more inward investment they attracted and the easier they found it to access state-of-the-art technology.

In the wake of 9/11, with the region facing increased geo-strategic instability, there was widespread public and media support across the GCC for further economic integration.[18] GCC governments responded by agreeing to fast-forward the start date of a long-planned customs union to January 2003. Initially, businessmen were less optimistic that a customs union, which is a free trade area with a common external tariff, could withstand the competing interests and outlooks that existed inside and between the GCC member states. In Dubai, for example, there were fears that a customs union might impact negatively on the emirate's status as the leading export and re-export hub in the region, as the new union required Dubai to raise its very low external tariff in line with the standard, unified, tariff rate across the GCC. Such concerns were misplaced. Following the launch of the customs union, Dubai saw its trade with Saudi Arabia, Kuwait, Qatar and Oman increase rather than shrink. So did Abu Dhabi and the five smaller emirates. Taken together, the UAE as a whole experienced a 30 per cent rise in exports and re-exports during the first year of the customs union. Other GCC states also benefited from the removal of barriers and, in particular, the unprecedented opportunity that the customs union provided them to sell into the much larger Saudi market. On top of these economic benefits, the launch of the customs union also provided an incentive for member states to work out long-time disagreements with one another over tariff levels, revenue collection and border inspections. A Riyadh-based Gulf authority for standardization with a mandate to monitor the implementation of the customs union was established to provide support for this deepening cooperation.

These years also saw renewed attempts to resolve a number of intra-GCC disputes that had hampered closer relations between member states in the past. Oman and the UAE settled a long-time disagreement over their border from east of Al-Aqeedat to Al-Daar in the north on the Arabian Gulf coast. This led to an immediate upgrade of bilateral relations. Saudi Arabia looked to settle its maritime differences with Qatar. It also held consultations with the UAE to reduce ongoing tensions over territory on their shared border that went back to the mid-1970s. This newly positive environment fuelled a growing consensus across the region over the merits of building on the customs union to extend integration further. At their annual summit at the end of 2003, leaders agreed to guarantee the full rights of GCC citizens in other member states. They also made a notable commitment to further cooperation in a number of key areas including water and power and talked of building a common rail system costing tens of billions of dollars that would link all members in the longer term. Most importantly, they also moved forward with their plans to establish a common market, and monetary union and a single currency by 2010. The common market was launched on 1 January 2008, on the eve of the global financial downturn. It opened the way for GCC citizens to live and work in other member states. This was an important move that would, in the words of Hamad Buamim, director general of the Dubai Chamber of Commerce and Industry, 'speed up cooperation and use the economy of scale in establishing the GCC single currency and monetary union'.[19]

As far back as the 1970s there had been calls for a single Gulf currency.[20] This was formalized as a long-term goal of the GCC in its first major economic agreement in 1981. Over the next two decades the Gulf partners made some practical moves in this direction. This included the establishment of a committee of central bank officials from all GCC states to coordinate initial discussions on monetary union. During the 1990s, the weak oil price and economic stagnation meant that progress on this front was slow and difficult. As the region's economic outlook improved along with the price of oil in the early 2000s, discussions on monetary union were renewed. By 2006, GCC central bank governors had agreed in principle to establish a monetary council that would serve as the basis for a GCC central bank to oversee the launch of a single currency when the time was right.

In the summer of 2008, GCC central bank governors announced their intention to establish a prototype central bank, to be known as the Gulf Monetary Council, in 2010.[21] Top Gulf finance officials met regularly after that to draw up a draft charter for monetary union. On the eve of the annual GCC summit in late December 2008, GCC secretary general Abdul Rahman bin Hamad Al-Attiyah told the media that the summit signalled a 'new start in GCC cooperation in all sectors'.[22] During the meeting, Gulf leaders all agreed that deeper integration would increase regional competitiveness and underpin stability in an increasingly unstable economic and financial environment. They also endorsed plans to build a unified power grid and a GCC rail network, and to work towards a unified currency. Despite this progress, GCC member states still needed to overcome several hurdles in order to achieve monetary union. There were ongoing barriers to intra-GCC investment, in particular in stock exchanges and property markets across the Gulf. It also took more time than planned to achieve a unified customs duty of 5 per cent across the GCC.

Within months, plans for monetary union and a single GCC currency fell apart when the UAE and Saudi Arabia clashed over whether the monetary council should be located in Riyadh or Abu Dhabi. Unable to get Saudi leaders to agree to the UAE capital, leaders in Abu Dhabi announced that the federation would not participate in any future Gulf monetary union. The UAE's decision was a much bigger blow to the project of regional integration than Oman's withdrawal a few years earlier, because the UAE economy was the second biggest GCC economy after Saudi Arabia. Just a couple of years earlier experts were speculating on a Riyadh–Abu Dhabi axis at heart of the GCC similar to that between Paris and Bonn during the heyday of the EU economic boom in the 1970s and 1980s. On a practical level the UAE's withdrawal has prevented the longer-term development of a common GCC capital market and has made it harder for the GCC central banks to deal with the financial challenges they face in unison. It has also made it harder for the GCC partners to develop a more unified trade policy, and to extend cooperation on large-scale infrastructural and science and technology projects.

The crisis over monetary union also highlighted the ongoing tendency within the GCC of members choosing to go it alone rather than take collective action in a number of key areas. This was also apparent in the way the GCC countries engaged with Afghanistan and Iraq following the overthrow of the Taliban and Saddam Hussein. They pledged significant sums of economic and humanitarian aid and funded refugee camps in both countries. In the case of Iraq, they also forgave the country billions in unpaid loans and, publicly at least, agreed to a joint GCC approach to the provision of aid at the Madrid Donor Conference in October 2003. In reality, Saudi Arabia opposed the preference of the rest of its GCC partners to make funds available to Iraq prior to any decision on who would take over power in Baghdad after Saddam. Riyadh refused to be swayed by the arguments of its partners that a lack of unity on this vital issue would be bad for the GCC, as well as Iraq.

At the time of Saddam's overthrow there was much discussion across the GCC over the benefits of a prosperous and stable Iraq for the rest of the region. It was hoped that the Arab Gulf would take the lead in reintegrating Iraq into the regional economy. There was even talk of a Gulf-funded railway linking Basra in the south of Iraq to rail and port networks across the Gulf. As time passed and businessmen and investors waited impatiently for the security situation on the ground to improve, Gulf governments became increasingly reluctant to participate in a unified approach to doing business in post-Saddam Iraq. Officials in Riyadh worried that a rejuvenated Baghdad might emerge as an economic challenger to its regional dominance. Leaders in the UAE, Kuwait and Qatar believed that intra-GCC bickering and bureaucracy would inevitably overshadow and undermine any coordinated economic action. On this basis, they refocused their efforts on building business links and networks independent of each other in the new Iraq. These decisions reflected a deep distrust of Saudi intentions. Since the birth of the GCC, its smaller partners believed that Saudi Arabia had a responsibility as the largest member to take the lead in uniting rather than dividing the regional grouping. Over the years this did not happen. Instead, Saudi Arabia's partners accused it of trying to control them by blocking inter-GCC trade and preventing other GCC states from working together free of Saudi influence. The Saudis, so the prevailing argument went, were intent on restricting and limiting GCC commercial cooperation and economic development because they wanted to prevent other GCC states from deepening ties with each other independent of Riyadh.

In the early 2000s, Saudi Arabia's GDP was still five times larger than that of the rest of the GCC member states. At the same time its traditional dominance over its GCC partners in all areas was being eroded. This was particularly true for Qatar and the UAE, both of whom looked to expand their influence across the Arab world in these years mainly at Saudi Arabia's expense. This was demonstrated by the UAE–Qatari agreement to build a causeway over the Khor al-Odeid waters that allowed them to bypass Saudi territory. Qatar and Bahrain also agreed in principle to interconnect directly by constructing a bridge. Saudi Arabia opposed both projects. It also blocked a Qatari plan to run a gas pipeline to Bahrain and Kuwait via Saudi territory. In 2006, six years after this multi-billion-dollar project was first announced, Qatar's energy minister blamed Saudi intransigence for the lack of progress. Apart from refusing to back ambitious infrastructural projects between other GCC member states, Riyadh also disagreed profoundly with them over how to proceed in establishing free trade agreements with external partners. For more than a decade the GCC had been engaged in unproductive and increasingly acrimonious negotiations with the European Union on a free trade agreement. In the early years of those deliberations both sides had hoped that a deal would be reached quickly and that once concluded it would set a precedent across the world as the first ever region-to-region free trade deal. By the mid-2000s such hopes had faded almost completely as round after round of talks between the two sides made little progress and eventually ground to a halt.

Gulf officials accused their European partners of 'foot dragging' and 'prevarication'. In one outburst, Kuwait's foreign minister publicly rebuked the EU for promising to sign an agreement but instead offering only 'excuses and premeditated delay'. They took particular offence at what appeared to be the European attempt to link a free trade deal to improved human rights in the region. Such interference in the internal affairs of GCC states, argued officials from the region, was unacceptable and would have no place in any final agreement. For their part, EU officials rejected claims that human rights had caused the impasse. They pointed out that a final agreement could not happen until the GCC had a single tariff system in place and that this had only occurred with the launch of the customs union in 2003. Others argued that the human rights issue provided a convenient smokescreen for Gulf States unwilling to meet another key

European demand – an end to government subsidies for the region's important petrochemical sector.

Whatever the reasons, the drawn-out and unproductive negotiations with the EU dampened the enthusiasm of GCC leaders for a collective free trade agreement with its biggest trade partner and it suspended negotiations on the matter in 2008. 'We don't mind the negotiations, but we do mind the delays,' explained one senior Kuwaiti figure in a statement that reflected the feelings of other top trade officials across the region. Midway through 2009 the GCC did sign its first region-to-region free trade agreement, with the European Free Trade Association (EFTA), the grouping made up of non-EU European economies including Switzerland, Norway and Iceland. The GCC's first region-to-region summit with the Association of Southeast Asian Nations (ASEAN) was held in Bahrain not long afterwards. Following these talks, Suri Pitsuan, then secretary general of the Asian trading bloc, summed up the gist of the discussions in a press conference with local journalists. 'You have what we don't have,' he explained, 'and we have in plenty what you don't have, so we need each other.'[23] This observation was not lost on the Gulf States. Within a year, GCC foreign ministers, again meeting in Bahrain, agreed to build up their links with ASEAN as part of their global push. The GCC states then signed a memorandum on commercial understanding with the ten members of the Common Market for Eastern and Southern Africa (COMESA), a regional grouping committed, like the GCC, to achieving sustainable economic and social progress for member states through increased cooperation and integration in all fields of endeavour.

Parallel to these moves there was also a push for bilateral alongside region-to-region free trade agreements. UAE officials, for example, approached the United Kingdom, Germany and France to enquire whether they would be willing to abandon the EU–GCC process in favour of one-to-one deals with individual GCC countries. Only Saudi Arabia rejected this evolving line of thinking. At a 2004 'Gulf Dialogue' meeting sponsored by a British think tank, foreign minister Saud Al-Faisal emphasized the need for GCC member states to act collectively on a regional level to ensure their long-term stability and security. There had to be, he argued, consensus among GCC partners that the signing of bilateral free trade agreements was 'not compatible with the spirit of the Charter of the GCC'. Saudi delegations also took a tough position on the issue at GCC meetings. They insisted that any free trade negotiations should take place on a multilateral level. To pursue bilateral negotiations, they argued, violated past GCC economic agreements, diminished the organization's collective bargaining power, prevented further economic integration and diluted GCC solidarity.

In 2003 President Bush announced an initiative to develop a free trade area in the Middle East. The following year Bahrain signed a historic free trade agreement with the United States. Prior to the deal, Saudi Arabia had exerted great pressure on Bahrain to pull out of negotiations. It halted the supply of some construction materials, threatened financial penalties and even warned Bahrain that it would be held responsible for the destruction of the GCC economy if it unilaterally agreed terms with Washington. Bahrain held firm in the face of this pressure. The king described himself as the 'father of the FTA', while his senior officials dismissed Riyadh's claim that a deal with Washington would profoundly damage the GCC. They also countered Saudi threats with their own threat to withdraw from the GCC customs union if the bilateral agreement with the US was blocked. American officials backed the Bahraini position and argued that bilateral trade agreements with individual GCC states were fully compatible with existing GCC agreements. As the US ambassador in Bahrain, William T. Monroe, put it, 'This is a positive step for Bahrain and the region.'[24]

The UAE, Qatar, Kuwait and Oman all agreed with this assessment. They saw the deal between Bahrain and the US as a precedent for similar bilateral agreements with the US as well as a host of other countries including Singapore, Australia and China. They also viewed it as an important test case over whether Saudi Arabia could successfully block its GCC partners from entering into such deals. For both these reasons they backed Bahrain, and the matter quickly became a 'five against one' battle inside the GCC, as Oman's foreign minister characterized it. All five of Saudi Arabia's partners took particular exception to Riyadh's attempts to politicize what they viewed to be a purely economic issue. They also suspected that the Saudi position had less to do with concerns over the future economic health of the GCC and more to do with fears that the Bahrain deal might erode Saudi Arabia's regional economic dominance. Such claims certainly had credibility. After Oman and the UAE publicly announced their plans to negotiate their own free trade agreements with the United States in early 2005, Saudi officials complained to their American counterparts that future bilateral free trade agreements between Washington and smaller GCC countries would weaken their kingdom.

In the mid-1970s, Saudi Arabia had pressured the UAE into signing a treaty in which the fledgling federation gave up its claim to the Zararah oilfield on their shared border and surrendered a piece of land that linked it to Qatar. Three decades later the UAE was harder to dominate. It was the third largest economy in the Arab world behind Saudi Arabia and Egypt, though its per capita income was far higher than that of either of these much larger countries. It had a GDP larger than those of Bahrain, Qatar and Kuwait combined. It was the top investor in other Arab countries, and had even recently overtaken Japan to become the number-one investor in Saudi Arabia itself. It had also made great strides in economic diversification. It had developed a manufacturing base, a hi-tech industry and an agricultural sector from scratch. The UAE's determination to step out of the Saudi shadow and realign the region's economic centre in its favour was evident during the GCC annual summit in December 2004, when the announcement to build a causeway linking Abu Dhabi and Doha was made. The UAE also opposed Saudi attempts to dictate the actions of its partners on free trade and looked to limit Saudi influence on a whole range of other regional economic issues.

Other GCC members also attempted to assert their right to independent economic action beyond Saudi control. This was even true in the case of Bahrain, which Saudi Arabia dominated more than its other GCC partners. Before the mid-twentieth century Bahrain had provided Saudi Arabia's link to the outside world via its Eastern Province. As one Saudi merchant recalled, Bahrain had been the 'centre of everything . . . everything came from Bahrain, shoes, matches, kerosene, cloth, everything'.[25] Following Saudi Arabia's emergence as an oil giant, resource-poor Bahrain became increasingly reliant on Saudi support. In a candid interview in the Kuwaiti press in the late 1970s, Bahrain's top soldier acknowledged that Riyadh provided his kingdom with all its 'economic, social and military requirements'.[26] Soon after the founding of the GCC, both kingdoms signed a formal cooperation pact. Over subsequent years Bahrain's ruling family acted increasingly like a Saudi client, voting with Riyadh at GCC meetings in return for economic and political support. In order to consolidate this relationship during the mid-1980s, Riyadh paid for the construction of a 25-kilometre causeway that linked Saudi Arabia to Bahrain. Two decades later, at the same time as the UAE and Qatar proposed the construction of their own causeway, the tiny kingdom of Bahrain showed that it was also willing to fight for its economic interests at a regional and global level. It refused to bow to Saudi pressure over its free trade deal with Washington. This gave Bahrain the distinction of becoming the first GCC state and only the third in the Arab world to have a free trade agreement with the US. This had immediate and highly visible benefits. Bahrain's king was the only GCC leader invited to attend the

G8 summit in Sea Island, Georgia, in the summer of 2004. He was also the first Gulf leader invited to visit the White House after George Bush's 2004 re-election victory. The kingdom used its growing relationship with Washington and its new international standing more generally to market itself even more aggressively than it had done in the past as the regional centre for education, healthcare, insurance and especially banking, which by now accounted for almost a quarter of its economy.

As the oil price increased rapidly after 2003, all GCC member states, including small-time energy players like Bahrain, Dubai and Oman, attempted to consolidate stability at home and influence abroad by integrating further into the world economy and financial markets. This expressed itself in investment strategies unprecedented in ambition, vision, scale and cost. In tourism and energy, real estate and luxury brands, the Gulf States established themselves as top investors across the Arab and Muslim world, in key emerging markets in the East and in the developed Western economies and Japan. As they did so, the recycling of petro-dollars became an important international economic and political issue just as it had been during the 1970s and 1980s. Much of this financial activity flowed through the Gulf's growing arsenal of sovereign wealth funds (SWFs). Andrew Rozanov, an analyst in the City of London, coined the term in the mid-2000s to describe state-owned investment funds managed independently of other state financial institutions and mandated to invest what Rozanov termed 'by-products of national budget surpluses, accumulated over years'. SWF investment strategies covered a diverse set of financial assets including treasury bonds, corporate stocks and real estate, all intended to contribute to economic diversification by moving Gulf economies away from dependence on oil and gas revenues.

Hamad bin Khalifa Al-Thani rose to power in Qatar in 1995. From then until his abdication in favour of his thirty-three-year-old son in 2013, he built a worldwide reputation as a visionary and ambitious leader. He was determined to make his tiny kingdom a major player on the world stage. In 2007, he gave an insight into the thinking behind this strategy of investing huge sums of money overseas as part of the ongoing search for alternative sources of income. 'Our energy sector won't last forever,' explained the emir, 'so we need to secure a good life so they [future generations] can continue the same standard of living.' Three years later, in another interview, he returned to this topic. He explained that his country had been devastated when its vital pearl industry collapsed in the 1930s and lamented the failure of Qatar to make wise investments during the oil boom of the 1970s. 'My concern now', he admitted, 'is how to invest both internally and externally towards the benefit of our future generations.'[27] In the same year, the UAE's president, Khalifa bin Zayed Al-Nahyan, made the same point. The 'future of the country', he explained, 'is linked to its ability to manage its wealth in the interests of future generations.'[28]

This sentiment was not new. In 1976, Kuwait had even created the 'Fund for Future Generations', into which 10 per cent of all state revenues were transferred annually. These resources were invested in diverse holdings across the globe from London office blocks to Australian wool farms to Fijian hotels. Nor was the idea of establishing an investment fund to serve as a long-term substitute for natural resources that novel: the earliest-known example can be found in quite an unlikely place – the Gilbert Islands in Micronesia. In the mid-1950s, British officials in charge of the tiny archipelago put a levy on the export of phosphates used in fertilizer, the economy's only significant natural resource and its main source of income. Over the decades this fund continued to earn a small percentage of all phosphate revenues and by the mid-2000s was worth an estimated half a billion dollars.[29] The majority of Gulf investment funds were much younger and much bigger than this and their money came from oil and gas, not fertilizer. But some could claim a longer lineage than others. In 1976 the Abu Dhabi Investment Authority (ADIA) was established with a mandate to invest the emirate's cash surpluses, again for the benefit of future generations.

By the early 2000s, ADIA was being run from the tallest building in Abu Dhabi and was seeking out investments all over the planet. As oil revenues poured in after 2003, the value of ADIA's assets under management jumped by about US$100 billion a year until 2008. It consolidated its position as one of the world's largest sovereign wealth funds, as well as one of the biggest institutional investors in the international markets. In 1982, the Kuwait Investment Authority (KIA) was founded as a successor to the Kuwait Investment Office that had been established in London in the early 1950s. In the decades following its launch, the KIA developed a reputation as one of the most efficient, disciplined and effective of all Gulf funds, as well as one of the biggest. By law it received at least 10 per cent of Kuwait's oil revenues to invest beyond its borders and by 2007 had over US$200 billion in assets, the most in the fund's history.

By the mid-2000s estimates of the number of Gulf SWFs in existence ranged from ten to forty. Few had either the experience or resources of the KIA or ADIA. Many were only a few years old. Qatar set up its SWF – the Qatar Investment Authority (QIA) in 2005. Oman and Bahrain set theirs up the following year with the establishment of the Oman Investment Fund and Mumtalakat respectively. All shared the same objective – to take advantage of the huge surpluses generated by the rapidly rising oil price and booming stock values across the world. During the late 1970s and 1980s, the Arab Gulf States had faced intense criticism when they capitalized on the high oil price to purchase assets abroad. In order to minimize such attacks subsequently they had learnt to be discreet and to place a premium on keeping their foreign investments out of the news. They also prioritized investments in safe assets like US Treasury securities and government bonds. When they did invest in global brands or participated in high-profile deals they preferred to play the role of 'quiet investors', taking small stakes and giving little cause for attention. This strategy meant that outside major financial centres like Wall Street and the City of London few were aware of the role or importance of funds like ADIA and the KIA. If they did have a reputation outside of the financial sector it was as passive and discreet investors who maintained a very modest public presence and limited the amount of discretionary information they made available to the markets.

Oil booms can be a blessing or a curse for producing economies, depending on how revenues are used. Initially, when the oil price surged after 2003, Gulf governments were cautious about how they spent their extra revenues. Compared to the 1970s, they spent much less on imported goods and services and saved a higher percentage. Most of the investments they made were in low-risk and low-profile bonds, stocks and shares.[30] Despite this sensible approach, oil and gas revenues were so large that it became increasingly tempting to use a growing percentage of surplus funds to move into non-traditional investments areas. These included private equity and emerging market deals, mortgages and commodities, all of which carried much more potential risk and reward than the investments they had mainly made in the past. These asset categories also tended to attract much more attention from the media and politicians, in the process making it increasingly difficult for these 'Masters of the Oil Universe',[31] as *Businessweek* magazine labelled them, to stay out of the spotlight.

As their reputations as funds with hundreds of billions of dollars available to spend grew, countries battled with each other to attract inward investment. This development was played out very obviously in Europe, a long-time destination for Gulf money. Delegations from across the continent descended on the Gulf. The Invest in Sweden Agency (ISA) pitched for money to fund Sweden's domestic IT, real estate, telecoms and biotech sectors. Several 'Invest in Italy' road trips promoted the country as a safe, secure and friendly investment environment.[32] Numerous European economies large and small – including the United Kingdom, Germany, the Netherlands, Austria,

Luxembourg and Malta – opened trade offices across the Gulf in the hope of attracting sizeable investments and attracting new business.

Though its economy was a sixth of the size of the US's, the United Kingdom was the world's number-two recipient of inward investment after the US during the first decade of the 2000s. It received more from Arab Gulf sources than any other European country. Dubai wealth funds, for example, took a 20 per cent holding in the London Stock Exchange, as well as a sizeable stake in the owner of the famed tourist attractions of the London Eye, Legoland and Madame Tussauds. They also bought the historic *QEII* cruise liner and several buildings in the heart of London's most pricey neighbourhoods. Abu Dhabi funds had a reputation for doing business in a much more conservative way than their Dubai counterparts. But their increasingly activist and public investment strategy earned them the title of 'the Gulf's new Bling Kings'. Some parts of the British media even speculated as to whether Abu Dhabi's recent 'readiness to flash the oil cash' could be explained by the fact that it had caught 'Dubai syndrome'.[33]

Taken together, the exploits of Abu Dhabi and Dubai made the UAE one of the three largest emerging-market buyers of companies in developed economies between 2000 and 2010. They were joined by funds from all over the Arab Gulf, all increasingly active and hungry for major overseas deals and eager to pump huge amounts of money into foreign assets. In 2007, Gulf Arab wealth funds signed off on over 300 major deals to the value of almost US$100 billion. This 'investment blitz',[34] as experts termed it at the time, was primarily a function of the energy revenues these countries now had available to spend. Even oil-poor Bahrain's mutual funds grew in value by over 70 per cent to US$15 billion in the mid-2000s. In line with their long-term strategies, the majority of SWF investments during this period were intended to add value to existing or future plans for domestic infrastructural or technological development, which explains why priority was often given to investments in companies or deals that provided access to cutting-edge technology or leading global brands, both of which were also often high-profile assets that gained international headlines. Wealthy private investors from the Gulf, including members of the region's royal families, also gained much publicity for their international investments. Prince Al-Waleed bin Talal, a nephew of King Abdullah, took major stakes in Twitter and Rupert Murdoch's NewsCorp, owner of Fox News. Abu Dhabi's Sheikh Mansour bin Zayed Al-Nahyan, a son of the UAE's founder, bought Manchester City football club. After that, Sheikh Mansour, as he is known to millions of football fans, established himself as a major figure in the world's most popular sport.

1. Muslim pilgrims circumambulate (tawaf) the sacred Kaaba during sunrise after fajr prayer in Mecca, Saudi Arabia.

2. President Nixon and Mrs Nixon welcome King Faisal of Saudi Arabia on a visit to the United States in May 1971.

3. Henry Kissinger (left), the US Secretary of State, meets the Shah of Iran (right) in Zurich in early 1975.

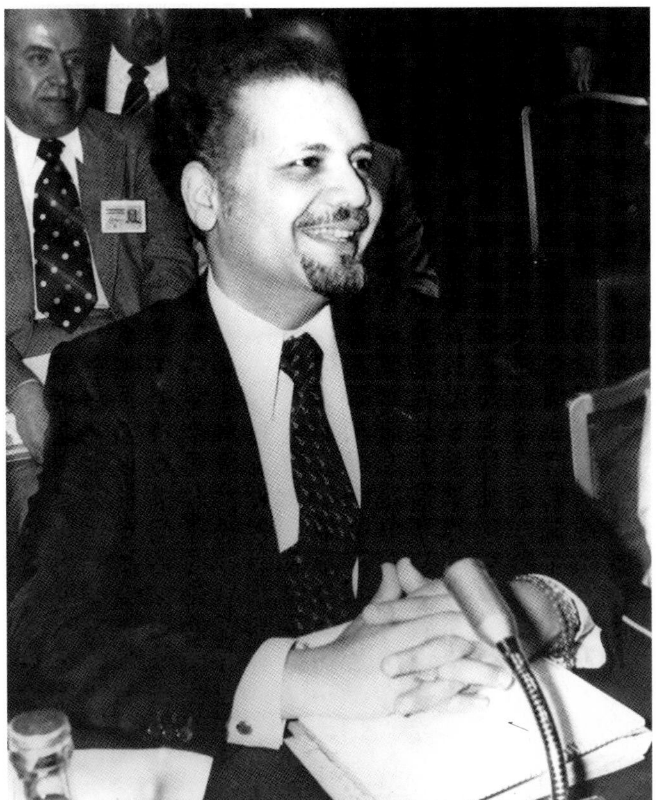

4. Sheik Yamani talks about oil and the Palestinian problem during a press conference in Saudi Arabia in July 1979.

5. Crowds of Iranian protestors demonstrate in support of exiled Ayatollah Sayyid Ruhollah Khomeini in 1978, the year prior to the revolution.

6. Iraqi leader Saddam Hussein addresses members of his armed forces shortly before the invasion of Iran in September 1980.

7. Saudi Arabian soldiers prepare to load into armoured personnel carriers during clean-up operations following the Battle of Khafji, 2 February 1991. The Battle of Khafji was the first major ground engagement of the 1991 Gulf war.

8. Palestinian women demonstrate with Palestinian and Iraqi flags and portraits of Yasser Arafat and Saddam Hussein in the West Bank during the Kuwait crisis of 1990–91.

11. On television from somewhere in Afghanistan, left to right: Sulaiman Abu Ghaith, the Al-Qaeda spokesman; Osama bin Laden; Ayman Zawahri of Egypt's Jihad; and Mohammed Atef.

12. Sheikh Hamad bin Khalifa Al-Thani, Qatar's emir between 1995 and 2013, meets with President George W. Bush at the White House in Washington, DC, in May 2003, less than two months after the American invasion of Iraq.

13. Saudi ambassador to the United States Prince Bandar bin Sultan, who served in that role from 1983 to 2005.

14. Prince Bandar, who served as Saudi ambassador to the United States from 1983 to 2005.

15. Sheikh Zayed Grand Mosque, Abu Dhabi, United Arab Emirates (UAE), in 2010. This impressive mosque was named after the ruler of Abu Dhabi who was the main driving force behind the founding of the UAE. He served as the first president of the UAE for thirty-three years until his death in 2004.

16. Prime Minister Khalifa bin Salman Al-Khalifa of Bahrain welcomes German Chancellor Angela Merkel in Manama, Bahrain, 27 May 2010. Merkel visited four Gulf Cooperation Council (GCC) countries during this trip to discuss politics and business in the midst of the global financial crisis.

17. The view towards Saudi Arabia from the halfway point of the King Fahd Causeway linking Bahrain and Saudi Arabia.

18. Protestors on the streets of Bahrain in April 2014, three years after the civil strife that divided the kingdom and led to an unprecedented GCC military intervention.

19. A Saudi soldier on duty at the largest oil refinery in the world, located at Ras Tanura, on the east coast of Saudi Arabia.

20. President Barack Obama delivers remarks alongside delegation leaders following the GCC–US summit at Camp David, Maryland, on 14 May 2015.

21. US Secretary of Defense Ash Carter meets in Washington with Prince Mohammed bin Salman, deputy crown prince and minister of defence of the Kingdom of Saudi Arabia, 4 September 2015.

22. US Secretary of State John Kerry stands with Foreign Minister Yusuf bin Alawi of Oman, Baroness Catherine Ashton of the European Union, and Foreign Minister Javad Zarif of Iran, before the beginning of three-way negotiations about the future of Iran's nuclear programme in November 2014, Muscat, Oman.

23. King Salman of Saudi Arabia with President Abdel Fattah Al-Sisi of Egypt at the end of an official five-day state visit to Egypt in April 2016. During this visit, both leaders announced the decision to build a bridge across the Red Sea to link the two countries, as well as connecting Asia and Africa.

24. A panoramic view of the Dubai skyscrapers and the Burj Khalifa tower, the tallest structure in the world, before sunrise in late 2015.

25. Preparations underway for a January 2016 performance at the stunning Royal Opera House, Muscat, Oman.

As deals like this became more common, the international media scrutinized the methods and motives of these wealthy Gulf funds and individual investors to an unprecedented extent. This started to have an impact far beyond those who paid attention to the financial news. In late 2007, a columnist with the influential *New Yorker* magazine even announced to readers that after all the problems in the financial sector, 'one new item has appeared on the list of things to worry about: so-called sovereign wealth funds'.[35] Along with the investment funds from the much bigger emerging economies of Russia and China, Gulf funds now stood accused of trying to buy up major stakes in important, cutting-edge and sensitive economic entities. Not only did they lack transparency, they were also under the control of unaccountable, often non-democratic governments, or single individuals and their extended ruling families. This was a particular concern in relation to the Gulf where it was often impossible to distinguish between wealth funds, national foreign reserves and the private wealth of Gulf rulers. Even the pro-business *Economist* magazine acknowledged that the implications of the Middle East's 'growing financial clout' were 'alarming'. At the very least, as one senior US official described it, there were 'legitimate questions about how we can ensure that investment continues to be commercially driven'. In a much-talked-about op-ed in the *Financial Times*, the highly respected former US treasury secretary Larry Summers pitched in. Government-owned SWFs, he warned, might not have the same profit-driven goals as other shareholders and might even be motivated by strategic or political objectives, or a desire to 'achieve influence'.[36] Nouriel Roubini, a professor of economics at New York University and one of the best-known and most respected commentators on the financial markets, went even further than Summers had done. He speculated that sovereign wealth funds, which he called 'US$200 billion gorillas', might raise greater issues and create more political problems than even the sub-prime mortgage crisis that had triggered the initial American downturn at the start of the global financial meltdown in 2007.[37]

The KIA's top official presented such concerns as appearing suddenly and unexpectedly. 'One day someone woke up in the morning', explained Bader Mohammed Al-Sa'ad, 'and considered these [sovereign wealth funds] to be a threat, a danger.' As chapter One showed, during the 1970s the newly rich oil-producing countries of the Arab Gulf had faced similar attacks for their international spending. In the following decade, as Japan's economy grew far faster than those in the rest of the developed world, Western officials and businessmen, as well as the media, railed against Japanese corporations buying up blue chip companies and iconic treasures like the Art Deco

Chrysler Building in New York (which, coincidentally, would be purchased in 2008 by an Abu Dhabi wealth fund). 'The Japanese are buying our country with our money', ran one representative headline as talk turned to the possibility of an 'economic Pearl Harbor' if the United States was not careful. In the 1990s, after the fear of aggressive Japanese business practices subsided, the spotlight turned on massive American multinationals, which were widely condemned in Europe for taking advantage of globalization to buy up some of the continent's best private companies.

France was the first major recipient of Gulf investment to adopt protectionist policies in response to the 'threat' posed by wealth funds. In 2005, Jacques Chirac's government issued a decree listing eleven sectors in which foreign investment would be subject to approval due to concerns over 'national defence interests'. Over the next few years, Chirac's populist successor as president, Nicolas Sarkozy, made several promises to protect his country's businesses from 'extremely aggressive' funds. He also appealed to other EU member states to set up their own SWFs to stop foreigners getting hold of prized assets.[38] German officials warned of 'mischievous' foreign buyers and pushed for legislation that would allow the government to block foreign investments worth more than 25 per cent of any company in order to protect 'public order and security'. All these proposals had the same objective. They were intended to enable policymakers to scrutinize foreign investments in order to 'protect European companies from unwanted foreign takeover'. Other developed economies took similar action. Australia issued principles to guide foreign investments in the country. Canada tightened existing laws that dealt with non-transparent overseas investors who might harbour 'non-commercial objectives'.

The Bush administration in Washington disagreed with these moves and was reluctant to follow suit. It argued that the investment process should be judged on commercial considerations only. The US Congress did not agree. There was widespread bipartisan political support in both the House of Representatives and the Senate for 'a lot more control over what they [sovereign-wealth funds] do and how they do it', as New York senator Hillary Rodham Clinton explained it.[39] Even before Clinton expressed these views in 2007, congressmen and senators had played a central role in one of the most talked-about attempts to block a Gulf investment.

DP World is one of the world's largest port operators and is owned by the Dubai government. In 2005, the company bid more than US$5 billion to buy P&O, Britain's biggest ports and ferries operator. As part of this deal it had acquired the contract for managing six US ports. Initially, there appeared to be nothing controversial with the deal. It received the unanimous approval of the Committee on Foreign Investment in the United States (CFIUS), a body set up in 1975 by President Ford to rule on the purchase of sensitive US businesses and assets during an earlier period of concern over massive foreign investment. It was rare for foreign deals to become the targets of this process and rarer still for them to be blocked. In 2006, the same year as the DP World affair, Qatar Petroleum underwent the slow and intrusive, though ultimately successful, process of gaining CFIUS approval for a joint project it had initiated with ConocoPhillips and ExxonMobil to develop the Golden Pass regasification facility in Texas. Unlike Qatar Petroleum's joint venture in Texas, the DP World deal encountered extensive opposition in Congress. New York senator Charles E. Schumer led the charge against the Dubai-based company. He was chair of the influential Congressional Joint Economic Committee and he targeted DP World as part of his wider campaign in support of tougher regulations to protect US assets from what he called 'non-economic motivations'.[40] Schumer gained bipartisan support for his efforts from those in the Senate and Congress preoccupied with the threat posed by Arab ownership of strategic infrastructure in major cities like New York after 9/11. In the case of Dubai World, the fact that two of the 9/11 hijackers were from the UAE and that Al-Qaeda was known to have raised some of its funds in the emirates was seen as particularly problematic.

Supporters of the deal dismissed such concerns. They pointed out that the government of Dubai, DP World's overall owner, had been an early signatory to the 'Container Security Initiative', by which US-bound cargo transiting through intermediary ports was pre-screened. President Bush actively urged Congress not to block the deal, and he reminded them that the war on terror demanded 'friendship with moderate Arab nations'. The following year Bush also backed Dubai's attempt to buy the NASDAQ stock exchange in New York, though in a concession to critics he promised that any such bid would undergo national security screening, a process that less than 5 per cent of inward investment deals had to undergo. Subsequently, the president spoke in more detail as to why he favoured such deals. 'We can protect our people against investments that jeopardize our national security', explained Bush, 'but it makes no sense to deny capital, including sovereign wealth funds, from access to the US markets.'[41]

Such arguments held little sway in Congress. There was widespread support for a much greater role for legislators in the process of approving acquisitions. Some congressmen and senators even supported a move to ban foreign governments from owning any vital US assets. Even after DP World sold the subsidiary that managed the US-based ports, ostensibly putting an end to the controversial affair, the House of Representatives passed a new law. This legislation – the Foreign Investment and National Security Act (FINSA) – mandated the CFIUS to investigate any business transactions undertaken by foreign governments or individuals who threatened national security or resulted in a controlling interest in anything that was deemed to be vital to the nation's security, safety and economic well-being. This included US critical infrastructure, notably water and power, as well as transportation companies, airports and ports and communications systems. In 2008, two congressmen from Virginia, Jim Moran, a Democrat, and Tom Davis, a Republican, set up a bipartisan task force to examine further the threat posed by SWFs to American economic and strategic interests.[42]

US-headquartered companies received more investment from Gulf SWFs than those based anywhere else in the world, but the US was not the only recipient country to take a tough stand against sovereign wealth funds. Dubai's efforts to buy Sweden's stock exchange and the international airport in Auckland, New Zealand, were both blocked. Investments emanating from other emerging economies faced a similar experience. In the United States, China's state oil company CNOOC was prevented from acquiring the Unocal oil company on national security grounds. Singapore's Temasek, one of the oldest and most respected funds, got into difficulties in Thailand after buying one of the country's largest telecom companies. In consultation with member state governments, EU technocrats in Brussels drew up guidelines that opened the way for the European Commission to act unilaterally to oppose investments on a case-by-case basis. Included in these measures was a mechanism that opened the way for legal action against investments that threatened public security, a free and diverse media and proper regulatory practices.[43]

In late 2007, the global banker's group, the Institute of International Finance (IIF), used open sources and insider knowledge to attempt to establish where Gulf oil revenues had ended up in the previous few years. Despite its expertise it could only trace the final destination of US$260 billion worth of investments, around half the estimated GCC spend.[44] Along with other anecdotal evidence, findings like this underscored the view that the biggest problem posed by SWFs was a lack of transparency. Norway's massive Government Pension Fund Global, which voluntarily disclosed its investments and returns on an annual basis, was a notable exception among the major players. Almost all the Gulf funds, including the biggest like ADIA, provided very little information about decision-making processes, strategies, goals or even asset holdings.

At the annual meeting of political, business and other global leaders at the World Economic Forum in Davos in early 2008, one of the main topics of conversation among delegates was the role of sovereign wealth funds. During a panel appearance the KIA's chief, Bader Mohammed Al-Sa'ad, was grilled so intensively about his fund's role and motives that he complained afterwards that he had been found 'guilty without having committed any crime'. By 2008, the US Treasury labelled SWFs 'large enough to be systemically significant',[45] and raised the issues of transparency and accountability with representatives of Gulf funds at Davos and at other high-profile international events and financial forums. A number of US Treasury and congressional delegations, including a bipartisan congressional fact-finding mission, also visited finance ministers and SWF chiefs across the Gulf specifically to address these concerns. More formally, officials from the EU, the IMF and the US Treasury also joined together to establish an International Working Group on SWFs. Based at the IMF's headquarters in Washington, DC, representatives from two dozen state-controlled funds, as well as officials from key nations and other multilateral organizations, also participated.

This working group was mandated to draw up a set of guidelines that would contribute to a more positive international investment environment by fostering trust between wealth funds and recipient countries. The upshot was the publication of a voluntary code of conduct made up of twenty-three 'Principles and Practices', known as the Santiago Principles. Initially, this document was not well received in Gulf financial circles. The governor of the UAE Central Bank issued a statement on behalf of thirteen countries that argued that the IMF lacked the expertise to draw up regulations to police wealth funds. The head of Dubai World, the parent company of DP World, called the new regulations 'discriminatory'. Bader Mohammed Al-Sa'ad of the KIA argued that they were unfair because they required SWFs to undergo more scrutiny than hedge funds or private equity funds.[46] Qatar's emir told overseas visitors that his country had money to invest but feared that restrictions might prevent good deals from taking place.

In private, some Gulf officials expressed the view that the hostile reception their funds had met had little to do with transparency or national security. They noted that although the oil price rise of the early 2000s was of the same order of magnitude as the one that occurred during the 1970s, it had not fuelled inflation, or resulted in economic downturn or unemployment on anywhere near the same scale. They also argued that critics of Gulf SWFs were unable to present even one major example of a regional fund abusing its power or using investments for non-commercial ends.

And they pointed out that the reinvestment of huge oil revenues in the international economy by SWFs, as well as other investment vehicles, had sustained economic growth and created many jobs, by some estimates over one million in Europe alone between 2003 and 2008. For all these reasons, the 'protectionist rhetoric and rash regulation',[47] as one top ADIA official put it, seemed unnecessary, alarmist and unfair. Others argued that the new restrictive regulations being proposed on the grounds of vague and undisclosed national interests made sense for dealing with Russia and China but were unnecessary for the Gulf. Others again went further and claimed that attempts to limit the freedom of action of SWFs undermined one of the fundamental pillars of the international economic system – an open investment and trade environment. Some even speculated that the targeting of wealth funds was the price that the Gulf and other emerging economies had to pay for daring to challenge the West's historic dominance of the financial markets. To back up the argument they noted that sovereign wealth fund spending reached its highest levels in the second half of 2007 and the first half of 2008 at exactly the same time as they faced the most vocal criticism and had to fend off the toughest demands for regulation.

Those who held the wealth funds to be the 'bogeymen of international finance'[48] had little time for such arguments but they did garner some sympathy among influential and informed financial commentators and policymakers. The attacks on wealth funds, explained one, had tipped over into 'outright prejudice and irrational finger-pointing', and critics should either prove their claims or 'cease chucking accusations around'.[49] US treasury secretary Henry Paulson worked hard to reassure SWF bosses not to be offended by either the criticism they received or the scrutiny they faced. In meetings with local leaders during a visit to the Gulf in the second half of 2008, Paulson dealt with SWF practices as a matter of priority, even above the issues of terror financing, Iranian sanctions and Iraqi reconstruction. Paulson's diplomatic efforts were part of an attempt by the Bush administration to improve relations with Gulf governments after the DP World affair. Top Gulf officials appreciated these conciliatory efforts. They did not want to risk strategic relations with Washington over one controversial business deal, especially as the White House had opposed Congress on the matter. They also welcomed the American decision to introduce legislation that only required the review of cases that raised national security concerns. They were much more resentful of moves in other parts of the world, especially in Europe, to place strict controls on SWF investments in a wide range of economic sectors. In order to prevent this from happening, funds began their own diplomatic offensive and even lobbied European recipient countries to adopt the more limited American approach.

ADIA cemented its position as the largest Gulf SWF in these boom years. In late 2007, it gained extensive international attention when it bought a 4.9 per cent holding in America's biggest bank, the struggling Citigroup. From the outset it actively attempted to minimize negative publicity surrounding this deal. First, it made sure that the stake it took in Citigroup was under the required reporting limit. It then declined its right to have a management role or even to appoint a representative to the institution's board of directors so that it could not be accused of trying to interfere in the running of the bank. Despite such caution, the deal unavoidably catapulted the debate on SWFs to the top of the international agenda. One commentator even described the ADIA investment in Citigroup as the 'single most important event' during that period.[50] To deal with this unwanted attention ADIA hired a major American public relations firm and embarked on a strategy of compromise and conflict avoidance in its investment dealings. Top ADIA officials visited numerous nations including the United Kingdom, France, Germany, Japan and Australia to reassure them over the fund's intentions and to restate their previous commitment not to use investments as an instrument of foreign policy. There was even a short-lived proposal to send ADIA goodwill ambassadors to every individual American state that was home to an ADIA investment.

Hamad Al-Suwaidi, a senior ADIA and Abu Dhabi government official, also agreed to co-chair the International Working Group of Sovereign Wealth Funds alongside Jaime Caruana, a high-level IMF official from Spain. The fund's boss, Ahmed bin Zayed Al-Nahyan, acknowledged that the unwanted attention it received over the Citibank deal had taken its toll, and stated that 'trust must be earned over time'.[51] In line with this thinking, ADIA became the first major SWF to reach a bilateral agreement with a recipient country on new principles for investment when it accepted the terms offered by the US Treasury in 2008. The agreement was categorical in its insistence that SWF investment decisions be made 'solely on commercial grounds' and that such decisions should not be made to 'advance directly or indirectly the geopolitical goals of the controlling government'. In return, the American government promised that it would not block legitimate deals or discriminate between different kinds of potential investors. According to officials in Abu Dhabi, the Bush administration had pushed for this bilateral code of conduct in order to pre-empt the introduction of much tougher new anti-SWF legislation in Congress.

Yousef Al-Otaiba, a senior Abu Dhabi official, also wrote to a number of foreign governments to inform them explicitly that neither ADIA nor any of the other, smaller, local wealth funds were motivated by power or political influence. 'It is important to be absolutely clear', Al-Otaiba explained, 'that the Abu Dhabi government has never and will never use its investment organizations or individual investments as a foreign policy tool.'[52] Sheikh Khalifa bin Zayed Al-Nahyan, Abu Dhabi's ruler and the UAE's president, also did his best to smooth over the situation on a political level. He played down the size of ADIA, telling the Arab media in early 2008 that the US$800 billion figure widely attributed to the world's largest SWF was 'exaggerated'. He also emphasized that all of the UAE's funds, not only ADIA, operated 'according to economic principles, not political considerations'.[53]

These wide-ranging efforts by ADIA and Abu Dhabi officials to cool passions and find common ground underscored the fact that, despite their frustrations, most senior decision makers in the Gulf wanted to find a compromise on this sensitive issue. In particular, they wanted to convince multinational organizations, such as the EU and the IMF, as well as the national governments of recipient countries, that it was unnecessary to introduce legislation to control SWF investments. With this in mind, and despite their initial scepticism about the Santiago Principles, in 2009 top KIA officials hosted a meeting of representatives from all the SWFs that had signed up to the framework. Those who attended this get-together in Kuwait City agreed to establish a permanent but informal forum for SWFs and also agreed on new proposals to make wealth funds more transparent and accountable. Commenting on this new willingness to embrace more regulation and transparency going forward, the Abu Dhabi-based media outlet *Al-Iqtisadiya* called on local SWFs to publish regular reports on investments and assets.[54] Soon afterwards, ADIA became the first Gulf fund to publish its financial results and make public its long-term investment strategy.

In the final account, the Gulf States needed to invest overseas as part of their long-term diversification plans. They had used their wealth funds to take advantage of the rising oil price and the massive redistribution of income from oil consumers to producers in the first decade of the 2000s to do this on a previously unprecedented scale. This undoubtedly, as one commentator aptly summed up, injected considerable 'fuzziness'[55] into the international financial system, which in turn generated an unprecedented level of international attention, concern, distrust and antagonism. Nor did it look as if this was about to change. A mid-2007 report by Morgan

Stanley estimated that the asset value of SWFs could reach US$12 trillion in less than a decade. The Gulf region, with its blurred lines between public and private ownership, would inevitably be at the centre of this evolving form of financial power. Three of the top six SWFs in the world by asset size were located in the UAE, Saudi Arabia and Kuwait. This made it impossible to overlook transparency concerns, especially as compliance with the new Santiago Principles was also limited in practice. A report by the Carnegie Endowment for International Peace found that only four funds were close to complying with the Santiago Principles, none of which was from the Gulf. Writing in mid-2007, Nouriel Roubini warned that if sovereign wealth funds grew too large while their activities remained 'opaque', financial protectionism on a global scale would be all but inevitable. Despite such stark predictions, concerns over the threat posed by Gulf wealth funds started to fade within the year as the global financial crisis began to preoccupy the thinking of politicians, bankers and economists alike and to play havoc with the lives of ordinary people across the world. As the next chapter shows, this led to a complete re-evaluation of the contribution that wealth funds, and their governments, could play in finding a solution to the financial turmoil that plagued the international community.

CHAPTER 6

SHEIKH DOWN

'Capital goes where it's welcome and stays where it's well treated.'
– Walter Wriston

On a balmy summer evening in July 2012, a laser show lit up the London skyline while the London Philharmonic Orchestra blasted out a selection of classic tunes across the River Thames. The occasion was not a national holiday. Nor was it a royal birth or wedding though there were royals, as well as other dignitaries, in attendance. The celebration marked the completion of a building. This was not any ordinary building. This was Europe's tallest building, the Shard, a seventy-two-floor state-of-the-art luxury tower located in the heart of the British capital at London Bridge. More than a decade earlier a British property developer named Irving Sellar had proposed building what he called Europe's 'first vertical town'. For the next eight years Sellar found himself in a constant battle with planners, environmentalists and local community groups. His plan to erect a giant building on top of a train station in a residential area in one of the busiest parts of central London led to a number of legal actions and government hearings. Finally, in 2008, just as he was ready to break ground and start construction, the global financial crisis foiled his chances of finding the money to fund such a risky project. His dream was only saved when the government of Qatar stepped in to take over 80 per cent of the equity in the project, ensuring that Sellar had the financial backing needed to bring his vision of the Shard to life.

This 'vertical town' in central London was completed four years later. Once launched it served as a potent reminder to all passing under it or gazing at it from far across the city that the Arab Gulf, home to only 1 per cent of the world's population, had successfully transformed its financial resources into a towering physical presence at the heart of the Western world. This achievement was all the more impressive given that Qatar took over the funding of this hugely ambitious and expensive project during a four-year period when the global financial markets faced meltdown and Western economies struggled to keep afloat. These near-calamitous events were triggered initially by the sub-prime mortgage crisis in the US housing market. This was made worse by high oil prices, a fall in the value of the dollar, rising inflation and the staggering collapse of Lehman Brothers, the global financial services firm, in mid-September 2008. Panic was rife and predictions of financial Armageddon were not far behind. Dominique Strauss-Kahn, the flamboyant and soon to be scandal-ridden IMF chief, even predicted a 'Great Depression'[1] that would wipe out fifty million jobs across the world.

In late October 2008, in an attempt to forestall such calamitous events, forty-three Asian and European leaders gathered in Beijing for a two-day meeting. A few weeks later, President George W. Bush hosted a summit of the Group of Twenty (G-20) in Washington, DC. The original proposal to convene this meeting of the world's twenty biggest economies had been made by European leaders. The US had endorsed the idea and agreed to serve as host. Those attending disagreed on many things, including who and what was responsible for the crisis, but there was consensus on a number of key points relating to what needed to be done to fix it. All agreed, for example, that it was vital to prop up the faltering banking system very quickly and that achieving this would require no less than US$750 billion up front and would ultimately cost trillions of dollars. World leaders also agreed on one further point – that the oil- and gas-rich Gulf Arabs would play a crucial role in averting possible global financial meltdown by buying assets and investing in struggling economies across the developed world.

By the time the West began to realize the severity of the economic crisis it faced in 2008, the oil price had hit US$100 a barrel. By July it had risen to US$147, further enriching the Arab Gulf, which by now was home to about 45 per cent of total global SWF assets. A study by the New York-based Council on Foreign Relations estimated that during 2008, as much of the world rushed towards economic crisis, the oil producers of the Gulf pocketed a total of US$300 billion in oil revenues. Estimates from other sources were even higher, placing GCC oil revenues in that same year at a staggering US$575 billion, a US$400 billion increase on 2003 revenues.[2] Whether the lower or higher estimates were correct was irrelevant. The Gulf States had massive reserves of cash at their disposal, between

US$1.5 trillion and US$2.5 trillion according to the US Treasury. Saudi Arabia had begun the decade as an economic basket case, heavily indebted and losing its dominant grip on the oil markets. By the time of the global economic crisis less than a decade later, revenues exceeded spending by the highest margins ever, with 2010 seeing the greatest cash surplus in the kingdom's history. Even Oman, traditionally the GCC member state with the lowest per capita oil revenues, saw a 50 per cent rise in energy income in the years leading up to the global crisis.

Officials tasked with preventing the possible collapse of the Western economic model now explored how these Gulf 'liquidity pools',[3] as former US treasury secretary John W. Snow termed them, could play a role in resolving the unprecedented crisis. Prior to the November G-20 meeting in Washington, senior Western officials like the US Treasury's Robert M. Kimmitt had visited the Gulf to brief regional leaders on the upcoming meeting, to coordinate follow-up action, and to address the role of SWFs in tackling the financial crisis. Kimmitt had published a widely discussed article in the January 2008 issue of the prestigious policy journal *Foreign Affairs* that presented SWF investment strategies in a positive light.[4] This earned him valuable goodwill during his trip to the Gulf. He also benefited from the fact, as the last chapter showed, that despite the DP World affair, the Bush administration was viewed as a much stronger backer of Gulf wealth funds than the governments of other major Western economies. During his visit Kimmitt made a promise to the Gulf States that they could expect much better treatment going forward than they had experienced during the DP affair a few years earlier. The US, he explained, had learnt much from the 2006 'controversy' and Gulf investors would find that 'much has changed, and changed for the good'.[5]

Some Western bankers, regulators and politicians were convinced that SWFs were inherently 'risk averse' and that this tendency made them unlikely to jump on the 'bail-out bandwagon'. Instead, they argued, these investment vehicles would choose to play it 'super safe' until calmer times prevailed. This view seemed to be supported by some statements emanating from senior Gulf figures. 'We move our ship at a slower pace,' explained Bahrain's central bank governor, 'avoiding the turbulence of the high seas.'[6] Many others rejected this assessment. They believed that Gulf governments would use their SWFs and other investment vehicles to become lenders of 'first resort' and that this would fill the vacuum caused by the contraction of the world economy. Henry Paulson, Snow's successor at the US Treasury, argued that the crisis offered the Gulf States 'an historic opportunity to make investments in foreign countries'. Speaking at a press conference in Dubai at the end of October 2008, at a time when the US was looking for financial support in the Gulf to save its failing car industry, Paulson's deputy at the Treasury, Kimmitt, offered a different explanation as to why the Arab Gulf would play a role. The GCC member states, he argued, had to get involved in rescuing the global economy because what happened had 'ramifications for all countries', not only those in the West.[7]

Top IMF officials and political leaders from across the Western world echoed the sentiments of senior American figures. Past worries over the national security threat posed by Gulf SWFs remained, but they were no longer a priority. In a matter of months those same characteristics that had made SWFs so problematic – their almost unlimited resources, lack of transparency and top-down structures that allowed for quick investment decisions – were now hugely attractive weapons in the war to stabilize the global financial system. It was not, as one incisive commentator on the rise of SWFs explained, the absolute size of these funds that made them so interesting, it was the pace at which they acted and the speed of their growth.[8] Observers marvelled over how, for example, it had only taken forty-eight hours of negotiations between ADIA and Citigroup before the Abu Dhabi fund agreed to pay out US$7.5 billion for a 4.9 per cent stake in the bank in 2007.

Some of the public statements coming out of the Gulf at this time also suggested that the region would play the role that many in the West hoped it would. The UAE's Omar bin Sulaiman predicted that 'if there is a light at the end of the tunnel, it is on this side of the world'. Abdullah bin Zayed Al-Nahyan sent out a similar message. Membership in the global system 'entails obligations', explained the UAE's foreign minister, and his government would do all it could to help find a solution to the crisis.[9] At the end of 2008, in a move that some interpreted as the Arab Gulf's practical acknowledgment of its new centrality in the international economy, delegations from all six GCC member states participated in a two-day 'GCC Europe Expo' held at London's massive Olympia Exhibition Hall. This was the first event of its kind ever held. It took place at a time when Gulf sovereign wealth funds and private investors from the region were spending vast amounts buying up Western, in particular European, assets. The purpose of the Expo event was to showcase the Arab Gulf as a dynamic, business-friendly and increasingly significant emerging market.

During the boom years, the United Kingdom was the Western state most open to SWF investments. Once those golden days came to a sudden end, British prime minister Gordon Brown took a lead role in the unfolding drama. In the summer of 2008, as the oil price climbed to record levels and

Saudi Arabia was reportedly making over US$2 billion a day from selling oil, Brown called for an oil summit and a 'new deal' between producers and consumers. Long before the full extent of the global crisis was known, he had been scheduled to visit Qatar, the UAE and Saudi Arabia in late 2008 at the head of a delegation promoting Anglo-Gulf trade and investment. As his trip drew nearer Brown became increasingly outspoken in singling out 'oil-rich countries', as well as major emerging economies like China, as having a 'vital role to play' in helping the IMF to stop the financial 'contagion' from spreading. He made his case in an uncompromising manner. He was going to the Gulf to raise funds for the IMF, he explained bluntly, because the Gulf States had the means to help and should do so. That did not mean, he insisted, that he would be going to the region with a 'begging bowl'.[10]

Over the course of his four-day visit Brown expounded on these points in several lengthy private meetings with rulers and top financial officials in Saudi Arabia, Qatar and the UAE. Eight months earlier the United Kingdom and Saudi Arabia had set up a new joint investment company to boost cooperation. Now in his meeting with King Abdullah, over dinner in the Saudi ruler's private aquarium, Brown was clear: Saudi Arabia was one of the most important economic players in the world and it had no choice but to play a central role in helping solve the financial crisis.[11] The British prime minister had chosen a risky strategy and his junior officials looked to play down his bluntness in their own briefings to the media. But his strategy appeared to be well timed and effective. After his own meeting with Brown, the UAE's president lauded the British leader's efforts on behalf of the international community, though he did not make any specific mention of what the UAE would do in terms of handing over hard cash.

The organizers of the November G-20 summit in Washington had refused Qatar's request for an invitation. US officials, led by Kimmitt, had tried to soften this rejection by promising that the meeting would discuss ways to bring valued partners like Qatar into the deliberations. Subsequently, Qatar joined more than twenty other small and medium-sized states in the World Economic Forum's Global Redesign Initiative (GRI), a mechanism that enabled them to feed into the G-20 process.[12] A few weeks after Brown's visit to Doha in late 2008, it was widely reported that Qatar's prime minister, Hamad bin Jassim Al-Thani, had made a substantive commitment of financial support. Brown met the Qatari prime minister again in Davos in late January 2009 and in London in early February in order to hammer out what this support meant in practical terms, as well as to discuss further possible Qatari investment opportunities in the United Kingdom.[13]

In a seminal article written in 1975, an earlier era also defined by Western economic stress and the flow of massive oil revenues into the Arab Gulf, the renowned Arab economist Yusif A. Sayigh argued that the oil-rich Gulf had no moral or economic obligation to help struggling Western economies.[14] Almost a quarter of a century later, similar sentiments continued to be heard all over the GCC and across the rest of the Arab world. There was an overwhelming belief in the Gulf region in particular that the financial crisis was a Western rather than a global problem in terms of causes and consequences. Resentment was also rife over the fact that those same governments that had only recently condemned Gulf wealth funds and attempted to regulate and place restrictions on them were now lobbying hard for their help in finding a solution to the global financial crisis.

In an interview in a Gulf newspaper, the financial commentator Mohammed Ali Yasin put into words what many were thinking – Western requests for help were nothing short of 'hypocrisy'. The high-profile Egyptian economist Ahmad El-Sayed El-Naggar argued that there was 'no acceptable justification' for the Western request for GCC financial support. His Kuwaiti counterpart Jassem Al-Saadoun cautioned policy-makers in the region to avoid 'politically motivated' decisions to invest sovereign wealth into struggling Western institutions. He also urged them to resist what he termed the long-time obsession of Gulf leaders, going back to the mid-1970s, to show the rest of the world that they were responsible and important global actors. The controversial Bahraini parliamentarian Jassim Al-Saeedi accused Brown of acting 'against the interests of the Gulf nations'. He also warned foreigners who wanted help that 'we are not ready to allow our wealth and [financial] power to be offered to help rescue the world for free'. Some in the region went further and presented the financial crisis as an instrument of Western military and political domination over the Arab world and even, according to one outspoken critic, a form of Western 'economic warfare' by other means.[15]

Mainstream Gulf officials at all levels refrained from making such charged statements but they did make it clear, in the words of one Saudi official, that they had no desire to become a 'milch cow' for the world economy. The Saudi finance minister, Ibrahim Al-Assaf, rejected the prevalent assumption that his government and other Gulf nations were 'coming to pay the bill'. Instead, he explained: 'We are not going to pay more or less than others. We have been playing our role responsibly and we will continue to play our role, but we are not going to finance the institutions just because we have large reserves.'[16] In an interview with a Kuwaiti newspaper soon after his meeting with Brown, King Abdullah of Saudi Arabia made a similar point. Neither his kingdom nor any of Saudi Arabia's allies in the GCC had any intention of bailing out the West. Apart from anything else, he explained, it was a matter of numbers. The crisis was so serious that it was going to cost trillions to fix. Gulf billions would not help even if they were made readily available.

Top Gulf officials also now stressed that any financial support should be linked to the reform of the global financial system that acknowledged the end of Western dominance and the increasingly important role of emerging economies in financial decision making. During his 2008 visit to the Gulf, Kimmitt argued that invitations to important forums including G-20 meetings should be based, at least in part, on the willingness of countries to contribute financially to solving the crisis. In line with this thinking, Qatar's prime minister called for the global financial system to be 'redefined'. The governor of the UAE's central bank was less diplomatic. There would be no more funds 'without extra voice and extra recognition'.[17] Other officials got into more detail on what this might actually entail. Saudi Arabia was already a top contributor to the IMF and for years had been pushing in vain for an increase in its power inside the organization, which instead wanted to prioritize the reallocation of quotas away from developed and wealthy nations towards poorer emerging markets. The kingdom's finance minister now demanded that in return for more money, Gulf States should receive a larger percentage of shares and voting rights in global financial institutions, first and foremost the IMF. He had the backing from many in the Arab world. Nasser Al-Saidi, the former Lebanese economy and trade minister, who served as the chief economist of the Dubai Financial Centre during the crisis, urged the Arab Gulf to remember that its role had changed. It was now, he argued, a 'global actor', its policymakers needed to transition from being 'decision takers to decision makers', and in line with this new standing should hold out for 'a place at the table'.[18]

During the early months of the crisis, Gordon Brown had insisted that he had not offered the Gulf leaders 'political promises' on the Palestine Question, Iran or anything else in return for their financial support. Rather, he held out the opportunity for Gulf States to engage in what he called 'a dialogue on opportunities' in exchange for any contribution they made to the stabilization of the global financial system. Brown also called for international financial institutions like the IMF and G-20 to hand over more power to emerging economies including those from the Arab Gulf. He even talked in terms of a 'new global order, fairer, more stable' rising from the ashes of the global crisis.[19] Other Western leaders put forward similar suggestions and made their own promises. Just a few years earlier Chancellor Angela Merkel had championed tough legislation in Germany to counter the threat of SWFs. Now she was linking SWF support to a greater global role for the Gulf States. Following her meeting with the king of Bahrain, Merkel promised that if the Gulf played a full in role solving the financial crisis, its 'responsibility' would 'grow', it would have a greater say in the power structures of international finance, and would even have more 'responsibility for peace and stability in the world'.[20]

One practical consideration that Gulf leaders had to take into account as they calculated the size of any financial contributions to the IMF-led bail-out was how much they could afford given their existing financial obligations and commitments. In the second half of 2008, as the financial crisis took hold, the Gulf States were hit by record agricultural commodity prices. Inflation was also on the rise. It had already reached double-digit levels in Oman, the UAE and Qatar and was hovering just below that level in Saudi Arabia. At the same time, the oil price was starting to fall. It peaked in July 2008 at around US$147 a barrel. By October it had fallen to under US$65 a barrel. By the time Gulf leaders met in Oman in December 2008 it had fallen again to a quarter of the level it had been the previous July. The global downturn in international travel and tourism that followed the outbreak of the financial crisis also hit the GCC hard and had a knock-on effect on a number of economic sectors including transport, construction, insurance and banking.

The collapse in the value of global stocks and shares posed a potentially much bigger financial problem for the Gulf States. In previous years, Gulf SWFs had all increasingly prioritized investments in riskier equities over safer options, like bonds. These were among the worst-hit investments when the global markets began to implode. Some of the most high-profile Gulf funds, in particular those from Qatar (QIA), Abu Dhabi (ADIA) and Kuwait (KIA), suffered major losses. As the KIA's Bader Mohammed Al-Sa'ad admitted somewhat sanguinely, his fund had 'not really hedge[d] against down turning markets' and was paying the price. By one estimate Gulf funds lost around US$350 billion between them when the world's stock markets crashed. This was about a quarter of the value of their assets. Other estimates put the figure nearer to 50 per cent, which roughly translated into a loss equivalent to one year's combined oil revenues – about US$450 billion. Individual funds reported massive losses in Europe. Abu Dhabi's Mubadala and IPIC funds lost around US$5 billion between them in 2011 alone.[21] The Saudi Arabian Monetary Agency (SAMA) was a notable exception to this trend. This fund managed the majority of the kingdom's foreign reserves. It had always taken a long-term and conservative approach to investments, and focused mainly on government securities. While other Gulf funds lost hundreds of billions between them from late 2008 onwards, SAMA increased the value of its portfolio by around US$150 billion as it built up its holdings of gold, cash and bonds.[22]

These massive global losses led to a discussion over whether the era of the Gulf sovereign wealth funds, short lived as it was, had come to an end. A senior official in Qatar's wealth fund, the QIA, told an audience in Dubai that his country was taking a 'long holiday' from investing in private deals in the West. But there was no consensus on this point, even within the same countries. Another Qatari government figure downplayed the impact of the credit crisis on investment plans, saying that the country had no intention of pulling out of global holdings in depressed economies.[23] In his own private discussions with foreign visitors to the kingdom, Qatar's prime minister, Hamad bin Jassim Al-Thani, was adamant that there would be no change in investment policies and that the QIA would continue to be active overseas. His emir was even more positive. He described the financial crisis as an investment 'opportunity that will not be repeated in the next 20 years'.[24]

ADIA and the eight other government-controlled state investment vehicles in Abu Dhabi took a similar position. All targeted developed Western economies in order to take advantage of the falling value of assets across numerous sectors. IPIC, for example, planned to grow its portfolio from US$15 billion to US$20 billion in the five years from 2009. Oman and Bahrain had only established SWF-like investment vehicles when the oil boom of the early 2000s got under way. Prior to that, both kingdoms had wanted to avoid drawing unnecessary attention to their financial activities overseas. But now they also recommitted to international investments. In 2009, for example, Bahrain's state-owned pension fund announced that it planned to put US$2.25 billion, the equivalent of half of its cash holdings, into bonds and shares in Europe and North America. Saudi Arabia had also refrained from setting up its first SWF – Sanabil Al-Saudia – until mid-2008 to avoid placing its international investment strategy in the spotlight. This fund was established with an initial cash injection of US$5.3 billion and was managed by the Ministry of Finance's Public Investment Fund (PIF). As a way of neutralizing any foreign backlash, Sanabil officials insisted that their fund was modelled on the most transparent SWF of all, Norway's Government Pension Fund Global.

Speaking at a meeting of GCC interior ministers in Doha in early November 2008, Saudi Arabia's Prince Nayef Abdul Aziz Al-Saud expressed 'confidence' that Gulf citizens would 'not be shaken' by the fallout from the economic downturn.[25] Other local leaders were just as adamant that despite the challenges they faced, their countries were sufficiently well protected to survive the global financial crisis intact. The oil price was down but compared to a decade earlier it was still very high. The region also continued to provide a quarter of the world's oil needs, and still controlled 25 per cent of the world's natural gas reserves and 45 per cent of its oil reserves. As GCC secretary general Abdul Rahman Al-Attiyah calmly observed, in the final account all Arab Gulf countries had the 'resources to weather this crisis'.[26] Others were even more positive. The UAE, explained the country's president, Khalifa bin Zayed Al-Nahyan, would not only absorb the impact of the crisis and 'overcome many of its ramifications',[27] it would also prosper during the crisis. The Saudi king confidently predicted that neither the falling oil price nor the ongoing global financial crisis would impact negatively on his kingdom's spending plans. His senior officials even argued that the global situation made Saudi Arabia the safest place to do business in the world. This was in line with the attempts by other key Saudi figures to promote the kingdom as an 'attractive alternative' to traditional markets at this time, as Ali Al-Naimi, the Saudi oil minister and a highly regarded former president and CEO of Saudi Aramco, put it.[28]

At the start of the financial crisis Joseph Ackerman, chairman of the board of Deutsche Bank Group, had argued that the Gulf's spending on infrastructure would compensate globally for the US economic downturn. Once the crisis started the UAE committed around US$300 billion to infrastructure and property-related projects. Qatar followed suit and announced that it would spend on average an extra US$20 billion a year in the medium term on new infrastructure.[29] Such demonstrations of positivity aside, the Gulf States were not immune to the fallout of what was happening around them. Initially, some, like Saudi oil minister Al-Naimi, had hoped that the crisis would have the beneficial outcome of drawing even higher levels of international investment into the region as traditional destinations for funds became less and less attractive. Others, like Ahmad bin Hamad Al-Nuami, the CEO of the Arab Petroleum Investments Corporation, disagreed.[30] He rightly predicted a decline in inward investment into the Gulf, especially for major infrastructural projects. There was also a flight of foreign money already in the region into more developed markets, which added to the lack of liquidity across the Gulf. Falling oil revenues, down by half in 2009 over the previous year, and a lack of available credit on the international markets, also contributed to the slowdown in domestic development, as projects worth hundreds of billions of dollars were put on hold. Kuwait's foreign minister, Mohammed Sabah Al-Salem

Al-Sabah, estimated that around 60 per cent of infrastructural projects had been postponed or scrapped across the region because of the worsening financial situation.

At an emergency meeting of finance ministers and central bankers in late October 2008, it was agreed that the GCC member states must present a united front in handling the crisis, especially as it impacted on their own economic well-being. This got off to a promising start when all the GCC partners endorsed Saudi Arabia's attendance at the hastily organized Washington G-20 summit in November. In the wake of that meeting Saudi Arabia hosted a second emergency meeting of Gulf central bank governors and finance ministers to brief them on the G-20 discussions they had participated in. During the final few days of 2008, Gulf leaders met in Muscat for the annual GCC summit. On its eve, GCC Secretary General Al-Attiyah promised that the global crisis would top the agenda. In his welcome address to delegates, Oman's sultan repeated this promise and called for joint efforts to deal with the global financial crisis.

Despite such rhetoric and the regular high-level meetings on the crisis that followed the Muscat summit, there was little coordinated GCC action. One day after GCC finance ministers agreed publicly that the entire region's banks could withstand the crisis in the global financial sector without any government assistance, Kuwait intervened to prop up Gulf Bank, the country's second largest bank. The other five GCC member states also chose to pursue their own independent responses to the crisis, judging this to be the best way to prevent the destabilization of their financial sectors and wider economies. Though they acted separately from each other they faced many of the same challenges and adopted similar responses to deal with them. They guaranteed bank deposits, cut the cost of borrowing and provided loans to citizens to boost saver and investor confidence and to stimulate the market. They also pumped capital into shaky stock markets and took major stakes in the investment and property portfolios of potentially vulnerable financial institutions.

The government of Qatar made the biggest commitment. It bought up the entire investment holdings of local banks to shore up their position. Later it purchased their toxic real estate portfolios at a cost of almost US$5 billion. The IMF described this move as a 'timely and decisive intervention'.[31] This understated the scale of Qatar's precautionary action. On a per capita basis and relative to the size of Qatar's economy, this was a greater financial commitment than the US$700 billion that Washington pumped into its own banks to keep them afloat over the same period. This had the desired effect and ensured that the kingdom was able to withstand any conceivable direct financial threat that emerged over the course of the crisis.

Some of Qatar's GCC partners fared less well. During the 1970s and 1980s, Kuwait had led the Arab Gulf in developing a cutting-edge financial services sector. In subsequent decades it was overtaken in a number of key areas by Saudi Arabia, Bahrain, the UAE and Qatar. For years senior officials had privately complained that short-sighted leaders and populist politicians had been responsible for the fact that their country lagged behind its GCC partners in everything from corporate governance to regulatory frameworks. The start of the global financial crisis highlighted these systemic vulnerabilities very clearly. The kingdom's stock exchange went into free fall, losing half its value in early 2009. Soon afterwards, Global Investment House, one of the biggest of the hundred or so investment companies in Kuwait, defaulted on a US$200 million loan repayment. At the same time, as noted above, the government had to pour millions in to prop up Gulf Bank.[32]

Traditionally SWFs had not been used to fund current spending at home. During the global downturn, Gulf governments began to redirect a much larger percentage of these funds' resources to support rising domestic spending at a time of reduced credit, falling oil revenues and shrinking stock portfolios. Gulf finance ministers and central bank governors first discussed using energy revenues at home at the end of 2008. This move was endorsed at the Arab Economic Summit held early in the following year. This inevitably impacted on the amount of money available to spend abroad. SAMA's top official Hamad Al-Sayyari explained that Saudi Arabia's first SWF had only been allocated US$5 billion on its launch because the country's main focus by that time was on domestic rather than overseas investment.[33]

Though contrary to the basic mandate of wealth funds – investment in income-earning assets that rise in value over time for the benefit of future generations – this diversion of funds back home was popular with local populations. From the very earliest days of the financial crisis KIA officials acknowledged that the main concern of the average Kuwaiti citizen was how the government was going to stop the fall in stock market values and stimulate the local economy. In the past, the KIA had rarely used its funds earmarked for overseas investments at home but as pressure mounted in the media and parliament, and as angry citizens protested outside the country's stock exchange, the fund's top official called a rare televised press conference. During his appearance, Bader Mohammed Al-Sa'ad reassured citizens that the KIA would not neglect the local economy and that its resources would be used at home rather than be sent abroad to bail out foreign institutions. There was a precedent for this. In 2006, the Kuwaiti government instructed the KIA to inject US$200 million into the country's stock exchange when it experienced sudden and significant losses after five years of growth. Now two years later, at the end of 2008, the KIA had new orders from the government to pump several billion dollars into plummeting Kuwaiti stocks. It was also tasked with propping up local banks and struggling financial institutions, keeping afloat investors and small businesses and helping fund current expenditure. Subsequently the KIA was required to institutionalize these new roles by establishing a fund worth billions to provide support for the fragile commercial property market and to invest long term in the country's stock market in order to provide a safety net for local investors.[34]

KIA officials attempted to put a brave face on their fund's new role. They explained that the decision to refocus on the domestic market was a voluntary one made free of government influence. They added, for good measure, that there were many attractive investment opportunities at home and that the KIA would not use its resources to keep failed companies, financial institutions or real estate deals artificially alive. In a direct challenge to this, in early 2010 members of Kuwait's robust and outspoken national assembly drafted a bill that, if passed into law, would have required the KIA to pay off up to US$20 billion of outstanding citizen loans.[35] There was one precedent for this. After the expulsion of Saddam's troops from Kuwait in early 1991, the government had paid off citizen debts. However, there was also a precedent for opposing this demand. In 2005, as the oil price rose, the government withstood pressure from politicians to use higher oil revenues to forgo the private debts of Kuwaiti citizens for a second time. Now, five years later, the government once more blocked such a demand in order to protect the KIA from squandering any more of its resources on lost causes.

The mini-crisis experienced by Kuwait paled into insignificance in comparison to events in Dubai. Between 2000 and 2008 Dubai's economy grew on average at 13 per cent a year, a growth rate higher even than that achieved by China and India over the same period.[36] Few expected Dubai to maintain its unmatched growth levels indefinitely. Donald Trump, the larger than life American real estate mogul who had several property and golfing interests in the emirate, even baulked at the situation. Dubai 'will never always grow at 25% per year', he rightly argued in 2006.[37] Most experts believed that the worst-case scenario for Dubai Inc. during the global financial crisis would be a slowdown in growth compared to previous astounding levels. The first half of 2008 showed little evidence that things were cooling down. Instead, it saw record levels of foreign investment with over US$2 billion pouring into the emirate to fund 300 projects in the first six months of the year.

Some informed critics had argued for years that Dubai faced problems other than an unsustainable growth rate. They argued that Dubai's financial model was vulnerable because it lacked regulation and oversight. In the emirate itself, these warnings were dismissed as the jealous musings of Dubai's partners and competitors inside and outside the Gulf. After all, by the summer of 2008 Dubai could claim to have achieved the Holy Grail of Gulf development and the one thing that all GCC member states had aspired to since the oil crisis of 1973 – a successful model of economic diversification. Dubai had never been oil rich but by the mid-2000s the non-oil sector of the economy accounted for more than 95 per cent of GDP. The free zones were booming, hotels were full, and major deals that attracted worldwide attention were being announced on a daily basis. The UN ranked Dubai as one of the twenty most attractive economies in the world for foreign investment. The emirate was home to the biggest, tallest and most expensive property developments under way anywhere. 'The World', for example, was constructed in the shape of the globe. It cost US$14 billion and on completion it comprised 300 islands ranging in price from US$15 million to US$250 million. It attracted an eclectic group of buyers. These included an Irish business consortium that planned to develop the island of Ireland into an Irish-themed resort. A Dubai-based fashion house also purchased an island with the goal of creating the first territory that was totally dedicated to fashion. There were also rumours that the singer Rod Stewart had bought Scotland even though a Scottish island was not part of the plans and that Brad Pitt and Angelina Jolie had purchased Ethiopia. Not content with having built 'The World', in January 2008 its developer announced plans for an even more ambitious project – 'The Universe'. On completion, this archipelago of islands designed to replicate the moon and planets would to take pride of place among the US$60 billion worth of offshore projects in the pipeline, all of which required extending the coastline from 70 to around 1,000 kilometres.

Below the surface this trend-setting, go-getting, no-limits emirate faced some profound structural problems. Government and public debt stood at US$147 billion, over 100 per cent of GDP. The real estate market, responsible for attracting much of the overseas investment and a source of huge profits over the previous decade, had peaked. Local banks and other lenders and investors found it increasingly hard to access the international funds needed to keep the whole operation afloat. In the last week of November 2008 Dubai World, the huge state-owned holding company created by the ruling Al-Maktoum family to run its business interests, requested a six-month suspension of loan repayments on its debts of US$59 billion. By December, foreign officials in Dubai were reporting signs of looming economic crisis. At first, neither officials in Dubai or the UAE's capital, Abu Dhabi, were willing to provide the international community with any information beyond providing reassurances that all was fine. Gradually, as the situation became harder to spin, the government conceded that the emirate faced some real challenges.

Dubai World was one of the most high-profile and ambitious investment groups in the world. It had gained almost iconic status as one of the architects of Dubai's rise to regional dominance and global prominence. It had developed 'The Palm' and 'The World'. It had also built the 160-storey Burj Dubai, the world's tallest building, which towered over Dubai and the region in testament to the emirate's achievements and ambitions. The video in its visitors' centre explained the thinking behind its height: 'You have to do something impossible, otherwise you'll be like any other company, or person. We have to grow higher and higher – grow like Dubai.'[38] The problem was that all these ventures, and many others, had been paid for with massive borrowings that had risen by almost 50 per cent in the year before the financial crisis. Dubai World now needed to restructure US$26 billion of debt. The government, which owned the company, offered 'backing'[39] but was in no position to provide real help. Lacking oil wealth and with total borrowings, according to Moody's credit rating agency, exceeding US$100 billion, Dubai's leaders refused to guarantee the conglomerate's debts.

The Gulf had experienced its fair share of economic crises in the past. Kuwait's stock market crashed in 1979 and 1982, when the failure of the unofficial Souk Al-Manakh ('camel market') erased billions in paper wealth overnight and forced the government to acquire major holdings in local banks and insurance companies to prevent panic and contagion. Stock markets across the region were also badly hit in 1997 and 2006. What happened in Dubai in late 2008 and early 2009 was different. Within a couple of weeks of the first sign of problems the Dubai stock exchange lost more than 20 per cent of its value. Property prices dropped by a quarter and around US$7 billion of funds – about 3 per cent of GDP – was moved out of the country by investors. Those working in the financial services sector did not know what fate awaited them. 'It's a nightmare,' one employee of a local bank told the media. 'We go into the office unsure if we will have a job at the end of the day.'[40]

Outside Dubai, the potential knock-on effect was also huge. Though other GCC countries did not face extensive exposure in terms of loans, they suffered as investor confidence took a real hit across the region. Qatar's stock exchange, the Doha Securities Market, lost almost 10 per cent of its value in the early days of the crisis. Major international financial institutions, including already battered British-based banks like Royal Bank of Scotland, fared even worse as they faced massive exposure to the crisis in Dubai. None of this did much to dilute the confidence and optimism of senior figures in the emirate. 'We are going to tighten our belts,' explained Mohammed Alabbar, a leading Dubai businessman who was appointed to a crisis oversight committee. After that, he continued, we will 'roll over and pay off debt, and be really trim over the next year'.[41] In a rare online discussion with reporters held during the crisis, Dubai's ruler Sheikh Mohammed was equally positive about both the immediate future and the longer term. The emirate, he told his audience, had already shifted 'from the crisis mood to the solution mood'.[42]

Such protestations aside, the near default of Dubai World raised real questions about the Dubai economic model, only a few years after US officials tasked with rebuilding post-Saddam Iraq had held the emirate up as the example for the new Iraq. They believed that the emirate's entrepreneurial spirit, its 'can-do' mentality and its mixed economy were exactly what was needed to make Iraq a success. Some perceptive observers pointed out the irony in all this. Despite its economic achievements Dubai had little interest in the sort of democracy championed by the Bush administration in its vision for Iraq and the wider Middle East. Under new plans for the debt restructuring of Dubai World, the real estate sector would take a less central place in the economy. Legislation was introduced to control future borrowing levels and there was a move to refocus on more traditional areas of trade, tourism and banking services. It was hoped that the void would also be filled by a new emphasis on the development of the emirate into a regional travel and transport hub and a leader in the areas of alterative energies, utilities, manufacturing and high technology. Dubai's oil-rich neighbour, Abu Dhabi, played down the threat posed by the crisis next door, which officials described as a short-term problem. They also expressed confidence that everything would soon be back to normal. Some even presented it as a valuable opportunity for Abu Dhabi to address vulnerabilities in its own economy. 'We will learn from Dubai's mistakes,'[43] explained one member of a new committee mandated to provide oversight for state-owned companies in Abu Dhabi to ensure that a crisis similar to the one taking place in Dubai was avoided.

In November 2008, Abu Dhabi acted to reassure the markets by injecting US$19 billion into Dubai. A further US$10 billion was handed over the following February. Such moves did little to convince many inside and outside of Dubai that Abu Dhabi, which sat on 94 per cent of the federation's oil reserves, was not a grudging and reluctant saviour of its neighbour. Recently named the richest city in the world by *Fortune* magazine, Abu Dhabi's initial November rescue package came two weeks after the crisis began, though some analysts believed that this delay was due to the fact that Dubai was reluctant to accept help from its neighbour because of the political ramifications.[44] The public statements that accompanied this move made it clear that this was not the beginning of an open-ended investment in Dubai. Rather, Abu Dhabi would 'pick and choose when and where to assist'.[45] This caution was necessary, as well as prudent, as Dubai World's collapse came at a time when Abu Dhabi faced its own, albeit much less troubling, liquidity challenges. Though not technically a bail-out, Abu Dhabi's financial assistance to Dubai did underscore the power imbalance in the relationship between the two neighbours. This was highlighted most clearly by the fact that Burj Dubai, the world's tallest building, was renamed Burj Khalifa in honour of Abu Dhabi's ruler after his emirate came to the rescue. There had always been healthy competition and, at times, strained relations between the two neighbours. They had even gone to war in 1946–7 over a territorial dispute on their northern border. These tensions continued in a more civilized manner after the establishment of the federation in the early 1970s. In more recent years Dubai's success had narrowed the power imbalance and, inevitably given this history, the financial meltdown in Dubai once more fed speculation that Abu Dhabi would now attempt to reassert its authority over its neighbour. Rumours even spread that Abu Dhabi might demand Emirates Airlines, the crown jewel in Dubai's portfolio, as payment for its help. Dubai's Sheikh Mohammed dismissed such speculation as a 'fabrication' and denounced the 'vicious attempts' to invent differences between Dubai and Abu Dhabi. 'I know that some people from outside the region have wished that [the] Dubai model will go down the river,' he explained in the course of dismissing the bad press he and his emirate had received in previous months. On another occasion, when journalists asked him about tensions with Abu Dhabi, he told them to shut up.

Even if outside observers and the international media overstated intra-UAE tensions, the crisis in Dubai opened the way for Abu Dhabi to consolidate its dominant position inside the federation by centralizing more power. Abu Dhabi also made a conscious attempt to position itself as the safe and sensible alternative to brash Dubai, as one commentator put it, playing the role of 'frugal parent, chiding a spendthrift child'.[46] When Abu Dhabi's most luxurious hotel, the Emirates Palace, boasted that it had spent US$11 million on the world's most expensive Christmas tree in the middle of the financial crisis, the government forced the hotel's managers to apologize publicly for their extravagance. This minor but illuminating incident occurred at a time when the financial crisis threatened to destroy European monetary union, the euro single currency and even the European Union itself. Sultan bin Saeed Al-Mansouri, the UAE's minister of economics, spoke for many in the Gulf when he argued that the region's exposure to Europe was 'small' and that European governments would soon overcome the challenges they faced without help from outsiders. He was wrong on both counts. Europe was not able to solve the crisis it faced on its own and the Arab Gulf could not insulate itself from the deteriorating situation in Europe. The two regions were connected deeply through trade, oil and investments. In 2010, for example, the EU was the GCC's number-one trade partner ahead of Japan, the US and China and two-way trade was US$110 billion. As noted above, Gulf investors had also invested heavily in European stock markets before they had collapsed.

During the boom years that preceded the crash, European critics of Gulf sovereign wealth funds complained that it was impossible to distinguish between public and private Gulf investment. This had not changed by the time the Eurozone crisis started and, combined with the discretion of recipient governments, makes it difficult to put an exact figure on total Gulf financial support for Europe during its time of need. By one estimate, Gulf States provided one-third of emergency funding to European governments during the autumn of 2008.[47] Speaking in Chile at exactly this time, John Lipsky, one of the IMF's senior figures, backed up this point when he praised the 'shock-absorbing role' played by the SWFs during the initial stage of the financial meltdown. Ben Bernanke, the US Federal Reserve chairman, later estimated that wealth funds from the Gulf and Asia provided about a third of the funding for Western financial institutions in the first year of the crisis. In 2011, the IMF announced that Saudi Arabia had provided around US$15 billion – around 3.5 per cent – of the US$430 billion raised by the institution to deal with the Euro-crisis. In the same year, the Gulf States were also important contributors to the EU directly as it looked to raise a further US$50 billion to shore up its bail-out plans across the continent. Early in the following year a group of European central bank governors visited the Gulf to discuss raising even more contributions. Following the meeting in Abu Dhabi, Mario Draghi, the European

Central Bank president, explained that the visit reflected the growing presence of GCC states in the global economy.[48]

In this environment, Gulf wealth funds were an increasingly necessary as well as attractive source of potential funds. On a national level some of the worst-hit victims of the Eurozone crisis – Greece, Spain, Portugal, Cyprus and Ireland – looked to the Gulf for massive infusions of cash to stabilize their faltering financial institutions and kick-start their economies. In doing so, they competed with much larger and less vulnerable EU partners like Germany, the United Kingdom and France. Delegations from these and other European countries toured the Gulf in the hope that they could gain support for distressed financial institutions and other struggling economic sectors back home. There was no one common Gulf response to such requests. When the UAE's minister for economics was asked whether his country planned to bail out crisis-ridden Greece, his answer was short and to the point – 'No we won't'. Qatar was more obliging. Various investment funds controlled by the Qatari government spent about US$5 billion on Greek assets during the worst of the crisis. This included a half a billion dollars to help restructure major Greek banks. In recognition of this, Greece's president described Qatari support as a key factor in any future national economic recovery. Qatar also signed several agreements with the Greek Cypriot government for major investments in the Mediterranean island's hotel and real estate sectors, the mainstays of the local economy. Between 2009 and 2014, various SWFs invested an estimated US$45 billion in Spain. Over half came from Norway but much of the rest came from the Gulf. Qatar's wealth fund alone bought several major assets and put US$300 million in the troubled Spanish financial sector in 2011. Abu Dhabi funds invested heavily in Cepsa, the multinational oil and gas company, Bankia, Spain's fourth largest bank, and Sener, the engineering and technology group.

In these circumstances, the earlier European preoccupation with the dangers posed by sovereign wealth funds evaporated. There was, in the final account, little appetite for implementing regulations that antagonized Gulf leaders in this environment. These funds, explained president of the European Commission José Manuel Barroso, were 'not a big bad wolf at the door'.[49] Rather, he argued, they played an important role in stabilizing Europe's financial markets. During the crisis, member state governments also acted to make their economies more attractive by dismantling existing obstacles to Gulf investment. In Italy, for example, the government scrapped a rule that blocked SWFs from buying more than 5 per cent of local companies. This opened the way for the launch of a US$2 billion fund jointly owned by the Italian government and Qatar's wealth fund to be used to make investments in several Italian economic sectors.[50]

There was also a sudden shift in the position of the Sarkozy government in Paris, which now became increasingly open to large-scale SWF investment in the struggling economy.[51] Kuwait's sovereign wealth fund made an offer of US$794.6 million for a 4.8 per cent stake in the French state-controlled nuclear firm Areva SA. ADIA paid US$750 million to acquire the assets of Docks Lyonnais, a property company owned by the Swiss bank UBS. In 2008, Sarkozy made the first visit to Qatar by a French president in over a decade. The local media described the trip as evidence of the 'growing and positive development of ties', especially in 'economic fields'.[52] Over the next few years France emerged as the number-two European recipient of Qatari investment after the United Kingdom. The kingdom bought up properties in some of the best locations in central Paris. Qatari funds also purchased major holdings in the Suez Energy Group, Dexia Bank, Paris Saint-Germain football club and the luxury leather goods company Le Tanneur. Smaller holdings were purchased in the country's largest company, oil giant Total, as well as Vivendi and LVMH, the owner of several of the world's most renowned brands including the fashion designer Christian Dior and Dom Pérignon champagne. In 2010, Qatar also invested US$1 billion in the heavily indebted French shipping group CMA CGM, the world's third biggest shipping group and one of the leading private sector employers in the southern French port city of Marseilles.

During his important visit to the Gulf in late 2008, Gordon Brown had been clear that as long as the region's investment funds 'play by our rules and operate in a commercial manner', the British economy would openly welcome them.[53] This promise was honoured during the financial crisis as the United Kingdom retained its position as the number-one European destination for SWF investments, attracting more than Germany, France and Spain combined. Gulf spending on British property in particular became one of the major stories of the global financial crisis. In 2009, almost 20 per cent of all foreign investment in the UK property market came from the Gulf.[54] Some of these purchases were made with a quick profit in mind. In 2010, for example, the Oman Investment Fund made almost US$120 million profit on an office block in the City of London that it had purchased less than a year before. The majority of the Gulf's big money property deals were intended to be longer-term investments. In 2010, Qatar was the largest overseas property investor in the world. To observers it appeared that much of this spending was going on in the

British capital, as Qatar established itself as a dominant force in the London property market. The kingdom, in the words of one journalist, had snatched up 'large chunks of London from London Bridge to Chelsea'.[55]

This was an exaggeration, but only just. Various Qatari investment vehicles became the major shareholder in Songbird Estates, the majority owner of Canary Wharf, London's financial district, giving it control over the headquarters of some of the world's biggest banks and financial institutions such as Credit Suisse. They backed the consortiums behind the development of the world's most expensive apartment block at One Hyde Park, the renovation of the Chelsea Barracks, and the redevelopment of the Olympic village in east London. They bought 20 per cent of Camden Market in north London, Royal Dutch Shell's headquarters, the long-time American embassy in Grosvenor Square and, as mentioned earlier, a majority holding in Europe's tallest building, the Shard.

Beyond property, numerous rumours spread in these heady years over Qatari plans to snatch up major British institutions. Included on this list were Arsenal Football Club and the blue chip department store Marks and Spencer. It was even rumoured that Qatar had set up a dedicated fund of billions to buy assets belonging to the British government. None of these rumours proved to be true, but this did little to change the widely held view of Qatar as an energy-rich shopaholic with an insatiable appetite for high-priced investments. As the *Financial Times* joked, the word Qatar was 'one of the sweetest sounding words' for anyone selling trophy assets or high-end luxury brands. 'How Qatar bought Britain' was the headline in another newspaper, while a profile of Qatar's prime minister described him as 'the man who bought London'.[56] Qatari officials were uncomfortable with this evolving reputation. After the QIA, the kingdom's wealth fund, purchased Harrods department store, a top official of the fund was adamant that his country was 'not chasing trophy assets'. Instead, he explained, the decision to buy this iconic store was part of a strategy to acquire 'prestigious top performing businesses and to buy them at the right point in the cycle'.[57] Qatar also took significant holdings in less glamorous assets including the J. Sainsbury supermarket chain, the London Stock Exchange and BAA, making it the third largest shareholder in the company that owned London's Heathrow Airport.

Nor did the money flow one way only. In 2011, Qatari liquefied natural gas (LNG) imports accounted for over half the gas consumption in the United Kingdom. This made the United Kingdom Qatar's most important European gas customer and resulted in a 160 per cent rise in the total value of Qatari exports to the United Kingdom. Qatar Petroleum was also the main shareholder in South Hook liquefied natural gas terminal. Located in Milford Haven in Wales, it has the capacity to provide up to a quarter of the United Kingdom's gas needs. The gas-rich kingdom of Qatar was, in the words of the British ambassador in Doha, a 'priority' that 'matters to my country'.[58]

It was not, however, the only Gulf State to establish itself as a key economic player in the British economy at this time. The UAE was Britain's largest export market in the GCC. In 2009, the United Kingdom and the UAE signed an agreement to boost bilateral trade even further. This opened the way for the establishment of a joint economic committee, intended to meet every two years, alternating between London and Abu Dhabi. Within weeks of taking office in 2010, David Cameron's new Conservative government went further. It set up a task force to 'elevate links' with the UAE. The aim, according to the recently appointed foreign secretary William Hague, was to double bilateral trade over the next five years. With this goal in mind the UAE, like Qatar, became a popular destination for senior British figures. The queen, Prime Minister Cameron and a host of other emissaries all visited Dubai and Abu Dhabi, often as part of a wider regional tour, to promote investment in Britain.

Like Qatar, the UAE also upped its investments across several sectors of the British economy during the financial crisis. It gained a particular reputation for supporting massive infrastructural investment projects in the British capital. This included the United Kingdom's most ambitious port and logistics centre, the London Gateway near the mouth of the River Thames. ADIA also took a 15 per cent stake in Gatwick Airport, and other Abu Dhabi funds provided Sony with the backing to bid for the British music company EMI, and invested in Rolls-Royce and EADS, the leading aerospace company. Soon afterwards, the British government's infrastructure strategy named Qatar's investment in Heathrow Airport's parent company BAA, as well as Abu Dhabi's stake in Thames Water, as examples of the kind of investments that it wanted to attract into the country. Only half jokingly, London mayor Boris Johnson described himself as 'mayor of the eighth emirate'. The City of London's lord mayor, David Wootton, publicly expressed the view that 'half the top 10 sovereign wealth funds had offices in London and we are glad to have them'.[59]

By the time of the global financial crisis, the UAE and Saudi Arabia were Germany's two most important markets in the Arab world. In 2009, Abu Dhabi, a country of five million people, bought three times more German goods than Egypt, a country of just under eighty million. The UAE also did more trade with Germany than the two Asian economic stars

Singapore and Hong Kong. A German–Emirati Chamber of Commerce and Industry was opened in Abu Dhabi in mid-2009 and top officials, including President Christian Wulff and Chancellor Angela Merkel, visited the region regularly to boost ongoing efforts to attract significant Gulf inward investment into Germany. This campaign was less successful in absolute terms than the one undertaken by Britain but Germany could still claim some major victories. Following numerous visits to Doha, Porsche's chief executive announced that Qatar had agreed to take a stake in the indebted luxury car maker. The QIA ultimately spent US$10 billion to purchase a 17 per cent stake in the integrated Volkswagen and Porsche firm following merger of the two companies. Dubai International Capital bought the large packaging firm Mauser AG and ADIA took a 13.4 per cent stake in Deutsche Annington, Germany's largest publicly traded residential property landlord. The Abu Dhabi investment fund Aabar paid US$2 billion for 10 per cent of another iconic German car maker, Daimler. The foreign media viewed the deal as a 'marriage of financial convenience dressed up as an industrial venture' that had saved the German government from 'begging for handouts'. But the German media took a much less judgemental view. The mass-circulation *Bild* dismissed the view that the investment was a sell out of 'our industrial pearls' that would turn the 'most German of all brands into Abu Daimler'. Instead, the paper argued that it was a great deal that would 'save and create' German jobs. *Die Welt* called on the German government to send a thank-you letter to Abu Dhabi for its willingness to invest in Germany so soon after the Merkel government had passed a law to restrict SWF investments flowing into the country.[60]

Even in the more welcoming climate of the global financial crisis and the post-crisis era, constituencies in some recipient countries continued to oppose the role of Gulf SWFs. British politicians warmly welcomed Qatar's investment in the Shard as a huge boost for the capital that could eventually create up to 10,000 jobs. Many others disagreed. A spokesman for a vocal and committed local residents group described the building as 'a massive pyramid slapped down here as a monument to the munificence of the Emirate of Qatar'. Qatari officials were sensitive to the potential backlash that high-profile property deals like the Shard aroused in some quarters. 'We respect local traditions, culture, ecosystems and architecture and leave behind a positive and sustainable footprint wherever we develop,' explained the chief executive of Qatar's real estate investment arm, Qatari Diar.[61]

The worst attack on the role of a wealth fund in a recipient country during the crisis occurred in France. Marine Le Pen, the outspoken leader of the far-right National Front, accused Qatar of taking a foothold in French national assets and posing a 'threat to our national independence'. More seriously, she accused Qatar of trying to finance Islamic fundamentalism through a multi-million-dollar fund that the country had pledged to invest in largely Muslim and impoverished Paris suburbs. Others with a more mainstream reputation made a similar argument. Writing in *Le Point*, in language reminiscent of the attacks on Gulf petro-dollar spending during the late 1970s, the celebrated philosopher Bernard-Henri Lévy described Qatar's planned investment as a 'source of humiliation for the recipient country, which appears bankrupt to the point of beggary'. He then dismissed Qatar's offer of financial support as 'nothing but a hoax or propaganda'.[62] In the face of this hostile reception, Qatar postponed its proposed project in order to avoid any controversy in the run-up to the French presidential election. Soon after his victory over Nicolas Sarkozy, the new socialist president, François Hollande, decided that Qatar's money would be used to fund small and medium-sized enterprises under the control of the industry ministry.[63]

Unpleasant as this whole affair was, it was an exception to the norm that had more to do with internal French politics in an election year than any non-commercial motivations of Qatari investment. For the most part the financial crisis forced a positive re-evaluation of the role of SWFs in bolstering the faltering global economy. It also served to highlight the valuable and important contribution that they could make in the longer term. In recognition of this, the number of sovereign wealth funds in the world grew from around ten at the beginning of the 2000s to eighty a decade and a half later, with major Western economies including France, Germany and the United Kingdom establishing them in the wake of the financial crisis. The mood had changed so much by this time that one highly respected financial commentator looking back at the previous decade from the vantage point of 2014 could joke how only a handful of years earlier wealth funds had been viewed as the 'financial equivalent of a James Bond villain: shadowy, powerful and potentially sinister'.[64]

If the global financial crisis had provided the world with an opportunity to reassess the role of wealth funds, it also provided the Gulf States with the opportunity to re-evaluate their economic and financial strategies at home and abroad. At home, governments acquitted themselves well in their response to the financial crisis and also made progress in tackling some of the more systemic problems in the financial sector that had been highlighted by events. Most notably, there was a move to clean up bank balance sheets, raise the level of bank capital in relation to risk, improve transparency, develop stronger regulatory frameworks and increase oversight. At the same time, in the wake of the crisis, the Gulf's wealth funds also exhibited a new sensitivity to domestic concerns over money being distributed abroad on the basis of political or altruistic considerations rather than profit. Going forward, this made senior officials very careful to present investments in terms of the bottom line. After the 'disasters in the US, some European countries or Asian countries', explained the head of the KIA, investment decisions would be made on the basis of potential returns only. His counterpart at ADIA was equally insistent that the fund's investment decisions would be 'driven solely by economic objectives'.[65]

Such public declarations of intent undoubtedly complicated the job of the wealth funds, especially as their growing acceptance and legitimacy during the crisis served to foster a new sense of international responsibility on the part of Gulf leaders, who started to think differently about the role their SWFs could play. On top of this, there were always going to be certain circumstances in which profits, or at least short-term profits, could not be the primary consideration. Sometimes more strategic factors needed to be taken into account as well. For example, in the summer of 2009, Qatar's sovereign wealth fund offered to provide the investment needed to rescue two struggling Polish shipyards. The move coincided with a long-term natural gas supply accord between Poland and Qatar, and with Warsaw's expression of hope that Poland would become a European hub for Gulf investment.[66] Six years later Qatar hoped to reap the rewards of these efforts once Poland's LNG terminal in Świnoujście became operational.

This refocusing on the profit factor also raised another question – how successful had the Gulf funds been in their investment decisions during the global financial crisis? Like many others, they paid dearly during the crisis for holding so many stocks and shares in publicly quoted Western companies whose values plummeted during the downturn. On the other hand, they could also claim some very big returns in some of the very same sectors – notably property, retail, financial services – in which they recorded some of their worst losses or overpaid hugely for inflated assets. This was most evident in the financial services sector.

In the early stages of the crisis the financial sector was a popular destination for Gulf funds. For the most part these were emergency investments and, along with similar support from China and Singapore, provided a lifeline to some of the world's largest and most renowned financial institutions at a time when public confidence in the banking system was at an all-time low. Apart from ADIA's massive stake in Citigroup, other UAE funds took significant holdings in Barclays Bank. Qatar put billions into

Credit Suisse, Citigroup and Barclays. Braving criticism from Kuwaiti parliamentarians who demanded it abandon all foreign investments, the KIA put US$5 billion into Citigroup and Merrill Lynch stock. The results were mixed. In 2009 ADIA entered into arbitration against Citigroup, alleging that it had been the victim of 'fraudulent misrepresentations' when it made its US$7 billion investment in the bank. Other investments proved to be hugely profitable. In the summer of 2009 a sister fund of ADIA made US$2.5 billion in profit when it sold its stake in Barclays only eight months after stepping in to help the struggling British bank. Soon after, the KIA made over US$1 billion profit on its US$3 billion rescue investment in Citigroup. This sale took place only three months after the KIA had said that it planned to hold on to its stake in the bank over the long term. Three years later, a Qatari fund, which was also the second largest shareholder in Credit Suisse, walked away with significant profits from the sale of part of its holding in Barclays without giving up its status as biggest shareholder in the UK bank.

Gulf rulers and their wealth fund managers also started to think differently during the financial crisis over the kind of investments their funds should prioritize. According to research commissioned by the OECD, until 2008 over 50 per cent of SWF investment measured by value took place in the financial sector, including US$25 billion in 2007 alone. This sector was attractive because it provided high rates of return and because financial institutions were high-value assets that could absorb significant amounts of surplus cash without drawing much negative attention. As noted previously, US$7 billion only got ADIA less than 5 per cent of Citibank in 2007. Despite offering the potential of huge returns as well as big risks, from 2009 onwards Gulf funds tended to avoid major investments in Western financial assets. Instead, they chose to build up their holdings in luxury brands, prime real estate and big-name companies. In mid-2008 Saudi Arabia, the most cautious of all Gulf investors, even launched a new fund with the express goal of investing only in those three sectors, while the kingdom's new wealth fund Sanabil Al-Saudia prioritized the purchase of overseas assets in the high-tech and financial services sectors as a way of contributing to the modernization of key economic sectors at home. As one of its officials explained, the new fund's mandate would be 'diversification – asset class, sectoral and geographic'.[67]

After having played such a critical role in recapitalizing struggling Western financial institutions and companies during the crisis, Gulf governments were more determined than ever to bring about an end to the 'inequalities in representation between emerging and developed economies and between different classes of emerging economies', as Qatar's minister of economy and finance Yousef Hussain Kamal framed the problem at a joint meeting of the IMF and World Bank in 2012.[68] Following her own meeting with GCC finance ministers and central bank governors in the October of the same year, Christine Lagarde, the IMF's managing director, thanked them for their important, positive role in the MENA region as well as the world at large. On a regional level, she singled out the generous financial aid that the GCC had provided to Arab countries in a very difficult period. On the global level, she commended the GCC countries for their oil policy that helped to stabilize oil markets and counter the price pressures that could have inflicted serious damage on the world economy. On this occasion, she refrained from making any commitment to consider the Gulf States' demands that the IMF be restructured to provide them with more power. Indeed, both during and since the financial crisis top IMF officials have been reticent in acknowledging explicitly the role of the Gulf States in the bail-out of the international financial system, though all, from Lagarde down, have repeatedly expressed their 'appreciation' of Saudi Arabia's 'important role' in supporting the global economy and its 'active participation' inside the IMF.

In these terms, the Gulf States failed to succeed in convincing the international financial community to recognize their efforts by meeting their demand for 'Arab participation in defining the new "post crisis" era', as one informed commentator put it. The Saudi king had attended the first G-20 meeting in Washington in late 2008, but he did not bother to turn up to the next one in Pittsburgh the following year. The UAE was invited to one in Cannes, France, at the end of 2011 in a gesture that was deemed insufficient acknowledgement of the contribution the federation was making to the rebalancing of the international financial system. What mattered now was not invitations but influence. A statement issued the following year by the UAE's minister of state for financial affairs in the name of the governments of Oman, Kuwait, Qatar and Bahrain called for the IMF to demonstrate its appreciation by doing two things: hire more Arab economists and policy advisers (only 3 per cent of the institution's employees were Arab, while IMF heads always tended to come from Europe); and end using national GDP as the major measure in deciding the votes of each member state inside the organization.

An IMF reform package had been agreed at the start of the financial crisis in 2008. It came into effect in early 2011 and gave fifty-four emerging economies an ad hoc increase in their voting power. In December 2010, the IMF board agreed to another reform package that became effective in late

2016. This move attempted to reflect the changing relative weights of member states in the global economy by doubling quotas and moving more than 6 per cent of existing shares to underrepresented emerging economies. Under these reforms Saudi Arabia actually saw a bigger fall in its shareholding than the other losers – Germany, the United Kingdom, the United States and Japan – as economies like India and Turkey saw their shareholdings rise, and China became the third largest IMF shareholder. Currently, 50 per cent of the existing quota formula is still based on GDP size, with economic openness counting for 30 per cent, economic variability 15 per cent and international reserves the final 5 per cent. On the basis of these criteria, the United States is still the major player inside the IMF, controlling 16.67 per cent of the vote. Between them, the six GCC states control 3 per cent of IMF voting rights, with Saudi Arabia accounting for just over 2 per cent of the total. This is less than the United Kingdom (4.07 per cent) but more than other influential small countries like Switzerland (1.19 per cent) and Norway (0.78 per cent).

Apart from wanting structural changes in the IMF that provided them with a greater say in economic decisions, following the financial crisis top Gulf officials also told Western counterparts that they wanted assurances that an open, non-discriminatory investment environment would be maintained that took into account their ambitions on the global stage. If not, they warned, they and other cash-rich emerging economies might start to prioritize unilateral rather than multilateral responses to international problems. Certainly, the Gulf's bargaining power in the immediate wake of the financial crisis was at an all-time high. It was home to over 20 per cent of the world's gas reserves and almost a third of its oil reserves. Between a third and a half of the world's entire SWF wealth was also concentrated in the region, which served as a home to four of the world's top ten SWFs, and seven of the top twenty. By the end of 2014, the combined assets of the GCC's sovereign wealth funds stood at an estimated US$2.4 trillion, out of worldwide sovereign wealth assets of around US$7 trillion, two and a half times greater than the combined value of the world's hedge funds.[69]

As chapter Ten of this book will show, during the financial crisis emerging markets like India, China and parts of Africa and Latin America also became increasingly attractive investment destinations for the Gulf. In short, the Arab Gulf States emerged from the global financial crisis with their economies intact, their wealth increased and with a number of viable investment alternatives to traditional Western markets. They also increasingly saw their role as a global hub for finance, business and travel between East and West, a development that provided the region with great opportunities to promote its economic interests and grow its international influence. Yet as the Arab Spring spread in late 2010 from Tunisia and Egypt to Libya and Bahrain, the Arab Gulf's achievements of the previous decade were threatened, and its capacity to ensure stability at home and influence abroad was tested to an unprecedented extent.

CHAPTER 7

SELF-DEFENCE

'I and my brother against my cousin, and I and my cousin against the stranger.'

– Arab Proverb

For the ordinary people of the Arab world, especially the region's huge population of under-twenty-fives, the Arab Spring was a spontaneous and unexpected expression of people power that, at least while it lasted, was simply the most significant reform movement in the Arab world in living memory. For those local leaders across the Arab Gulf, the events of 2011 – popular revolt in Tunisia, Egypt and Libya; large-scale anti-regime protests in Bahrain; smaller-scale unrest in Oman, Kuwait and the oil-rich Eastern Province of Saudi Arabia; and the start of the ongoing quasi-civil war in Syria – threatened to undermine all their hard-won success in consolidating stability at home and projecting influence abroad over the previous decades. Though the root causes of the Arab Spring ran deep and cannot be traced to any one event, there is wide agreement that the drastic action of Mohamed Bouazizi, a downtrodden twenty-something street vendor in the rural Tunisian town of Sidi Bouzid, was the catalyst that sparked subsequent events across the Arab world. Bouazizi was not remarkable in any way. Like millions of others in the region he was a high-school dropout with few prospects struggling to deal with the harassment, corruption and the callousness of daily life. When he could take no more he set himself on fire on the same busy city streets where he had plied his meagre trade.

His act of defiance sparked mass protests in villages, towns and cities across Tunisia against the rule of President Zine El Abidine Ben-Ali. A soldier and security technocrat turned politician, Ben-Ali had seized the presidency in a bloodless coup in 1987. After a quarter of a century in office he was forced out amid the countrywide revolt in January 2011, less than a week before Bouazizi died from his burns and wounds. The Jasmine Revolution, as the revolt against Ben-Ali in Tunisia came to be known, inspired millions of angry citizens in half a dozen Arab countries to take to the streets. They protested against elite indifference and corruption, a lack of jobs and economic opportunities and, worst of all, a lack of hope.

Soon after Ben-Ali was overthrown, thousands of protestors set up camp in Tahrir Square in central Cairo. They called for Egyptian president Hosni Mubarak to give up power. For most of the modern era, Egypt had been the pivotal state in the Arab world – the big pebble on the Arab beach, as British diplomats had referred to it in the past. Mubarak had led the country for three decades. During those years he played a central role in regional politics and diplomacy and was a highly visible figure on the world stage. Few imagined that the protests in Cairo would lead to his overthrow. Mubarak was a much more important figure than Ben-Ali, but like the ousted Tunisian leader he was also a former senior military officer who had lost touch with his people after a generation in power. He no longer even pretended to serve their interests or needs, and he had even lost much of his core support in his main constituency, the conservative upper echelons of the military.

As shocked policymakers and pundits across the world speculated on what the end of Mubarak meant for the future of the Middle East, the protestors on the streets of Cairo were jubilant. Ahmed Raafat Amin, a twenty-two-year-old Cairo college student, described events as a 'national dream that we all share'. Mohammed Abdul Ghedi, a lifeguard in his early twenties, who had travelled to Cairo from the Red Sea resort of Sharm el-Sheikh, carried a sign during the protests that read, 'Mubarak you are nothing'. Once Mubarak was gone, he was effusive: 'Now Egyptians are free. All of Egypt is liberated.' It was not only younger Egyptians who felt this way. 'We have done something unprecedented in 7,000 years, we have brought down the pharaoh,' proclaimed Tareq Saad, a fifty-one-year-old carpenter, before adding: 'Egypt is free, it will never go back to what it was. We won't let it.' While sixty-five-year-old tailor Saad el Din Ahmed summed up succinctly what many young and old alike were thinking in the early days of the revolution: 'Nightmare over . . . Now we have our freedom and can breathe and demand our rights.'[1]

Protests against Colonel Muammar Gaddafi began in Libya a couple of weeks after they had started in Cairo's Tahrir Square. Gaddafi had ruled oil-rich Libya with an iron fist since 1969. The trigger for the revolt against his regime was the mid-February arrest in the city of Benghazi of a human rights lawyer who represented the relatives of political prisoners massacred by Gaddafi's security forces more than a decade earlier. This marked the beginning of an eight-month uprising that culminated in the brutal death of a brutal dictator at the hands of rebels in his hometown of Sirte. Few mourned the end of Gaddafi. He had been one of the most unpredictable and unstable rulers in the Middle East and was more detested at home and abroad than either Ben-Ali or Mubarak had ever been. Lamin El-Bijou, a resident of Benghazi where the revolution had started, captured the exhilaration of many in the days and weeks after the dictator was overthrown. 'It's freedom. There's no Gaddafi, unbelievable. I feel the freedom. I smell the freedom.' Libyans living outside the country were no less happy. 'It's a collective sigh of relief,' explained one second-generation Libyan exile based in the United States, 'forty-two years under his rule – and then to see him reduced to a dead corpse in a rat hole. Everybody's happy to see this thing.'[2]

The GCC had always been a deeply conservative regional bloc and its ruling elites instinctively recoiled from the idea of revolution anywhere at any time. As its first secretary general explained in the mid-1980s, the organization was a 'council for development and not for change'. 'It was not', he continued, 'a mechanism for storms and hurricanes; it seeks adherence to heritage and to maintain the balance of power.'[3] Indeed, the GCC had been born, in part at least, as a reaction to the Iranian revolution, which Gulf leaders viewed at the time as setting an unhealthy precedent for the removal of long-time hereditary rulers. Their distaste of revolution was further compounded over future decades by the ongoing threat they faced from the same Islamic revolutionaries in Tehran who had overthrown the shah.

By the time of the Arab Spring, GCC rulers had deftly weathered the challenge posed by Iran. They had managed to survive the fallout from 9/11 and the war on terror and the US invasion and occupation of Iraq far better than many onlookers thought possible. They had even outlived Saddam Hussein, their most dangerous Arab adversary, in the process. On the economic front, they had overcome extended periods of economic stagnation and low oil prices without abandoning the rapid and ambitious development programmes initiated in the 1970s. They had also consolidated political stability at home. There were few viable protest movements and, with the exception of Bahrain, low levels of citizen dissatisfaction with the status quo across the GCC. No less important, despite deep and divisive historic, political and economic differences, the Gulf States had managed time and again to find a modus vivendi with each other on issues that threatened to pull the GCC apart. Nothing highlighted this better in the years before the Arab Spring than the relationship between Saudi Arabia and Qatar.

As far back as the 1930s, Saudi Arabia's founder, Abdul Aziz Ibn Saud, had attempted to claim large parts of Qatar for his kingdom. Thereafter, Qatar, like the other small Gulf kingdoms, found itself located on what one understated commentator writing in the late-1970s termed 'the immediate fringe of Saudi influence'.[4] On the GCC's birth, officials insisted that neither the history of Saudi domination nor the fact that the GCC's headquarters was located in Riyadh meant that Saudi Arabia had a 'stronger voice' than other partners in the new organization. 'Member states are equal', explained secretary general Bisharah at an early GCC press conference, before adding that this would be the case 'whatever their position, resources, foreign policy or affiliations might be'.[5] Such protestations failed to convince many onlookers that the fledgling GCC was a partnership of equals. In its early years informed observers of Gulf affairs had no doubt that the GCC was a Saudi-run show. *The Economist* magazine called the GCC the 'one plus five' organization in recognition of Saudi Arabia's dominance. 'Everyone knows', added a regional expert, 'that greater cooperation between the GCC would mean greater integration with – and subordination to – Saudi Arabia.'[6]

The other GCC member states resented this threat to their own integrity, sovereignty and independence. This situation was compounded by the fact that rulers in Riyadh never attempted to hide what foreign diplomats working in the region termed their 'instinctive feelings of religious and cultural superiority'.[7] These feelings found expression in various ways. When it was announced during the late 1990s that Abu Dhabi's Sheikh Zayed Mosque would be the biggest in the world when completed, Saudi officials requested that the plans be scaled back so that Mecca could continue to retain that particular honour. Despite this state of affairs, during their formative years the other Gulf nations all needed Saudi support and they had no choice but to defer to their much more established and powerful neighbour. 'The stability of the Saudi regime', as one UAE official explained in 1982, 'is essential to the stability of the region'.[8]

It was not until the early 2000s that the UAE was in a position to compete with Riyadh for the title of number-one economic player in the GCC. In the same years, Qatar began to capitalize on its flourishing relationship with Washington to challenge Saudi Arabia's dominance in matters of foreign affairs. Doha scored some notable successes in establishing itself as a key diplomatic player in the wider Arab world. It outmanoeuvred

Riyadh and Cairo to mediate between Fatah and Hamas in Palestine following the latter's rise to power in Gaza in 2006. This culminated in early 2009 when Doha played host to an emergency meeting on the Gaza crisis, attended by Hamas political director Khaled Meshaal and representatives from thirteen Arab states but boycotted by Saudi Arabia, Egypt and the leadership of the Palestinian Authority. In an impressive display of diplomatic ambition and pragmatism, Qatar also marginalized Riyadh in 2008, when it brought together all the opposing Lebanese factions, including the pro-Iranian and anti-Western Hezbollah, at a peace conference in Doha. The Qatari-sponsored deal succeeded where attempts by other major political players from inside and outside the region including the US and Saudi Arabia had failed. Qatar's success paved the way for the formation of a new government and a new election law. This went some way towards resolving the country's eighteen-month political crisis and ending over two years of political stalemate that had brought Lebanon to the brink of civil war. In acknowledgement of this, billboards were erected on the road from Beirut Airport saying, 'Thank you Qatar'. It also resulted in a visit to Doha by then UN secretary general Kofi Annan to express his own appreciation on behalf of the international community.[9]

Qatar's mastery of 'riyal politik',[10] as one astute commentator described its innovative use of financial diplomacy in these years, served to threaten Saudi influence beyond its borders to an extent that no other local player had ever previously managed. At the same time Al-Jazeera, Qatar's prized cable news network, posed a direct threat to internal stability in Saudi Arabia itself. It was founded in 1996 by Qatar's new emir one year after he came to power. The channel, he predicted at the time, would 'help put tiny Qatar on the map'.[11] Within two years of its launch it had more than thirty million viewers across the Middle East. Al-Jazeera gained so many viewers so quickly because it fundamentally changed the way news and current affairs were reported and presented in the Arab world. As it grew in popularity and influence, it developed into a major irritant of policymakers from north Africa to the Levant. Within five years of its launch, almost every Arab government had lodged a formal complaint with the Qatari government over the network's critical reporting. They also took more direct action. They summarily closed down local Al-Jazeera offices, refused the channel's correspondents entry visas and withdrew their diplomats from Doha in protest at the station's coverage of what was going on in their countries. When these measures failed to stop citizens from watching the channel's round-the-clock unforgiving news coverage and commentary they resorted to even more drastic action. In 1999, for example, the authorities in Algeria cut the power supply to prevent citizens from seeing an Al-Jazeera documentary about the country's decade-long bloody civil war that was only then winding down after claiming hundreds of thousands of lives.

For its part, an indignant Saudi leadership was openly furious over Al-Jazeera's willingness to provide a platform for the kingdom's legion of dissidents. In front of an audience of millions, these outspoken opponents of the Saudi royal family accused their rulers of corruption, human rights abuses and incompetence. In response, Saudi officials accused Qatar of financing radical Saudi opposition groups exiled in London. During the GCC summit in Muscat at the end of 2001, Saudi Crown Prince Abdullah went much further. In a strongly worded speech, he labelled Al-Jazeera 'a disgrace to the GCC countries' and accused it of 'threatening the stability of the Arab world and of encouraging terrorism', an extremely serious allegation only a few months after the 9/11 attacks. The following year, Riyadh broke diplomatic relations with Doha and worked hard to discredit Al-Jazeera at every opportunity. It was later acknowledged that the Saudi government had even established its own news channel, Al-Arabiya, in order to challenge Qatar and undermine Al-Jazeera. Bahrain banned the channel. Policymakers in Oman, Kuwait and the UAE warned Western officials that Al-Jazeera was inciting hatred and destabilizing the entire region and urged them to use their influence over the Qatari leadership to rein in the channel.[12]

And yet, on the eve of the Arab Spring, following years of open hostility and despite ongoing tensions, Qatar and Saudi Arabia had managed to overcome their differences over the role of Al-Jazeera. This reconciliation began in September 2007 when Qatar's emir made a surprise visit to Riyadh in the company of senior Al-Jazeera officials. The following December the Saudi king attended a GCC summit in Doha. This led to the immediate return of a Saudi ambassador to the Qatari capital after an absence of more than five years. Several high-level visits between the kingdoms and the signing of a comprehensive new agreement followed soon after.

The Al-Jazeera case underscores the impressive capacity of the Arab Gulf States to bounce back from major disagreements with each other in the interests of cooperation under the GCC banner. So does the clash between the UAE and Saudi Arabia over the location of a future GCC central bank. As recounted earlier, in May 2009 the UAE had pulled out of plans for GCC monetary union following the choice of Riyadh rather than Abu Dhabi to host the new GCC central bank. In retaliation, Saudi Arabia closed a major border crossing and refused to allow UAE citizens to enter the kingdom using their national identity cards. This caused long delays for thousands of drivers trapped in traffic jams in the summer heat. Rather than escalate the situation, the UAE's leadership instead chose to accept the official Saudi explanation that the problems on the border had been caused by technical difficulties. This unwillingness of GCC member states to let major differences with each other in general, and with Saudi Arabia in particular, impact on their cooperation on vital matters made the GCC one of the most reliable and resilient regional groupings in the world. When President Bush travelled to the Middle East on a farewell tour in 2008, he visited four GCC states and only one non-GCC Arab state. The following year Joseph LeBaron, the American ambassador in Qatar, sent a confidential document to superiors in Washington. LeBaron's report, like thousands of other secret American documents written on the region, subsequently came to public attention as part of the WikiLeaks release. Titled 'The Rise of the Gulf States', LeBaron's report expressed a sentiment that had increasingly come to dominate thinking about the wider Middle East. 'The Arab world's center of gravity is clearly moving south-east, to the Arabian Peninsula,' explained this deeply knowledgeable veteran diplomat. 'The rise of the Gulf – economic, and increasingly, political', he explained, had huge implications. Most importantly, it paved the way for the member states of the GCC to consolidate their position as 'a vehicle for and anchor of stability in a volatile region'.[13]

Once the Arab Spring got under way, the Arab Gulf States had the opportunity to demonstrate if LeBaron was correct. Fighting between anti-government protestors and security forces cost the countries most affected – Tunisia, Libya and Egypt in particular – billions by the middle months of 2011. In the midst of this chaos, as the feverish push for change spread like wildfire, the Arab Gulf States pumped vast amounts of money into the wider region in the interests of stability and in order to protect their extensive holdings in the tourism, real estate and financial sectors. In Egypt, for example, most of the outside money flowing into the country during the anti-Mubarak uprising and after his removal from power came from Saudi Arabia, the UAE, Kuwait and Qatar.

As this chapter will show, GCC members did much more than become the main financial backers of their poorer and increasingly unstable Arab partners across the region. Saudi leaders were deeply conservative and reviled revolution. They had done all they could to prevent the overthrow of Mubarak and they provided refuge for Ben-Ali and his family when they fled Tunisia in mid-January 2011. There was no similar Saudi desire to come to the aid of Gaddafi. Leaders in Riyadh had long despised the

Libyan ruler. They resented his constant accusations that they were American stooges and they blamed him for a failed attempt on the life of King Abdullah in 2003 when he was still crown prince. Now they played a crucial role inside the Arab League, gaining support for a UN Security Council resolution calling for a no-fly zone over Libya. Although most other Arab states were reluctant to take a stand against the Libyan leader this early in the uprising, Saudi Arabia's move gained the backing of all its GCC partners. Soon afterwards it was reported that Riyadh had sent weapons to anti-Gaddafi rebels.

Qatar and the UAE went even further. They became early and outspoken advocates of the overthrow of Gaddafi. They were the first Arab countries and two of the earliest countries anywhere to call for military intervention. They took their stand long before it was inevitable that the Gaddafi regime would fall or that major international actors like the United States and China would back the rebellion. Qatar and the UAE also took the unprecedented, and symbolically important, decision to contribute fighter planes to the air campaign that eventually toppled Gaddafi. Qatar's prime minister and foreign minister, Hamad bin Jassim Al-Thani, explained that his country had agreed to participate in military action, because 'we believe there must be Arab states undertaking this action, because the situation is intolerable'.[14]

Qatar's engagement in Libya was a continuation of its previous proactive diplomacy from Palestine and Lebanon to Darfur in western Sudan. Once it decided to join the battle against Gaddafi, its support for Libyan rebels was unstinting. It was one of the first countries to recognize Libya's National Interim Transitional Council. It sent military advisers to support rebel groups and it established training camps in Benghazi and the Nafusa mountains. There were even unconfirmed reports that Qatari special-forces teams participated in the offensive to take the Libyan capital from pro-Gaddafi troops in the late summer of 2011.[15] On the diplomatic front Qatar also assumed the daunting role of holding together the international anti-Gaddafi coalition, hosting negotiations between NATO and senior anti-regime militia leaders and pressuring and lobbying key members of the international community, most notably China,[16] to back the forces of change in Libya.

If Qatar's very public lead role in the Libya crisis highlighted the kingdom's new standing as a key Arab player on the regional and world stage, Al-Jazeera's role in the Arab Spring also underscored how far it had come in terms of global power and influence in the decade and a half since it had been established. In 2006, the network launched an English-language news channel that soon rivalled the BBC and CNN. By the time the Arab Spring was under way, Al-Jazeera was more than one of the world's most important media organizations. It was also one of the world's best-known brands alongside Apple, Google and Ikea and a regular on *Time* magazine's annual 'Most Influential' list.[17]

From the earliest days of protest in Tunisia, Al-Jazeera had led the way in reporting events on the ground unfiltered, uncensored and on a minute-by-minute basis twenty-four hours a day. It used cutting-edge social media outlets – Facebook, Twitter, YouTube – to get the message of revolution out in real time. It also produced and broadcast a series of well-received documentaries on the Arab Spring under the provocative title 'Death of Fear, End of a Dictator, Seeds of a Revolution'. In a desperate and futile response, the Tunisian authorities barred Al-Jazeera reporters from the country. In Libya, Colonel Gaddafi accused the network of inciting rebels, while a photograph of a slogan on a wall in the city of Tobruk that read 'Freedom=Al Jazeera' went viral and gained worldwide exposure.[18]

Al-Jazeera's coverage of Tunisia also fuelled the initial protests against Mubarak in Egypt. Thereafter, the channel played an important role in sustaining the anti-regime sentiment that led to Mubarak's downfall. Egypt's state-controlled television channels tried to play down what was happening by showing pre-recorded scenes of empty streets, free-flowing traffic and happy customers going about their daily business. Al-Jazeera, on the other hand, showed hundreds of thousands of people gathered in the centre of the city, causing gridlock and calling for regime change. In recognition of this contribution to the cause, the giant television screen hanging over Tahrir Square for the entire duration of the revolution broadcast the network live, as thousands in the crowd chanted 'Long live Al-Jazeera'.[19] The Egyptian state media and besieged government officials accused the Qatari network of 'inciting the people'. It also accused it of serving as a 'sophisticated mouthpiece' of the government in Doha. The robust Qatari rejection of this charge did not help its Egyptian employees, who were accused of treason. The network's Cairo headquarters was stormed by pro-Mubarak supporters; its offices across the rest of the country were closed down. None of these moves succeeded in silencing Al-Jazeera. Finally, Nilesat, the Egyptian-owned satellite that broadcast the channel, stopped its transmission.[20]

At the same time as these momentous events were taking place across the wider Middle East, protests in support of political, social and economic reform were gaining momentum across the Arab Gulf. In the decades since the establishment of the GCC, its member states had made some progress in liberalizing their political systems, as well as their economies. In Oman, the GCC's second largest state, a consultative council that advised the government on key issues was established in the early 1980s. At that time it was presented by Sultan Qaboos as the 'first step towards people's participation in government'.[21] In the early 1990s, the country's lower house, the *Majlis al-Shura*, had become a fully elected body with a sizeable female membership. In 1996 a constitution was promulgated that enshrined human rights protections and judicial independence. By the early 2000s, the country had introduced universal suffrage and was holding direct elections to a national assembly. These moves earned Oman the top spot among Arab states in terms of government submission to the rule of law, a key indicator of political liberalization. Yet the sultanate's State Council, an unelected upper house made up of members of the elite and former high-ranking government officials, continued to grow in both size and influence at the expense of more democratic reforms. As the Arab Spring gained pace, demonstrators in Oman demanded further political reforms, including changes to the State Council. They also called on the government to tackle rising unemployment and official corruption. Clashes between protestors and the security forces were sporadic but at their most violent they left a handful of dead in the Omani industrial city of Sohar.

In Kuwait, like Oman, most of the demonstrators were young. They also took to the streets to express their deep frustration over their lack of available economic opportunities and to demand political reforms, including constitutional amendments. In particular, the protestors called for the resignation of the prime minister, who had been linked to bribery claims the previous year. Kuwait had introduced female suffrage in 2005 and its active and outspoken parliament had proved itself repeatedly willing to challenge the government and the ruling family. It had even set a GCC precedent by attempting to intervene in the highly sensitive area of royal succession. This competition between an ambitious parliament and a distrustful ruling family unwilling to cede power to elected officials had resulted in the fall of seven governments between 2005 and 2011. The protests in Kuwait took the form of strikes and non-violent action. At their height nearly 100,000 took to the street in the biggest protest marches in the kingdom's history. Government services were also disrupted and the country's national assembly was briefly occupied. Members of the stateless Bedoon ethnic group also took advantage of the wider expression of dissatisfaction to step up their own protests. During the 1970s and '80s, its members had made up the vast majority of serving soldiers in the Kuwaiti army and now they wanted the Kuwaiti government to recognize their citizenship.

Though Saudi Arabia had always been the most politically conservative and reform-averse of the GCC states, there had been some move towards liberalization over the previous decade. The kingdom's consultative council was expanded in 2001 and again in 2005, the same year that the first municipal elections in forty years were held. These years also saw senior royal figures, with Crown Prince Abdullah at the forefront, call for greater political participation across the entire Arab world, as well as at home. Most notably, Abdullah acknowledged the legitimate grievances of the country's three million Shia citizens, who accounted for more than 10 per cent of the Saudi population. For decades this community had called for an end to religious and political discrimination, the release of political prisoners and political reform.[22] In the second half of February 2011, as uprisings across the Middle East gained momentum, protests started on the streets of Al-Ahsa, Al-Qatif and other parts of the oil-rich Eastern Province, where the majority of Saudi Arabia's Shia population resided. At the same time, 100 Saudi intellectuals and public figures from the majority Sunni community published an open letter that called for political reform and a greater role for the people in the kingdom's political life. There were also calls for a more equitable distribution of wealth across society, and greater official efforts to combat corruption, bribery and the misappropriation of public land.

The protests in Kuwait, Oman and Saudi Arabia were much more contained and, for the most part, smaller and less violent than those taking place elsewhere in the Middle East. This was due in part to the speed with which the authorities in all three countries moved to stem dissent among dissatisfied constituencies. Some of these strategies were intended to build bridges with protestors. Ruling elites had room for manoeuvre because of the political structure of the Arab Gulf kingdoms. As one incisive commentator explained at the height of the crisis, rulers could cede legislative power as a concession to protestors, without ceding actual control. If that did not satisfy demands they also had the further option of promoting younger members of the royal family to positions of influence to show their commitment to extensive reform.[23]

Qatar had held municipal elections in 1999 and introduced a new constitution in 2003. In a proactive move at the start of the Arab Spring, intended to pre-empt any citizen demands for more political participation, the emir restated his commitment, as set out in the constitution, that two-thirds of *Shura* council seats would be decided at the ballot box in the upcoming 2013 elections. In Kuwait the government resigned after a court-imposed dissolution of the parliament. The emir then changed the voting procedures. In Oman, the sultan removed several government ministers for failing to address the needs of his people and appointed eleven new ministers. A controversial police chief was replaced and a number of civil servants accused of corruption were fired. There were also promises that the semi-elected *Shura* council would receive some real legislative power. In Saudi Arabia, a promise was made to establish a National Anti-Corruption Commission, a new date for municipal elections was announced, and the king declared that women would be allowed to vote and run in the elections scheduled to take place in 2015.[24]

F. Gregory Gause III, a leading expert on Gulf politics, would subsequently argue that these and other political concessions blunted popular demand for reform and played a crucial role in consolidating the grip of ruling families on power across the Gulf.[25] At the same time, they also underscored just how limited progress on the political front had become in the region by the time of the Arab Spring. Nor were the region's young thinking only, or even primarily, in terms of a right to vote at the ballot box every four years. When they talked of political representation they meant the right to speak, to advocate, to agitate, to have a fair chance to change policy and to influence the direction and priorities of society towards more foundational values like free speech, gender equality, minority rights, human rights and the right to protest. These aspirations not only aroused the suspicions of the ruling elites across the Gulf, they were also anathema to many older and more conservative citizens who already resented the erosion of the traditional order and feared the societal consequences of further political concessions and more extensive reform.

For these reasons, Gulf leaders complemented their relatively minor political concessions with other more aggressive and less consensual and conciliatory attempts to neutralize opposition before it got out of hand. From the mid-1980s onwards the Saudis had repeatedly pressed the rest of the GCC to introduce more stringent measures to combat the subversive activities of political dissidents and radicals, including new joint mechanisms to exchange information and improve security cooperation in order to deal with domestic dissent. Riyadh's proposals were viewed with suspicion by its GCC partners, all of whom feared they were a pretext for Saudi interference in their own internal affairs. In the middle of the Arab Spring, as all the GCC states worried over the prospect of unrest at home, they finally adopted many of the tough measures that Saudi Arabia had championed for decades. There was heavy investment in state-of-the-art software used to monitor communications, as well as the widespread arrest of protestors. Some, like Qatari blogger and human rights advocate Sultan Al-Khalafi, were released quickly before trial without being charged. Some were found guilty and then pardoned and released. Others were jailed without trial or held for extended periods of time without access to lawyers. Others still had their day in court and received prison terms for minor offences – including insulting government officials – which many observers believed to be disproportionate.

In a move intended to reduce further trouble, some of those detained during demonstrations were required to take a pledge to refrain from future protests before being set free. Others were banned from travelling abroad after their release. Security services and interior ministries across the Gulf all received far greater powers that allowed them to ban demonstrations at will. Bahrain passed legislation that allowed for citizens to be stripped of their citizenship for terror offences. In Saudi Arabia, the authorities extended anti-terror laws to cover civil rights protestors and political activists. This opened the way for those arrested in the future to be charged with far more serious crimes including subversion and money laundering that carried long jail sentences.

There were no anti-regime demonstrations in the UAE, though 100 intellectuals signed a petition in March 2011 calling for laws that gave the elected Federal National Council proper powers. In a gesture to their erstwhile pro-democracy movement the government greatly increased the number of citizens eligible to vote in the next ballot, scheduled for later in the year. The federal government also took much tougher measures. It revoked the citizenship of dissidents and expelled NGO workers viewed to be sympathetic to protestors in neighbouring countries demanding reform. In the summer of 2011, five bloggers living in the UAE, including Ahmad Mansoor, who was affiliated to Human Rights Watch, were charged with undermining public order and national security after using the Internet to attack the political system and call on people to take to the streets in protest. They were jailed but pardoned after a few months in the run-up to the UAE's National Day celebrations. Subsequently, one of the five was rearrested and, though not charged with any offence, was given the choice of a long jail term or deportation on national security grounds.[26] Within a couple of years of the start of the Arab Spring, the Emirates Centre for Human Rights estimated that the UAE authorities had detained more than 100 political opponents.

New laws limiting media criticism of political and religious leaders were also introduced in other parts of the GCC. Before the Arab Spring, Kuwait was the only GCC country ranked partly free in terms of press freedom and the ministry of information had been abolished in a demonstration of good faith. Yet during the Arab Spring, newspapers were closed down and editors were imprisoned for incitement. The government also tried to get a law passed that carried fines of up to US$1 million for insulting the emir and his senior officials. Oman's ministry of information had a reputation as a conservative institution that enforced censorship of the print and electronic media. It now moved to amend the existing press and publications laws to allow the government to ban any published writings that threatened public safety or state security. Some thirty nationals were also arrested in the sultanate for 'defamatory postings' on social media.[27] Living up to its contrarian reputation, Qatar broke with its GCC partners on these issues and during the Arab Spring introduced a draft law that prevented journalists from being detained by security officials without a court order and proposed removing jail time as a punishment for defamation.[28]

A massive programme of government spending intended to buy the loyalty of citizens complemented the political reforms and the tough legal and security measures referred to above. In 2010, the Arab Gulf States earned collectively more than US$450 billion from selling oil and gas. These vast revenues provided the means to pay for generous cash handouts, higher wages and better pensions to citizens. The cost was truly staggering. In Kuwait the bill topped US$70 billion, as the emir increased wages and social welfare payments and gave every citizen a one-off payment of US$4,000. He also offered a year's worth of free food to all those who wanted it. In Saudi Arabia, King Abdullah made an unprecedented 'royal gift' to his citizens that, according to the state-controlled media, proved their ruler was 'not isolated from his people, unlike most leaders'. This largesse was accompanied by significant increases in social welfare spending, and unemployment and housing benefits. The government also announced the construction of around half a million affordable homes, as well as pay rises for the large public sector, which employed many of the country's educated middle classes. This cost upwards of US$150 billion. With an eye on further underpinning the ruling family's legitimacy, the government also earmarked another US$100 million dollars for educational institutions devoted to teaching the Quran and Islamic studies.[29] Even the rulers of poorer GCC states made exceptional efforts to keep their populations happy. Backed up by financial support from his GCC partners, Oman's sultan announced some 50,000 new jobs and increased benefits for the unemployed, doubling monthly welfare payments. In total, the combined spending of GCC states on citizens and society in direct response to the Arab Spring was about US$250 billion.

Gulf leaders justified their sweeping political, security and financial responses as legitimate and necessary actions that were required to defend citizens, ensure security and protect sovereignty. The Gulf States were deeply concerned about addressing this final point. They not only insisted that they alone had the right to decide how they should react to the Arab Spring within their own borders; they also lobbied their international partners to accept that right. This effort paid off in April 2011 when the concluding statement of the twenty-first annual EU–GCC ministerial meeting acknowledged 'importance for the respect for sovereignty of the GCC Member States' and recognized that the GCC was 'entitled to take all necessary measures to protect their citizens'.

During the Arab Spring, it was not only Gulf governments who began to think differently about the risks associated with democratization, political participation and reform. Growing numbers of citizens of all ages and socio-economic backgrounds also started to place more and more importance in stability, prosperity and living in a safe region. This was even true in Qatar and the UAE, the Arab Gulf States least affected at home by demonstrations, protests and unrest. Polling undertaken by Qatar University in December 2010 and June 2011 confirmed this evolving attitude among Qatari citizens. The proportion of respondents who claimed to be 'interested' or 'very interested' in politics fell by almost 20 per cent over the first quarter of 2011, the crucial months of the Arab Spring. Eighty per cent now felt that social and economic stability was the most pressing national priority compared to just over 10 per cent who felt that it was political participation.[30] The proportion of Qataris who agreed that living in a democratic country was 'very important' also fell. When asked their opinion on the most pressing national priority over the coming decade, 13 per cent said 'giving people more say over important government decisions', compared to 82 per cent who prioritized either social stability ('maintaining order') or economic stability ('fighting inflation').[31]

A second survey, commissioned by the Doha Debates, backed up these findings. This high-profile affair founded and chaired in 2004 by former BBC journalist Tim Sebastian regularly brought together experts, practitioners, policymakers and intellectuals to discuss some of the most important and controversial issues of the day. In June 2011 the televised topic for debate was 'This House believes resistance to the Arab Spring is futile'. The YouGov organization undertook the fieldwork for the poll that accompanied this event. It showed that support for 'more freedom and democracy' was higher in the Levant and north Africa than in the GCC. Respondents from the Gulf were also less convinced than those in other parts of the Arab world that the Arab Spring was the dawn of a 'new era'. Far more GCC citizens felt that their governments could effectively withstand the pressures of the Arab Spring better than those in other Arab countries. Far more GCC citizens also expressed a reluctance to take to the streets against their governments than their counterparts in north Africa or the Levant.

This final finding was only contradicted by events in one GCC country in the first half of 2011 – Bahrain. The protests that occurred there against the rule of the Al-Khalifa royal family were much larger, more violent and longer lasting than any others that occurred in the GCC. For decades Bahraini officials had carefully nurtured an image of their kingdom as a haven of stability, progress and prosperity in the Arab world. 'The basic fundamentals for political, economic and social life', explained a senior cabinet member in the mid-1990s, 'had already been laid down' and it was time to move on to the next phase. A few years later, King Hamad bin Isa Al-Khalifa expounded on what this meant. 'We in this dynamic location, which the world cannot do without, are aware of the important dimension of our role in the field of international energy, strategic balance, economic exchange and dialogue of civilizations.'[32]

The reality was very different. Informed observers had long viewed this tiny island as the 'most sensitive politically'[33] of all the Gulf kingdoms. It was a hotbed of socio-economic and political unrest, and it had experienced some form of mass protest during almost every decade of the twentieth century. In 1923 internal unrest had even led to the abdication of Bahrain's then ruler after fifty-four years in power. It was the only Arab Gulf State in which Shia Muslims made up a majority, accounting for 70 per cent of the population by the time of the Arab Spring. This constituency had long complained of discrimination at the hands of the Sunni minority. They resented their status as a second-class community and they felt excluded from playing a key role in the development of the kingdom's political and socio-economic life. They were angry over being blocked from serving in the police, the army and security services, which instead preferred to recruit Sunnis from Yemen, Lebanon, Syria and Pakistan to fill their ranks.

Protests began in Bahrain in early February 2011. Like those in the rest of the GCC, they were triggered by events in Tunisia, Egypt and Libya. The earliest demonstrations, for example, took place as hundreds of people gathered around the Egyptian embassy in the capital of Manama to express solidarity with protestors in Tahrir Square. At the time they did not raise much concern. As late as the second week of February 2011, *The Economist* only ranked Bahrain as the thirteenth most likely Arab state to fall victim to the social unrest sweeping the wider region. Small gatherings of protestors soon turned into much larger, peaceful mass demonstrations in the area around the GCC roundabout in Manama, near the Central Market and the marina. Thousands of commuters and holidaymakers passed through this well-known and easily distinguishable traffic circle daily. It even had a nickname – the Pearl Roundabout – in recognition of the statue of six sails holding a pearl at its centre. Its transformation into the headquarters of anti-government protests happened quickly. Within days, food stands had been set up and a stage had been erected on which speakers could make impromptu speeches. There was even a barber on site so that protestors could maintain their appearance as they rallied against government injustice.

The protests in Bahrain were some of the largest in the Arab world when measured as a percentage of the total population taking part. From the start there was no consensus among protestors over what they wanted. Some prioritized better social and human rights. Others wanted increased political representation similar to that being demanded on a much smaller scale in other parts of the Gulf. 'We want a kingdom with a king but where the people have the right to choose their government,' explained one young protestor. Such demands had a long and divisive history in Bahrain. In 1975, only a few years after independence, the emir had dissolved the national assembly and placed power in the hands of an unelected cabinet, suspending the constitutional requirement that elections be held within two months of any dissolution of the elected body. It took three widely backed petitions and several high-profile public demonstrations before the government finally agreed to constitutional and political reforms in the mid-1990s.[34] These promises were set out in a National Action Charter (NAC) introduced in 2001. It was backed by 98 per cent of voters in a national referendum. The following year Bahrain held its first parliamentary elections in almost three decades. This move was widely welcomed by Bahrain's international partners. The White House even issued a presidential statement that praised Bahrain as an 'important example of a nation making the transition to democracy'. At home the main opposition parties, all Shia-dominated, disagreed with Washington's assessment and refused to participate in the election.

Intercommunal relations improved following the 2002 vote as a number of opposition parties agreed to register with the government as political societies in order to be eligible to participate in the next election in 2006. This new spirit of cooperation and compromise was short lived. In 2005, marchers in the annual Al Quds International Day demonstration in support of Palestinian rights carried the flag of Lebanon's pro-Iranian

Hezbollah group, as well as pictures of Iran's two supreme leaders, ayatollahs Khomeini and Khamenei. This open support for Iran alarmed senior members of the ruling elite. As one official explained to foreign diplomats, there was growing uncertainty over whether Shia activists were 'trying to negotiate a place at the table, or maybe more than that'. These suspicions had a negative impact on the 2006 elections. After the polls closed there were public allegations that government officials had manipulated the results in order to prevent Shia candidates from winning too many seats. Anger over the possibility that the election was rigged led to a further deterioration in relations between the government and the opposition groups in the years before the Arab Spring. In the run-up to the October 2010 election, one of the main Shia opposition groups, the Al-Wefaq party, was accused of supporting terrorism and working for Iran. The authorities also arrested hundreds of opposition supporters and activists in the months prior to the vote. The elections themselves were marred by clashes between pro- and anti-government supporters and the arrest of a large number of opposition activists.

Less than six months later, as the demonstrations of early 2011 gathered momentum, protestors called on the king to make good on past promises of political reform. They wanted him to agree finally to back the establishment of a constitutional monarchy in which the toothless elected assembly rather than the royal-appointed *Shura* council would hold the real power. Along the same lines, leaders of the Al-Wefaq party called for the 'people to be the source of all authority' and argued that this would only happen if the ruling family gave up its right to govern and a democratically elected parliament was allowed to choose the government. On the surface these were non-sectarian demands that had little to do with the divide in society between the ruling Sunni minority and the Shia majority. 'Not Sunni, Not Shi'ite, Bahraini!' was the most popular slogan chanted by protestors in the early days of the protests. Jaffar Al-Jazeery, an elderly religious leader, encapsulated this kind of thinking. 'This isn't about religion,' he explained, 'it's about rights . . . we are protesting for our rights as Bahrainis.' No matter how sincerely held, such arguments could not change the fact that most of the protestors came from the Shia community. Nor could they hide the fact that beside demands for improved human rights and political reforms, many among the crowds occupying the Pearl Roundabout were also calling for the resignation of the king's uncle. Khalifa bin Salman Al-Khalifa had become prime minister at the time of independence. Forty years later he was viewed by many within the Shia community as the person most responsible for their marginalization in society. Not satisfied with the removal of the long-serving prime minister, some protestors now also called for the removal of his nephew the king.

Bahrain's royal family had long presented itself, in the words of justice minister Khalid bin Ali Al-Khalifa, as a 'buffer zone' between Sunni and Shia citizens.[35] As the protests gained strength, more than twenty political prisoners were released as a concession to opponents of the regime. In early February, at the start of the crisis, the king also gave every family in the kingdom a one-off gift of US$2,650. Yet, a few notable senior exceptions aside, the ruling family refused to acknowledge that the protests against them had anything at all to do with the Arab Spring. The situation in Bahrain was 'totally different' from the turmoil in other parts of the Arab world, explained one top official, because the kingdom was a 'model of democracy'. Officials also dismissed the 'frail excuses and frivolous pretexts'[36] used by protestors to justify the sit-ins, road closures, marches on official buildings, and clashes with the authorities.

As anti-regime demonstrations became more frequent and disruptive over the course of February, the Bahraini military and security services started to intervene on a regular basis. In an interview in the Saudi press in early April, not long after a semblance of order had been restored, Bahrain's top soldier explained that the authorities had handled the unrest of the previous few months with 'extreme wisdom, flexibility, and efficiency'.[37] In reality, from their earliest engagement with protestors, Bahrain's security forces had used strong-arm tactics to break up demonstrations. This crack-down resulted in a number of deaths and scores of injuries, and hardened the commitment of protestors to their cause. 'Before we only wanted the prime minister out,' explained Sawsan Mendeel, a twenty-four-year-old engineer who had been participating in the protests from the start. 'Now, after all this killing, we want the King gone too. Pray for us'.[38] Al-Haqq, one of Bahrain's largest Shi'ite political groups, and a key member of the Bahrain opposition Coalition for the Republic, along with Al-Wefaq and the Bahrain Freedom Movement, openly called for the end of the monarchy and the establishment of a republic.

Surrounded by crowds of young demonstrators and draped in the Bahraini flag, Nabeel Rajab, president of the Bahrain Centre for Human Rights, who would later be sentenced to six months in jail for tweeting that Bahraini security services conspired with Islamic State (ISIS), led chants of 'Down, down with the Khalifa'. Other Shia communal leaders tried to play down these demands for regime change. 'I don't think these young kids really mean it,' explained a middle-aged Shia businessman. 'No one wants to be a republic – but they are angry and want revenge.'[39] Bahrain's Sunni citizens were sceptical of such conciliatory words coming from their Shia fellow citizens. They had long worried that any political concessions made to opposition parties would threaten their dominant position in society. It was, for example, widely presumed that the Al-Wefaq party would win any fully democratic and open election. Now, increasingly vocal calls by protestors for the removal of the king and prime minister from office provided the pretext for Sunni Bahrainis to oppose any concessions to anti-government protestors. Opposition leaders claimed that most of their Sunni friends, neighbours and co-workers supported their cause. They argued that many of those participating in pro-government counter-demonstrations were not fellow citizens but foreign labourers from Bangladesh and other places forced to take part in events staged by the authorities. In reality, large numbers of Sunni citizens chose to take to the streets in support of the royal family rather than turn out to lend support to the opposition. 'We are here supporting our king, our country. We are here hand in hand to show our loyalty,' explained one Sunni citizen making his way through the streets of Manama in one of the many long convoys of trucks, cars and jeeps bedecked in the national flag, banners and pictures of the king.

As violent clashes between the two opposing sides became more frequent, the world's media descended on Bahrain to cover the crisis. Journalists based in the region and international correspondents who made a living parachuting into danger zones described the situation on the ground as a 'battlefield'. Day after day, before a worldwide audience of millions, they reported on the rising number of attacks, random and orchestrated, on demonstrators and critics of the regime by pro-government militias and the security services. The international media also focused much of its coverage on the government's targeting of local journalists, bloggers and social media activists. Officials repeatedly denied these allegations but human rights and advocacy groups stood by their claims. In 2012, for example, Reporters Without Borders classified Bahrain as an 'enemy of the Internet', only one of eleven nations worldwide to earn this status. Four years later, in a comprehensive report on human rights in the Arab world five years after the Arab Spring, Amnesty International was no less critical. The Bahraini authorities, it was noted, continued to target those using social media to take a political stand against the government.[40]

In the middle of the protests in February 2011, in a move intended to restore calm, Bahrain's crown prince, Salman bin Hamad Al-Khalifa, went on state television and called for a national dialogue between the government and the officially recognized opposition parties. A graduate of the

American University in Washington, DC, as well as Cambridge University, he had a reputation as a reformer, and had headed up the committee tasked with implementing political change in the early 2000s. 'Let's work together,' he pleaded on television. He followed this up with a proposal to hold talks with protestors on their key demands, including the establishment of an elected parliament, if they called off their demonstrations. In response, the kingdom's largest trade union threatened to call a general strike if the government refused to agree to all the opposition's demands. Shia politicians staged a mass resignation in protest at the violent tactics used by the security services. For their part, the crowds of anti-regime protestors on the ground turned their focus more and more on the symbols of royal power. They blocked access to the *Shura* council and gathered in large numbers outside the king's Manama residence. By early March the situation on the ground threatened to spiral out of control. Outside observers speculated over whether Bahrain's emir would soon follow Ben-Ali and Mubarak out of office. The possibility that this might happen and that a long-time GCC ruler might become the first hereditary monarch to succumb to the people power of the Arab Spring appalled other Gulf royals.

It is very difficult for revolutions to succeed. Rulers, as Jack A. Goldstone has explained, only tend to lose power in a revolution under two conditions: when they no longer have credibility and legitimacy across a wide cross-section of societal actors, including elite groups like the military; and when they cannot get powerful foreign actors to intervene to prop them up in power.[41] This is exactly what happened in Egypt, Tunisia and Libya in 2011. Arab Gulf leaders were determined that this would not happen in Bahrain. In the second half of February, the foreign ministers of Bahrain's five GCC partners travelled to Manama to show their support. This visit coincided with an emergency meeting of GCC rulers that agreed to send an aid package to Bahrain worth US$10 billion over ten years. In the short term it was hoped that this money would reduce antagonism towards Al-Khalifa rule. The hope for the longer term was that it would fund a GCC-sponsored socio-economic plan covering everything from education and housing to job creation.

The Arab Gulf policymakers who championed this ambitious proposal argued that the situation was deteriorating so rapidly that only a response on this scale would prevent chaos, civil war and revolution in Bahrain. These concerns were communicated to Bahrain's king during a visit he made to Saudi Arabia in late February. Even before he returned home, rumours circulated that Saudi leaders had warned him that they would act to defuse the situation if he could not. This was not an idle threat. Senior royals in Riyadh were convinced that Shia agitation in Bahrain posed an existential threat to their kingdom's internal stability. They feared that the turmoil in Bahrain might spread to Saudi Arabia's interconnected oil-rich Eastern Province. Only 25 kilometres off the Bahraini coast, this vital region was home to a significant Shia population that had already taken to the streets to protest against government policies. To prevent any spillover from the turmoil next door, the King Fahd Causeway connecting Bahrain to Saudi Arabia was closed. The Saudi authorities also installed infrared cameras, laser sensors and ground radar to increase their early warning capability. Dozens of German police instructors were also hired on a private contract to train Saudi security forces to search and occupy houses and deal with protests and uprisings.

The fear that insurrection in Bahrain might some day trigger sectarian conflict in Saudi Arabia had preoccupied Saudi leaders for decades. Ever since Bahraini independence in 1971 the Saudi intelligence service had maintained a strong presence in Manama to ensure that Riyadh was fully informed of any evolving threat from Iranian-sponsored subversives. Saudi officials labelled the failed coup attempt in Bahrain in 1981 as an Iranian 'sabotage plot'. Saudi interior minister Prince Nayef Abdul Aziz Al-Saud went further. He claimed that the failed insurrection in Bahrain was first and foremost an attack 'directed against Saudi Arabia', and he promised that future attempts to undermine the existing order in Bahrain would be met with Saudi intervention 'in a very short time'.[42] This was an illuminating insight into two things: the profound impact that the Islamic revolution in Iran had on the Arab Gulf, and in particular Saudi Arabia's feelings of insecurity; and how senior Gulf officials, especially top Saudis like Prince Nayef, viewed Bahraini security as a function of Saudi security. This deep conviction gained its most concrete expression in 1986, when the 25-kilometre causeway linking the two kingdoms was opened. Paid for by Saudi Arabia, this project was publicly presented as an investment in deeper GCC integration. The fact that the four-lane highway was wide enough to accommodate tanks and was designed to withstand bombing from the air was rarely mentioned.

In 1994, in response to serious Shia-led unrest, hundreds of plainclothes Saudi security personnel were dispatched to Manama to help the government suppress this challenge to its authority. The following year, Prince Saud Al-Faisal told US officials that he believed that the sectarian issue in Bahrain was 'very serious' as the Shia in the kingdom took their lead from Iran and were committed to causing trouble. He also dismissed Iranian claims that they had no role in fomenting agitation in Bahrain. Over the following years, the Bahraini authorities regularly accused Iran of interfering in the domestic affairs of the kingdom. They even provided detailed information on Iranian-sponsored terror and subversion, including a plan to set up a Bahraini version of Lebanese Hezbollah.

Following the US invasion of Iraq in 2003, Riyadh once more stepped up its security and intelligence role in Bahrain. The worry was that Iran would attempt to take advantage of the turmoil in post-Saddam Iraq to try to overthrow the existing order in the GCC's most vulnerable member state. Bahraini officials looked to capitalize on Riyadh's obsession with the Iranian menace for their own benefit. In 2008 they claimed that Iran was training rebels in the Syrian mountains to attack the kingdom. Two years later, on the eve of the Arab Spring, they claimed that pro-Iranian cells were operating on the ground inside Bahrain with the goal of destabilizing Sunni rule. The kingdom's foreign minister Khaled bin Ahmed Al-Khalifa explained that his government had 'never seen such a sustained campaign from Iran'.[43] Other officials linked the events of 2011 to past Iranian-sponsored plots going back to the failed 1981 coup attempt. 'Iran always starts with Bahrain' was a common refrain of Bahrain's king in meetings with his GCC counterparts and high-level Western visitors. During their late February 2011 visit to Bahrain, the other GCC foreign ministers jointly issued a statement that warned of 'foreign meddling' in the country, shorthand for an Iranian role. The Saudi authorities were more to the point. 'There is no doubt Iran is involved,' explained one official in Riyadh.

As the Arab Spring raged across the wider Middle East and the threat of local uprisings loomed large, Saudi policymakers were no longer willing to ignore this dangerous situation. On the morning of 14 March, between 1,500 and 2,000 members of the Saudi National Guard, as well as 100 tanks and armoured vehicles, crossed the Saudi–Bahrain causeway to help put down the uprising, secure Bahrain's royal family in power and contain Iranian influence. They were accompanied by hundreds of federal police officers from the UAE. Within hours these ground forces had set up camp and awaited further orders, while Kuwaiti naval vessels secured Bahrain's coastline. 'This is the initial phase,' a Saudi official explained. 'Bahrain will get whatever assistance it needs. It's open-ended'. This deployment was unprecedented. It was the first time that Arab forces had crossed an international border in response to the events of the Arab Spring. It was also a new departure for Saudi Arabia. During the 1960s, the Saudis had provided military aid for royalist forces in the North Yemen civil war and the kingdom's troops had played a central role in the military campaign against republicans backed by Nasser's Egypt. Since then Saudi rulers had preferred to protect their kingdom's unique position at the heart of the Islamic and energy worlds by acting behind the scenes, and using money and traditional diplomacy in defence of the status quo.

The decision to act militarily in Bahrain was a repudiation of this long-time approach. Despite the challenge posed by Qatar in the foreign policy arena in the pre-Arab Spring era, the Saudi intervention in Bahrain was a reminder that it was the only GCC member state capable of sending a military message to Iran that the Sunni Gulf could not be undermined through subversion or proxy wars. The recent revolution in Egypt made such messages all the more necessary. Mubarak had demonstrated an almost visceral distrust of Iran and he had viewed Shia communities as potential fifth columns in the service of mullahs in Tehran. Like Saudi leaders, Mubarak viewed Bahrain as the Arab Gulf's most vulnerable point and a vital bulwark against Iranian influence across the Persian Gulf and Arabian Peninsula. Under his leadership, Egypt was Saudi Arabia's main partner in the anti-Iranian Sunni Arab bloc.

Top Iranian officials revelled in the turmoil that engulfed the Arab world in 2011. The country's supreme leader, Ali Khamenei, took credit for the revolutions in Egypt and Tunisia as 'natural extensions of Iran's Islamic revolution'. He denounced Mubarak as a 'traitor and dictator'.[44] Many other Iranians took pleasure in the fact that Mubarak handed over power to Egypt's Supreme Military Council on 11 February – the anniversary of Iran's 1979 revolution. During the initial stage of the crisis in Bahrain, Iranian rhetoric was more restrained. The public statements coming out of Tehran applauded the demonstration of people power and urged Bahrain's leaders to use restraint and wisdom in defusing the situation. They stopped short of openly calling for revolution and there was little substantive evidence of official Iranian involvement in fomenting unrest in the kingdom. Following the Saudi-led GCC intervention in March, the Iranian response became tougher, and foreign minister Ali Akbar Salehi described the military response as 'unfair and un-Islamic'.

The Saudi-led operation in Bahrain took place under the aegis of the GCC's Peninsula Shield force almost thirty years after it had been established. In the early 2000s, in response to the start of the war on terror and the US invasion of Iraq, GCC member states endorsed a Saudi proposal to turn the lacklustre military unit into a rapid deployment force, only to be activated for pre-planned joint military training exercises or in response to specific crises. With these principles in place the Peninsula Shield force grew rapidly. It developed the most comprehensive unified operational procedures and joint training programmes in its history. By the time of the

Arab Spring it had more than 40,000 men in its ranks, based in their home countries and under the military command of the GCC secretariat in Riyadh. This was no small achievement. The GCC's secretary general, Abdul Rahman Al-Attiyah, expressed the hope that this reconstituted force would consolidate its position as 'one of the pillars that will support stability and security in the region' and that, in doing so, it would serve as the 'main safeguard' of GCC collective security doctrine.

This made the Peninsula Shield's military operation in Bahrain a key moment in the evolution of the GCC as a unified military player. It was, GCC officials explained, evidence of the 'spirit of collective cohesion' that now bound GCC member states together. Bahrain's king, who had invited this force into his country, described it as an 'impregnable shield', as well as a 'force for good, security and peace'. His top general explained that the arrival of GCC troops had 'raised the ceiling of ambitions and aspirations' to build a 'unified army'; the state-run Bahrain News Agency talked of the deployment in terms of 'common destiny bonding'. Saudi and GCC officials also insisted that Shield troops had been deployed to protect infrastructure and to play a supporting role to Bahraini police and soldiers. They were adamant that they were not there to fight civilian protestors and certainly 'not there to kill people'. The Bahraini government sent contradictory messages on this point. At times it explained that the GCC force would stay out of internal politics. On other occasions it made it clear that the force had been invited into the kingdom to help restore and preserve public order and that it would intervene when and where necessary to achieve this.

Opposition leaders, Shia political organizations and human rights advocates united in their condemnation of the GCC military intervention. They described it as the 'overt occupation of the kingdom' as well as a 'conspiracy against the unarmed people of Bahrain'. They accused GCC troops of taking part in house raids, manning checkpoints and generally acting to suppress the opposition's efforts to foster change.[45] The London-based Islamic Human Rights Commission was a not-for-profit organization that had close links to the Bahraini opposition from the time of its founding in the 1990s. It condemned the intervention as further evidence of the ruling family's preference for 'blaming outsiders whilst relying upon others to justify and secure its power'. The Al-Wefaq party went further, describing the Saudi-led intervention as a 'declaration of war'.[46]

Bahrain's ruler had announced the start of a three-month state of emergency, the State of National Safety, less than twenty-four hours after the arrival of GCC soldiers in his kingdom. This provided the army and security services with the authority to use extreme measures to end the uprising. In a series of raids that followed, several of the most high-profile and vocal anti-regime protestors were arrested, and the headquarters of the biggest opposition groups, Al-Wefaq and Al-Wa'ad, were attacked, though neither group was disbanded. From early on in the crisis, scores of injured anti-government protestors had been treated at the Salmaniya Medical Complex. A large public teaching hospital in central Manama, this institution quickly found itself at the centre of the movement for political and economic reform. Many of the 2,000 doctors, nurses and other medical professionals working there had regularly joined the protests and the hospital served as a quasi-official base for opposition groups. Once the crackdown on anti-government protests gained pace in mid-March, Bahraini security forces and Sunni militias stormed the hospital. Those suspected of treating demonstrators and of backing the anti-government protests were detained.

Soon afterwards, tanks entered the Pearl Roundabout to demolish an even more prominent symbol of opposition to the regime. In quick order the protestor encampment was scattered, the roundabout bulldozed and the pearl statue, built in late 1982 to commemorate the first time that Bahrain hosted a summit of GCC leaders, was knocked down. The government renamed the site the Gulf Cooperation Council Square and blamed its demolition on protestors who had 'desecrated' a long-time symbol of cooperation and harmony. This marked the end of the most intense period of anti-regime protests in Bahrain. In mid-April, the causeway linking Bahrain and Saudi Arabia was reopened. In early June the state of emergency was lifted. Though the Saudi-dominated Peninsula Shield force remained in the kingdom indefinitely, soldiers were taken off the streets of Manama and other towns and replaced by police patrols.

According to Amnesty International, the uprising in Bahrain had left an estimated seventy dead and thousands injured. Thousands more were imprisoned, fired from their jobs or expelled from college for involvement in the protest movement. Even after the end of the state of emergency, the international media and human rights groups continued to report attacks on journalists, opposition leaders and protestors. An Al-Jazeera English-language documentary 'Shouting in the Dark', dismissed by Bahraini officials as 'one-sided propaganda', chronicled the ongoing struggle to an audience of millions around the world. In late June, King Hamad bin Isa Al-Khalifa appointed five international lawyers and human rights experts to head an investigation known as the Bahrain Independent Commission of Inquiry (BICI). Over the following summer months he also dismissed the charges against some of those detained during the protests and urged those who had been poorly treated while in detention to lodge official complaints. Senior royals also announced the beginning of a national dialogue with opposition groups but ruled out talks on the opposition's key demand, a democratically elected parliament.

Despite the recent threat of catastrophic sectarian revolt, there was no will to initiate a process that might ultimately lead to the diffusion of political power along ethnic lines. Sunni political control was not, in the final account, negotiable. This ensured that the underlying tensions in the kingdom between the Sunni rulers and the Shia-dominated opposition could not be resolved. Talks between the government and its political opponents that got under way in July 2011 reflected this stalemate. From the beginning they were conducted in an atmosphere of suspicion and mutual distrust. Officials accused members of the Al-Wefaq party of being Iranian agents, while protestors gathered outside chanted 'Dialogue is suicide'. Clashes between demonstrators and the police continued across Manama as the talks took place. The situation was aggravated further by the victory of pro-government candidates in a September 2011 by-election boycotted by Shia parliamentarians and voters. The widely anticipated publication of the BICI report at the end of 2011 also aggravated the situation. Over 500 pages long, it charged the Bahraini authorities with gross human rights violations, including the use of torture and unlawful killing during the protests. It also called for the establishment of an independent human rights body. In response, the Bahraini government announced a number of concessions, including the prosecution of twenty security personnel for using excessive force during the protests.[47] Such moves did little to quell ongoing anti-regime demonstrations in Shia strongholds like the township of Bani Jamrah and Sitra, south of Manama, which had earned the title of 'capital of the revolution' over the previous year.

At the outset of the crisis in Bahrain, Saudi officials had been adamant that they would not tolerate a Shia-dominated government in the kingdom that would serve as an Iranian strategic base at the heart of the Arab Gulf. In an important speech to the *Majlis al-Shura*, made seven months after the Bahrain crisis had started, King Abdullah expressed 'relief' that Bahrain had finally been secured and he restated his government's commitment to GCC defence cooperation. The security of the GCC, he declared, was 'indivisible' with his own kingdom's security.[48] From the Saudi perspective the uncompromising GCC response in Bahrain was also a clear message to Tehran that the Arab Gulf would use force to prevent Iran from taking over the kingdom and destabilizing the region. Iran, explained a joint statement issued by GCC foreign ministers in the same period, needed to refrain from meddling in GCC business and from 'violating the sovereignty' of member states.

The Saudi-led intervention in Bahrain may have averted the immediate threat to the region's delicate equilibrium but it did nothing to neutralize fears over the proxy war being waged by Iran and its respective allies across the wider Middle East. Just as importantly, the turmoil in Bahrain, on top of the other upheavals in the Middle East during the Arab Spring, also convinced Gulf leaders that sustainable socio-economic development was no longer simply an economic or human right. It was a strategic priority that was needed to ensure stability and influence in coming decades. This realization made it imperative that Gulf States act quickly at home to empower their increasingly vocal, and ever-growing, young populations through greater economic opportunities and a stake in the future of society. As the next chapter will show, this required rapid diversification away from oil, and a massive overhaul of the bloated public sectors and patronage systems that together had provided the basis for social stability and prosperity across the Gulf since the oil boom of the 1970s.

CHAPTER 8

OIL CHANGE

> 'The new Arab will re-enter history, contribute to civilization, not with his oil but with his brains.'
>
> – Ahmed Yamani

Evolution of Man is a work of art consisting of five silk-screen prints. It begins with an X-ray of a man holding a gun to his head; over the course of the next four prints the gun gradually morphs into a gasoline pump. The message is very clear – overdependence on oil can be dangerous; it can even have deadly consequences. Ahmed Mater, the artist who created this piece, is a doctor at a hospital in the city of Abha, the capital of the southern Saudi province of Aseer. In his spare time Mater is a key figure in the innovative Edge of Arabia artists' collective. He is also one of the founders of the Al-Meftaha Arts Village based in his hometown, where talented young artists work with a variety of different mediums including painting, photography and video installations. This project has developed into a vibrant cultural hub in a region previously best known for its farming, its national park and for having the highest levels of rainfall in the kingdom.

Mater has built up a large international following for his art, which mainly deals with the impact of globalization and modernity on Islamic culture and society, in particular in his native Saudi Arabia. Critics of art like Mater's, that also serves as a trenchant if somewhat gloomy social commentary, would argue that since the mid-1970s the Arab Gulf has benefited more than any other part of the world from oil and gas wealth. Petro-dollars, they would point out, have paid for the region's impressive modernization and development programmes, as well as the treasure trove of high-end overseas assets that ruling families and their wealthy citizens now own.

Without energy revenues Qatar would not be the richest nation in the world on a per capita basis. Kuwait, Qatar and the UAE would not have the world's fourth, fifth and sixth largest number of millionaires as a proportion of the population. Without gas and oil money it would not have been possible for the Gulf States to establish themselves as some of the world's most generous providers of humanitarian and development aid. According to the World Bank, the Arab Gulf States between them have contributed more than twice the United Nations target of 0.7 per cent of their combined gross national income since 1973. The Kuwait Fund for Arab Economic Development alone has funded almost 1,000 projects in 100 countries at a cost of nearly US$20 billion since its establishment. Nor, as the last chapter showed, could ruling families across the Gulf have spent hundreds of billions of dollars at home to defuse potential crises before they got out of hand during the Arab Spring. In short, without their control of vast energy resources, Gulf leaders would not have been able to achieve stability at home and influence abroad on the scale they have over the last four decades.

That's the upside. The downside is that overreliance on any single source of income leaves a country vulnerable to external economic forces beyond its control. This is especially true in the case of oil. Those who produce and sell it can do nothing about economic downturns or mild winters, technological breakthroughs in alternative energies or the decisions of consumer countries to move to other kinds of fuel. Nor can they prevent consumers using fuel in more efficient ways. Europe uses less oil now than it did at the beginning of the 1980s. American oil consumption has only risen very slightly in the last four decades even though its economy is twice as big now as then. All these factors make oil an unpredictable commodity subject to extreme swings in price over relatively short periods of time. In fact, the only thing that anyone really knows for sure about the oil market is that the price goes up and down, often in a dramatic fashion. A barrel of oil cost US$3 in 1970. By the end of that decade it had reached US$40. During the 1980s its price halved, falling back to pre-1973 levels in real terms. In the late 1990s it fell to almost US$10 a barrel. By the time the global financial crisis began in 2008, after six years of rising prices, it was at a record US$160. By early 2016 it was down to under US$30. This pattern of profound fluctuation in the oil price is responsible for much volatility in the international system. In the Gulf, it means that energy revenues cannot be relied upon to serve as an alternative to substantive and viable long-term solutions to socio-economic problems.

Even in the 1970s, informed members of the Gulf's elite understood the economic problems they would one day face if they relied only on oil revenues to fund their future. The establishment of Saudi Basic Industries Corporation (SABIC) in 1976 by royal decree was a testament to that. Launched as a manufacturing company focused on chemicals, fertilizers and metals, over the years it has developed into the crown jewel of the Saudi diversification project. The 1970s also saw the rise of a small but growing class of technocrats and business leaders in the Gulf who preached the need to reduce oil dependence. Born and raised in the region but often trained abroad, they play an increasingly important role in public life. In the late 1960s, only two major Saudi government ministries – oil and finance – were in the hands of non-royals. The new Saudi cabinet appointed by King Salman after he came to power in January 2015 included twenty-two technocrats and only four royals.

In 1995 the Kuwaiti economist Jassem Al-Saadoun, an adviser to his country's parliament, warned that unrest across the region would be inevitable in subsequent decades without the introduction of programmes that addressed the causes, rather than the symptoms, of economic instability, inequality and discontent.[1] On the eve of the Arab Spring, a UAE government official made a similar point. 'Energy revenues', he explained, would never be the answer, and they only provided the Gulf States with a 'cushion and the luxury of time'[2] to get their socio-economic houses in order. In late July 2013, the high-profile Saudi investor Prince Al-Waleed bin Talal received worldwide media attention for posting on Twitter a letter he had written a few months earlier to top Saudi policymakers warning that 'almost total dependency on oil' posed a 'continuous threat' to the kingdom. Others have made the related point that neither security deals with outside powers including China, the United States, Great Britain and France, nor spending billions on state-of-the-art military equipment are sufficient substitutes for proper socio-economic development. Speaking in 2007, Hamad bin Jaber Al-Thani, the US-educated secretary general of Qatar's planning council, encapsulated this sort of thinking. Security, he explained, requires much more than 'defence or military protection'. Just as vital, he continued, is 'formulating and adopting strategies and ... policies that ensure continued development in social, economic and political sectors'.[3]

Until the Arab Spring, most Gulf citizens did not pay too much attention to the warnings of their more astute leaders, jet-setting tycoons and Western-educated technocrats. They believed that oil and gas provided them with immunity from the social and economic cleavages that had plagued the rest of the Arab world for generations. They were equally convinced that the dangers they faced were solely external in nature and they conceived and measured those threats to domestic stability and even regime survival only in terms of hard power. Guns not butter were the order of the day, and they failed to see the link between socio-economic progress and security. The events of the Arab Spring demonstrated just how wrong they were. More than any other group of nations, the Arab Gulf States had reaped the rewards of the unprecedented rise in oil prices in the first decade of the 2000s. High oil prices meant high oil revenues and that made possible massive spending at home and abroad as well as record levels of growth. Neither the drop in the oil price after it hit its peak in the second half of 2008, nor the global financial crisis that followed, seemed to slow down the advance of Gulf economies on the global stage. This made the Arab Spring protests in Kuwait, Saudi Arabia and Oman, not to mention Bahrain, so troubling. Historically, local agitation for socio-economic or political reform occurred during or following prolonged periods of low oil prices that had forced government spending down. The expressions of frustration in 2011 did not take place in an era of downturn. They took place after years of high oil prices and ambitious government spending programmes across all economic sectors. This was something new and highlighted for the first time that the Arab Gulf was vulnerable to unrest at home even at times of high oil revenues and prosperity.

To make matters worse, the Arab Spring also showed that even wealthy countries could not take their domestic stability or security for granted. Tunisia was one of the most economically developed countries in Africa, with a large middle class. That did not save Ben-Ali. In the four years preceding the Arab Spring, the World Bank had named Egypt one of the world's top economic reformers. That did not stop the march of revolution or the end of Mubarak. Bahrain was the eighteenth most 'economically free' and the nineteenth richest country in the world when unrest broke out. In per capita terms it was almost as rich as Kuwait and the UAE and much richer than Oman and Saudi Arabia. It could boast annual economic growth of 7 per cent, less than 4 per cent unemployment and an average per capita income of US$24,000. As a top Bahraini official pointed out at the time, the people of the kingdom, including many within the large Shia population, lived prosperous lives and enjoyed high living standards, higher even than some in western Europe. Yet Bahrain still experienced one of the largest and longest-lasting protest movements in the Middle East, with nearly one out of every five citizens taking to the streets.

Speaking in 2004, Saudi foreign minister Prince Saud Al-Faisal made the point that no two Gulf States faced identical problems at home. This, he continued, demanded that any proposed solutions to their problems had to be country-specific. He was right – no two GCC countries are the same and their problems are not uniform. They differ in both size and nature. Most obviously, Bahrain differs from other Sunni monarchies in the region in having a deeply alienated and frustrated Shia majority. This constituency's grievances are not limited to the real disparities in wealth and influence that exist between the Sunni and Shia communities there. They also spring from deep and historic sectarian divisions and geo-strategic pressures that the troubled kingdom has had to grapple with for decades.

Saudi rulers have always attempted to coopt powerful religious constituencies in society as a way of facilitating and consolidating their own power. The kingdom also faces a far greater demographic challenge than any of its much smaller partners. Between 1960 and 2015 the kingdom's population grew by more than 650 per cent, from four million to over thirty million people, out of a total GCC population of around fifty million. One consequence of this population explosion over the last fifty years is that oil revenues per capita are now substantially less in real terms than they were in the 1970s. Another is that despite its wealth, per capita income is much lower in Saudi Arabia than it is in other GCC countries. What makes the Saudi problem worse is that three out of five of its citizens are under twenty years of age. An estimated 150,000 young nationals enter the workforce every year. Unemployment among Saudis aged between fifteen and twenty-nine is around 30 per cent, placing the kingdom in the unenviable position of ranking second in the world, after parts of sub-Saharan Africa, for youth unemployment. There is a glut of graduates from large public universities who complete their studies without the skills needed to get productive jobs. They lack language and technical knowledge, as well as other basic business and office skills. Even graduates with Masters and PhD degrees from well-regarded local and foreign universities struggle to find decent jobs.

None of the other Gulf countries has to deal with the demographic challenges faced by Saudi Arabia. But they all have their own particular circumstances and priority concerns. Kuwait has a vibrant elected national assembly that provides a constant challenge to the ruling family. As far back as 1967 *The Economist* was applauding Kuwait's royals for 'having marvellously handled their co-existence with democracy'.[4] This dynamic has much to commend it but it has also made it impossible for a consensus to be reached on how to build a competitive business environment and how to move the political process forward. The UAE has to balance the interests and needs of many disparate groups in a federation made up of seven emirates, each with their own ruling families, economies and political bases, and all at different stages of development. This throws up all sorts of complications and anomalies. The UAE is, for example, the only state in the world where offshore oil rights belong to the individual parts of the federation rather than the federation itself.

Qatar is spared many of these concerns. It has the world's highest GDP per capita and the world's lowest unemployment rate. Unlike Bahrain it can boast a remarkable level of social cohesion. Unlike Kuwait, its rulers do not have to worry about competition from an ambitious political class vying for influence and authority. Unlike Oman it is resource rich and unlike the UAE it has only one ruling family making decisions about the country's future. Nor do its rulers have to worry about the demands of powerful religious constituencies or growing armies of out-of-work citizens like their Saudi counterparts. On the other hand, tiny Qatar finds itself in the difficult position of having to share its most valuable and important economic asset – the North Field or North Dome gas field – with its much bigger and more powerful neighbour, Iran.

Despite variations in wealth, population size, sectarian make-up and resources, all the Gulf countries share the same basic structures of government and economic management and, no less importantly, the same relationship between rulers and the ruled. Overwhelmingly reliant on oil and gas for economic growth and development, they are classic rentier states. The ruling elites are in total control of the use and allocation of wealth and they have developed an impressive system of patronage intended first and foremost to buy loyalty and preserve their own power. This means that they also share to a large degree the same socio-economic challenges and a common understanding of what needs to be done to overcome these challenges – 'optimal rationalization of state revenues and spending',[5] as a Bahraini technocrat once put it. In layman's language this means that all the GCC states have to earn more and spend less while at the same time moving beyond dependence on oil and gas revenues to balance their budgets.

From a practical perspective this is not easy to achieve because it demands the gradual dismantlement of the vastly expensive welfare state. For decades the cost of everything from healthcare and education to cars, homes and utilities has been heavily subsidized. For many Gulf citizens this is all they know or remember. Not only are they unwilling to give up such valuable benefits, they are even reluctant to pay the small amounts they are charged for the use of public goods like fuel and electricity. A few years back it was estimated that Kuwait's national power grid was owed over US$1 billion from citizens who ignored bills because they did not think they should have to pay anything at all for electricity. This sense of entitlement is made worse by the fact that GCC citizens are some of the biggest per capita users of oil and gas in the world. Energy consumption across the region is rising faster than economic growth. This is due to rapid urbanization, population growth, large-scale infrastructural development and, believe it or not, air conditioning units that eat up electricity day and night all year long in these hot desert kingdoms. Saudi Arabia is the sixth biggest oil consumer in the world. The kingdom uses more oil than industrial heavyweights like Germany, Canada and South Korea.[6] At least Saudi Arabia is the world's top producer of this precious commodity. By the standards of the region at least, Oman is oil-poor and has few other natural resources. Yet annual per capita electricity consumption is double the world average. To cushion its citizens from the cost of their high energy use, the Omani government has spent just under one US$1 billion a year to maintain a generous fuel subsidy programme that results in some of the world's cheapest energy prices.

Since the summer of 2014, the oil price has spiralled downwards. It lost half its value between July 2014 and April 2015 and hit an eleven-year low in December 2015. This has forced the Gulf States to take measures to streamline costs by reducing subsidies on electricity, water and energy, the latter of which exceeded US$70 billion in 2015 alone. Towards the end of that year, the head of Qatar's ministry of development planning, Saleh bin Mohammed Al-Nabit, spoke for many officials across the Gulf when he said that his country's generous programme of subsidies was in 'urgent' need of reform. In line with this thinking, Qatar, Oman and Kuwait have introduced significant increases in the price of diesel. Bahrain has increased fuel prices and reduced subsidies on meat. Abu Dhabi was already home to the highest gas prices in the GCC. It went further in the second half of 2015 when it scrapped fuel subsidies and increased petrol prices by more than 20 per cent. It also increased tariffs on electricity by 40 per cent and on water by 170 per cent.[7] At the end of December 2015, Saudi Arabia increased the fuel price by over 60 per cent – though it was still cheaper than bottled water in the kingdom. This is not the first time that Gulf States have moved to cut subsidies in order to reduce spending. They did it in the mid-1980s and at the end of the 1990s when the oil price slumped to new lows and economic growth stagnated. On both occasions, subsidies rose again once the economic situation improved.

There is no personal income tax or value added tax (VAT) anywhere in the GCC. Corporation tax does exist, but it is only levied on a small number of mainly foreign companies. Consultants, economists and international organizations, including the IMF, have repeatedly called on the six Gulf States to establish a functioning tax base. Recent proposals include the introduction of VAT on goods and services with the exception of food items, health and education; extending corporation tax to include local as well as foreign firms; the launch of a 'sin' tax on cigarettes and sweet foods and drinks; and even a tax on car sales in order to shift the cost of driving from the state to the individual. There has been much more reluctance to put forward plans for income tax and the UAE has already ruled that option out. In a system where traditional networks of tribe, family and community have long served as channels for the distribution and redistribution of wealth and patronage, it is hardly surprising that such proposals for reform face staunch local opposition. This makes it tough for rulers preoccupied above all else with keeping stability at home to start introducing radical new policies on taxes and subsidies. No less politically sensitive is the need to reform the public sector. The Gulf patronage system is not based on monetary reward alone. It also extends to the allocation of government contracts, loans and well-paid government jobs. Most Gulf nationals – up to 95 per cent in some countries – find employment in the public sector. The wages and benefits bill for overstaffed and underproductive government departments across the region is massive. They amount to between 40 and 50 per cent of government spending in Saudi Arabia alone.

The population boom of recent years also means that Gulf governments can no longer rely on the public sector to absorb high school and university graduates as a way of keeping unemployment down as it did in the past. When the global financial crisis began in 2008, small states like Ireland and Greece with large, expensive and unproductive public sectors were among the worst hit. The experiences of both offered some stark but valuable lessons. To avoid the same fate in future economic downturns, other states need to create more efficient, competitive and cost-effective public sectors. To do this, however, strikes at the heart of the socio-economic pact between ruler and ruled in the Gulf, and governments are reluctant to implement even the least aggressive moves like capping the number of government jobs or eliminating non-essential positions once they become vacant.

The only way to reduce the size of the public sector without undermining the fundamental tenets of the existing social order is to find jobs for nationals in the private sector. The problem is that millions of foreign workers dominate almost every area of private economic endeavour. The entire regional economy is, in the words of Hadi Ghaemi of Human Rights Watch, 'run on the backs of migrant workers'. As discussed earlier, this dependence on expatriate workers is not a new phenomenon. It has been necessary to import foreign labour into the Gulf for generations because the local labour force has always been too small. Most countries have to deal with the problems caused by a surplus of labour and a shortage of capital. For generations the Gulf States have faced the opposite predicament. They have had plenty of money but too few people to undertake the rapid industrialization and modernization of their economies and societies. This makes the provision of services and infrastructure also very expensive because the cost per unit of the population is very high when populations are small or spread out, as was the norm before modern cities rose up out of the desert. The upshot has been a massive influx of foreign workers that continues up to the present day.

These workers currently account for around twenty million (40 per cent) of the GCC's total population of 49–50 million. Most are unskilled and come from south-east Asia and the Horn of Africa. They work as labourers, drivers, maids and nannies and dominate the food and hospitality industries, retail outlets and back offices. The UAE is the largest recipient of foreign labour in the Gulf, as well as the fifth largest recipient in the world. In 2015, non-nationals made up almost 90 per cent of the federation's population. The largest ethnic groups are Indians, Pakistanis, Bangladeshis and Filipinos, who between them make up over 50 per cent of the entire population. Qatar has the second highest percentage of foreigners in relation to the citizen population in the Arab Gulf. As of 2015, there were 278,000 Qatari nationals. They represent a mere 12 per cent of the country's total population. Indians and Nepalese, the two biggest national groups in the country, account for 545,000 and 400,000 respectively. Foreigners also make up 70 per cent of Kuwait's population of less than four million, and account for substantial minorities in Oman, Saudi Arabia and Bahrain.

The massive use of cheap, unskilled foreign labour has been a key reason for the economic success of the Gulf since the 1970s. But it is also, in the words of Gulf expert Steffen Hertog, the 'Achilles Heel' of Gulf society.[8] It profoundly retards private sector development and makes it v ery difficult to attract nationals into, or find room for them in, privately owned companies. Before the oil era Kuwait was considered a leading merchant hub and home to a thriving boat-building industry. Now less than 10 per cent of its citizens work in the private sector, which only contributes around a quarter of the country's annual GDP. Fewer than one in ten Saudis works in a private company and a recent report showed that over 250,000 small and medium-sized Saudi businesses do not even employ one Saudi national.

All immigration into the region is temporary and it is practically impossible for a foreigner living in any of the GCC states to acquire citizenship. Instead, a highly efficient form of local sponsorship, known as the kafala system, has developed to regulate residency status and worker rights in host countries. It functions well in terms of providing a constant flow of cheap labour but it raises a number of deeply problematic issues. It often fails to provide workers with the necessary protections for dealing with exploitative working and housing conditions, poor pay and even physical or financial abuse. Workers are banned from joining trade unions and are not allowed to strike. This limits the opportunities they have to express their discontent. Sometimes frustrations boil over into car torching and other forms of property damage inside the sprawling labour camps and residential compounds in which they reside. On very rare occasions protests spill out into the public or there are attempts to initiate illegal strikes. Such actions almost invariably result in the protestors involved being deported back to their home countries by the local authorities.

There are some signs that this situation is changing. Kuwait set a precedent in 2015 by acknowledging the rights and providing protection under the law for more than 600,000 domestic workers, mainly women from Asia and Africa, living in the country. In the same year the governments of Qatar, Saudi Arabia and the UAE all improved their own labour laws to offer better protection to migrant workers, but unlike the Kuwaiti legislation none of these laws addressed the rights of the large armies of domestic workers in the three kingdoms. In the case of the UAE, for example, the three new decrees that were passed explicitly excluded domestic workers, who are not covered under labour law. There are self-interested, as well as moral and ethical, reasons for improving further the current system for workers in the construction and service industries and for bringing domestic workers under the law. Playing host to an army of resentful foreigners distrusted by the local population is not a recipe for long-term stability. This situation threatens the fabric of local culture and inevitably raises sectarian and ethnic challenges. It negatively impacts on the relations between the various Arab Gulf countries and the governments of the home nations of these armies of workers. In recent years, Sri Lanka has placed limits on how many female citizens are allowed to work in Saudi Arabia as maids after the beheading of a seventeen-year-old citizen convicted of killing her employer's infant son. When it was alleged that a Saudi employer chopped off the arm of an Indian domestic worker after she complained to police that he was mistreating her, the Indian government made a 'strong complaint', and promised to 'pursue justice'. This affair sparked a wide-ranging debate in India over what the *Times of India* called the 'never-ending agonies of Indian workers in Gulf'.

Indonesia, the world's most populous Muslim country, has also taken steps to ban its citizens from taking domestic jobs in all six GCC states after two Indonesian maids were executed by beheading in Saudi Arabia for allegedly killing their abusive employer. It is not just Saudi Arabia. In the summer of 2015, a video of a Bahraini slapping a south Asian migrant worker went viral, adding to the woes of the government in Manama. This has become such a hot international topic that the highly influential *Financial Times* dedicated its 2015 Christmas appeal to the cause of the Gulf's 'Vulnerable Migrant Workers', and led its reporting with an interview with the founder of a Nepali organization set up to help fellow citizens trapped in the Gulf, who described the situation as 'twenty-first century slavery'.[9] The negative media attention and the outrage expressed by the home governments and populations of migrants erodes the international legitimacy of Gulf States and makes it harder for them to project themselves as bastions of progress in the wider Middle East. It also has the potential to hurt foreign investment, tourism and the wider economy. As chapter Ten will show, all are vital if the Gulf is to be successful in establishing itself as a global hub between East and West. The current system is also very expensive to maintain. Foreign workers transfer vast sums of money out of the Gulf each year. At the beginning of the 2000s it was reported that Saudi Arabia spent 1 per cent of its total annual income on paying non-Saudi drivers employed in the kingdom. Most of that money left the country as overseas remittances. Currently, foreign workers living in Saudi Arabia remit funds to the value of 10 per cent of the kingdom's GDP, around US$60 billion; workers in the UAE send around US$12 billion a year home to their families. In 2014, some twenty million foreign workers sent home more than US$100 billion in remittances. These funds have transformed some of the poorer countries whose migrants travel to the Gulf in large numbers. In Nepal, for example, where just under 10 per cent of the population works abroad, remittances make up over 30 per cent of the economy, up from 2 per cent at the beginning of the 2000s.

Finally, and perhaps most importantly from an economic perspective, the current system reduces the opportunities for indigenous development, and closes down potential avenues of employment for locals. 'The GCC employs 17 million foreign workers but has more than 1 million unemployed citizens,'[10] Bahrain's labour minister Majeed Al-Alawi declared regretfully on the eve of the Arab Spring. The region has always needed foreign workers but this state of affairs is a relatively new phenomenon in terms of composition. Until the end of the 1970s the majority of immigrant workers in the Gulf were Arab and came from Palestine, Jordan, Sudan, Yemen and Egypt. In those years Gulf citizens still did many of the jobs that they would rarely consider doing now. For example, most truck drivers in Saudi Arabia were nationals until the spoils of the oil boom started to be redistributed across society in the late 1970s. Now the entire industry is dependent on drivers from south-east Asia and parts of Africa.

For decades, Gulf governments have adopted a proactive and interventionist approach to solving this problem. They have championed worker nationalization programmes – known as Qatarization, Saudization, Omanization, Kuwaitization, Emiratization – as a way of opening up the private sector to locals. As far back as 1980, the Saudi government had started to prioritize what it officially termed 'incisive manpower development policies with the objective of replacing foreign manpower by Saudis to the maximum possible extent'.[11] Since then all the other GCC countries have followed suit. The UAE's president, Khalifa bin Zayed Al-Nahyan, has dedicated many of his recent National Day speeches to promoting a 'strategy for the future' that centres on a 'real program to develop local young people' that would 'only [be] complete when private sector works as a full partner in the national development process'.[12]

In order to make this happen, Gulf governments have introduced numerous laws, regulations and policies over the years. As Steffen Hertog has shown in his research, these are either prescriptive or 'incentive'-based programmes.[13] The more prescriptive require private sector firms to meet minimum quotas of nationals in their companies. Saudi Arabia, where 70 per cent of working nationals are employed in the government and even the private sector remains dependent on government spending, has introduced dramatic regulations. Under the *Nitaqat* proposals of 2011, for example, Saudi private companies must employ a specific number of nationals, depending on the sector and the size of the firm in question. Those who refuse to comply face fines. Other common policies include the levying of monthly fees from employers for every foreign worker on their books as a way of making non-national labour more costly and less attractive.

In response to domestic political pressure, the Kuwaiti government has acted most decisively. It has pledged to increase the number of nationals working in the private sector by 50 per cent by 2020, and has also announced its intention to reduce the foreign population in the kingdom by 60 per cent by 2030. As an initial step in achieving these interconnected goals, the number of foreign residents allowed to work in the country has been frozen and newcomers are now only allowed in to replace those leaving. Oman has regulated the percentage of nationals in different sectors, with 65 per cent of those working in insurance companies required to be Omanis, and has imposed sporadic six-month bans on the recruitment of foreigners working as maids and nannies and in the construction, carpentry and aluminium sectors. From January 2016 the authorities in Oman also began charging companies the equivalent of US$50 to process new visas and to renew visas for foreign workers, a service that had been free up until then.

These policies can claim some success. Since the launch of the *Nitaqat* regulations in 2011, 40 per cent of all new jobs created in Saudi Arabia have been in the private sector. A job-placement and job-training scheme introduced as part of the same labour reforms and targeting the kingdom's less well-educated male population has also led to the number of registered Saudi jobseekers receiving training rising tenfold to over one million in the same period.[14] Unlike in previous decades, stories of Saudi nationals working in the service industries are no longer newsworthy as growing numbers of nationals with few other options take jobs in restaurants, hotels and shops. One in three employees at a large McDonald's in Riyadh, for example, are Saudi nationals. What is still striking is not the number of young citizens preparing Big Macs for hungry customers but what they get paid. They make almost US$1,500 a month, some of it subsidized by the government, compared to non-citizen co-workers who earn just over US$300 a month.[15]

Such flawed progress aside, none of the GCC states has so far succeeded in building up an indigenous labour force. Nor have they managed to wean their countries off their reliance on foreign workers. The majority of private sector employees are still non-nationals. Between 2000 and 2010, about seven million jobs were created across the GCC (excluding the UAE, for which data is unavailable). The vast majority of these jobs, 5.4 million, were created in the private sector, 90 per cent of which were filled by foreigners. On average, expatriates now do more than 80 per cent of all low-skilled private sector jobs across the six GCC member states and 60 per cent of the more skilled work. At the same time, the employment of nationals as a percentage of all those employed in the region is falling. One reason for this is demographics. In some places – notably Dubai and Qatar – there are simply not enough nationals leaving school and university and entering the job market every year to fill all the private sector positions that need to be filled. This is not a problem in Saudi Arabia, where it is estimated that 250,000 school leavers enter the workforce every year.

The much bigger problem is cheap foreign workers distorting private sector wages. This makes hiring expensive nationals far less attractive to employers looking to make a profit. Foreign firms operating in free zones almost always take advantage of the quota reductions and exemptions they receive as an incentive for locating there. Companies not eligible to avail of these terms immediately rehire low-wage, low-skilled foreigner workers whenever Gulf governments reduce quota numbers for nationals. During the global financial crisis, for example, the number of foreign workers in the Gulf fell briefly as jobs in construction and the service industries dried up. When the economic situation improved, companies once again looked to refill posts with the cheapest possible available labour. Many firms are even willing to risk criminal penalties in order to employ illegal foreign workers. A few years back the Saudi authorities launched a major crack-down to address this problem. There were raids on ports, offices, shops, hotels and restaurants across the country. Roadblocks were set up in all the kingdom's major business centres to check employment documents. This nationwide operation did little to reduce the appeal of cheap foreign labour but it did cause chaos. Shops, restaurants and hotels were unable to function as hundreds of thousands of legal and illegal non-citizen workers stayed away from work to avoid undue scrutiny.

The problem is not only a consequence of employers looking to maximize profit by minimizing labour costs. It is also structural. The majority of private sector jobs in the Gulf are in low-skilled and low-paid sectors like construction and the service industries. This makes it very hard to attract nationals, who view themselves as middle class and upper middle class and will rarely apply for what they view to be menial or unskilled jobs. Instead they will only consider better-paid, white-collar, managerial and supervisory roles commensurate with their status in society. The upshot is that many firms cannot afford to hire nationals even if they are willing to do so. In an attempt to overcome the problems caused by the significant disparity in wages and benefits received by nationals working in the public and private sectors, governments have introduced various programmes and policies intended to make private sector jobs attractive to locals. These include offers to pay newly hired nationals half of their first year's salary in advance and sizeable bonuses for locals who complete their first full year of work in a private company. Kuwait introduced a wage support programme in 2000 that extended some public sector benefits to private sector employees. The programme has expanded since its launch and is one reason the number of private sector workers in Kuwait has increased in the last decade in comparison to Qatar and the UAE. The Kuwaiti educational NGO, INJAZ-Kuwait, has also provided almost 30,000 young citizens with some form of private sector workplace experience in the hope that this will influence them to think more positively about a private sector career when they enter the job market. In a similar programme in the UAE, the government's *Tawteen* programme has focused on tackling the social and cultural impediments that locals face in trying to find jobs in private companies.

Despite such efforts, Gulf nationals still prefer to find employment in the public sector. Wages are often several times higher and employment conditions and non-wage benefits including working hours and job security are far better. Those nationals who do not land one of these government jobs often end up joining the growing ranks of disaffected, struggling citizens, a constituency that is going to increase exponentially in the future in a region where 50 per cent of the population is under fifteen years of age. A 2007 newspaper headline in the Dubai-based *Khaleej Times* summed up a growing sentiment of many young in the region: 'Large number of nationals seeking meaningful work'.[16] A decade on, the problem is even more acute. The number of GCC nationals entering the labour force will grow by 1.2–1.6 million by 2018. International consulting firms like McKinsey estimate that between them the GCC states will need to create several hundred thousand jobs a year on top of those currently available to employ young citizens graduating from schools and universities.

Economic diversification is the only way policymakers can succeed in creating new private sector jobs that nationals are willing and able to do and that reflect true market forces. Attempts to move beyond oil and gas into other areas of economic endeavour are no newer than attempts to nationalize the workforce. Economists, regional experts and policymakers have argued for decades that diversification is the only really effective way to generate non-oil-based income, increase the number of well-paid private sector jobs and wean populations off government handouts. In the late 1970s, some informed commentators gave the Gulf States a maximum of twenty-five years to bring their economies to the point where they could move beyond energy dependence and compete in the global economy.[17] At that time, local policymakers were confident that they could meet such deadlines. In Saudi Arabia, officials pointed to the fact that even before the oil boom the number of Saudi industrial enterprises, though mostly small, had grown from five in 1954 to sixty-seven in 1964. The Saudi plan to build a massive industrial economy in the heart of the desert from the mid-1970s onwards was simply a much more ambitious, and expensive, continuation of this strategy. Speaking in the final months of the 1970s, Ghazi Abdel-Rahman Al-Gosaibi, the Saudi Arabian minister for industry and electricity, predicted that within ten years the majority of his country's revenues would be coming from industry rather than oil.[18] The kingdom's third five-year development plan launched in 1980 earmarked almost US$250 billion for the diversification of the economic base. Previous plans had invested hundreds of billions of dollars in developing commercial and residential infrastructure, communications, roads and essential utilities like water and electricity. It was now time, as a Saudi Ministry of Planning document made clear, for a significant portion of the kingdom's 'capital and manpower'[19] to be reallocated to productive economic sectors including, but not limited to, agriculture and industry.

Writing in the *New York Times* at the end of the 1970s, the celebrated Middle East expert Foud Ajami noted how Saudi Arabia had 'mounted the horse of industrialization', but asked rhetorically, 'Can it stay atop?'[20] In some ways, subsequent events have shown that it could. King Fahd was lauded by admirers for making diversification a 'key achievement' of his time in power between 1982 and 2005. When he suffered a stroke in 1995, reform slowed significantly until his successor, Crown Prince Abdullah, established himself in his new role and launched a number of his own economic reforms. In particular, he focused on modernizing the education system, tackling corruption and increasing foreign investment coming into the country. During the oil boom of the mid-2000s there was real hope that Abdullah's efforts, combined with rising oil revenues, would accelerate the structural shift in the Saudi economy and that other smaller GCC states would follow. 'We have a tsunami of opportunities here,' explained one Saudi businessman in 2005 at the height of this era of optimism.

Saudi diversification policy, in particular in the area of industrialization, can boast some real achievements and successes under both Fahd and Abdullah, who ruled until 2015. These included the transformation of many towns and cities into vibrant and productive economic hubs. Yenbo, for example, was a sleepy fishing port in the Hejaz province that had served as a base for Arab and British forces fighting the Ottomans during the First World War. Following a royal decree of 1975 it became a new centre of the emerging Saudi petrochemical industry, as well as the kingdom's second port after Jeddah. Jizan, another Saudi port city in the south-west of the country in an area bordering Yemen, was a major pearling and trading centre a century ago, before falling on hard times. Now it is home to the multi-billion dollar Jizan Economic City and is an increasingly important centre of the kingdom's steel and copper industries. It is also home to a number of major infrastructural and industrial projects in the areas of transport, renewable energy and agriculture and has a world-class petrochemical industry.

In the 2000s Saudi Arabia announced plans for a giant industrial zone and six new 'economic cities' at a cost of more than US$150 billion. These new centres of economic endeavour focused on light and heavy industry and finance (King Abdullah Economic City), transport logistic services and agribusiness (Prince Abd al Aziz Bin Mosead Economic City) and IT and communications (Medina Knowledge Economy City).[21] The most ambitious and biggest of these projects is King Abdullah Economic City, about 100 kilometres north of Jeddah, on Saudi Arabia's Red Sea coast. Launched in 2005 and expected to cost US$100 billion, on completion in 2030 it will offer cutting-edge communications, transportation and other infrastructural links that will attract companies from all over the world to set up manufacturing plants. Already Mars, Pfizer and Danone are among the foreign companies operating there and it is hoped that the city will provide one million new jobs by the time it is finished. The success of high-risk, high-value projects like this will determine whether Saudi Arabia can successfully transition to a post-oil economy.

It is impossible to deny that Saudi Arabia, along with its GCC partners, is committed to a massive experiment in diversification. At the same time, since the 1970s, the kingdom's plans for moving out of oil through industrialization have suffered from major problems of resource allocation and inefficiencies in implementation. Nor is it possible to ignore the fact that despite the introduction of nine development plans between 1970 and 2013 that prioritized diversification, Saudi Arabia, as one commentator put it, remains a 'one-product wonder' as oil continues to be a main driver of the economy. This reality is troubling for all other GCC leaders because Saudi Arabia has more potential for development than other GCC states due to its larger population, talent pool and market. Nonetheless, other Arab Gulf States have attempted to replicate the Saudi industrialization strategy, albeit on a much smaller scale, as part of their own efforts to diversify their economies beyond energy. Initially these plans focused on establishing a globally competitive 'downstream' oil business in the areas of refining and transporting petrochemicals and other oil-related products. These efforts made some headway, despite scepticism over whether such moves truly constituted diversification out of oil. They were followed by more ambitious plans across the Gulf to develop a non-oil economy in a wide range of areas including agriculture, healthcare, tourism and finance.

Bahrain has always had the least oil but some of the most educated citizens and advanced communications networks in the Gulf. In the early 1980s, it began to capitalize on its local talent and capabilities to drive forward diversification. The kingdom quickly developed into one of the most open and diversified GCC economies. It built up its heavy industry, retail, tourism and banking sectors and for years could even boast the most successful financial services sector in the Middle East. Billions of dollars flowed through Bahrain's offshore banks and it made great strides in establishing itself as the regional centre for Islamic finance and insurance. More recently, Qatar and Dubai launched their own financial services centres to much fanfare as the sector developed into an important part of region-wide diversification plans. In both Qatar and Bahrain, financial services are the second largest sectors, accounting for just under 15 and 17 per cent of GDP respectively in 2014.

Oil and gas only makes up 30 per cent of the UAE's export revenues. This is the lowest percentage for any GCC country. In total, the UAE's oil and gas revenues account for just under 40 per cent of GDP. This is in no small part due to Dubai's long-time status as the Gulf's most successful non-oil economy. Following the emirate's own financial crisis, manufacturing, transportation and logistics filled the vacuum left by real estate and investment as the key sectors driving the economy forward, while technology and communications were also prioritized in the new urban economic zones of Internet City, Silicon Oasis, Media City and Incubator City. In the early 1970s, non-oil income only accounted for 2 per cent of oil-rich Abu Dhabi's revenues.[22] By 2012 this had risen to around 65 per cent of the economy, up from 40 per cent only five years earlier. Ambitious projects, including the building of the world's largest single site aluminium smelter, Emirates Aluminium, in record time, were central to Abu Dhabi's diversification plan. Unlike Abu Dhabi, Oman is not rich in natural resources. Deserts and mountain ranges account for over 95 per cent of its territory. Like Bahrain, it never produced enough oil to qualify for OPEC membership. It was also the last GCC country to start exporting oil. Even so, in 1970 oil revenues accounted for 70 per cent of the country's GDP. In 1975, the Omani government set out a development strategy for the next twenty-five years. It has launched eight plans since then and economic diversification has been central to all, with the primary focus on luxury and activity tourism, commerce and shipping. The government has also built a giant container port and free zone at Salalah, one of the fastest growing in west Asia, to compete for a share of the Indian Ocean transhipment business. It has also spent US$1.5 billion constructing the Middle East's second biggest dry dock at Duqm and has built a US$400 million steel plant.

The news is not all positive. Hydrocarbon revenues still constitute on average 46 per cent of nominal GDP across the Gulf. Though export diversification into non-oil goods and services, a key driver of sustainable growth, has increased from 12 to 30 per cent between 2000 and 2013, non-oil GDP as a share of total revenue is falling. Since 1970, Oman has reduced its dependence on oil revenue from 70 to 50 per cent. Its officials now predict that the contribution of oil to real GDP could even fall as low as 10 per cent over the next decade. Yet Oman's oil and gas revenues still amount to two-thirds of its export income and linkages between oil and the rest of the economy remains weak. The same is true for Bahrain. Despite being one of the most diversified GCC economies, the kingdom still relies on oil for almost a third of its GDP and over 70 per cent of its export income. Kuwait has also undertaken hugely ambitious diversification projects like the proposed Silk City in Subiya. By 2030 this is intended to provide a home for hundreds of businesses and a population of 700,000, all linked to Kuwait City by a 40-kilometre causeway. Yet Kuwait remains the least diversified and most oil-dependent of all the GCC nations. Oil revenues make up an incredible 94 per cent of its exports. Oil and gas make up 92 per cent of Qatar's exports. For Saudi Arabia the figure is still 86 per cent. On top of this, the Gulf's private sector remains too reliant on oil-financed government stimulus. In short, far too much vital spending across all socio-economic sectors comes from government-controlled energy revenues rather than private sources.

According to the World Bank, tourism is a key vehicle for both diversification and privatization in developing countries, especially small ones where opportunities for economic diversification are limited. The sector provides employment for around one in twelve of the world's workers and makes up over 5 per cent of world trade. In theory, a bustling Gulf tourist trade offers real job opportunities for nationals and also boosts construction, as well as the restaurant, leisure and other service-driven sectors. The UAE's tourism industry has long been held up as a successful example of diversification. However, tourism has made only a negligible contribution to the UAE's nationalization objectives as cheaper foreign workers take most of the jobs across this sector. Nationals only make up 1 per cent of those working in the UAE's tourism sector, and most of those work in the state-owned airlines of Emirates and Etihad. When the Emirates Taskforce for Tourism launched a two-month programme to train nationals to work in the hospitality industry, fewer than 1,000 applied.

There have been some moves towards privatizing state industries including telecoms, airports, airlines and banks across the GCC. Yet with the partial exception of Oman, traditionally the Gulf state most open to the privatization of its state-owned assets, the region's governments have been cautious in selling off public assets and businesses. Even in Oman, there have been recent strikes by civil servants opposed to the government's plans to privatize the postal service. Somewhat understandably, it is the less educated and unskilled Gulf citizens who most fear that the privatization of state-owned companies will result in job losses. This is a legitimate concern. There are also widespread concerns that the privatization of state-owned enterprises is an attempt to shrink the welfare state and put an end to the culture of government subsidies. A Saudi proposal to earmark up to 70 per cent of total spending between 2000 and 2010 to develop the private sector was scaled back because of extensive domestic opposition. Critics dismissed the plans as an attempt to erode the 'handout' culture that so many citizens had come to rely on and expect. The Saudi government's plans to privatize twenty key economic sectors, promoted as the 'sale of the century' in 2002, also made little headway for the same reason. The vast majority of those polled in surveys in Kuwait over the last decade have expressed an overwhelmingly negative view of privatization. The kingdom's 2010 privatization bill, for example, was attacked across society as 'a law for the sale of Kuwait' that targeted workers and the middle classes.

Not surprisingly, state intervention is a far more common phenomenon than privatization. Like so much else in the Gulf, this situation has its roots in the pre-oil and early oil periods when rising revenues went directly to rulers. This meant that the government had, almost by default, an overwhelmingly dominant role in the economy from the outset of the modern era. Even today, many projects that at first glance appear private are actually state-funded or state-controlled enterprises that enable governments to retain control of key economic sectors and to drive development in line with their preferences. Currently twenty-nine of the thirty-two state-owned enterprises listed in the top 100 MENA companies are from the GCC. 'We have to change the culture,' explained one top Kuwaiti businessman recently, in reference to the government's dominant role in the local economy. This does not detract from the contribution of a number of the Gulf's leading state-owned enterprises to the overall development of the region in the last four decades. Along with Aramco, SABIC is the star of the Saudi economy. It has played a vital role in fostering industrialization and improving business practices and standards far beyond the oil and petrochemical sectors.

There is no proven correlation between an abundance of natural resources and poor or ineffective socio-economic development. As the SABIC case demonstrates, it is by no means inevitable that oil-rich nations are unable to develop world-leading industrial enterprises. There is much more evidence to suggest that energy-rich developing countries tend to have inefficient non-oil sectors and that this makes it hard to shift the economy away from oil dependence. The Gulf States are not alone in experiencing such problems. Countries like Algeria, Nigeria and Venezuela have made limited progress in their attempts at diversification. Malaysia, Indonesia and Mexico have fared better, but all of these cases provide one lesson for the Gulf States above all others – it is vital to implement diversification polices before the decline in oil revenues becomes irreversible.

The highly ambitious, socio-economic development strategies unveiled across the Gulf in recent years have all acknowledged this. Oman's 2020 Vision, the UAE's Vision 2021, Saudi Arabia's 2025 strategy and the 2030 visions of Abu Dhabi, Qatar, Bahrain and, most recently, Saudi Arabia, all include an overarching commitment to prioritize economic diversification. For example, drawing on the experience of transformative small economies who pursued successful development models in the past including Singapore, Norway and New Zealand, Abu Dhabi's *Vision 2030* describes economic diversification as both 'common and fundamental' to the government's 'stated priority areas', as well as to its 'policy agenda as a whole'. Diversified knowledge economies that can compete globally to attract foreign direct investment and create jobs cannot exist without investment in physical infrastructure – power generation, construction and transportation. Over the last two decades, all of the GCC countries have invested heavily in these areas. They have built modern transport systems, urban areas and economic zones and even whole new cities. Yet, physical infrastructure, no matter how central to the Gulf's socio-economic model and no matter how state of the art, is not enough. In today's highly competitive and globalized economy, a potential investor will not invest only in order to move into a modern, well-designed building. They also want to know that their investments are safe.

This requires strong institutions, a robust regulatory environment and protection for physical and intellectual property rights. The judicial system needs to function effectively and efficiently and there needs to be a willingness to introduce, where necessary, regulations and administrative practices that protect foreign investments from corruption, bureaucratic incompetence and political and social instability. Arab Gulf countries have acted to address these issues in recent years. Since 2011 Qatar, Kuwait and Saudi Arabia have all set up autonomous anti-corruption commissions and authorities. The UAE has a long record in tackling corruption and has even established a State Auditing Court tasked with prosecuting cases of government corruption. On a regional level, in June 2013 the GCC established a committee of heads of agencies involved in the fight against corruption and the promotion of integrity. They meet on a semi-annual basis to discuss ways to develop mechanisms to coordinate their work and build cooperation. All the GCC states have also backed the Pearl Initiative, an independent not-for-profit organization that works in partnership with the United Nations across the Gulf to promote corporate accountability and transparency. Despite these efforts, a united anti-corruption and integrity vision for the Gulf remains a long way off as member states still struggle on a national level instituting reforms. There is also the deeper issue of defining what constitutes corruption in a region were patronage is rife and the lines between public money and private interests is unclear.

Potential investors also need to know that a stream of talented labour is available, and that it has access to the right training and education. Across the Gulf this has made it very difficult for private companies to find and retain sufficiently qualified local candidates for posts. By one account, in the mid-2000s around 40 per cent of Saudi students were enrolled in Islamic studies, compared to 19 per cent in science. More recently, a survey of GCC residents aged between fifteen and twenty-four found that only 19 per cent believed their education prepared them properly for the job market. This makes it vital for Gulf governments to prioritize the 'role of knowledge and human capital', as UAE president Khalifa bin Zayed Al-Nahyan has repeatedly argued since taking power in 2005. Many years ago, while serving as director general of Dubai's department of economic development, influential real estate developer and business mogul Mohammed Alabbar succinctly summed up the importance of connecting human capital with a suitable regulatory environment. 'Liberalization, privatization and transparency,' he explained, 'coupled with a strong emphasis on human resources development through education programmes for the younger generation – this is the way forward.'[23] Speaking at the Doha Forum 2010, on the eve of the Arab Spring, Qatar's dynamic emir, Hamad bin Khalifa Al-Thani, made a similar point. Before an audience of hundreds of senior policymakers, scholars and public intellectuals from all over the world, he drove home one point: the rule of law, development and innovation, access to education, a commitment to promoting female participation in the workforce, and investment in sustainable growth are not only important, they are 'fundamental basics' of prosperity and domestic stability.[24]

The academic and commentator Abdulkhaleq Abdulla, a former general coordinator of the Gulf Development Forum, has argued that human capital is not only the 'key', but is also the 'most significant challenge' that the Arab Gulf needs to address.[25] In September 2011, with the most critical events of the Arab Spring still fresh in everyone's mind, King Abdullah of Saudi Arabia made a timely and important speech before the *Majlis al-Shura*, whose members include government officials, tribal and religious leaders, businessmen and scholars. 'We have harvested what parents and grandparents planted,' the king explained. He went on to make it clear that 'our responsibility multiplies for children and grandchildren to reap the maximum benefit, quantity is not as important as the quality of the crop'. In order to ensure that this happened going forward, Abdullah promised that the kingdom's future economic strategy would focus on 'diversification, sustainable and balanced development and a focus on the private sector'. To show his commitment on this matter he then announced that the largest single amount in the next budget, around US$40 billion, would be allocated to secondary and third-level education and training.[26] The following year the government announced plans to spend a record US$219 billion at home on a wide range of related programmes.

The entire Arab world has always found it difficult to combine a business-friendly environment with progressive strategies for developing human capital. The Arab Human Development Reports co-published by the United Nations Development Programme and the Arab Fund for Economic and Social Development have consistently highlighted how much every Arab state suffers from a knowledge gap and an acute shortage of investment in human capital.[27] Yet the Arab Gulf States have a number of advantages over other developing countries in their attempts to address this problem. They are mainly urban and have high per capita incomes. They also have vast cash reserves that allow them to put money into whatever projects they choose to prioritize. GCC citizens are also more literate and better educated than those living in other developing regions. Average adult and youth literacy rates are over 90 per cent and 97 per cent respectively, levels that are comparable to some European economies.

The GCC countries have all made progress in streamlining their legal and regulatory environments in a number of areas, including start-up and licensing procedures for businesses, competition policies, investor and consumer rights, and bankruptcy and company laws. The GCC states are all also consistently rising up the international rankings and indexes that measure e-government, technological readiness and innovative capacity, productivity and competitiveness. In the Global Competitiveness Report for 2014–15, the UAE was ranked the twelfth most competitive economy out of 144 countries, followed by Qatar (sixteenth) and Saudi Arabia (twenty-fourth), with Bahrain, Kuwait and Oman also ranking in the top fifty countries. The World Bank classifies the GCC countries as high-income developing countries and by some measures they are also high human capital development countries. Yet they are still overwhelmingly dependent on energy revenues, patronage and subsidies. This makes them inherently less efficient and less competitive than their non-energy counterparts. They also tend to be poor at implementing reforms. In the Arab Gulf, one explanation for this is the pushback from important local constituencies, Islamist and conservative, who oppose widespread and rapid change across society. This has forced leaders to search for a delicate balance between upholding tradition and promoting modernization. This inevitably slows down the process of reform. For example, efforts to change the GCC's educational curriculum so that it prepares students for jobs in the private sector have faced stiff opposition from Islamists and traditionalists. In the Saudi case this has even included intense debate over whether schoolgirls should be allowed to participate in physical education classes.

This tension is even more apparent in the move to bring women into the workplace. Historically, one significant reason why the Gulf has been so dependent on foreign workers is that women have been excluded from so much economic activity. Females have higher literacy rates and make up a larger proportion of recent university graduates than men. By the time they reach twenty-five, more than twice as many Qatari women have university degrees than men. A higher percentage of female secondary school students go into third-level education in the UAE than in any other country in the world, and 70 per cent of all UAE university graduates are female. This is all the more notable when one remembers that when the UAE was founded in 1971, only two nationals had university degrees and both were male. Female university graduates also outnumber males in the five other GCC states.

This situation is mainly the result of state-led initiatives to boost female enrolment in education. Yet other barriers to female entry and participation in the economy remain. According to the World Economic Forum's most recent Global Gender Gap report, the Arab Gulf States have levels of female educational attainment on a par with the world's most developed nations but they rank among the worst in the world on female economic and political inclusion.[28] Gulf leaders have acknowledged this failing and the vital importance of 'upgrading the development status of women', as King Abdullah termed it shortly before his death. Regular announcements, made to much fanfare, point to progress in this area – for example, the introduction of a 20 per cent quota for female membership of the advisory *Shura* council in Saudi Arabia in 2011, or Bahrain's 2014 decision to allow women to join the country's military. Yet, even taken together these sporadic and disjointed moves have done little to deliver female economic empowerment or to enable women to decide their own professional destinies. Qatari females make up the majority of local college graduates but less than a third of them work. In Oman, which has a much higher percentage of nationals in the workforce, female labour force participation is still only around 16 per cent. Even in the UAE, home to the highest percentage of college-educated women in the world, females only make up 12 per cent of the workforce.

Parallel, and directly related to the challenges of achieving diversification and worker nationalization, all Gulf governments aspire to building a world-class research culture and cutting-edge knowledge economies. In some areas of research, including alternative energies, they even aspire to world leadership. In order to do this, they have invested heavily in third-level education. There was only one university in the Arab Gulf in the 1950s; there were three in the 1960s, and forty in the 1990s. In the first decade of the 2000s alone the number doubled. By 2011 there were 120 universities operating across the GCC. In Saudi Arabia, which has by far the biggest student body, enrolments in universities quadrupled between 1996 and 2011. That does not even take into account the 100,000 students the kingdom sends abroad every year at huge expense on university scholarships. The pay-offs have been obvious in some areas. Almost 15 per cent of working doctors in Saudi Arabia are Saudi nationals, up from only 2 per cent in 1990.

As well as establishing home-grown public and private universities and technical colleges and sending top students abroad to study in some of the world's best third-level institutions, a number of the Gulf States have also opened branch campuses of leading international research universities. Abu Dhabi can boast NYU Abu Dhabi, the Sorbonne and INSEAD, as well as Zayed University and the higher colleges of technology. Qatar is home to Education City, the largest enclave of American universities overseas, with six branch campuses of prestigious American universities including Georgetown, Northwestern and Cornell. The Gulf States have also built science and technology parks to ensure that appropriate research is brought to market – Masdar City in Abu Dhabi and Technology City in Qatar are two notable examples. These parks provide facilities, commercialization support programmes and tax incentives for international companies to develop new technologies in partnership with local universities, and as an incubator for start-up ventures. Impressive as these moves are, public spending on education in the GCC as a share of national income over the last decade has averaged 3.9 per cent, relative to an average global spending ratio of 4.6 per cent, while standardized test scores on mathematics and science consistently reveal a comparatively low level of academic achievement across the region. This has led some critics to argue that what is most needed is immediate reform of pre-school education upwards, not the opening of more high-profile foreign research universities with global reputations.

The development of a dynamic entrepreneurial class tends to go hand in hand with building up the education system, research capacity and a culture of innovation. Writing in the mid-1980s, Ghassan Salameh provided a scathing assessment of why the Gulf found it hard to develop its own entrepreneurs. 'Hyper-monetized, accustomed to easy profits and government subsidies', he explained, 'the Gulf's new bourgeoisie prefers speculation to investment and is more at home as the middle man than the entrepreneur.'[29] Controversial as these words were at the time, Salameh, a Lebanese intellectual, politician and UN adviser, had a point. Historically, a number of wealthy merchant families held a disproportionate share of private sector wealth. In recent decades they have been joined in this privileged position by an army of princes and key royal retainers who run important business enterprises across the Gulf. In Saudi Arabia where the royal family runs to an estimated 7,000–8,000 members, this has not only enriched many royals. It has also created an unofficial economic structure, which has led to the rise of more interest groups and power blocs inside and outside the ruling family. This phenomenon complicates further the already complex socio-economic situation in Gulf society.

The dominant position of the state in the economy has also been detrimental to building an entrepreneurial class. So have the problems of attracting the right local talent to start-ups and gaining the necessary funding from banks and venture capitalists. On top of all these obstacles, would-be entrepreneurs have had to operate in an economy where public sector wages and benefits are so high that there is little incentive to take risks. In November 2010, 2,000 budding and established entrepreneurs met in Dubai to celebrate Arab entrepreneurship. Two years later, Dubai hosted the high-profile Global Entrepreneurship Summit. Events like this have raised awareness throughout the region of the importance of an entrepreneurial class that can contribute to job creation, and can play an important role in reducing the percentage of Gulf citizens working in the public sector.

According to Global Entrepreneurship Monitor (GEM), there are still far too many laws in the GCC that do not help businesses and need streamlining in order for a viable entrepreneurial culture to fully emerge. There needs to be much more transparency, much more support for commercializing inventions and research and better skills and training. Local banks need to provide accessible credit to those with new business ideas that demonstrate potential. For their part, governments also need to introduce mechanisms that provide fledgling entrepreneurs with support through export subsidies and public–private partnerships. If developed correctly, an entrepreneurial sector that maximizes the opportunities provided by human capital development can also impact positively on improving worker nationalization programmes and can bring women into the workforce. It will also result in the repatriation of some of the hundreds of billions of dollars that Gulf citizens have deposited in overseas savings accounts and invested in foreign assets.

For all these reasons, the Gulf States have backed strategies to spur citizens into finding what Qatar's minister of commerce Ahmed bin Jassim Al-Thani has called the 'entrepreneurial spirit'. Qatar has declared public–private partnerships a priority. Oman and Kuwait have both launched state funds to back small entrepreneurs. The Kuwaiti fund, established in 2013, with working capital of US$7 billion, is the world's largest fund for SMEs. It has backed many new projects, including those of female entrepreneurs like Mona Al-Mukhaizeem, whose company, Sirdab Lab, provides space, training and networking for other start-ups. Other recent and notable home-grown start-up and entrepreneurial success stories across the Gulf include: the business information website Zawya.com, launched in the early 2000s with funding from Abraaj Capital, a Dubai venture capital fund;[30] Careem, the Gulf's version of Uber; Fetchr, the first Silicon Valley-funded app in the MENA region; Gossip Desserts, an Emirati-American-European fusion café; OMENA, a Dubai-based, women-only angel investing group; and Beehive, the region's first peer-to-peer finance platform.[31]

During the first decade of the 2000s the oil price was at record levels and the Arab Gulf economy was one of the fastest growing in the world. There was, in other words, little pressure on the Gulf States to make hard choices or to take the tough decisions about spending priorities. There were also few political incentives to implement much-needed reforms that alienated citizens by shrinking the welfare state and prioritizing diversification. As recently as 2012, then Saudi oil minister Al-Naimi expressed confidence that the oil price would remain over US$100 a barrel in the short term at least. He was half right. Oil remained at high levels for the rest of that year, earning the Gulf States a combined annual surplus of almost US$350 billion, more than 80 per cent larger than China's surplus in the same year.[32] Subsequently, a fall in demand for oil in China, Europe and Japan at the same time as non-OPEC producers, in particular Russia and the US, increased supply resulted in a drop in the oil price. It lost half its value between July 2014 and April 2015 and hovered between US$35 and US$40 for the first quarter of 2016. Abdullatif Al-Othman, head of the Saudi investment authority, has made the case that the recent plunge in oil prices has given plans for economic diversification more urgency.

Majid Jafar, CEO of the UAE-based Crescent Petroleum, the oldest private oil and gas business in the region, has made a similar argument – the falling oil price is good because it has forced producers to refocus on diversification and achieving better efficiency.[33] Kuwait's deputy prime minister and minister of finance Anas Kalid Al-Saleh has made the same point, arguing that the lower oil price 'definitely helps to sell the idea' of diversification and 'brings urgency to the notion'.[34]

The view that the falling oil price is a positive factor that will serve as the catalyst to reform and lead to the transformation of Gulf economies is one we have heard before. It is given credibility by the fact that the wealth of the Arab Gulf States, including the most economically vulnerable – Bahrain and Oman – does provide them with both the time and the resources they need to undertake the challenges they face. Whether it happens will depend on how committed Gulf rulers are to moving beyond the existing economic model and how willing they are to take on the daunting and very risky tasks of reforming government spending, the patronage system and the public sector, while simultaneously tackling the problem of foreign workers and empowering increasingly vocal young and female populations through greater economic opportunities and a stake in the future. Yet without such moves, as one Western banker who has worked for years in the region recently commented, it is about as realistic for the Gulf States to pull off their ambitious plans as your 'three year old son saying he wants to become an astronaut'.[35]

CHAPTER 9

DIVIDED WE STAND

'The security of the Gulf will remain part of the responsibility of the sons of the Gulf.'

– Hamad bin Jassim Al-Thani

The dense forests and lush grasslands of the Catoctin Mountain Park to the north-west of Washington, DC, on the Eastern Ridge of the Appalachian Mountains, are a long way from the urban modernity and desert landscapes of the Arab Gulf. This picturesque setting little more than an hour's drive from the US capital is home to Camp David, the presidential retreat that has played host to many world leaders since its establishment at the beginning of the Second World War by Franklin D. Roosevelt. In its early years, Camp David was named Shangri-La after the mythical, harmonious sanctuary described in James Hilton's novel *Lost Horizon*. But the emirs of Kuwait and Qatar and the high-ranking figures from the four other GCC states attending a summit there as the guests of US President Barack Obama in May 2015 were not feeling very harmonious.

Beyond the diplomatic niceties of the conference table and the photo-ops in front of Camp David's iconic wooden cabins, the mood was distinctly downbeat. Gulf leaders were feeling agitated, vulnerable and not a little worried. The few years since the Arab Spring had seen regional crises spiral out of control as state and non-state actors battled for advantage across the Middle East. This threatened to undermine regional stability and Gulf security. Yet it seemed to many in the Arab Gulf that the Obama administration was unwilling or even incapable of defusing the situation. In October 2013, Saudi Arabia declined its invitation to join the UN Security Council as a non-permanent temporary member in order to demonstrate its displeasure with Washington's Middle East policy. Soon after, Saudi billionaire investor Prince Al-Waleed bin Talal shared his thoughts on American policy in his home region in an interview with the *Wall Street Journal*: 'Complete chaos. Confusion. No policy' was his verdict. On the eve of the Camp David meeting, the UAE's ambassador in Washington, Yousef Al-Otaiba, was no less scathing in his own diplomatic way. 'We definitely want a stronger relationship,' he explained, before adding, 'We have survived with a gentleman's agreement [on security]. I think today, we needed something in writing.'[1]

That four Gulf rulers stayed away from the summit, choosing instead to send lower-ranking officials to meet the US president, was also offered as evidence at the time of growing Gulf Arab disillusionment with their most important strategic partner. Just five years earlier, on the eve of the Arab Spring, the Arab Gulf's political, economic and diplomatic power and influence was at an all-time high. Years of massive oil revenues had helped ruling families to consolidate stability and development at home. Proactive diplomacy aided by an impressive soft power arsenal had added to the Gulf States' credentials as key mediators and political brokers in the wider Middle East, from Palestine to Yemen and Lebanon to Darfur, while their role in the global financial crisis had cemented their standing as economic powers on the world stage and had provided them with the opportunity to further stamp their mark on leading international institutions, including the G-20 and the IMF.

Relations between Washington and the Gulf capitals, though already under some strain, were also, for the most part, still in good working order. American diplomats stationed in the region reported home on the GCC's rising power and the golden opportunity that this provided for Washington. The US National Security Strategy issued by President Obama in May 2010 acknowledged this explicitly. It described strategic ties with the GCC as among America's 'key security relationships', and promised to 'work together more effectively' in the future.[2] As this book has shown time and again, working together had never come easy to the GCC member states. Local feuds and diverging national interests, as well as a fear of antagonizing regional actors like Iran and Iraq, had repeatedly prevented them from developing a united and consistent foreign policy approach on key regional issues. It had also prevented them from playing a sustained leadership role in the Arab world, either individually or collectively. In that sense, the disjointed and contradictory responses of the Arab Gulf nations to the anti-government uprisings in Tunisia and Egypt, Yemen, Libya and Syria from 2011 onwards was business as usual.

Nowhere were the 'simmering political tensions and confrontation'[3] inside the GCC during the Arab Spring more evident than in its members' varying responses to the fortunes of the Muslim Brotherhood in Egypt once President Hosni Mubarak lost power in early 2011. The Brotherhood had been founded in Egypt in the late 1920s as a conservative, pan-Islamic social and religious movement. Though first active in the Gulf in the following decade, it only established itself as a significant player in Kuwait, the UAE, Bahrain and Qatar during the 1960s and '70s. It never gained traction in Oman. During the Cold War, the authorities in Saudi Arabia used the Brotherhood to counterbalance the challenge they faced from leftists, Arab nationalists and anti-Western forces. Otherwise the group was marginalized and suppressed as its message was held to be in direct competition and conflict with Saudi Arabia's own brand of conservative Islam.

The soul searching and rising anti-Western feeling that followed the Kuwait crisis of 1990–91 led to a wave of renewed support for Islamists of all stripes across the Gulf region. This benefited the Brotherhood, but it also drew unprecedented attention to its activities. Though in disagreement on many issues, the UAE and Saudi Arabia were now increasingly in accord over the threat that the Brotherhood posed to domestic security and stability. Known members were closely monitored, its activities were restricted and its influence was curtailed. Anti-Brotherhood policies and actions further intensified after 9/11 and continued up until the Arab Spring.

Just as Saudi Arabia had done with Osama bin Laden in the 1990s, the UAE responded to the uncertainty of the Arab Spring by revoking the citizenship of a dissident linked to the Brotherhood. Hundreds of citizens and other residents with ties to the organization were arrested and charged with conspiring to undermine domestic stability.[4] In Kuwait, home to the most dynamic and dysfunctional political system in the Gulf, leaders tried to contain the influence of the small band of Brotherhood parliamentarians who worked closely with other Islamist parties and independents in the national assembly. In Bahrain, concerns over the Brotherhood also increased during the early 2000s as the group gradually shifted its focus in the kingdom from educational and charitable work to politics, winning parliamentary seats in the 2002 and 2006 elections.

Qatar was a notable exception to this trend. The Brotherhood had first established itself there in the 1960s and '70s, when Egyptian teachers and intellectuals linked to the movement found work in the country's developing education sector. One of those to settle in Doha at that time was

Yusef Al-Qaradawi. Though not affiliated officially with the Brotherhood, this Egyptian theologian is often described as one of the group's most influential 'spiritual guides'.[5] For many years he was also the charismatic host of a hugely popular show on Al-Jazeera, 'Shariah and Life', which beamed into millions of homes around the Muslim world. Over the years, Qatar also provided a refuge for many other less eminent figures associated with the Brotherhood. These have included senior members of the Syrian branch involved in the anti-Assad opposition movement and leaders of Hamas, the Palestinian branch of the Brotherhood. In 2012, after the group closed its office in the Syrian capital of Damascus, the head of Hamas's political bureau, Khaled Meshaal, moved his operation to Doha.

Prior to the Arab Spring, the Mubarak regime had been suspicious of Qatar's relationship with the Brotherhood. It had accused the country of trying to help Hamas take over Gaza after the group won the 2006 Palestinian legislative elections. For their part, Qatari officials were critical of President Mubarak's anti-Hamas policies and presented him as an obstacle to Israeli–Palestinian peace. Once the Brotherhood had established itself as a key member of the anti-Mubarak opposition in early 2011, Al-Jazeera portrayed the group in a very positive light to its many millions of viewers in the Arab world and beyond. The Qatari government also provided significant funds to Mohammed Morsi and the Brotherhood during the immediate post-Mubarak era and after the party won the July 2012 Egyptian elections. During the same year, all six GCC states pledged to support a 'secure and stable transition in Egypt'. That did not stop Saudi Arabia and the UAE from backing the Egyptian military when it ousted Morsi from power in the summer of 2013 at a time of widespread demonstrations against Brotherhood rule. During Morsi and the Brotherhood's brief time in power, Qatar had provided crucial financial backing estimated to have totalled US$7.5 billion. Following Morsi's overthrow, the UAE, Kuwait and Saudi Arabia provided an estimated US$12 billion to the military-led government that replaced him.[6] Riyadh also supported the new government's blacklisting of the Brotherhood as a terror organization and the purge of its members in a nationwide crackdown that resulted in hundreds of deaths and the arrest and trial of thousands, including most of its leadership. The deposed Morsi was subsequently charged with a number of crimes, including spying for Qatar.

Shortly before stepping down from his official roles in the summer of 2013, Hamad bin Jassim Al-Thani, Qatar's globetrotting, multitasking prime minister and foreign minister, expounded in detail on his country's recent involvement in Egypt. Qatar's policy, he explained, at all times backed the 'popular will'. He also pointed out that, far from only supporting the Brotherhood, Qatar's emir had been the first GCC leader to meet with Egypt's post-revolution de facto ruler, Field Marshal Mohamed Hussein Tantawi, a year before the Brotherhood's election victory. Khalid bin Mohammed Al-Attiyah, who replaced Al-Thani as foreign minister, expressed a similar view. 'Qatar does not support the Muslim Brotherhood, full stop,' he explained in a 2015 interview, before adding that the group had been elected by the 'Egyptian people'. Like his predecessor, he also emphasized that his country had provided economic and financial support to Egypt both before and after the Brotherhood held office.[7]

The clash between Qatar and its major Gulf partners over the future of Egypt during, and in the immediate aftermath of, the Arab Spring illustrated the competitive tendencies of GCC member states in the realm of foreign affairs. It also exposed their profoundly different strategic, as well as political and ideological, visions for Egypt and the wider Middle East after the Arab Spring. Saudi Arabia and the UAE desired a return to the status quo, a new era of old 'Mubarakism', as one insightful commentator put it.[8] Qatar was open to something much more novel and unpredictable. As foreign minister Al-Thani argued in late 2011, the Islamists of the Brotherhood should be 'tried' to see if they could make a positive contribution to the region.[9] At the same time, the role of the UAE, Kuwait, Qatar and the Saudis in Egypt during and since 2011 has demonstrated their determination to use their financial power and other resources, such as Al-Jazeera in the case of Qatar, to play a pivotal role in the fate of a key regional state. More generally, the capacity to promote their own individual and collective interests, to back friends and undermine opponents in a number of places simultaneously, also served to shine a bright light on just how weak once mighty Arab nations like Iraq, Syria and, of course, Egypt had become.

Traditionally the most important Arab military and political players, these countries were divided, increasingly impotent, political entities unable to keep order at home or project power beyond their borders. The contrast with the Arab Gulf States was obvious. It was also unprecedented. As commentator Fares Al-Khattab rightly pointed out in 2012, the success of the Arab Gulf in challenging the traditional order in the Arab world broke down a 'moral and material barrier' that had never previously been breached.[10] As Ambassador LeBaron had forecast only a few years earlier, the Gulf had established itself as the undisputed centre of the MENA region as newer players consolidated their diplomatic credentials alongside the seasoned Saudi veteran. Nor was this limited only to the UAE and

Qatar. During the post-Arab Spring era, Oman served as the broker for talks between the United States and Iran, and hosted Iran's nuclear negotiations with the major powers. The sultanate also developed its own distinct policies in response to the crises in Yemen and Syria, which have separated it from the rest of the GCC. Oman, as *The Economist* summed up, consolidated its position as 'a country apart' in the foreign policy sphere.[11]

The Arab Gulf States have also demonstrated an unprecedented willingness to take risks beyond their borders. Sometimes they have done so acting alone, like Qatar in Egypt and Oman in Syria, Yemen and on the Iranian nuclear issue. On other occasions they have taken risks in small groups as the UAE and Qatar did in Libya. They have also, though less frequently, worked together as a cohesive unit of six as they did in Bahrain during the Arab Spring. Indeed, by cooperating with each other to suppress revolt and rebellion in Bahrain, they not only successfully managed to preserve the status quo in their own backyard; they also exhibited a real seriousness of purpose and provided a reminder to the world that at times of existential danger they had the capacity to put aside differences and work together in the defence of their common interests and goals. The upshot was that the Arab Gulf States emerged from the turmoil of the Arab Spring as the only local actors with the requisite financial resources, stability at home and influence abroad to set the political and strategic direction of the wider Arab world. This not only made them even more important regional players, it also greatly increased their standing on the international stage.

In 2004 the UAE, Kuwait, Bahrain and Qatar joined the NATO-sponsored Istanbul Cooperation Initiative (ICI). This forum was intended to contribute to long-term global and regional security by offering the countries of the broader Middle East practical bilateral security cooperation with NATO. Less than a decade later, in early 2012, NATO secretary general Anders Fogh Rasmussen praised the 'active and positive role' of the GCC during the Arab Spring and expressed his organization's desire to move closer to the GCC in order to enhance security in the wider Middle East.[12] During the same year, British Foreign Office minister Lord Howell was effusive in his assessment of the GCC's evolving political, as well as economic, role. Describing the GCC countries as 'a network with an increasingly influential voice', and with a 'growing role to play in shaping the region's wider political future', he argued that it was a British 'national interest' to 'step up its engagement with these Gulf countries – both on regional and wider international issues'.[13] The same sort of thinking was behind the request by François Hollande's government early the following year for the GCC to provide material, financial and political backing for the French military campaign against Islamist rebels in Mali.[14]

Speaking at an early GCC summit in 1982, Muhammad Al-Khalifa, Bahrain's then foreign minister, had expressed his belief that the GCC states would one day play a unique role in both the Arab and international arenas. In the immediate wake of the Arab Spring it appeared, if only briefly, that this day had come. To some it even seemed possible that the GCC might now become, as King Fahd of Saudi Arabia had hoped during the Iran–Iraq war, 'a solid brick made to shield the Arab and Islamic nation'.[15] Things have not quite worked out that way. The new assertiveness demonstrated by the Arab Gulf since the Arab Spring has not resulted in more stability at home or influence abroad. It has resulted in less. As Gulf leaders made very clear to President Obama during their 2015 Camp David summit, the regional situation is more precarious now than at any time since Saddam Hussein's tanks rolled over the Kuwaiti border a quarter of a century earlier. Obama was already well aware of such feelings. The purpose of the Camp David summit, he explained, was to 'work out ways' to strengthen security cooperation 'while resolving the multiple conflicts that have caused so much hardship and instability throughout the Middle East'.[16]

Of the 'multiple conflicts' Obama was referring to, the one that concerned his guests at Camp David most, and which has preoccupied Gulf leaders above and beyond all others, is the overarching and multifaceted challenge they face from Iran. As earlier chapters showed, the rivalry between the Sunni Arab monarchies of the Gulf and Shia Iran long predated the 1979 revolution. In the modern era it can be traced back to the heyday of the shah. The threat may be overblown. It may represent a breakdown of conventional diplomacy. Yet it also reflects a common strand of thinking in the Arab Gulf, where suspicions run deep that the revolutionary leaders in Tehran, like the pro-Western shah they replaced, are striving to build a 'Greater Iran' that can dominate the entire Persian Gulf and Arabian Peninsula and project power across the wider Middle East and Muslim world.

'Iran is a paper tiger, but one with steel claws,' explained Prince Turki Al-Faisal in an interview in the German media. The former Saudi intelligence chief and ambassador to London and Washington then listed off all those Muslim countries from Iraq, Lebanon and Syria to Turkey, Bahrain, Afghanistan and even Pakistan, where Iranian intrigue is at work.[17] Prince Turki's opinion is shared by those within the Gulf elites who view competition and rivalry with Iran as a zero-sum game. In the words of one Gulf commentator, Iran is 'interfering, instigating, creating sleeping cells, resorting to espionage and stirring sectarian strife'.[18] The deployment of the Saudi-led Peninsula Shield force to Bahrain in March 2011 was partly a declaration of Saudi Arabia's new, somewhat reluctant, status as the champion of counter-revolution in the region. It was also an act of self-defence in response to the perceived, if exaggerated, view of Iranian interference in the internal affairs of the Gulf. This made the consolidation of Al-Khalifa rule in Bahrain in 2011 an important victory. Yet that military operation in itself did little to convince Gulf leaders that Iran had abandoned its attempts to undermine the GCC by radicalizing and subverting Shia communities inside their borders. In the immediate aftermath of the Bahrain crisis King Abdullah warned those 'deviant groups' targeting his kingdom to desist. At the same time, the Saudi ministry of the interior blamed a number of localized attacks against security forces in cities in the Eastern Province on 'instigators of sedition, discord and unrest' working on behalf of a foreign country.[19] Since then security has been stepped up at government buildings and in areas frequented by foreign visitors and there has been a noticeable increase in the number of police patrols and random checkpoints across the kingdom.

Many other incidents across the GCC have also been held up as further evidence of Iranian attempts to undermine the dominance of the Sunni monarchical order from within. The authorities in Bahrain have blamed almost every street protest and violent attack since 2011 on disloyal Shia citizens working for Iran. They have also accused Iranian Revolutionary Guards of plotting to assassinate public figures, and of planning attacks on the local airport and on government buildings. Citizens have been arrested and charged with membership of a group known as the 'Imam Army', trained and funded by Iran. Others detained in relation to the seizure of bomb-making equipment and explosives have been accused of having links to Iran and Hezbollah. As far back as the mid-1980s, the Kuwaiti authorities had linked sporadic bombings and the discovery of hidden weapons and ordnance to Shia militants operating in the kingdom. This fuelled fears of a disloyal fifth column at the heart of Kuwaiti society. Subsequent events have done little to diminish these concerns. In 2015, the Kuwaiti ministry of the interior announced the seizure of a major weapons cache that included large amounts of explosives, weapons, grenades and ammunition. More than twenty suspects were arrested, all allegedly Hezbollah members who had received training in Lebanon and had met with Iranian diplomats in Kuwait prior to their apprehension.[20]

Some experts on Iran have bemoaned the failure of the country to craft a proper Gulf policy since the revolution.[21] Others, like Seyed Hossein Mousavian, the former senior Iranian diplomat and spokesman for Iran's nuclear negotiators, believe that a strategy is in place but have argued that it needs to be upgraded as a 'necessity'.[22] When Hassan Rouhani won the Iranian presidential elections in August 2013, some predicted that it would result in a new era of positive bilateral relations as his new government initiated a series of high-level contacts. Rouhani visited Oman. His foreign minister made a rare trip to Riyadh following the death of King Abdullah and to Kuwait after the nuclear deal was signed in July 2015. Earlier in the same year, Ali Larijani, the influential speaker of the Iranian *Majlis*, visited Qatar.[23] Many Gulf leaders, including some in Saudi Arabia, welcomed such moves. They view Iran as a regional rival but not an existential threat and do not view the relationship between the Arab Gulf States and Iran only in adversarial terms. They have always looked to find ways of co-existing with their powerful neighbour with whom they share historical, cultural and familial links, as well as extensive and intertwined trade and business interests.

Qatar shares its North West Dome (North Field) gas field off its north-east coast with Iran. Oman shares the Straits of Hormuz with Iran and has positioned itself to serve as a transit point for Iranian natural gas exports. Hundreds of thousands of Iranians live and work in Dubai and over 2,000 Iranian companies do business in the dynamic emirate. The smaller northern emirates also trade extensively with Iran. Ras Al Khaimah is working to establish itself as a hub between Iran and the Gulf and Farsi is one of the main languages spoken in Sharjah's fishing port. One obstacle that has prevented capitalizing on such wide-ranging ties is the fact that, historically, Arab and Iranian elites have tended to interact much less regularly with each other than their respective merchants, traders and fishermen. That said, Iranian leaders have long argued that if the Arab Gulf States truly want regional stability, they should distance themselves from Washington and work with Tehran to find regional solutions to regional security problems. On a visit to Kuwait, Iranian foreign minister Mohammad Javad Zarif declared that 'no country can solve regional problems without the help of others', before adding, 'Our message to the regional countries is that we should fight together against this shared challenge' of extremism, terrorism and sectarianism.[24] Since then he has followed up with a similar appeal: 'We and Arabs in the region are in one ship,' he explained in October 2015, 'and if this ship sinks, everyone will drown together, and there is no one that will save us'.[25] Even Iran's supreme leader, Ayatollah Ali Khamenei, has argued that regional security depends on 'sound' ties between the GCC and Iran.[26]

After the Iran–Iraq war ended, Iran made numerous diplomatic efforts to build bridges with the Arab Gulf and bilateral relations improved gradually along these lines from the mid-1990s until the early years of the new millennium. Before and since, such arguments have rarely resonated at any level of Gulf society. Mutual contempt runs deep on both sides and though its roots are historic, in the shorter term this hostility can be traced back to the Islamic revolution of 1979. The events of that tumultuous time have had a profound impact on the Arab Gulf's subsequent strategic and security thinking. As one top Gulf official recently stated, the GCC will only 'pivot to Iran' if Tehran first agrees to 'de-escalate its destabilizing behaviour'.[27] This worldview has, in turn, even affected the internal dynamics of countries like Saudi Arabia and Kuwait up to the present day. In short, almost four decades after the downfall of the shah, it is impossible to overestimate the hold that the revolution in Iran continues to have on the psyche of the Sunni Arab Gulf. This explains why over 90 per cent of those polled in a national survey in Saudi Arabia published in September 2015 viewed Iran's recent policies in either 'fairly negative' or 'very negative' terms. Only 12 per cent expected any improvement in Iranian behaviour over the coming years. A survey of Kuwaiti citizens in the same month returned similar results. Seventy-four per cent of those polled held a 'fairly negative' or 'very negative' view of Iran. The clash with Iran also tied for first place alongside the closely related sectarian conflict between Sunni and Shia as the biggest concern of those polled.[28]

At different times, and for different reasons, Qatar and Oman have backed engagement and dialogue with Iran more than any of their GCC partners. The temperaments of policymakers in both kingdoms, as well as their histories, geographies and economic interests, have inclined them to search for accommodation and cooperation with Iran whenever possible. Yet they too share a deep suspicion of Iranian hegemonic intentions across the wider Middle East. At the end of 2012, for example, both joined their four GCC partners in signing up to a communiqué that described Iran as their 'main rival' and called for an 'end' to the country's interference in the region. More than three years later, in January 2016, a meeting of GCC foreign ministers once again backed an uncompromising statement that condemned Iran's 'terrorist acts' and demanded that it stop 'meddling' in Arab affairs. Such feelings came into sharp relief at the time of the US invasion of Iraq and the overthrow of Saddam Hussein's regime in 2003–4. Once Saddam was gone, his army disbanded and his war machine decimated, GCC military chiefs had little doubt that the number-one danger they faced going forward would come from Iranian revolutionary forces. Already active in Lebanon and Iraq, according to some Gulf officials they were also gaining influence in Bahrain, Saudi Arabia and Kuwait. As the issue of the Iranian nuclear programme also made its way to the top of the international agenda, alarmed Gulf policymakers came to view their neighbour's quest for nuclear weapons as further, potentially devastating, evidence of the country's nefarious intentions. The election of hardliner Mahmoud Ahmadinejad to the Iranian presidency in 2005 fuelled existing anxieties.

As the nuclear stand-off heated up following Ahmadinejad's consolidation of power, these interrelated fears became even more pronounced. In an attempt to avoid antagonizing Iran, many of the GCC's public expressions of concern over the nuclear issue were couched in environmental terms, and focused on the devastating impact of nuclear fallout from an industrial accident. A much greater, though often unspoken, concern was that a nuclear Iran would pose a profound threat to the regional security balance, and even lead to a nuclear arms race as other countries attempted to get hold of their own weapons of mass destruction to deter Iranian aggression. In order to prevent this from happening, the Gulf States did what they had done in times of trouble since the 1980s – they looked to the US as a way of counterbalancing Iranian ambitions. Washington was happy to oblige. As secretary of state Condoleezza Rice explained on the eve of a visit to the region in the summer of 2007, the military equipment made available to Arab Gulf partners, including Patriot missile batteries to counter any Iranian missile attack, was intended to 'secure peace and stability'.[29] The Gulf States welcomed the opportunity to purchase advanced weaponry. Ever conscious of unnecessarily antagonizing their neighbour, they were less enthusiastic over the Bush administration's plans for them to serve as the frontline in the containment of Iran.

During the Obama era, the US, alongside France and Great Britain, sold more than US$100 billion dollars' worth of state-of-the art military technology to Gulf States eager to update their war-fighting capabilities. The Arab Gulf also looked to Washington, and to a lesser extent these other European powers, for more explicit defence and security protection to help them prepare to deal with the threat posed by Iranian-sponsored subversion and proxy warfare, as well as more conventional forms of engagement. Top US officials repeatedly looked to reassure Gulf leaders that they could always rely on American support in their quest for security. In the summer of 2009, US secretary of state Hillary Clinton announced that the Obama administration would consider extending a 'defense umbrella' over the region to prevent Iran from intimidating and dominating its neighbours.[30] The following February, in a televised Town Hall meeting at the Doha branch of Carnegie Mellon University, Clinton listed the three options that the GCC could adopt to deal with the Iranian nuclear threat. They could, she explained, 'give in to the threat; or they can seek their own capabilities, including nuclear; or they ally themselves with a country like the US that is willing to help defend them'. This third alternative was, in her considered opinion, 'by far the preferable option'.[31]

The Obama administration has repeated similar arguments regularly since Clinton stepped down as secretary of state. Speaking in mid-2014 on the issue of ballistic missile defence in the Gulf, Frank A. Rose, the State Department's senior official dealing with arms control, was clear: 'Security cooperation has long stood at the core of the US–Gulf partnership. The United States is not only committed to enhancing US–GCC missile defense cooperation – we see it as a strategic imperative.'[32] In order to back up such statements, Washington has declared on many occasions a willingness to expand military ties with the GCC and to develop a new 'security architecture' in the Gulf that integrates air and naval power and missile defence in order to enhance regional stability. In 2012, GCC foreign ministers and top US officials meeting at the newly established US–GCC Strategic Cooperation Forum set out a framework for drawing up plans to prevent an Iranian airborne attack on GCC territory. This is important not only for Kuwait City and Dubai, the urban targets nearest Iran and thus most vulnerable to a missile strike; it is also vital for cities further away like Abu Dhabi, Manama, Doha and several coastal Saudi cities that are within reach of longer-range Iranian Shahab-1 and -2 missiles.[33] Almost three years later, at the Camp David summit meeting in May 2015, it was agreed to prioritize missile defence once more as part of the agreement to improve further the US–GCC strategic partnership'. Two months later, precisely one day after the Iran nuclear deal was signed in July, Obama expressed the hope that by the time his successor was elected in late 2016, the US would have 'strengthened' its 'security partnerships' with its Gulf allies. Secretary of State Kerry followed this up with a commitment to expand regional security through cooperation in several key areas, including intelligence sharing, the training of special forces, maritime security cooperation and the protection of critical infrastructure.

Important as such moves are, they have not served to overcome or neutralize the Arab Gulf's growing disillusionment with Washington since the Arab Spring. In the tumultuous days of early 2011, Saudi leaders had lobbied their US counterparts to fully and openly back Egypt's Hosni Mubarak. King Abdullah had condemned the protestors in Egypt as 'infiltrators' guilty of 'malicious sedition'. Along with other senior Gulf officials, he tried to influence the US president on the matter and, according to several reports, pleaded with Obama on the telephone not to humiliate Mubarak, who was a close friend as well as a key ally. Instead, the Obama administration offered cautious support for Egyptian protestors and then called for Mubarak, a long-time American partner, to give up power after only days of popular protests. This shocked and infuriated GCC leaders. According to Saudi officials, King Abdullah's faith in the US completely 'evaporated'[34] following the debacle in Egypt. Soon afterwards, planned visits by secretary of defence Robert Gates and secretary of state Hillary Clinton to Riyadh were cancelled. Though the official reason provided was that King Abdullah was unwell, many speculated that he was unwilling to meet with these top American officials because he was so angry over the Obama administration's handling of the ongoing crises in the region. Washington's subsequent public rebuke of Bahrain's royals and the calls by US officials for the ruling family to 'address the legitimate grievances' of the protestors and undertake a 'process of meaningful reform' appalled Gulf leaders even more. In response, Riyadh undermined American efforts to mediate a compromise agreement between the Bahraini leadership and local protestors.

Unlike previous presidents, Obama had never been an enthusiastic partner of the Saudis. As far back as 2002, in one of his first major public statements on foreign policy, as a member of Illinois' state senate, Obama had referred to the Saudis (together with Mubarak's Egypt) as America's 'so-called allies in the Middle East'.[35] Almost a decade later, his administration's response to events in Egypt and Bahrain raised real questions over the US commitment to its long-time partners in the region. In particular, though Clinton and her successor John Kerry talked tough on Iran, statements emanating from other top officials including secretary of defence Robert Gates seemed to suggest that the Obama administration was intent on reducing its engagement in the Gulf. The US Defense Strategic Guidance, announced by President Obama in 2012, seemed to confirm these changing priorities, and underscored a shifting focus of US military planning towards the Asia–Pacific theatre away from the Middle East.

This further eroded Arab Gulf confidence in the US as a long-term security partner. A usually inoffensive magazine published by the Saudi foreign ministry and distributed in Riyadh hotels complained of 'America wiping its hands of its responsibilities' across the region. The respected

UAE businessman Khalaf Ahmad Al-Habtoor asked rhetorically in an op-ed written in the Arabic media: 'Do we still imagine Uncle Sam will send in the cavalry? If so, we should think again.'[36] Iranian rhetoric fuelled these fears. Speaking soon after Mubarak's demise, Iran's supreme leader Ayatollah Ali Khamenei noted that when Washington realized Mubarak could not be saved, 'they threw him away'. This, he added, should serve as a 'lesson' for other local leaders dependent on the US: 'When they are no longer useful, it will throw them away just like a piece of old cloth and will ignore them.'[37]

It is hardly surprising that in this climate of distrust, Gulf leaders exhibited growing agitation over what they viewed to be the weakness of the US-led international coalition involved in negotiations with Iran on the nuclear issue. In particular, they questioned the value of what Prince Turki called a 'carrot and stick approach', in which the 'stick was never used'.[38] Arab Gulf leaders had been refused a seat at the nuclear talks. After being denied this opportunity to have a say in any final agreement, Gulf leaders pressured American and other Western officials to stand firm in their negotiations with Iran. They also warned them that Iranian negotiators could not be trusted, that they would bargain relentlessly until they got what they wanted, and that they would interpret any compromise as a sign of tacit acceptance of the inevitability of their nuclear programme.

In July 2015, after receiving reassurances from the US and the other members of the P5+1 (the five permanent members of the UN Security Council plus Germany), the Gulf States cautiously and resignedly endorsed the agreement that had been finalized with Iran. Qatar's emir, for example, expressed the hope that it would prove to be a 'key factor for stability in the region'. His foreign minister described it as 'the best option among other options' during an August meeting of GCC foreign ministers in Doha attended by Kerry. That meeting concluded with the publication of a joint statement that again welcomed the agreement with Iran, as long as it was 'fully implemented' and contributed to regional security and prevented Iran from gaining nuclear weapons.[39] Yet Gulf leaders still worried that Iran might renege on its commitment or that even if the agreement held it would leave Iran unchecked and free to promote its hegemonic intentions across the region. There were also growing concerns that the nuclear deal would serve as the basis for a 'grand bargain' between Washington and Iran, and that the GCC would be the first and biggest casualty of any American–Iranian reconciliation.

As far back as 2002, when it became inevitable that the Bush administration planned to remove Saddam Hussein from power, Gulf leaders feared, and some even predicted, that the US would pull out of Iraq before the job was done, leaving the country in turmoil and open for Iran to intervene and take control. The Sunni Gulf viewed Iranian dominance of Iraq as a nightmare scenario that would force them to deal with two large, aggressive, Shia-controlled states on their doorstep. This appalling prospect became more likely in the summer of 2010 when President Obama declared that the American combat mission in Iraq had ended. The following year he confirmed that he would be honouring the agreement made between his predecessor in the Oval Office and the Iraqi government to withdraw all US troops from Iraq by the end of 2011. The last few hundred departed the country in the week before Christmas 2011. An estimated 20,000 diplomats, technicians and advisers, as well as 5,000 private security officers contracted by the US government, remained behind to advise the government, to liaise with local partners and to staff and secure the massive embassy compound in Baghdad and the consulates in Basra, Mosul and Kirkuk.

Fears of an Iranian-dominated Iraq heightened as Sunni communities became increasingly alienated from the Shia-controlled government in Baghdad. By late 2015, there was growing speculation in the Gulf media that dozens, and by some accounts, hundreds of thousands of Iranian revolutionary guards, as well as Shia fighters from Lebanon, were entering Iraq without proper entry visas or under the pretext of visiting Shia holy sites. Their mission, it was alleged, was to consolidate Iranian gains across Iraq at the expense of Sunni citizens by meddling in the country's domestic affairs. The success of the Sunni extremists of the Islamic State of Iraq and al-Sham (ISIS) in capitalizing on this situation to extend the territory under its control may have provided a block of sorts on Iranian and Shia aspirations, but it inevitably complicated matters for the Gulf States. The perception of the Obama administration as an increasingly unreliable and fatigued ally, in retreat and unwilling to stand up to Iran and extremist non-state actors in the region, gained further currency as the situation in Syria deteriorated. It was reported that the UAE's Crown Prince Mohammed bin Zayed Al-Nahyan even described President Obama as 'untrustworthy' on the Syria issue in meetings with foreign visitors.[40]

Iran had been a major beneficiary of the chaos in Iraq that followed the US invasion in 2003. It had also succeeded in consolidating and even extending its influence in the Arab world following the 2006 Israeli war in Lebanon and the 2008–9 Gaza conflict between Hamas and Israel. The overthrow of Hosni Mubarak, one of Iran's major Arab opponents, strengthened the Iranian position during the Arab Spring. The role of Shia communities in uprisings and protest movements in the Sunni Gulf during this same period also provided a psychological and morale boost to Tehran. The civil war in Syria provided the Arab Gulf with the opportunity to overturn all these Iranian gains. After taking power in the early 1970s, Hafez Al-Assad had transformed Syria into an important regional player and the dominant external actor in Lebanon. Backed by the ruling Ba'ath Party and the Alawite elite, he also established Syria as Iran's only dedicated Arab ally following the 1979 revolution. Damascus sided with Iran during its war with Iraq in the 1980s. In the 1990s it joined Iran as the only major Middle East player to wholeheartedly oppose the Oslo peace process between Israel and the Palestinians. First under Hafez Al-Assad and then under Bashar, his second son and unintended heir who became president in 2000, Syria also worked closely with Iranian-backed Hezbollah in Lebanon. The high point in Syrian–GCC relations occurred in the early 1990s when leaders in Damascus excoriated Saddam for his invasion of Kuwait and sent troops to participate in the anti-Iraq military coalition. Once the crisis ended, Gulf leaders even considered stationing Syrian troops on their territory to strengthen anti-Iraqi defences.

The GCC–Syrian relationship was nowhere near as intimate by the time of the Arab Spring. Though Saudi Arabia had been the second country Bashar Al-Assad visited after becoming president, ties soured following the 2005 assassination of Lebanon's prime minister, Rafik Hariri, a very close associate of the Saudi ruling elite. When Hariri was blown up by a massive car bomb in central Beirut, his supporters, the media and international observers immediately accused his killers of having links to Syrian intelligence. This outraged leaders in Riyadh and relations deteriorated the following year when Syria backed Hezbollah, the Shia group closely aligned to Iran, in its war with Israel. In defending his backing of pro-Iranian forces in Lebanon, Assad accused other Arab leaders, in particular the Saudis, of being 'half-men' for not joining him in standing up to Israeli aggression. Though differences on Lebanon remained unresolved, a rapprochement of sorts took place following King Abdullah's visit to Damascus and two trips by President Assad to Riyadh during 2009.

Anti-regime demonstrations began in Syria in March 2011 when mostly peaceful protestors took to the streets demanding political and economic reform, an end to official corruption and the abolition of the government's oppressive state of emergency laws. Arab Gulf leaders, who had criticized Assad's regime for its harsh treatment of protestors in the past, immediately urged the government in Damascus to adopt a non-violent and conciliatory response to the growing unrest. They hoped that their status as key players in inter-Arab politics and major investors in the Syrian economy would add weight to their appeal to Assad to compromise with his opponents. Qatar, in particular, had high hopes that it could influence Assad's actions. It had channelled vast amounts of money into Syrian real estate and other economic sectors and had lobbied for Syrian interests while a non-permanent member of the UN Security Council at the time of the 2006 Israel–Hezbollah war in Lebanon.

Assad was unmoved by these pleas from the Gulf. Instead, he violently crushed the protest movement, sending his army into trouble spots across the country. Within weeks, 1,000 demonstrators had been killed. Outraged at what top officials would repeatedly describe as the 'slaughter' and 'carnage' taking place in Syria,[41] the Gulf States donated hundreds of millions of dollars to the Syrian opposition and activated a wide array of diplomatic tools as part of a 'get tough' approach to dealing with the Syrian regime. Qatar hosted several meetings of the broad-based Syrian opposition and, in July 2011, became the first Gulf country to withdraw its ambassador and close its embassy in Damascus. Saudi Arabia, the UAE, Kuwait and Bahrain soon followed. Oman chose to maintain full diplomatic relations with Syria and in the summer of 2011 the sultanate's foreign minister Yusuf bin Alawi bin Abdullah visited Damascus to urge an end to the violence. Backed by other GCC states, Qatar also used its rotating presidency of the Arab League to build an Arab consensus in favour of financial and economic sanctions against Syria. The GCC member states were also the driving force behind the late 2011 decision to suspend Syria from the Arab League.

As the violent protests turned into civil war, the Gulf States became increasingly outspoken in their condemnations of the Assad regime. They championed the dispatch of Arab observers to the country to monitor the crisis and to implement a stillborn peace plan that was rejected by Assad, who instead vowed to crush his opponents with an 'iron fist'.[42] In early 2012, in a widely reported interview with the American broadcaster CBS's flagship news programme, *60 Minutes*, the emir of Qatar became the first Arab leader to call for military intervention in Syria in order to 'stop the killing'.[43] This was a very bold move at a time when most of the international community was only willing to provide political support, commit humanitarian supplies or, at the very most, supply covert military aid to the anti-Assad rebels. As GCC pressure on Assad grew, the Syrian president moved closer to Iran as a way of consolidating his rule. The Gulf States had never believed that Iran or its Hezbollah proxy had a special interest in Syria. Now they came to view the Assad regime as little more than an instrument of Iranian hegemonic intentions.

Though united in their opposition to the Ba'athist regime and sharing the same goals – an end to Assad rule and containment of Iranian influence in Syria and the wider Levant – the Gulf States still found it very difficult to cooperate with each other in responding to the crisis. Qatar and Saudi Arabia threw their weight behind different political opponents of Assad and funded, supplied and armed rival rebel and insurgent groups in Syria via Turkey and Jordan. Though often competing with each other, and at times even clashing, these various proxy groups tended to share an extremist Sunni ideology. At the same time, all the GCC states, along with Egypt, Iraq, Jordan, Lebanon and the United States, signed up to the Jeddah Communiqué of September 2014. This committed the Gulf States to a 'strategy to destroy' Islamic State. As part of this commitment, several GCC states contributed to the air strikes against the extremist group in Syria and Iraq. At their Camp David summit with Obama in May 2015, GCC leaders also agreed to do more to 'degrade and ultimately destroy' Islamic State, which by this time was in control of large parts of northern and eastern Syria.

As the threat from Islamic State grew, the Arab Gulf States demonstrated a new willingness to acknowledge the dangers posed by other extremist Sunni non-state actors fighting in Syria. This included groups that they had backed in the past, like the Al-Qaeda-linked Nusra Front, a major rival of Islamic State, as well as connected militias such as Jaysh Al-Islam, Ahrar Al-Sham and Jund Al-Aqsa.[44] Anwar Qarqash, the UAE's minister of state for foreign affairs, went further, announcing that his country would participate in any 'international effort' on the ground in Syria to fight terrorists.[45] Since taking office in 2015, Saudi Arabia's young but influential deputy crown prince and defence minister Mohammed bin Salman has also promised that his kingdom will confront 'any terrorist organization that appears in front of us'.[46] These increasingly vocal condemnations have engendered a response from Islamic State. The group has pledged to overthrow the pro-Western Arab Gulf monarchies and it has launched several attacks on Shia mosques and other targets in Kuwait and Saudi Arabia with the objective of sowing the seeds of sectarian strife in the heart of the Gulf.

A number of those radical groups backed by the Gulf States in Syria have inflicted important defeats and setbacks on army units loyal to Assad, Hezbollah fighters and even regular Iranian troops in the north and south of Syria. Of these, the Nusra Front, along with Islamic State, were excluded from the historic meeting of Syrian opposition groups in Riyadh in December 2015. Representatives of Jaysh Al-Islam and Ahrar Al-Sham were invited and did attend this gathering, the largest get-together of the anti-Assad opposition in four years of fighting. But the crisis in Syria has also emphasized the limits of Arab Gulf power as much as it has underscored its extensive influence and involvement in regional strategic and political affairs. No single Arab Gulf State, nor any coalition of them, has been able to manage the conflict in the war-torn country in line with its own interests. Instead, they have had to address criticism that their interventions have made the problem worse by escalating tensions on the ground. In an implicit acknowledgement of this, Oman attempted to mediate talks between all the key actors in Syria. In the first meeting between senior GCC and Syrian officials since 2011, Oman's top diplomat Alawi met his Syrian counterpart in Muscat and President Assad in Damascus in August and October 2015 respectively.

At their annual summit, held in Riyadh in the same week in December 2015 that Syrian opposition groups met in the city, GCC leaders attempted to present a united front on the crisis. Qatar's endorsement of a common approach was of particular note given the past differences between Doha and Riyadh on the Syria issue. On coming to power in the summer of 2013, Qatar's new emir, Tamim bin Hamad Al-Thani, demonstrated a willingness to heal the worsening rift between his kingdom and Saudi Arabia. He visited Riyadh and made a commitment to avoid any actions that damaged the interests of his GCC partners or destabilized the Gulf region. In the immediate term these moves did little to mitigate tensions. In March 2014, Saudi Arabia, the UAE and Bahrain recalled their ambassadors from Doha and all three countries threatened to implement sanctions against Qatar. This unprecedented coordinated diplomatic boycott was intended to send a clear message to Doha that its backing of the Muslim Brotherhood and its policies in Syria, Egypt and Libya, where it was supporting factions opposed by the UAE, would no longer be tolerated.

Relations continued to be strained until mid-November 2014 when GCC leaders attended an unannounced and impromptu meeting in Saudi Arabia dedicated to overcoming internal differences. This was followed the next day by a phone conversation between the rulers of Saudi Arabia and Qatar that opened the way for a new beginning at the thirty-fifth annual GCC leaders' summit in Doha the following month. This meeting was not without disagreement. The UAE delegation expressed concerns regarding the proposed establishment of a Turkish military base in Qatar due to fears that a Qatar–Turkey alliance might increase the regional influence of the Muslim Brotherhood. Yet outstanding concerns aside, all attending this meeting worked hard to foster improved relations and cooperation, if not harmony, on most issues. Qatar's foreign minister Al-Attiyah even briefed journalists that intra-GCC differences were 'something from the past now'.[47]

The accession to power of King Salman in Saudi Arabia in January 2015 contributed further to improved relations. Immediately on taking office, Salman demonstrated a real willingness to work together with Qatar in defence of Sunni Gulf interests. This move towards reconciliation was part of a broader Saudi strategy intended to bring as many Sunni parties as possible into an anti-Iranian coalition. It has led to closer ties between Riyadh and the AKP government of Recep Tayyip Erdoğan in Ankara. It also resulted in the relaxation of Saudi hostility to the Muslim Brotherhood, an organization that Salman's predecessor Abdullah had compared to Hezbollah and designated a terrorist group as recently as 2014. It is of little surprise that these Saudi efforts have deeply antagonized Iran. One senior revolutionary guard declared that Saudi Arabia had moved from being a 'regional rival' to a 'proxy threat'; another predicted the 'collapse of the House of Saud . . . in the footsteps of Zionist Israel'.[48]

Even before Salman rose to power, the conflict in Syria had become a key event in the historic conflict between Sunni and Shia. This pitched the GCC states, Turkey and the West against the Alawi elite of Assad's Syria, Russia, Iran and its Shia Lebanese and Iraqi proxy forces. In recognition of this, seventy-six Sunni Islamic groups issued a declaration in Cairo calling for jihad against the Syrian regime, and its Iranian and Hezbollah backers. In response to this and other religious edicts, hundreds if not thousands of young Saudis and lesser numbers of citizens from other parts of the Arab Gulf have made their way into Syria by way of Turkey or Jordan to join volunteers from other parts of the Arab world, Russia, North America and Europe waging 'holy war' against the Assad government. This epic struggle also spilt over into Yemen. The country borders two GCC states – Oman and Saudi Arabia – and it had been a constant source of concern for the Arab Gulf since long before the establishment of the GCC. For decades, the Gulf States poured hundreds of millions of dollars into the country's economy, healthcare and educational systems in the hope that this would bring some stability to their conflict-ridden and poverty-stricken neighbour. They also intervened diplomatically to mediate clashes between local rivals in the hope of defusing crises before they spiralled out of control and caused instability inside the GCC. They even considered, but ultimately rejected on several occasions, Yemeni requests to join the GCC. This possible option for pacifying Yemen has roused passionate debate among member states. In 2006, for example, Kuwait threatened to leave the GCC if a Saudi–Qatari proposal for Yemeni membership over the longer term was not dropped.

As the Arab Spring unfolded across the wider Middle East in late 2011, hundreds of thousands of demonstrators took to the streets of Yemen. They demanded improved social and economic conditions and called for the resignation of veteran president Ali Abdullah Saleh. He had served as president of North Yemen since 1978 and became president of the entire country following unification in 1991. In order to stem instability, the GCC states engaged in proactive mediation between President Saleh and opposition groups in 2011. By the middle of that year, Saleh had agreed to resign, only to renege on this promise subsequently. Under intense GCC pressure and with the threat of civil war looming, he finally stepped down from the presidency at the end of 2011. All GCC states apart from Oman backed the transition to power of Saleh's deputy, Abd Rabbuh Mansour Hadi, who won an election in which he was the only candidate. Following this election, the Gulf States won widespread international praise for their role in facilitating a peaceful transition in Yemen. They were also applauded for following this up with the launch of a national dialogue intended to address the grievances of those constituencies still unhappy with Hadi's accession to power. This GCC-sponsored dialogue failed to deliver consensus or compromise. Instead, fighting spread across the country as anti-Hadi forces attempted to overturn his election victory. Hadi had the support of the predominantly Sunni south of the country. Yemen's security forces were divided. Some remained loyal to Hadi while others backed his predecessor. The Houthis of Yemen's northern provinces make up a third of the country's population. They are adherents of a branch of Shia Islam known as Zaidism. They initially joined the protests against Saleh, but after Hadi's election victory they established themselves as Saleh's most powerful domestic backers and the main threat to Hadi's continued rule. In 2014, they led the military campaign that forced Hadi and the official Yemeni government out of the capital, Sana'a. They then seized the presidential palace and established a committee to take over the functions of the presidency, actions Hadi condemned as a coup. With the exception of Oman, all the GCC states and their close ally Jordan agreed with Hadi's description of what had happened. In late March 2015, less than twenty-four hours after Hadi had fled to the safety of Riyadh, the air forces of Saudi Arabia, the UAE, Bahrain, Qatar, Kuwait and Jordan launched Operation 'Decisive Storm'.

From its outset, this operation, under the direction of Salman's deputy crown prince and youngest son, Mohammed bin Salman, has been framed in sectarian terms. Senior Gulf diplomats justified the intervention on the grounds that Lebanese Hezbollah and Iran were active in Yemen on the side of the Houthis. This made it impossible for the Arab Gulf to abstain from involvement. The conflict, explained Saudi foreign minister Adel bin Ahmed Al-Jubeir, was a battle 'between good and evil'.[49] The Gulf States have never been able to demonstrate how much backing Iran has actually provided to Hadi's enemies in Yemen, though in early 2016 the Saudis claimed that they had intercepted a shipment of Iranian arms intended for the rebels, and the American navy made a similar claim a few months later. For its part, Iran has denied providing practical support for the Houthis or any of the other rebel groups fighting against Hadi, and many commentators tend to agree that Tehran's role is 'limited and low-cost'. The local rebels acknowledge links to Iran, with some even going so far as to admit having received training from Iranian-backed forces, but reject claims that they are merely pawns and proxies serving Iranian interests.

Aided by American and British political, technical and logistical support, the Saudi-led air war quickly developed into a ground offensive. Local Yemeni anti-rebel forces were joined by an initial deployment of 300 Sudanese troops, a number that grew to several thousand in the following months. More than 1,500 Moroccan paratroops and military police, 2,500 soldiers from the west African nation of Senegal and just under 1,000 from Egypt also joined the war in its early stages. Thousands of troops from the GCC were also deployed, including Saudi special forces, an armoured brigade from the UAE, and Qatari infantry backed up by armoured vehicles and Apache attack helicopters. Reportedly, these Arab and Muslim forces were supplemented by hundreds of mercenaries from Panama, Colombia and Chile paid for by the UAE government.

At the end of November 2015, top Emirati official Anwar Qarqash argued that the Saudi-led intervention in Yemen might provide a viable 'alternative model' to Western intervention in the Middle East.[50] Yet the cost of this conflict has been high for countries with falling oil revenues and little experience of sustaining battlefield casualties in a drawn-out war. In one day, in early September 2015, forty-five UAE troops, ten Saudis and five Bahrainis were killed in a rebel missile attack, the worst day of losses for GCC forces since the conflict began. Since then Qatar has also taken combat casualties, and the UAE and Saudi Arabia have lost some of their most senior officers on the ground as total GCC losses creep towards the mid-hundreds. Though costly in money and men, many in the Arab Gulf consider this to be a price worth paying to prevent a pro-Iranian group from seizing power in Yemen. Such an eventuality would leave Gulf Arab oil producers vulnerable to enemy forces positioned on the Bab el-Mandeb Strait, a strategic point between the Horn of Africa and the Middle East through which millions of barrels of oil pass every day. Yemen could also become a breeding ground for radicalism that would pose a direct threat to Saudi Arabia and Oman, both of which border the country. As Oman's Alawi explained, 'This is an area of chaos, and chaos gives a chance for . . . extremists and terrorists'. Worst of all, from a Saudi perspective, it would result in the extension of the frontier of the dreaded Shia crescent to the borders of the kingdom itself.[51]

In December 2015, in his opening speech at the first annual summit of Gulf leaders he hosted as Saudi king, Salman acknowledged all of these potential threats. He also told his audience at the Diriyah Palace in Riyadh that any political solution to the war in Yemen had to be followed by an international conference to support the reconstruction of the country, and the deeper integration of Yemen into the GCC economy. This last proposal – to use the GCC as a mechanism to pacify and stabilize Yemen – underscores the long-time importance that Saudi leaders have attached to the GCC as an instrument of security and stability. For decades, Saudi Arabia's GCC partners have been distrustful of such thinking. They have feared that Riyadh wants to hijack legitimate security concerns in order to extend its own influence across the region. This has made them all ultra-vigilant in searching for ulterior motives in the many Saudi proposals for a comprehensive GCC regional security agreement. Such suspicions are understandable. In an unequal power relationship, closer cooperation on security and defence can lead to reduced sovereignty and can even breed dependence. But mistrust inside the GCC has not been limited to fears over Saudi hegemony. Multiple, overlapping, border disputes between various member states, not to mention the desire to protect external relationships, have also conspired to limit the appeal of further security and defence cooperation. Unperturbed by past experience, in early December 2011, speaking at a security conference in Riyadh, Turki Al-Faisal called for the establishment of a 'united military force' in the Gulf, even if it meant 'ceding bits of individual sovereignty'.[52] This and other calls by Saudi officials for the GCC to be transformed into a fully fledged diplomatic and military union culminated in a proposal by King Abdullah known as the Riyadh Declaration. Issued at the end of the GCC summit in December 2011, this landmark statement made the case for a 'single unity' in several areas. In the area of defence and security it proposed the establishment of a joint GCC military command as a way of facilitating much closer security and military coordination. Again only Bahrain, itself subject to rumours at the time that it would imminently enter a political union with Saudi Arabia, provided open support for this proposal. Qatar, Kuwait and the UAE responded diplomatically, offering support for the idea in principle but requesting more time to fully consider its ramifications. Oman expressed serious reservations from the start.

Subsequent discussions were overtaken by the rapid escalation of crises in Egypt, Syria, Libya and Iraq, all of which served in their own ways to underscore the importance of closer GCC security cooperation. Ironically, they all also illuminated the profound differences among the GCC member states themselves. It was not until the final months of 2013 that GCC secretary general Abdullatif Al-Zayani once more spelt out the mutual benefits of defence and security cooperation based on King Abdullah's 2011 proposals. 'Military integration', Al-Zayani argued, was a central component of the move to 'full integration into one entity'. On that basis, he urged Gulf leaders to embrace the opportunity to approve a 'comprehensive security agreement'.[53]

Within weeks, this issue was being addressed at the annual GCC's leaders' summit in Kuwait City. Once again, Bahrain's prime minister backed the Saudi position, describing defence and security integration as a 'pressing demand [now] more than ever'.[54] He also endorsed the move to political union in its broadest form. Qatar, the UAE and Kuwait were once again much more cautious. They expressed their support for improved cooperation and integration but refused to commit to anything more at this stage. Oman categorically ruled out the possibility that it would participate in anything that resulted in deeper political union. 'We will not prevent a union, but if it happens we will not be part of it,' Alawi explained, adding that if other GCC member states did decide to go ahead and form a union, 'we will simply withdraw'.[55]

Despite the Omani refusal to countenance deeper integration at this time, the role of the Peninsula Shield force in Bahrain during the turbulent first six months of 2011 had highlighted the important contribution that a GCC regional military structure could make to Gulf security and even regime survival. Concerns over Saudi hegemony and disagreements on a multitude of foreign policy issues aside, this engendered a new willingness to consider, in principle at least, closer security and defence cooperation. Gulf rulers agreed to back the establishment of a Defence Planning Committee based on the NATO model, in which civilian and military experts would contribute to military planning and oversee issues of deployment, the standardization and interoperability of training and, where possible, the procurement of weapons systems.

Meeting in Abu Dhabi, senior GCC military figures also agreed to improve cooperation in securing and protecting critical infrastructure, especially in the oil and gas sectors. This was followed by a call from GCC defence officials to set up a joint naval force. GCC interior ministers lobbied for a joint police force and criminal database, as well as the establishment of a GCC counter-terrorism training centre in Abu Dhabi. By the end of 2014, these and other proposals were gaining high-level backing across the GCC. This was due in part to the new-found willingness of the UAE, Saudi Arabia and Qatar to look beyond their disagreements on political and ideological matters in order to work together. Speaking on the eve of the 2014 GCC summit in Doha, Qatar's foreign minister was adamant that on the issue of defence and security cooperation, 'we need to double [our] efforts'.[56] The Doha summit that followed was unprecedented in its backing for more unified policies and actions. The possibility that the US might withdraw from the region, leaving a security vacuum that played into the hands of Iran, also served as an incentive for GCC members to embrace closer cooperation. The Obama administration has encouraged the Gulf States to prioritize integration with each other over bilateral ties with Washington, and attempted to sell weapons systems to the GCC as a bloc whenever feasible in support of this position. At the Camp David summit in mid-2015, President Obama once more pushed his GCC guests on this matter, laying out the benefits of further intra-Gulf integration of their military capabilities and increased coordination on security issues.

This American emphasis on GCC self-help was taken as yet another sign that the Obama administration was increasingly reluctant to commit itself to the safety and security of the Arab Gulf. The problem is that there are not many viable alternatives to the security relationship with Washington. France and the United Kingdom – the two 'big' European military players – are important Gulf arms suppliers and both have signed major security and defence agreements with Gulf States in recent years. In 2009 France opened a military base in Abu Dhabi, its first new foreign military base in fifty years, and its first ever outside French or African territory. In 2014, Britain signed an agreement with Bahrain to establish a permanent naval base on the island. But neither of these countries nor the European Union as a whole has the military capacity, resources or political will to replace the United States as the Gulf's main provider of external security and defence. In 2007, India launched a new strategic initiative called the Indian Ocean Naval Symposium, mandated to develop 'cooperative, consultative and inclusive' mechanisms to address threats to Indian Ocean security. India's evolving security relationship with the Gulf States was included in this framework. Since then successive Indian governments have also signed several bilateral defence and security agreements with individual GCC states, including Qatar in 2008 and Saudi Arabia in 2010.

In recent years, there have been calls from within for the GCC to 'boost ties'[57] with an increasingly proactive and assertive Russia. Under Putin, so the argument goes, Russia has succeeded in re-establishing its Cold War standing and influence in the Middle East, while its close ties with Syria and Iran make Moscow much more able than Washington to moderate the behaviour of both. In reality, Russia proved to be Tehran's closest ally on the nuclear issue and, in the company of Iran, propped up the Assad regime in Syria. During Russia's six-month military intervention in Syria, the divide between Russian interests and those of the GCC grew even wider. On the same day as the first Russian bombings of anti-Assad strongholds took place in September 2015, Saudi foreign minister Adel Al-Jubeir stated that there was 'no future for Assad' and warned that if he refused to give up power the Saudi-led alliance would be forced to embrace a military option that would potentially place it in direct conflict with the Russian military. Since then, Gulf commentators have become increasingly agitated by the evolving Iranian–Russian axis. In particular, Putin's gift of a replica of Russia's oldest handwritten Quran to supreme leader Ali Khamenei during a meeting in late 2015 was the subject of extensive comment, much of it incredulous.[58] A group of Saudi religious leaders even declared a 'holy war' against the Putin government for backing the Assad regime and Iran in Syria.

Since the early 2000s, China has worked to institutionalize ties with the GCC as a regional grouping, as well as with individual GCC member states. This resulted in the establishment of the China–GCC Strategic Dialogue, which held its first meeting in 2010. On a bilateral level, Beijing and several GCC states regularly hold strategic and political consultations. When Chinese president Xi Jinping visited Kuwait in 2014, during the kingdom's rotating presidency of the GCC, he promised that his country 'stands ready to work with countries in the region to promote political solutions of regional issues and safeguard local peace and stability'. Later in the same year, President Xi hosted Qatar's emir on a three-day visit to Beijing, on the eve of Qatar's chairmanship of the GCC. During their meetings, the Chinese premier called for enhanced cooperation on matters of security, law enforcement and counter-terrorism.[59] These two encounters demonstrate China's new willingness since the Arab Spring to take into account the strategic and security concerns of its important trade and energy partners in the Arab Gulf. Yet Beijing has little interest in drawing regional states away from their reliance on the US security guarantee and even less of a desire to play the role of strategic balancer in the Gulf, a region it still considers an American sphere of influence.

Despite its growing credibility deficit, the United States, not China, India or Russia, is still the only major external player in the Persian Gulf and Arabian Peninsula capable of protecting and defending GCC interests. This has not stopped the Gulf States from building up alliances with major Muslim nations like Indonesia and Malaysia, as well as Turkey and more traditional partners like Bangladesh and Pakistan. These last two have cooperated closely with Saudi Arabia on military matters for decades. Pakistan also provided military backing for GCC operations in Bahrain in 2011 but declined an initial Saudi request to join the military campaign in Yemen in order to avoid entanglement in that increasingly sectarian conflict. Two other majority-Muslim countries – Senegal and Sudan – did agree to send troops to Yemen. They explained their decision in terms of their commitment to defend Saudi Arabia, the land of the Two Holy Mosques. They also had more practical reasons to get involved, as the Saudis paid them billions for their participation in the Yemen operation. Turkey has also become an increasingly important security partner for Qatar, and more recently Saudi Arabia, in the context of Riyadh's efforts to build up an anti-Iranian Sunni coalition and because of its unique interests in Syria and Iraq and its key role in NATO.

The involvement of Jordan in the air war in Yemen and the role of Morocco and Egypt in the subsequent ground war in the country also underscores the Saudi-led GCC's desire to enhance security relations with Arab Sunni monarchies and republics from across the wider region. Cooperation with all these countries goes back many decades. In the middle years of the 1980s during the Iran–Iraq war, there were rumours that GCC officials and their Moroccan counterparts had held secret talks over military cooperation.[60] At the conclusion of that conflict the Gulf States considered bringing Jordan and Egypt into the GCC's military framework. Three years later, at the end of the Kuwait crisis, a request went out to Egypt and Syria to station troops in the Gulf to help deter future threats from Saddam Hussein. Though none of these proposals ultimately got off the ground, they did point to a pattern – in the immediate aftermath of major crises the GCC states tend to prioritize the consolidation of security and defence ties with friendly Sunni Arab countries. This was evident once more in the immediate aftermath of the Arab Spring. In May 2011, in the wake of the most turbulent months of unrest in Bahrain, Saudi leaders proposed that Morocco along with Jordan join the GCC. The informed Gulf commentator Abdullah Al-Shayji believed this development 'marked a tectonic shift'[61] in GCC thinking. It was certainly not driven by geographic considerations. Though Jordan shares a border with the north-west of Saudi Arabia, neither is located in the Gulf, and Morocco is 5,000 kilometres from Saudi Arabia. Nor did it make much financial sense. As the insightful Saudi-based economist John Sfakianakis noted in the *Financial Times*, both Morocco and Jordan are poor and the former, with a population of over thirty million, would be very hard to absorb into the GCC.[62]

Yet this bold invitation did have its own strategic logic. It was intended to extend the GCC's security structures beyond the Gulf, in order to shore up two other pro-Western, pro-GCC, battle-hardened Sunni Muslim (albeit constitutional) monarchies and bind their fate to that of the GCC. It was also intended to serve as a reminder of Saudi Arabia's standing in the Arab and Islamic worlds. Finally, it was meant to send a message to opponents, in particular Iran, that the Saudi-led GCC would act in defence of its interests across the entire MENA region, not only in its own backyard. The emir of Bahrain had emerged from the Arab Spring calling on the GCC to establish 'multiple bases everywhere'. He eagerly endorsed the 'Six Plus Two' plan, as the proposed entry of Morocco and Jordan into the GCC became known. The rulers of Qatar, Oman, Kuwait and the UAE were less enthusiastic. Though they had all taken unprecedented risks in the international arena in the previous few years, they had concerns over the implications of any enlargement. They did not want to overextend the GCC or turn it into a 'mini-NATO', nor did they want to antagonize Iran unnecessarily or pay for the privilege of having Morocco or Jordan join their ranks.

Their scepticism, and ultimately their veto of this proposal, was also linked to their long-time distrust of Saudi intentions. Three years later, in 2014, all except Oman were much more willing to contemplate, in principle at least, an amended version of the 2011 proposal. This called for President Abdel Fattah Al-Sisi's post-Muslim Brotherhood Egypt to join Jordan and Morocco in a more integrated GCC security framework, known as 'GCC Plus'. The return of Egypt to its traditional position as the number-one strategic and military player in the Arab world may still be some way off, but its inclusion in this proposed framework demonstrated a general desire among Arab Gulf States to move closer to Cairo in the post-Muslim Brotherhood era. This was followed by the announcement of a Saudi–Egyptian plan to establish a joint military force at the end of 2015; and the announcement of dozens of Saudi investment projects in Egypt in mid-2016 valued in the billions. As President Sisi explained in a live television conference with King Salman in Cairo, Saudi Arabia shared with his country a 'unique quality of the relations' that allowed both 'to face mutual challenges'.[63]

In his first GCC summit as host in December 2015, King Salman presented a new and comprehensive vision intended to transform the GCC into a stronger and more effective entity in the regional and international arenas. This proposal received unanimous support from fellow Gulf leaders in attendance. Yet a truly integrated, autonomous regional security and defence capability is very difficult to implement. Most recently, this has been evident in the reluctance of GCC member states to agree to move ahead with plans to develop an integrated ballistic missile defence. This could effectively neutralize the threat from Iran's large arsenal of missiles, leaving the GCC's larger and more advanced air forces in control of the region's skies. Yet it is a very complex and ambitious undertaking that requires much more than technical integration and the coordination of defence spending. It also requires a shared vision of the benefits that regional defence and security integration will bring, as well as closer political ties and a willingness to cede – at least some – national sovereignty. This can only happen if there is real trust between Saudi Arabia and its partners. Currently that does not appear to exist. In 2015, for example, Qatar, Oman and Kuwait fiercely opposed the establishment of the joint missile system after Saudi officials demanded that only Saudi personnel run the programme. This once more clearly demonstrates how GCC states still think nationally and short term, and not regionally and long term. They remain very far from functioning in a coherent fashion in the realm of defence and security. They have not yet managed to build on their achievement in Bahrain in 2011 or their more recent cooperation in Yemen to develop a viable joint security and defence strategy. If they are unable to do this in the face of the disintegration of Iraq, the rise of Islamic State and the challenge of Iran, one must wonder if they will ever be able to achieve self-reliance or even attempt to rely primarily on each other rather than on a host of non-Gulf actors in their ongoing quest for stability at home and influence abroad.

CHAPTER 10

THE HUB

'We are part of the Arab world and the Islamic world . . . we're also part of humanity and the international community.'

– Sheikh Tamim bin Hamad Al-Thani

Speaking on live television during a visit to Cairo in April 2016, King Salman of Saudi Arabia announced plans to build a bridge between his kingdom and Sharm el-Sheikh, on the tip of Egypt's Sinai Peninsula. The decision to move forward with this ambitious construction and engineering project, to be named the King Salman Causeway, not only underscored the rapidly growing strategic and economic ties between the two countries since Salman took power in 2015; it also represented, as the king explained, a 'historic step to connect Africa and Asia'. He did not go further, but if he had, he could also have mentioned that the bridge is the most recent, and perhaps one of the most significant, demonstrations of the intent of the Arab Gulf States to turn their home region into a business, trade, finance, leisure, culture and travel hub between East and West at the centre of the world.

In purely geographic terms, the Gulf States have a comparative advantage in pursuing these ambitions. Located between Asia, Africa and Europe, at least a third of the world's population lives within a four-hour plane journey of the Gulf on the Indian sub-continent or in east Africa. Half of the world's seven billion people are within an eight-hour flight of the region. The Gulf's ambitions are also fitting for a region that can claim a 'rich mélange of cultural influences',[1] as one scholar recently put it. Indeed, by the middle of the nineteenth century, the Gulf was a multicultural hothouse brimming over with Persians, Indians, Europeans,

Africans, all buying and selling goods and sampling the local customs and culture.

In more recent times, at least since the oil boom of the 1970s, the Arab Gulf States have been at the heart of the global energy system and have become more and more integrated into the international economy as some of the world's leading oil exporters. By 2000, all had invested significant sums of money in overseas assets and had increasingly open economies. Measured in terms of economic openness – exports and imports as a percentage of GDP – the GCC states were among the most open nations anywhere in the developed or the developing world by the beginning of the twenty-first century. They all also relied on the outside world for technology, a very important source of economic growth, as well as for most of their professional expertise, unskilled labour and food. All apart from Saudi Arabia were also members of the WTO by the end of 2000. The kingdom became the last GCC member state to join the organization in 2005, twelve years after it first applied. The Arab Gulf's progressive integration into the multilateral trading system by the dawn of the new millennium was demonstrated very clearly in November 2001. Top officials from all over the world travelled to Doha to attend the most important meeting on global free trade since the founding of the WTO six years earlier. This meeting was viewed as crucial to stimulating the global economy and strengthening the trading system. The many years of negotiations that followed were known as the Doha Round, and though they were suspended in 2008, while they lasted they were a constant reminder of Qatar and the wider region's commitment to the building of a liberal international trade system.

Globalization has always been at the heart of the liberal trade regime and the world is now more globalized and more interconnected than ever before. Money, talent and ideas flow freely in all directions. Scholars have argued for over a decade now that the Arab Gulf provides a 'laboratory par excellence'[2] to test the theories of globalization. Gulf rulers are doing everything they can to help in this endeavour as part of their efforts to turn their home region into a global hub. Of course, dreams do not always become reality, not even in the oil-rich Gulf where money is rarely an obstacle to ambition. With this in mind, this final chapter will examine the Gulf's globalizing adventure over the last decade and a half and assess the very real difficulties that the Gulf States continue to face in their efforts to turn the region into an all-encompassing hub between East and West.

The start of the global financial crisis in 2008 highlighted how deeply the Arab Gulf had integrated into the heart of the international financial system in previous years. The near collapse of Dubai in particular underscored how interconnected, and thus vulnerable, the Gulf was to the crises affecting the world's major stock markets, trading blocs and lenders. By the mid-2000s, Dubai was home to more than a dozen successful free zones. Between them they housed thousands of companies from almost 100 countries. It was also the Arab world's most globalized economy. It revelled in the phrase 'Shanghai, Mumbai, Dubai, or goodbye', which was coined at the time, and its leaders took great pleasure in having their emirate regularly compared to major emerging entrepreneurial players like China and India. The global crisis also provided the Gulf States with the opportunity to solidify their positions as a focal point for finance at the heart of the international system. The Dubai International Financial Centre and the Qatar Financial Centre were established in 2004 and 2005 respectively. From the time of their launch, both were conceived in global rather than regional terms, and unlike Bahrain, a long-time offshore financial centre in the region, they were established in free zones. They were governed by their own set of laws and regulations based on English common law rather than local civil law and shariah courts.[3] In 2003 Dubai had hosted the annual meeting of the IMF and World Bank. Just as Qatar had hosted the 2001 WTO meeting to highlight its relevance to the international trading system, this meeting in Dubai was intended to announce the emirate's financial credentials to the world on the eve of the establishment of its financial centre. As one senior official involved in the early years of the Dubai Financial Centre admitted, 'Our goal is to put Dubai's clock up on the walls of the world's financial institutions, in a slot between Hong Kong, Singapore and London.'[4]

Along with Malaysia, Pakistan and Iran, all the GCC states except Oman have also established themselves at the forefront of Islamic banking and finance. They are key players in developing what one expert has called 'a new form of Islamic capitalism'.[5] They are leaders in Islamic insurance (*takaful*), retail and investment banking and shariah-compliant asset management. All except Oman are among the top nations in the world in terms of holding shariah-compliant financial assets. Some of the most popular Islamic financial mechanisms and exchange transactions, notably *murabaha* and *ijara*,[6] were pioneered and refined in the GCC. Islamic bonds (*sukuk*) were first issued in Pakistan and Malaysia in the 1980s and '90s. In the early 2000s, Bahrain, intent on establishing itself as a major global centre of Islamic finance, introduced the first sovereign *sukuk*. Its capital city, Manama, subsequently became home to the International Islamic Financial Market (IIFM), an organization that promotes common trading standards across the Islamic finance industry. These efforts have paid off for Bahrain, which is now the number-one Islamic finance market in the GCC and one of the top two or three in the world. For its part, in 2013, Dubai launched the first ever Global Islamic Economy Summit. Under the personal sponsorship of the emirate's ruler, its objective since its launch has been to introduce the world to the possibilities of a cohesive global Islamic ecosystem with Dubai as its capital.

The recent preoccupation of the Arab Gulf States with global integration has complicated their relations with the rest of the Arab world. From its very beginnings, Arab critics described the GCC as an 'exclusive club for the rich'.[7] In line with this thinking, the twin processes of GCC integration and globalization have been interpreted as an attempt to isolate the wealthy Gulf region from the rest of the problem-riddled Arab world. Gulf leaders have always played down such concerns. The preamble to the GCC charter stated clearly that the organization's duty was to 'serve Arab and Islamic causes'. Speaking at the height of the Iran–Iraq war, Secretary General Bisharah explained that the organization was 'operating in the Arab framework; we do not wish to appear to be a group separate from the Arabs'. It was not, he continued, an independent bloc, indeed if anything the 'role and responsibilities' of its members across the Arab world 'have increased and widened because of the GCC'.[8] Three decades later, Gulf leaders continued to present the GCC as the eastern flank of the Arab nation, a sub-regional grouping committed to strengthening the entire Arab world.

As the Arab Gulf becomes more and more integrated into the global economy, it has continued to set out ambitious plans for deeper regional integration. Recently these have included proposals to spend hundreds of billions of dollars on 6,000 kilometres of track connecting the entire GCC by train. At the same time, the rest of the Arab world has stagnated and, in many cases, gone backwards. For example, as the Gulf States rose up the rankings in all areas of global interconnectedness, the Middle East and North Africa as a whole was the only region to suffer a large drop in its connectedness in the years since the Arab Spring. This has further highlighted the differences between the Arab 'winners' and 'losers' in an era of trade liberalization and globalization. It has also fuelled further suspicion as to whether the Arab Gulf is looking towards or beyond its Arab brethren. Soon after coming to power in 2013, Qatar's new emir, Tamim bin Hamad Al-Thani, provided his own take on this dilemma. 'We are part of the Arab world and the Islamic world,' explained the thirty-three-year-old British-educated ruler, before adding, 'We're also part of humanity and the international community.'[9]

Partly to address this tension, the Arab Gulf States have poured vast sums of money into business ventures, real estate, infrastructure projects and utilities across the Middle East and North Africa. Their investments dwarf those of much bigger traditional Arab powers like Egypt. The UAE, Saudi Arabia, Qatar, Kuwait and Bahrain are the first, second, fourth, sixth and seventh ranked investors in the rest of the Arab world. Up to 50 per cent of Egypt's stock market and 75 per cent of Jordan's are owned by institutional or private investors from the GCC.[10] This 'financial statecraft',[11] as the Gulf's involvement in cross-border business has been termed, serves as a constant reminder of the dominant role of the Gulf States in the wider Arab region. The annual Gulf Business poll of the 100 most powerful Arabs for 2015 is instructive in this regard. Of the top fifty in the rankings, only five come from Arab countries outside the GCC and one of those is the Mexican multi-billionaire Carlos Slim who is included because of his vast holdings in Lebanon.

During the global financial crisis, funds were temporarily diverted back home. This did not last long and by the time of the Arab Spring the Gulf States were once more pumping vast amounts of money into the rest of the Arab world in the form of aid, debt relief and large deposits of currency in faltering banks. Jordan and Morocco, two of the GCC's closest Arab partners, received billions in emergency assistance and investment funds in vital economic sectors like tourism at the height of the Arab Spring. As the last chapter showed, there was even a Saudi proposal to open membership of the GCC to both as a way of improving regional security. For their part, most senior Moroccan and Jordanian figures favoured this proposal for economic reasons. Jawad Anani, a former Jordanian foreign minister and deputy prime minister, even observed that when measured in terms of its existing economic, financial and labour relations Jordan was 'already a member' of the GCC.[12]

The IMF estimates that from the time of the Arab Spring until the downward spiral of the oil price in 2014, GCC assistance to non-oil-producing Arab states rose from 1 per cent to 5 per cent of recipient state GDP.[13] As long as oil revenues remained strong, the Gulf States showed no signs of cutting back on their funding for the Arab world. At a GCC economic summit in Riyadh in late January 2013, Saudi Arabia's then crown prince called on his partners to agree to a 50 per cent increase in the amount of money they put up for development projects across the wider region.[14] As well as being the biggest providers of aid and investment, the Gulf States have also been the main sources of tourist income in Arab countries and the biggest employers of labour from the rest of the Arab world. Every year, millions of Arab workers in the Gulf send home billions of dollars in wages.

Historically, the major trading centres of the Gulf thrived as bridges linking the Middle East and Asia. Since the early 2000s, three distinct but overlapping factors have fuelled the Gulf's renewed focus on building up economic ties with the East. The first was the determination of Gulf rulers to establish their own region as a global hub between East and West. The second was the Gulf's geographic appeal to Asian firms looking for a launch pad to Europe and Africa. The third was the cash-rich Gulf's growing hunger to find new investment opportunities in emerging markets at a time of rising oil revenues. The start of the global financial crisis added more impetus to this shift eastwards, as Western markets that had long served as the destination for most Gulf petro-dollars imploded. In Europe in particular, the Gulf States faced multi-billion dollar losses as they watched the value of their major holdings plunge. The title of an op-ed in one English-language Abu Dhabi paper summed up the evolving reality from the GCC perspective: 'Asia ascends, Europe sinks, and the US remains the same'.[15] Nobody could ignore the fact that at the same time as the Eurozone crisis caused a Europe-wide recession, many Asian countries were achieving almost double-digit growth. 'Why invest in 2 per cent growth economies', asked Bader Mohammed Al-Sa'ad, the head of Kuwait's sovereign wealth fund, 'when you can invest in 8 per cent growth economies?'[16]

On top of this, as local economists, commentators and businessmen explained, Asia was home to four billion people – 60 per cent of the world's population – and there were huge investment opportunities in everything from agribusiness, energy and infrastructure, to real estate and financial services. In recognition of this the KIA opened a new office in Beijing to mark its status as a qualified foreign institutional investor (QFII) in China. This was only the Kuwaiti fund's second overseas office ever and came four decades after its London base opened its doors. Tellingly, the massive fund has never had an office in the United States. Before the crash, ADIA of Abu Dhabi placed between 60 and 85 per cent of its investment capital in North America and Europe. In the midst of the crisis it started to look increasingly towards emerging markets that offered greater returns. ADIA's boss, Sheikh Hamed bin Zayed Al-Nahyan, summed up the thinking behind this decision. The Eurozone crisis, he explained, made the European investment environment 'unpredictable and unwelcome'. This made it wise to refocus on other regions that were 'more resilient to economic shocks'.[17]

There was also growing consensus among Gulf policymakers, as well as economists and commentators, that Asia was not only the better bet during the financial crisis but was also likely to emerge from the crisis stronger than traditional Western economies. 'The world's economic geography has shifted east. China and India and, increasingly the GCC at the center, account for a larger part of the world's trade,'[18] explained Nasser Al-Saidi, the former Lebanese economy and trade minister and chief economist at the Dubai International Financial Centre. On this basis, Gulf leaders prepared to refocus eastwards for the longer term, as well as during the crisis. Sultan bin Saeed Al-Mansouri, the UAE minister of economy, described Europe as 'kind of secondary for us now', and played up future ties with 'our partners in East Asia'.[19] This widely held view was primarily influenced by the growing economic power of the two Asian giants – India and China. The majority of Gulf experts polled in a late 2008 survey agreed that in the next few years India would become the top destination for Gulf investments and that China would become the most influential external actor across the Arab Gulf.[20]

Over the previous decade, the Chinese and Indian economies had both benefited from rising domestic government expenditure and massive government stimulus packages, as well as structural reforms and a rapidly growing middle class. These developments resulted in an explosion of domestic demand and infrastructural and other investment projects, making both countries increasingly attractive destinations for Gulf money. For their part, India and China welcomed the flow of inward investment from the Gulf as it partially offset the huge cost of importing Gulf oil and gas. From the time China and India became net oil importers in the mid-1990s the Gulf States had evolved into increasingly important energy partners. In 2002, Saudi Arabia became China's number-one supplier of crude oil and Beijing officially acknowledged its 'strategic oil relationship' with Riyadh for the first time. Since then, some of the largest foreign investment programmes in Chinese energy infrastructure have been made by the Gulf, sometimes on their own and sometimes in partnership with oil companies.

Between 2001 and 2006, Chinese–GCC bilateral trade increased three-fold from US$10 billion to US$30 billion a year. Chinese officials heralded the beginning of a 'new partnership' with the GCC. A China–GCC Strategic Dialogue and a China–GCC Economic and Trade Cooperation Forum were established to formalize these rising ties. In 2010, China and the GCC agreed to upgrade existing relations to the level of a strategic partnership. By then Saudi Arabia was China's number-one trading partner in west Asia and Africa and the UAE was number two and served as a key hub for Chinese goods entering Middle Eastern and north African markets. Since then, GCC trade with China has grown more rapidly than with any other major partner. In 2014, China spent US$100 billion on GCC exports. Many Chinese companies continue to view the Gulf as the launch pad for entry into the rest of the world. By 2020 China is expected to be the largest buyer of GCC exports, spending an estimated US$160 billion a year in the region and also selling more goods and services to the Gulf than any other trade partner.[21]

Between them, seven million Indian citizens living in the Gulf send home around US$40 billion in remittances annually.[22] They have long been at the heart of the relationship between India and the Gulf. In recent years, other factors have become more and more important as well. On a visit to Oman in 2008, India's then prime minister, Manmohan Singh, talked of the 'unique opportunity' for India to leverage the 'vast surplus funds in the Gulf for our development needs', and to accelerate trade and investment flows.[23] During Singh's time in office, New Delhi prioritized a multi-billion dollar joint fund with Saudi Arabia to focus on the development of infrastructure, and the promotion of joint exploration and the production of hydrocarbons.[24] A GCC road show was also organized by Indian officials as part of the government's plan to raise US$1 trillion between 2012 and 2017. The hope, as one finance ministry official explained, was that a 'positive response' in the Gulf would open the way for further road shows in the United States and other major economies.[25]

In terms of the volume and value of bilateral trade, relations between India and the Gulf are growing all the time. The GCC is one of India's top trade partners and the region is viewed more and more as part of India's 'natural economic hinterland', as one informed commentator recently put it.[26] Prime Minister Narendra Modi and his senior officials place great emphasis on the Gulf as a key partner for India. On a 2015 visit to the UAE, Modi made a firm commitment to strengthen economic relations with the region. This is vitally important for the Gulf's future economic development, as well as its success in establishing its position as a truly global hub. The Indian economy grew faster than any other major emerging economy in 2015, outpacing Russia and Brazil, as well as China. Though Indian GDP per capita is less than half that of China, it has a dynamic and increasingly educated young population – there are fifty million more Indians between the ages of fifteen and twenty-four than Chinese – and it offers huge potential for the Gulf nations. This is all the more important as the era of uninterrupted Chinese double-digit growth is over. This has raised inevitable concerns in the Gulf over the longer-term health of the Chinese economy. In the more immediate term, it has already cost the Gulf economies dearly. It is estimated that the Chinese stock market crash of 2015 wiped out up to 6 per cent of the total portfolio assets held by GCC countries. The second market collapse that followed in early 2016 is likely to have had a similarly detrimental impact on Gulf holdings.

China and India are not the only Asian nations to record a rapid rise in ties with the Gulf in recent years. By 2006, Gulf oil exports to Asia accounted for two-thirds of the GCC's entire output and Gulf leaders lobbied their counterparts across the entire Asian continent for permission to reinvest billions into rapidly growing capital markets. A City of London banker with years of experience working in the Gulf explained what this meant for his sector. 'Today,' he explained, 'when an investment bank approaches the Arab SWFs to offer them financial products in Europe or the US, they are not shy to refuse to buy them; instead, they express huge interest in the Asian markets.'[27] Gulf leaders also travelled across the region closing deals and making promises of further cooperation and investment in the areas of trade, agriculture, financial services, labour, tourism, education and training, from South Korea to Thailand, Sri Lanka to Vietnam, the Philippines to Bangladesh and Indonesia to Malaysia. There were even predictions that up to 50 per cent of all future Gulf real estate investments would occur in Asia. During a two-day state visit to the Philippines in early 2012, to take one of many examples, Qatar's then emir, fresh from a similar visit to Vietnam, pledged to launch a US$1 billion fund to support projects in agriculture, energy, halal food, labour, mining, petrochemicals, real estate, steel, tourism, trade and infrastructure development.[28]

All this activity fuelled speculation that rising commercial, financial and investment ties between Asia and the Gulf States marked the beginning of a 'new silk road' tailored to the needs of the twenty-first century. Kuwait committed billions to Silk City, a massive economic area in the north of the country, intended to serve as a free trade zone linking Asia and Europe. King Abdullah Economic City has similar aspirations. From its conception it has been presented as an international rather than a Saudi city. On completion, it hopes to be a global logistics and manufacturing hub located on the Red Sea that can connect Asia to Europe and the Mediterranean through the Suez Canal. 'Asia', announced one local commentator in 2012, 'is now writ large into Gulf business plans.'[29] It was not only Asia. 'Buying the World', ran one headline in *The Economist* at the end of 2008. Two years later, in a high-profile interview with the *Financial Times*, Qatar's then emir explained, 'We are investing everywhere.'[30] Australian mineral and energy companies, banks from Brazil to Bosnia, Irish leasing companies, Mexican holiday resorts, were all added to the Gulf's collective list of possessions in non-traditional investment markets all over the world. In Africa, Saudi Arabia alone provided funding for infrastructural and other projects in over twenty countries and was the lead investor in the financial sectors of a number of the continent's major economies, including Ethiopia.

Along with other Gulf States, Saudi Arabia also moved into other important African markets like Nigeria, Kenya and South Africa, as well as smaller ones like the Central African Republic, one of the world's least developed countries, where one Qatari investment firm committed over US$1 billion.

The Gulf States also entered major Muslim markets, including Asia's two Muslim powerhouses, Indonesia and Malaysia, which established its first trade office in the Middle East in the UAE. Etisalat, a telecoms operator based in the UAE, took a majority stake in Pakistan Telecom. In the financial sector, the Kuwaiti Islamic bank, Kuwait Finance House, established itself as a major player in Turkey, where it quickly became the country's largest Islamic bank, with eighty-eight branches. Along with Saudi Arabia's Al Rajhi Bank, Kuwait Finance House also made inroads into the Malaysian banking sector, before expanding into Australia and Singapore. The world's oldest Islamic financial institution, Dubai Islamic Bank, also expanded into Pakistan, Sudan, Egypt, Yemen and Turkish-controlled Northern Cyprus. Gulf investment in Turkey rose from US$300 million in 2007 to about US$1.7 billion in 2008. In early 2009, the head of Turkey's investment office expressed confidence that his country could attract up to US$10 billion from the Gulf in the form of various investments over the short term.[31] One Turkish partner in a massive real estate deal in Istanbul put into words what many businessmen in Islamic countries across the world were thinking in these heady days. 'They have so much money and they want to spend money, Europe is not doing well and Turkey is cheap. We are Muslim. They are Muslim.'[32]

The Arab Gulf's global investment strategy has been characterized by a real willingness to acquire major holdings in markets in Africa, Asia, Latin America and the wider Middle East with unresolved regulatory, transparency and investment protection issues. Their success in winning so many prized deals in these and other markets is also impressive given the stiff competition they have faced from equally ambitious and cash-rich Chinese funds and other investors looking for attractive long-term opportunities in emerging markets. As mentioned previously, the vast majority of Gulf investments in these years were driven by financial considerations and potential returns. Others have been made with more strategic objectives in mind. All GCC members suffer in varying degrees from water shortages, and they have among the highest per capita water consumption rates globally in a region with the highest water scarcity. On a per capita basis, Saudi Arabia and the UAE consume 91 per cent and 83 per cent more water than the global average. Qatar and Oman are also above the global average for water consumption. To address this major problem, GCC governments earmarked more than US$100 billion for investment in desalination technologies involving solar energy and other water-related technology in the five years up to 2016. They also established themselves as some of the biggest backers and promoters of competitions and prizes for innovative ideas and inventions dealing with water technology; Abu Dhabi even hosts the International Water Summit every year.

The Arab Gulf suffers from food shortages, in part because of its severe lack of water. The surge in the price of commodities including soya beans and rice, as well as a reduction in the grain supply from the start of 2007 to the middle of 2008, saw food move up the global political and security agenda. This development underscored the importance of sourcing and securing reliable produce for the 'oil rich, cash rich but food poor'[33] Gulf, as one contemporary commentator put it. 'Agriculture is now a priority for us,'[34] explained Qatar's influential finance minister, Yousef Hussein Kamal, in the early years of the global financial crisis. To address this problem the Gulf nations sped up their investments in agriculture across the developing world. One Kuwaiti official involved in implementing his country's food investment strategy in these years explained how parts of Asia and Africa – with land but little money – offered real potential to develop into the 'bread basket of the world'.[35]

Some of these ventures are purely commercial in nature. Kuwait's investments in rice, wheat and corn in Asia are one case in point. Similarly, Saudi Arabia launched a US$800 million company to support private sector investment in overseas farms, and the government has made large 'for-profit' investments in Brazilian beef farming and sugarcane production. The vast majority of Gulf agri-investments have been driven by long-term food supply needs rather than short-term profit. This growing 'food-energy security nexus',[36] as Kristian Coates Ulrichsen has termed it, has served to deepen ties between the Gulf States and many parts of the developing world. Saudi Arabia and Qatar have invested vast sums in dozens of food security projects in Sudan, one of Africa's largest countries. This in turn has had a significant, and some would argue negative, impact on the country's socio-economic priorities. The Sudanese government set aside one-fifth of its cultivated land for sale to Gulf funds, as investment in Sudanese agricultural holdings rose from 3 per cent of all investment in the country in 2007 to 50 per cent in 2010, and totalled US$7.5 billion. Billions of dollars more have been invested in millions of hectares of farmland in a number of other countries in Africa (Ethiopia, Democratic Republic of Congo, Algeria, Mauritania, Mozambique), south-east Asia (Cambodia,

Vietnam, Malaysia, the Philippines, the Seychelles, Thailand), central Asia and eastern Europe (Kazakhstan, Ukraine) and south Asia (Bangladesh, Pakistan). Between 2007 and 2009, the Gulf States and other major agri-investors, notably China and South Korea, spent as much as US$30 billion on farmland covering territory the size of France.[37] Given the scale of this move into food security – described by some informed experts as a 'land grab of epic proportions' and a type of 'twenty-first century . . . land grab'[38] – it is not surprising that the Gulf States, as well as China and other major players in the sector, have had to deal with resentment, protests and even occasional violent clashes in several African and Asian countries where deals have gone ahead. Critics have complained in particular about a lack of transparency and the exclusion from negotiations of those most directly affected – local farmers and their communities.

At the other end of the spectrum – and far less controversial, but no less central to the Gulf's global expansion in recent years – has been the clearly defined strategy of investing in foreign know-how and technology linked to plans for diversification and sustainable economic development, a priority in the Gulf. Abu Dhabi hosts the Middle East's largest annual meeting on sustainability policies, technologies and investment. The emirate is also a major investor in cutting-edge engineering and manufacturing assets as part of its attempts to build up its shipping and aviation sectors. Its purchase of large shares in Rolls-Royce, as well as the European Aeronautic Defence and Space Company NV, the name of the Airbus Group prior to 2014, were intended to help kick-start an aerospace industry in the emirate. Aabar, the Abu Dhabi investment fund, went one better. It bought a major stake in Virgin Galactic, the US-based commercial space venture set up by serial entrepreneur Richard Branson. The plan is to locate a spaceport in the emirate as a way of establishing it as a destination for high-end tourists who want to experience sub-orbital flight. Like the UAE, Qatar has also developed an investment strategy that prioritizes investment in cutting-edge global technology that fosters sustainable development. As Saleh bin Mohammed Al-Nabit, secretary general of Qatar's ministry of development and planning, has explained, 'Sustainable development is crucial to Qatar's National Vision'.[39] Within a few months of the launch of its 'Vision 2030' in 2009, Qatari officials announced a partnership with the United Kingdom that would establish a US$400 million fund to invest in pioneering clean-energy companies. The objective was to develop technologies that could help produce low-carbon-emitting energy. In return for its financial commitment, the United Kingdom's Carbon Trust, a government body, made its own commitment to attract investment from private companies and pledged to transfer technology to Qatar, allowing it to 'develop and commercialize' these projects domestically. Subsequently, the QIA made a further significant investment in the Carbon Trust as part of its contribution to develop cutting-edge low-carbon technologies.[40]

To further facilitate sustainability, the Qatari government also established the Sustainability Development Industry (SDI) initiative, a pledge by companies to improve their environmental record, as well as their corporate governance, social progress and human development efforts. The QIA has also become a lead partner in the Agreement on the Establishment of the Global Green Growth Institute (GGGI) – with a mandate to develop a new model of economic development by linking economic performance to sustainability. This commitment has influenced many of Qatar's recent international investments. In mid-2015, for example, it purchased a 100 per cent interest from Hine, the international real estate firm that specializes in sustainable projects, in Porta Nuova, a transformative city-centre development in Milan, Italy. All of these purchases and many more besides illuminate a clearly defined Gulf strategy to invest in overseas tech companies and tech know-how that adds value to plans for diversification and development.

As the most globalized place in the Gulf, Dubai tops the list by almost every measure, including the Trade Freedom Index, as the most open Gulf market. It is the centre of Gulf commerce, travel, finance, communications and transport and, for now at least, the one truly global location in the region. It is hard to argue with the government of Dubai's own description of the emirate as one of the 'most inspirational, exciting and successful cities in the world' and the 'perfect gateway' between East and West. Many Asian firms choose the emirate as their base for doing business across the Middle East, Europe and East and sub-Saharan Africa. This growing engagement with Asia is one reason why Dubai was able return to growth within a few years of its 2009 financial crisis. Though its post-recovery growth was at a much more modest rate than before, it was still higher than the GCC average. Dubai also quickly re-established itself as a magnet for funds. During the oil boom earlier in the decade, vast amounts of petrodollars flooded into the real estate and hospitality sectors. Once the Arab Spring began in 2011, record amounts of money once more returned to the emirate in search of a regional safe haven in a period of unprecedented instability.

By 2012, hugely ambitions development projects that had been suspended during the downturn were relaunched. These included plans to open the world's biggest shopping mall to complement Dubai Mall, already one of the world's largest in total area. On completion, this new project, named Mall of the World, will occupy 700,000 square metres. It will be connected to 100 new hotels, the Middle East's largest entertainment centre, and an indoor recreational space larger than London's Hyde Park. The world's tallest Ferris wheel, the Dubai Eye, will also be located in the massive complex. This renewed programme of 'big' domestic development is at the heart of Dubai's ongoing attempts to consolidate its position as an international hub for tourism, leisure and entertainment. The story of Dubai's Global Village demonstrates how far this strategy has come since the 1990s. At the time of its launch in 1996, it was nothing more than a few small kiosks stocked with arts and crafts, foodstuffs and knick-knacks from around the world. Two decades later it is home to forty large pavilions, hundreds of kiosks and shops and even more stage shows. It has more than six million visitors each year and it is one of the world's largest global cultural events.

Travel and tourism is one of the world economy's fastest-growing sectors. In 2012 the number of annual world travellers topped one billion for the first time. Dubai has worked hard not only to attract visitors but also to establish itself as a leading global player in this ever-expanding market. Emirates Airline, Dubai's flagship carrier, was established in the mid-1980s to accelerate the transition of Dubai International Airport from a regional into a global travel hub. Three decades on, Emirates has the world's largest fleet of Airbus A380 super jumbos and Boeing 777 wide-body jets. It is one of the world's top airlines when measured by key indicators – revenue, passenger miles, fleet size and international passengers carried. Between 2000 and 2015 Dubai, along with Turkey and China, accounted for almost 30 per cent of the emerging market air travel growth. From its Dubai base, the airline flies to almost 100 countries on six continents. It has a reputation for targeting markets in Asia, Africa and even Latin America that have been poorly served in the past by international carriers, who focused on easier, more established and profitable routes. Its ambitious approach to connecting the world was underscored in March 2016 when it launched a direct service from Dubai to Panama City. At just under eighteen hours, this was the longest non-stop commercial passenger flight in history at the time of its announcement.

The success of Emirates has contributed greatly to Dubai's reputation as a top global destination. It was voted the world's number-one destination at the 2013 World Travel Awards. The runner-up was Abu Dhabi, which has pursued a broadly similar strategy to its UAE partner, also centred on its own airline, Etihad. In a 2015 survey conducted by

MasterCard, Dubai ranked fourth, behind London, Bangkok and Paris, of the world's 132 most visited cities in terms of annual international overnight visitor arrivals (14.26 million) and cross-border spending (US$11.68 billion). This placed it ahead of Istanbul, New York, Singapore, Kuala Lumpur, Seoul and Hong Kong in the top ten. Dubai predicts that it will attract twenty million foreign visitors in 2020 when it hosts World Expo. As well as being a centre for tourism, leisure and entertainment, Dubai is also an international transit hub. In 1980, Dubai did not make the world's top twenty-five container ports. By 2011, Jebel Ali had broken into the world's top ten busiest and Dubai also ranks sixth globally in terms of volume of air cargo traffic. Nor is there any sign of Dubai slowing down its development of this key sector. Dubai World Central, a logistics base located near the new airport, will be twice as large as Hong Kong Island on completion.[41]

The success of Dubai is due to a specific set of circumstances that its Gulf partners currently cannot replicate, not least its unparalleled infrastructural base – which ranks very high in terms of global connectedness. According to recent research published by McKinsey only six international cities can be classified as global hubs in at least four of the five areas that measure global flows and interconnectedness – goods, services, finance, people, and data and communication. These cities are London, Singapore, Hong Kong, New York, Tokyo and Dubai.[42] This has not deterred other Gulf States from attempting to make the most of their own geographic advantage to offer their own connected bridge between East and West. Doha ranks high in two areas – finance and communication. The Saudi port of Jeddah also scores highly in terms of connectedness and the kingdom has ambitious plans to build up its port capacity to match that of Jebel Ali. For example, the main developer of King Abdullah City, which happens to be a Dubai-run company, is constructing a port there that will become a major East–West maritime transhipment location.[43] More generally, Saudi Arabia gained nineteen places between 1995 and 2012 to reach sixteenth place in the world in terms of global connectedness.

Abu Dhabi launched Etihad Airlines in 2003, almost two decades after the establishment of Emirates in Dubai. In recent years its global growth strategy has revolved around buying stakes in, or building alliances with, several airlines in Europe, Asia and Australia. In early 2016 its partnership with Jet Airways made it the fastest-growing airline in India. This has enabled Etihad to get a foothold in India and boosted Abu Dhabi's status as a hub between this vast market and the rest of the world. Five other Gulf airlines – Emirates, Oman Air, Saudi Arabian, Air Arabia and Qatar

Airways – also made it into the top ten carriers in India by passenger numbers in 2015.

Qatar Airways operates across the world from a hub at the new Doha International Airport. Launched a decade after Emirates in the mid-1990s, it was the first Gulf carrier to join an international airline alliance, when it became a member of OneWorld in 2012. It has an aggressive strategy of adding numerous new international routes on an almost monthly basis. In mid-2015 alone, it announced that it would be adding three major American routes – Los Angeles, Boston and Atlanta – a move that enabled it to offer direct flights from Doha to the ten largest metropolitan areas in the United States for the first time. Between June 2016 and 2017 the airline plans to add another seventeen routes – six in Europe, four in Africa, three in Australasia, two in south-east Asia and one in the United States. At the 2015 World Airline Awards, Qatar Airways was named the world's number-one airline. The Doha-based carrier topped the poll of 245 airlines based on a survey of millions of customers from over 100 countries. Emirates came fifth and Etihad came sixth. Following in the footsteps of Emirates, in January 2016 Qatar Airways looked to make aviation history of its own when it announced plans to launch a non-stop Doha to Auckland, New Zealand, service. At over 14,000 kilometres, the almost nineteen-hour journey would replace Emirates' Dubai–Panama City route as the world's longest direct flight.

Gulf governments have presented the rise of their national carriers to international prominence in recent years as evidence of two things: the region's status as a global hub; and the innovative and ambitious policies of visionary leaders who have succeeded in changing the way the world thinks about international travel. The Gulf States understand that a global hub needs a global brand. As Qatar's National Strategy for Branding explains, a strong brand increases international recognition and helps develop an image of 'an economically successful, globalizing, pro-business, and independent state'.[44] Some of the most successful recent examples of national branding have included the Irish 'Celtic Tiger', 'Incredible India' and 'Cool Britannia'. In 2012, as a way of underscoring the importance of branding to its citizens, Dubai's ruler sponsored a UAE-wide competition to find a 'nation brand' that would fully represent the achievements of the federation in all areas of endeavour.

The hosting of major sporting events adds value to national brands and raises national profile. The 1992 Barcelona Summer Olympics was Spain's announcement to the world that after decades of dictatorship and only a few years after joining the EU, the country had arrived on the global scene.

More recently, Beijing's 2008 Summer Olympics was intended to send a similar message about China's rising status and fortunes. Speaking on the eve of the global financial crisis in 2007, Dubai's entrepreneurial ruler, Sheikh Mohammed Al-Maktoum, described massive Gulf spending on sporting events as a multi-billion dollar 'charm offensive'.[45] The five-year strategic plan launched by the Abu Dhabi Tourism Authority in the same year prioritized bidding for several major sporting events in order to achieve maximum 'exposure well beyond our shores',[46] as its head, Sultan bin Tahnoon Al-Nahyan, poetically explained. For their part, Qatari policy-makers acknowledged that they wanted to attract major sporting events in order to draw attention to the major strides the kingdom had made in recent years.[47]

Qatar received due acknowledgement of its recent success in 2010 when it became the first Arab and Muslim country to win the right to host the world's most watched sporting event, the FIFA football World Cup in 2022. This decision, as one leading Gulf expert acknowledged at the time, was not only a victory for Qatar, it was also a testament to 'the remarkable rise of the GCC states to international prominence'.[48] Delighted Qatari leaders also presented their successful bid in regional terms. 'Thank you for having such bold vision,' the head of Qatar's bid team, Mohammad bin Hamad Al-Thani, told the rest of the world. 'Thank you also for acknowledging this is the right time for the Middle East. We have a date with history, which is summer 2022.'[49] Football has a vast global audience, a massive fan base, hugely lucrative and high-profile advertising deals and even top-selling video games. From the moment it won the right to host the World Cup, Qatar started to use World Cup-related content to promote the country internationally. The prospect of a big sporting event is not only good for the national brand and national pride; it also helps speed up domestic infrastructural development. When Doha became the first Gulf city and only the second in west Asia to host the Asian Games in 2006, the government initiated a massive building programme of roads, shopping malls and hotels to prepare for the arrival of teams, fans and the international media. Since winning its 2022 World Cup bid, Qatar has unveiled plans to spend around US$60 billion on an even more ambitious programme of domestic development. This includes US$24 billion worth of transport infrastructure, including the construction of a 340-kilometre public transport network serving Doha and its environs by way of a metro and a suburban rail network. There was even a promise of high-speed rail lines to Bahrain and Saudi Arabia, to link local football fans across the region to the mega-event.

Hosting major sporting events also attracts tourists and generates revenue. Oman recorded a 15–20 per cent rise in holidaymakers after it hosted the Asian Beach Games in 2010. Annual foreign visitors to Brazil rose above six million for the first time ever in 2014, the year it hosted the World Cup. The country's tourism ministry explained the record-breaking figures almost entirely in terms of the global attention the country received from hosting the tournament. Apart from winning bids to host to flagship global events like the Asia Games, the World Athletics Championships, the World Swimming Championships, the World High Diving Championships and the World Cup – and that's just Qatar – over the last decade the Gulf States have also won the right to host numerous smaller but still high-profile events across a whole variety of sporting endeavours. These include some of the most anticipated annual events on the world golf calendar, including the Dubai Desert Classic, known as the 'Major of the Middle East', and the Abu Dhabi HSBC Golf Championship. Since it started in 2006, this tournament has become one of the top events on the PGA European Tour, with an estimated television audience of around half a billion. Annual ATP and WTA tennis events in Doha, Dubai and Abu Dhabi attract many of the world's top male and female tennis players and are beamed across the world to a global audience of millions.

Bahrain and Abu Dhabi host two of the twenty-one Formula One Grands Prix held every year. Motor racing's premier competition has always marketed its races as a great way for countries to increase their profile before an affluent global audience of fans. Since they began in Bahrain in 2004 and Abu Dhabi in 2009, these races have provided both kingdoms with 'global resonance', as Abu Dhabi's Crown Prince Mohammed bin Zayed Al-Nahyan has termed it. They are among the most popular on the circuit, attracting hundreds of thousands of locals, as well as holidaymakers and race aficionados from all over the world. Formula One's bosses and team owners view them as cash cows for the rich sponsors they attract. They also appreciate the willingness of the local organizers to experiment in order to keep the attention of a global television audience that has been falling in recent years. In 2014, for example, Bahrain switched to a night race in part so that television viewers could watch sparks flying from the undercarriage of the cars in the dark skies. This adds to the spectacle and entertainment value of Formula One but cannot be easily seen during daytime races.

The Arab Gulf strategy goes beyond hosting major sporting events. It also attempts to connect the region with sporting brands and franchises that have global recognition and fans in every corner of the planet.

Manchester City in the English football Premier League is owned by an Abu Dhabi royal. Paris Saint-Germain, one of the top French football teams, is owned by Qatar's sovereign wealth fund. The club's two main sponsors are the Qatar Tourism Authority and Emirates Airlines. Prior to the club's first Asian tour, the airline presented it with a branded aircraft in club colours so the millions of football fans eagerly awaiting the team's arrival would associate Emirates with the team they devotedly follow. Emirates Airlines also pays millions every year for the privilege of having its name on the Arsenal stadium in north London. It also sponsors some of the most high-profile tennis events, including two of the four Grand Slams – the French Open at Roland Garros Stadium in Paris and the US Open in New York's Flushing Meadows. Emirates' sponsorship of the three biggest international cricket competitions – the ICC's Cricket World Cup, World Twenty20 and Champions Trophy – illuminates the way such deals are linked to the development of Dubai's brand as a global hub. As the company explains, its investment in cricket provides a 'strong synergy' and a 'powerful platform to connect with fans and communities' across Asia, Australasia and the United Kingdom.

In 2010, Barcelona Football Club in Spain's 'La Liga' ended its long-time policy of not advertising sponsors on players' jerseys when it accepted a deal with the Qatar Foundation, a private, non-profit organization founded in 1995 and chaired by Sheikha Moza bint Nasser Al-Missned, the former queen and mother of the kingdom's current emir. The following year Qatar Airways took over the club's sponsorship in a five-year deal estimated to be worth US$150 million. At the same time, the Qatari airline became the sponsor of the world's most famous cycling race, the Tour de France, which by some accounts has a global television audience of more than three billion. This move by the airline coincided with discussions between Qatari officials and race organizers to bring the ceremonial first leg of the Tour to Doha at a future date. This demonstrated very clearly the fusion of the two interconnected Gulf sporting strategies – hosting high-profile events in the region and sponsoring them in their home locations.

Apart from positioning themselves as leading players in sport and international travel, the Arab Gulf States have also looked to turn the region into a global hub for culture. Jazz and film festivals, as well as classical music concerts headlined by the world's most famous conductors and orchestras, take place regularly. They are held at ultra-modern performing arts centres and, in the case of Oman, the Muscat Royal Opera House, established by royal decree by the music-loving sultan. In 2012, Qatar hosted artists, curators and collectors from across the world at the Global

Art Forum. The following year it staged exhibitions by renowned contemporary artists Takashi Murakami and Damien Hirst, as well as a Louise Bourgeois retrospective and the installation of an 25-metre-high Richard Serra statue in the middle of the desert.

The UAE also holds two major international art shows – Art Dubai and the Sharjah Biennial. The former is the leading international art fair in the Middle East, Africa and south Asia and is presented by its organizers as 'one of the most globalized meeting points in the art world today'. The latter has grown from a traditional and regionally focused exhibition on its launch in the early 1990s into a major event on the global art calendar. Sheikha Hoor bint Sultan Al-Qasimi, the daughter of Sharjah's ruler, is president of the biennial. She is also a regular on the art world's annual 'Power 100' list. So is Sheikha Al-Mayassa, head of the Qatar Museums Authority who has led the kingdom's art-buying spree in recent years and, in the process, earned the nickname 'Qatar's culture Queen' from *The Economist*. In 2011, under her leadership, Qatar spent US$250 million on Cezanne's *The Card Players*. This was the highest price ever paid for a piece of artwork up to that point and, as one commentator put it, 'reflected the new multi-polarity and shifting power structure of the art world'.[50] The same year the *Art Newspaper* ranked Qatar as the world's biggest buyer in the art market in terms of value. In 2015, a work of two Tahitian women (*Nafea Faa Ipoipo?*), painted by French Post-Impressionist Paul Gauguin in the 1890s, was purchased by the Qatar Museums Authority for US$300 million, making it the most expensive piece of art ever sold.

Such exhibitions, events and purchases are linked directly to ambitious plans to create a world-leading and cutting-edge cultural heritage sector across the Gulf. New museums and galleries have opened up on an unprecedented scale since 2000, with more than a dozen in Dubai alone. World-famous architects have been commissioned to make these ambitious dreams a reality. I. M. Pei designed the Museum of Islamic Art in Doha. It houses rare manuscripts, textiles and ceramics from age-old Muslim communities in Europe, Asia and the Middle East. Not far away on the corniche, Doha's coastal road, a building designed by renowned French architect Jean Nouvel is under construction and on completion will house Qatar's National Museum. Along with Frank Gehry, Norman Foster, Tadao Ando and the late Zaha Hadid, Nouvel is also among those appointed by Abu Dhabi since the early 2000s to design several major cultural institutions. Some of these projects, including the Sheikh Zayed National Museum, look to preserve Abu Dhabi's local history, and project national distinctiveness. Others, most notably the Louvre Abu Dhabi and the Guggenheim Abu

Dhabi, are more about connecting the Gulf with some of the world's leading cultural brands.

This process of 'Guggenheiming' – a term that describes the use of globally recognized cultural institutions to achieve rapid economic and cultural growth – is not specific to the Gulf. The Guggenheim Abu Dhabi follows in the footsteps of the flagship museum in New York, as well as other branches in Las Vegas, Venice, Bilbao and Berlin. One is also planned for Lithuania's capital of Vilnius. The one in the German capital closed in 2013 and the one in Vilnius is stalled over allegations of financial impropriety. The Bilbao branch has fared much better. In 1991, the regional government of the Basque country in northern Spain agreed to fund the building of the Guggenheim Museum Bilbao as a way of rejuvenating the town's rundown port area. Designed by Frank Gehry, it opened in 1997 and has been a phenomenal success. In 2007, ten years after his Bilbao gallery opened, Gehry was commissioned to design the Guggenheim Abu Dhabi, the largest of all the Guggenheims.

Cities all over the world also employ 'starchitects' like Gehry to maximize publicity around new buildings. What makes the case of the Gulf different is the number of these projects that have been initiated since the early 2000s, as well as the way they have been presented – as part of a regional attempt to bring together different cultures, religions and even civilizations. In 2006, when the plan to build the Guggenheim Abu Dhabi was announced, the director of the Guggenheim Foundation, Thomas Krens, declared that the project was about bringing together the world's cultures and setting the 'standards' for global culture 'for decades to come'. The following year French and UAE officials explained that, once completed, the Louvre Abu Dhabi would be a 'universal museum' that would transform Abu Dhabi into one of the 'great cultural nations'. More than that, they argued, it could even serve as a 'central arena for dialogue between civilizations and cultures'. When the stunning Royal Opera House in Muscat opened in 2011, it was lauded not only as a magnificent venue for opera lovers; it was also heralded as a centre of excellence that facilitated 'global cultural dialogue'.

In her foreword to the catalogue of Damien Hirst's 'Relics' exhibition in Doha in 2013, Sheikha Al-Mayassa addressed the thinking behind her own country's cultural engagement. Qatar, she explained, was not only interested in art for art's sake. The kingdom also wanted to become a 'leader in making, showing and debating the visual arts' in order to help to 'unlock communication between diverse nations'.[51] Admirable as these sentiments are, some commentators and observers have wondered whether they represent a view held only by a small group within the ruling elite rather than society as a whole. There is also some scepticism over whether the massive investment in cultural hubs across the Gulf is driven primarily by less idealistic goals, first and foremost a desire to transform the region into a fashionable arts destination that can attract high-end tourists.

Taken together, this hyperactive and wide-ranging engagement with travel and tourism, sports and culture has undoubtedly increased the international standing of the Arab Gulf as a hub of cutting-edge activity at the centre of the world. At the same time, the strategies embraced by Gulf players in all these areas have generated significant controversy and raised a number of difficult questions at a time when the region has been commanding a great deal of global attention. They have also served to highlight the political and social costs and challenges, as well as the great opportunities and benefits, resulting from the move to establish the region as a global hub in so many areas simultaneously.

The success of Qatar Airways, Emirates and Etihad in their commercial air war with more established though less well-resourced international competitors is a case in point. In the summer of 2015, the three biggest US long-haul carriers, American, Delta and United, accused the three mega-Gulf carriers of achieving their dominant position in air travel through receiving billions in state aid and by 'divert[ing] global traffic to their hubs'. The governments of France and Germany have made similar complaints on behalf of European-based airlines, arguing that the subsidies that Gulf carriers receive distort the market and reduce competitiveness. Since the entry of the big Gulf carriers, Frankfurt, Lufthansa's biggest hub, has lost nearly a third of its market share on routes between Europe and Asia. It has also had to cut dozens of flights all around the world on other routes because it is unable to match the fares and the quality of service offered by Gulf carriers. Air France-KLM has been forced to abandon several of its own routes to the Middle East and Asia for the same reasons.

Gulf airline executives and senior government officials have dismissed the allegations they face as nothing more than the unsubstantiated claims of jealous and disgruntled competitors. They have also argued that for years hypocritical Western airlines received substantial support from their own governments and still continue to deny some Gulf carriers access to major airports like Paris Charles de Gaulle, in order to protect national carriers, in this case Air France. Even if their defence is to the point, the accusations that Gulf airlines and their governments face are particularly troubling because they take aim at the Arab Gulf's long-cultivated image as a bastion of free-market enterprise in a region not known for such openness.

According to one story, several years ago when the chairman of Emirates asked Dubai's ruler for financial protection, the pro-business Mohammed Al-Maktoum allegedly replied that he could not help out because, although he loved the airline, he 'loved Dubai more'. Whether true or not, this story does highlight just how concerned Gulf leaders, especially in Dubai, are to maintain their hard-won reputations as paragons of the liberal global trading system. On the other hand, the same story also draws attention to one problem inherent in the Gulf business model – its lack of transparency and accountability and the almost absolute power and control that tends to be vested in a few individuals. As mentioned previously, the lines between private wealth and public assets are blurred in the Arab Gulf. In part this is a hangover from an earlier era when national budgets did not exist and rulers were entirely responsible for collecting and distributing money. Over the years this has often made it impossible to establish who owns what in the region. In 2007, the *Financial Times* shone a bright light on what this actually amounts to in practice in the case of Dubai's financial services sector:

> Dubai Holdings belongs to Dubai ruler Sheikh Muhammad bin Rashid Al-Maktoum, and in turn owns financial conglomerate Dubai Group, a 20 per cent shareholder in Borse Dubai – the holding company for DFM [Dubai Financial Market], and DIFX [Dubai International Financial Exchange]. DIFX is a centrepiece of the government's Dubai International Financial Centre, a financial business park, which owns another 20 per cent.[52]

The above example indicates just how complex and non-transparent business practice can be in the Gulf. Whether it is inimical to the basic tenets of capitalism or not is debatable. There is broad consensus that building an attractive and sustainable global hub requires transparent and efficient laws and regulations, as well as high-quality physical infrastructure like those on offer in the Gulf. It is also true that when governments, rulers and their families are also the main shareholders of what are ostensibly commercial concerns, the profit motive may not always be the number-one priority. International influence, power projection and domestic economic or political considerations, including regime protection, may be even more important drivers of business decisions.

China's economic rise over the last two decades has somewhat challenged the view that rapid development requires a move towards more progressive political systems. In the Gulf, rulers have found it easier to embrace and deal with globalization and free trade than they have political liberalization. Yet, the Gulf's success in the sporting and cultural arenas has also placed a spotlight on domestic politics and on issues like human rights and political participation like never before as the recent experience of the Bahrain Grand Prix and Qatar's World Cup bid demonstrate. Until the start of the Arab Spring, the Bahrain Grand Prix was an annual event cherished by the kingdom's ruling elite for presenting a positive image of the country around the world. This brought in tourist dollars and provided the regime with legitimacy. Anti-government forces knew that very well and once civil strife began in 2011 during the Arab Spring, they targeted the race in order to delegitimize the ruling family in the international arena. The 2011 Bahrain Grand Prix was scheduled to take place in March, one month after widespread anti-government demonstrations started, and only one day before the Saudi-led GCC military force intervened to prop up the royal family. Demands to postpone or cancel the Grand Prix gained saturation coverage on the international news. The campaign by human rights groups to have the race called off gained over 300,000 followers on Facebook.

Pressure on the race organizers intensified when it became known that Shia staff working at the Manama event had been fired for allegedly participating in anti-government protests. Bowing to international criticism and global media attention, the race was eventually postponed until the following October. The debate over whether it was right or even safe to proceed with the race continued during the intervening months. Finally, after a number of Formula One teams went public with their displeasure over having to return to Bahrain to participate in the rescheduled event, it was eventually cancelled. The following year, anti-government groups ramped up their demonstrations during race week to once more draw attention to their cause. The race still went ahead and a heavy police presence around the track and in Manama's hotel district ensured that most foreigners in town for the event were insulated from the protests. These security measures could not prevent many of the journalists, in the country ostensibly to cover the race, from filing reports that had more to do with the local political situation and the ethical issues of holding the race than with the race itself, once more embarrassing the Bahraini authorities.

In December 2010, thousands gathered on Doha's streets to watch live coverage of the World Cup vote from Zurich, Switzerland, on giant television screens. When the decision to award Qatar the competition in 2022 was announced, these crowds were jubilant. Thousands more flooded on to the streets to celebrate over the course of the day. Long convoys of cars and vans descended on the corniche to celebrate, and their horn beeping and flag waving continued into the early hours of the next morning. Even after this initial euphoria died down, there was huge excitement over what hosting the World Cup would do for the tiny kingdom's economy and how it would boost its global, as well as regional, reputation and ambitions. 'Expect Amazing' was the slogan for Qatar's World Cup bid, but within weeks things had started to go sour. Rumours circulated that Qatar's success was the result of bribery and corruption. Soon these allegations were making headline news. Ongoing revelations over endemic bribery and corruption inside FIFA have continued to attract relentless media attention. The Swiss and American authorities have both launched official investigations of football's governing body that continue, even if only indirectly, to cast a shadow over the World Cup in Qatar. Unfortunately for Qatar, allegations over financial irregularities are only one problem plaguing its World Cup preparations. There is even a Wikipedia page entitled 'List of 2022 FIFA World Cup controversies' that covers the biggest problems Qatar faces, one by one. These include climate; transportation; cost; cultural and political issues; and human rights. As one media outlet summed up, Qatar has an uphill struggle to convince sceptical fans that World Cup 2022 will not be 'a sweltering, boring and alcohol-free tournament'.[53]

The most damaging allegations connected to the World Cup relate to the poor welfare, living and working conditions of migrant labourers employed to carry out the massive infrastructural projects that need to be completed in time for the event. During 2011, calls for Qatar to respect workers' rights on World Cup construction sites got louder. Human Rights Watch, the International Trade Union Confederation (ITUC), Amnesty International and the UN's International Labour Organization all took up the cause of this army of unskilled workers. They have lobbied the Qatari government to address several major issues, including exorbitant recruitment fees, the confiscation of passports and restrictions under the kafala sponsorship system that limits the mobility of workers to move from one job to another.[54] They have also become the voice of hundreds of primarily Indian and Nepalese workers who have died in building site accidents. The international media's coverage of these tragedies has been unsparing: 'How many more must die for Qatar's World Cup?' and 'Thousands Dead on World-Cup Construction Site: The Qatari Hunger Games' are just two examples from the British and German media respectively.[55]

As far back as 2004, Qatar had introduced legislation that regulated labour in the private sector, limited worker hours and set better health and safety standards. Since the country's policies have come under intense scrutiny and criticism more recently, the government has acknowledged that much more needs to be done and has passed new regulations and laws to ensure that those improvements take place. In 2015, the emir approved important changes to the kafala system, which opened the way for workers to challenge a sponsor's decision to refuse them permission to leave the country. He also endorsed the introduction of an electronic wage protection system to regularize the payment of salaries by requiring all businesses to pay workers online rather than with cash. At the same time, Qatari officials have counselled that real change will take time to achieve, though this argument has done little to dampen international anger on the issue. 'The Qatari government', argued the Human Rights Watch annual report for 2016, 'should understand that protecting the rights of migrant construction workers is a necessary part of hosting a 21st century football tournament.'[56] In the middle of the same year, the International Labour Organization (ILO) threatened Qatar with a possible investigation. If this is launched it would make Qatar only the fifth country ever to face such an inquiry and, in the most extreme case, could open the way for international sanctions.

It is possible that the World Cup, intended to be the crowning achievement of Qatar's global strategy, will do more damage to the country's reputation and standing across the world than any other single issue. It was reported in 2015 that Barcelona Football Club, arguably the biggest brand in world football, is considering replacing Qatar Airways with another sponsor when the current deal ends in 2016 because of the ongoing controversy over workers' rights. Similarly, when top German team Bayern Munich announced a new sponsorship with Doha International Airport at the beginning of 2016, the news was met with vocal criticism and protests from fans, trade unions, human rights groups and politicians.

Apart from having to overcome scepticism over its motives, the Gulf's cultural sector, like the sporting world, has also had to deal with negative publicity on the workers' rights issue. There were claims that the migrants building the UAE's cultural hub, including the Louvre and the Guggenheim museums, had to endure 'prison conditions' both on site on Saadiyat Island in Abu Dhabi and off site in the hostels and labour camps where they live. In order to draw attention to the curfews, monitoring and restrictions of movement these workers faced, Gulf Labor, a coalition of international artists working to ensure that migrant worker rights are protected during the construction of the museums, presented their findings at a series of high-profile events over ten days at the Venice Biennale, the world's most prestigious contemporary art event, in July 2015. The protest group followed this up with the publication of a book, *The Gulf: High Culture/*

Hard Labor, chronicling the cultural activism of fighting for the rights of workers in the Gulf. In a related case, and at the cost of much negative comment in the art world, the UAE government denied entry visas to two artists, Walid Raad and Ashok Sukumaran, scheduled to attend the Sharjah Biennial, because of their public criticism of labour practices in the region.

On one level, such problems are to be expected, given the scale of the Arab Gulf's ambitious plans to become a central player in sport, culture, transportation, travel and trade, and the speed with which they have looked to make this happen. This is compounded by the fact that the region is still in the developmental stage and still working out how to implement profound socio-economic reform in an era of massive domestic development without overturning decades of stability and progress. All the GCC states apart from Oman are in the top fifty nations in the world in terms of social globalization, which measures the level of worldwide social relations, which influence how local developments are shaped by foreign events. At the same time, only Qatar, at number eighty, makes it into the top 100 nations in terms of political globalization, which measures the trend towards multilateralism, NGO and civil society involvement in political life. This means that as long as issues like workers' rights remain unresolved, it will be difficult for the Arab Gulf States to ignore external pressures for change. It will also make it harder for them to attract foreign investment, to present themselves as bastions of governance and economic freedom and to move beyond consultative political representation to a more substantive type of political engagement that signals a real move towards democratic reform. This situation may even retard somewhat the goal of becoming a dynamic global hub for the twenty-first century, even as the region consolidates its important position at the heart of the global trading system alongside established players like the EU, US and Japan and newer ones like China and India.

The Economist Intelligence Unit, in a report published in 2009, predicted that by 2020 the Gulf region would be an increasingly important trading and economic hub, with a US$2 trillion economy, deep links to Asia and Africa as well as more traditional partners in the West. Nothing that has happened since then has challenged the validity of this broad assessment. If anything, events since then, despite the backlash over workers' rights and anti-competitive practices, have pointed to the Gulf exceeding those expectations well before 2020. According to the most recent Global Connectedness Index, all the Gulf States are among the top forty-five most connected countries in the world.[57] As the UAE gears up to host World

Expo in 2020 and Qatar prepares for FIFA World Cup 2022, rulers in all six Gulf States continue to pursue numerous strategies intended to turn their own countries and the region as a whole into a hub at the centre of the world. It would be a mistake to underestimate just how much the Gulf's efforts to become a hub have been one of the defining factors shaping the region's experience in the new millennium. Nor should we ignore what these developments say about the Arab Gulf's rising confidence and power in the world over the last four decades.

CONCLUSION

(IN) CAPACITATED

In the early 1970s the Arab Gulf States took control of their own fortunes. Since then they have used their oil and gas wealth to pursue stability at home and influence abroad. They are now an influential group of small and, in the Saudi case, medium-sized states projecting their power all over the world in the service of their interests. Across north Africa, in the Levant and on the shores of the eastern Mediterranean, the traditional heartland of the Arab world, one can see the fruits of their financial and traditional diplomacy all around. If the Gulf States are the new Arab powerhouses in the Middle East, they are also major players in the wider Muslim world, over and beyond the authority and legitimacy that Saudi Arabia derives from its special position at the heart of Islam. In Sudan, one of Africa's biggest nations, and in Turkey and Pakistan, as well as in a host of smaller Muslim nations, their political and economic influence is extensive.

Gulf standing in both the Arab and Muslim worlds was demonstrated twice in quick succession in late 2015 and early 2016. First, Saudi Arabia announced that it would lead a newly established thirty-five-nation Islamic military coalition (excluding Iran) to fight terror from a joint operations command centre in Riyadh. Then, only months later, the kingdom hosted Operation Northern Thunder. This was the largest military exercise ever held in the Middle East. Almost 350,000 ground troops, as well as combat planes and tanks from twenty nations, including all six GCC member states and partners big (Malaysia, Turkey and Pakistan) and small (Chad, the Comoros and the Maldives) participated in the twelve-day battlefield simulations in the Saudi desert on the borders of Kuwait and Iraq. Some questioned the viability of these unprecedented projects; others waited in vain for proper details to emerge on what exactly, beyond photo-ops, these new alliances planned to do. Yet both underscored Saudi Arabia's key role in the Islamic and Arab worlds and demonstrated the kingdom's willingness, in the company of its GCC partners, to spend its political capital and oil dollars on novel and ambitious cooperative security arrangements.

The power differential in the energy markets is shrinking, but Saudi Arabia remains the single most important oil producer, and Qatar is still the world's number-one exporter of natural gas. More broadly, the Gulf is still home to more than half of the world's oil reserves and over a third of its natural gas. This fact alone ensures that the Gulf States remain important global players, and some of the wealthiest nations anywhere. The World Bank, the IMF and the CIA all rank Qatar number one in the world in terms of per capita income. Kuwait and the UAE are in the top ten, Bahrain and Saudi Arabia are in the top fifteen and Oman is in the top twenty-five. This has enabled them to consolidate their position as some of the world's top overseas investors, as well as leaders in both mainstream and Islamic finance. While the region's push to become a global hub is both a tribute to its rising role in a number of sectors that drive global connectivity – travel, logistics, sport – and a testament to its evolving capacity to provide a state-of the-art infrastructural link between Europe, Asia, Africa and the rest of the world.

These achievements, especially when combined with an unparalleled ambition that is both insatiable and 'soaring',[1] as *The Economist* recently described it, have earned the Gulf States the recognition of the entire international community. Even much bigger, and traditionally much more powerful, global players like Europe, China, the United States and Russia, all regard the Gulf States as important partners and, in what is an acknowledgement of their status, regularly take their interests into account before they act on any number of economic and political issues.

Survivors

Whether all this can last is the vital question. Some believe it cannot. On the foreign policy level it has been argued that the current elevated position of the Gulf States in the Arab world will never endure over the longer term because both individually and collectively they lack the indigenous populations, the military might, the ideological appeal and the political skills to turn their oil wealth into real influence in the way that past dominant players, like Nasser's Egypt in the 1950s and '60s, have done before them. Others link the upcoming 'pandemonium' in the oil markets and the end of 'big oil' to the end of Gulf influence in the region and beyond.[2] Gulf energy producers do face a major challenge from rivals in the energy sector, in particular American firms exploiting unconventional sources of oil and gas, including shale.[3] This has become a 'big issue' for Gulf oil producers, in the words of the UAE's oil minister, Mohammed bin Dhaen Al-Hamli. The International Energy Agency (IEA) has even predicted that the exploitation of new sources of unconventional fossil fuels, including shale, will redraw the world's energy map in the next decade. By some other estimates, the United States will overtake Saudi Arabia to become the world's largest oil producer by 2020. At the same time, the Gulf also faces new competition from gas suppliers, including Australia and the United States, which could potentially export as much LNG as Qatar, the world's largest exporter, by 2020.[4]

Real as these challenges are, they do not foretell the end of the Arab Gulf States' global powers, never mind their demise as viable and functioning players on a regional level. History has shown that most states, most of the time, even when they are small, weak, poor and vulnerable, tend to withstand significant internal and external pressure before they succumb. 'Once created, states have little intention of surrendering their power,' noted the late Fred Halliday, an insightful and distinguished thinker on international affairs.[5] In the final account, sovereign states have a great capacity to survive the challenges they face and they are very hard to destroy. The record of the Arab Gulf States since the boom years of the 1970s seems to bear out this argument in favour of state resilience. They successfully navigated the Iranian revolution and the brutal war between Iran and Iraq during the 1980s that threatened to tear asunder all that they had achieved in the previous decade. At the start of the 1990s, and with the backing of almost the entire international community, they overcame the threat and trauma of the Iraqi invasion and occupation of Kuwait. Exactly a decade later they weathered the maelstrom of anti-Muslim sentiment and rising domestic insecurity following the 9/11 terror attacks on America and the subsequent US invasion of Iraq. During the Arab Spring, the Gulf States had their diplomatic skills and seriousness of purpose tested like never before. In response, they demonstrated a deep commitment to upholding the status quo in their home region. They also exhibited a new willingness to take a leading military, as well as economic and diplomatic, role across the wider Middle East to protect and promote their individual and collective interests when necessary.

On each of these occasions of profound regional turmoil, the Gulf States adapted to meet the challenges they faced. In doing so they consolidated their status as the key Arab political players, not only in the region but also on the world stage. Of course, past achievement and current status does not mean that regime change or societal collapse cannot happen at some future point. Ever since Britain abandoned its long-time role as their protector at the beginning of the 1970s, the region's rulers have worried endlessly about this possibility, and have done everything within their power to avoid it happening. Certainly, as this book has shown, the Gulf States continue to face numerous threats outside their borders and beyond their control. First and foremost among these are Iran and Iranian-controlled or -inspired Shia 'Resistance Networks', including Hezbollah in Lebanon and Syria, Houthi tribesmen in Yemen, and government-backed militias in Iraq, not to mention the threat of sleeper cells at home.

As long as the Gulf States continue to feel threatened by Iran, they will continue to search for a way to re-establish a regional balance. Their difficulty in achieving this objective highlights their ongoing reliance on the United States as the key external security guarantor. For this reason, Gulf policymakers do not want Washington to abandon the region, convinced that this move would create a larger vacuum that could only lead to further chaos. In his final year in power, President Obama did little to reassure Gulf partners on this matter. In a series of foreign policy interviews with President Obama, published in *The Atlantic* magazine in April 2016, Jeffrey Goldberg presented a president with little time for the Arab world in general, and Saudi Arabia in particular. Obama, Goldberg reported, was 'irritated' at being required to treat the kingdom as an ally. More worrying for the Gulf States was Goldberg's recounting of Obama's belief that Saudi Arabia should 'share' the Middle East with Iran by finding some form of 'cold peace'.[6] This is not what Gulf leaders wanted to hear from their closest and most powerful ally in a period of unprecedented uncertainty and insecurity across the region.

Capacity, Not Legitimacy

Yet the Gulf's recent history – including its experience of the Arab Spring – has shown that socio-economic problems pose a much greater danger to the status quo in the Gulf than the Iranian challenge, the poor state of the American alliance or any other matter of external security. Many argue that the existing socio-economic and political pressures faced by Gulf rulers are so profound that they cannot be overcome and will ultimately lead to the 'collapse of the Gulf monarchies, or at least most of them in their present form',[7] as one expert on the Gulf has recently argued in a book-length study predicting the downfall of regimes across the region. Others argue that the profound shifts in the energy markets will result in the inevitable collapse of Saudi Arabia and, with it, the end of stability across the Arab Gulf.[8]

These are real causes of concern but those in power in the region can find some comfort in the fact that they do not face a legitimacy problem at home. With the exception of the Al-Khalifa in Bahrain, the region's royal families can claim popular consent over their right to rule. There is widespread acceptance of their authority and they do not have to rely on the level of coercion to maintain order that has been the norm in other parts of the Arab world. At the same time, with every passing year Gulf rulers are being held to higher and higher standards by their peoples. Few may deny their right to hold power but more and more are demanding that they deliver greater progress and prosperity. In short, the major challenges that Gulf elites must address as a priority are capacity-related and revolve around managing available resources for the benefit of current and future generations.

For their entire time as sovereign states, the success of the Gulf States, as well as the legitimacy of their rulers, has been based on the capacity to redistribute oil revenues to various interest groups and stakeholders in society and to transform the remaining oil surpluses into valuable tangible assets – roads and hospitals at home and real estate, art, stocks and shares abroad. Gradually over the years, and especially since the Arab Spring, rulers have come to realize that their legitimacy is increasingly dependent on their capacity to deliver a more productive and competitive economic base; more and better private sector jobs; and an entrepreneurial business environment that has been all too absent from the region in the modern era. As the recent establishment of a ministry for youth in Kuwait acknowledges, this also requires a greater willingness to address the mounting concerns of frustrated young populations, who lack opportunities and a stake in society, and who are ripe for further alienation if not radicalization unless they are properly engaged.

In these terms, the types of sustainable socio-economic reforms examined in this book, those intended to increase economic opportunities and reduce the feelings of inequality and exclusion that cause social unrest, are evolving into an increasingly vital component of regime security and even regime survival. This is a profound shift away from the long-time social contract between family and tribe and ruler and ruled that has been held together by an expensive, expansive and often non-productive patronage system that can be traced back to the pre-oil era when Britain controlled the region.

Energy Saver

The continuing centrality of this age-old socio-economic structure, together with much more recent demographic pressures, does not complement the processes of reform; it makes it far harder to achieve. This was clearly illuminated following the fall in the oil price in 2014. Subsequently, economic growth slowed, revenues fell and budgetary pressures rose. This situation was made worse by concerns over the break-even price of oil across the region. This is the price that producers need to sell a barrel of oil for in order to generate enough income to cover their annual spending on everything from education and health to new roads, public service salaries and military hardware. In 2008, the average break-even price across the GCC six was US$43. The spending spree that took place during the Arab Spring forced up the break-even price of oil across the region and, by the end of 2011, it was almost US$79. Since then, it has continued to rise across the region to average out at US$94 in mid-2016. Qatar requires the lowest break-even price in order to balance its budget (at around US$55), while Oman and Bahrain require a barrel of oil to sell at around US$100 to balance theirs.

This evolving reality has forced policymakers to acknowledge more publicly than ever the need to embrace serious reform without delay. Recently in Saudi Arabia, the minister for economy and planning, Adel bin Muhammad Al-Fakih, promised that his government planned to 'seize the moment and take the right decisions to change our economy'.[9] Soon after, Mohammed bin Salman, the kingdom's deputy crown prince, defence minister and the cabinet member with overall responsibility for the economy and unprecedented control over the state oil monopoly, bluntly acknowledged that the key challenge his country faced was 'overdependence on oil and the way we prepare and spend our budgets'.[10] He followed this up in April 2016 with the launch of a new '2030 Vision' intended to end oil dependence by the mid-2030s at the latest. He even proposed a radical way to make this happen – he would sell off around 5 per cent of Saudi Aramco, the state-run oil giant, which produces about 10 per cent of the world's daily oil production and is by some estimates the world's most valuable company, worth more than US$2 trillion.

More immediately, all the Gulf States moved to reduce subsidies and put billions of dollars of planned expenditure on hold in non-priority areas. They were far more reluctant to reduce spending on diversification and domestic development programmes. In Kuwait, for example, though public spending was cut, there were no plans to cut capital spending under the kingdom's US$100 billion 2015–2020 Development Plan, which is funded in part by the kingdom's sovereign wealth fund. As the country's finance minister explained, the intention was 'to maintain expenditure and run a higher deficit rather than cause stagnation in an economy that depends on government spending'. The Gulf States also continued to allocate significant sums to welfare programmes in order to ensure the maintenance of social order. The most extravagant example of this occurred when the authorities gave away US$32 billion to all workers and pensioners as a coronation bonus when Salman became the Saudi king in early 2015. This was paid for with Saudi cash reserves, which peaked in August 2013 at US$737 billion. By the middle of 2015 they had fallen to under US$700 billion. By mid-2016 it was estimated that the Saudis were spending their reserves at about US$10–15 billion a month and total reserves had fallen to around US$600 billion. None of the five other GCC states have anywhere near the same reserves to draw on as Saudi Arabia and none have drawn down on their reserves at anywhere near the same rate as the Saudis. At the beginning of 2016, the five had just over US$250 billion in reserves between them, with the UAE holding US$80 billion and Bahrain bringing up the rear with just over US$5 billion. These reserves, along with other major pools of liquidity held in sovereign wealth funds and assets held in other investment vehicles, provide the Gulf States with a buffer in tough times, as well as the resources required to implement public sector reforms, promote diversification and human capital programmes, and tackle the problem of foreign workers. But they cannot compensate for the lack of political will needed to phase out free services, subsidized prices and large welfare payments, on top of highly paid government jobs. As long as all remain the norm, there will be little motivation for many citizens to acquire education, skills or a career or to embrace the radical and sweeping plans for socio-economic restructuring that leaders now admit need to be introduced.

Integrate

The GCC customs union was completed in 2015, ensuring that a common external tariff is collected at all points of entry across the GCC. This has led to the harmonization of standards, and has extended free movement and opportunities for citizens to invest and do business across the Gulf. But more still needs to be done on a regional level to improve the mobility of capital, labour, goods and services across the GCC. The market for financial services is also very fragmented. There is little regulatory convergence and each member state has developed its own regulatory system for banks and other financial institutions. To address these problems, Gulf leaders need to work together to overcome the scepticism of their citizens and provide the collective political will required to deliver deeper economic integration in the interests of all. This would be a big step towards turning the entire GCC into one large, single, domestic market of fifty million people and would open the way for more interregional trade, greater economies of scale, improved competitiveness and more foreign investment.

The lure of all this continues to inspire those determined to push for Gulf economic and monetary union. In 2010, three years after Oman and one year after the UAE withdrew from this process, Bahrain, Kuwait, Saudi Arabia and Qatar came together to form a monetary council. Since then, the official position of all four is that monetary union should continue 'without a delay'. Few believe that this is likely to happen any time soon. In 2013, fourteen out of fifteen experts polled by Reuters were emphatic that there would be no GCC single currency in the medium term. And, while some continue to view the plan for monetary union as a long-term project that is viable from both economic and political perspectives, others have dismissed it as an unrealistic scheme that has already passed its expiry date.

Invested

The GCC economies can attain many advantages if they work together to deepen integration and create a single market. One important goal of turning the region into a dynamic hub for travel, trade and tourism has been to increase the amount of foreign direct investment. Even super-rich oil producers value inward investment for domestic development, especially when the oil price is low. It is a more attractive and less volatile source of capital than bank loans, and it brings technology, market access and organizational skills to the host country. Since the 1970s, the Arab Gulf States have all been net exporters of capital, as huge amounts of money have flowed out of the region. Much of this has flowed into overseas investments that have increasingly come to be viewed as a key sector of non-oil growth. 'The region is seen as a source of capital,' explained Nazem Al-Kudsi, one of Abu Dhabi's top investment figures. 'From our perspective,' he added, 'we also think the region should be seen as a destination of capital.'[11] In order to improve their record in this area all the Gulf States have become much friendlier to foreign businesses operating in their markets. Qatar has topped the world rankings in terms of market attractiveness for foreign investment, according to the United Nations' FDI potential index. Along with the UAE, it is also now part of the

MSCI Emerging Markets index. An FDI law passed in Kuwait in 2013 allows for up to 100 per cent ownership of all Kuwaiti companies with the exception of those in ten key sectors. Even Saudi Arabia has become more open in allowing foreign ownership across a number of areas, including energy, aviation and financial industries, and in the summer of 2015 opened the stock market to foreign investment. Yet, overall, the Gulf still only attracts relatively small amounts of foreign direct investment every year. In fact, foreign investment flows have halved since 2010, as the tightening of local funds has led to the exodus of many foreign companies, notably law firms, financial services companies and business consultancies that relied on high levels of Gulf spending to fund their work.

When measured as one single market instead of six separate ones, the GCC is the ninth largest economy in the world today – similar in size to Canada and Russia and not far off the size of India. If it is able to keep growing at an annual average of around 3 per cent over the next fifteen years, it could challenge Japan for a spot in the world's top five economies by the early 2030s. Yet to make this happen over the next decade and a half, all the Gulf States will have to work together in order to deal with the socio-economic challenges they face. If the ruling elites can do this in a way that brings sustainable economic development and maximizes capacity, their legitimacy will be further consolidated, and they will ensure continued stability at home and influence abroad for future generations.

NOTES

Introduction: Paradise Found

1. For an informed and informative history of the region excluding Saudi Arabia see Rosemarie Said Zahlan, *The Making of the Modern Gulf States: Kuwait, Bahrain, Qatar, United Arab Emirates and Oman* (Reading, Ithaca Press, 1989).
2. Jill Crystal, 'Coalitions in Oil Monarchies: Kuwait and Qatar', *Comparative Politics*, 21:4 (July 1989), p. 427.
3. *The Economist*, 5 May 1975.
4. J. B. Kelly, *Arabia, the Gulf & the West: A Critical View of the Arabs and Their Oil Policy* (New York, Basic Books, 1980), p. 175.
5. Husain M. Albaharna, *The Legal Status of the Arabian Gulf States: A Study of Their Treaty Relations and International Relations* (Manchester, Manchester University Press, 1968), p. 9.
6. Ibid., p. 11.
7. James Onley, *The Arabian Frontier of the Raj: Merchants, Rulers and the British in the Nineteenth Century Gulf* (Oxford and New York, Oxford University Press, 2007), p. 10.
8. Tore T. Petersen, *The Decline of the Anglo-American Middle East 1961–1969: A Willing Retreat* (Portland, OR, Sussex Academic Press, 2006), pp. 118–19.
9. Kelly, *Arabia, the Gulf & the West*, p. 92.
10. *The Times*, 14 July 1970.
11. Petersen, *The Decline of the Anglo-American Middle East 1961–1969*, p. 118.
12. See Miriam Cooke, *Tribal Modern: Branding New Nations in the Arab Gulf* (Berkeley and Los Angeles, University of California Press, 2014), especially pp. 1–15 and 50–63.
13. *Middle East International*, July 1971, p. 19.
14. Abdullah Baabood, 'Dynamics and Determinants of the GCC States' Foreign Policy, with Special Reference to the EU', in Gerd Nonneman (ed.), *Analyzing Middle East Foreign Policies and the Relationship with Europe* (London and New York, Routledge, 2005), p. 159.
15. See press conference by Prince Sultan bin Abdulaziz, Saudi deputy prime minister and minister of defence, 5 October 1985, reprinted in R. K. Ramazani, *The Gulf Cooperation Council: Record and Analysis* (Charlottesville, University of Virginia Press, 1988), p. 90.
16. Report on 9th Annual Emirates Center for Strategic Studies and Research (ECSSR) Conference on Gulf Security, Abu Dhabi, January 2004.

17. Manama Supreme Council Summit: Opening Statement by Sheikh Isa Ibn Salman Al-Khalifa, emir of Bahrain, reprinted in Ramazani, *The Gulf Cooperation Council*, p. 146.
18. *Monday Morning Magazine* (Beirut), 7–13 November 1983.
19. *Al Jazirah*, 22 March 1983.
20. Kamal Al-Kilani, *Progress of a Nation: A Biography of King Fahd bin Abdul-Aziz* (London and New York, Namara Publications, 1985), p. 31. See also the comments by Saudi King Fahd at 5th GCC Summit, 29 November 1984, reprinted in Ramazani, *The Gulf Cooperation Council*, p. 164.
21. *The Hindu*, 21 August 2014.
22. *Financial Times*, 24 November 2010.
23. Janet Abu-Lughod, 'Urbanization and Social Change in the Arab World', *Ekisitcs*, 50:300 (1983), p. 227.
24. *New York Times*, 24 March 1974.
25. Ibid., 7 July 1997.
26. *Le Monde*, 12 March 1979.
27. Interview with Prince Abdullah of Saudi Arabia, Gulf News Agency, 21 April 1979.
28. For an interesting account of this crucial period in the evolution of the Arab Gulf see Yusif Abdalla Sayigh, *The Economies of the Arab World: Development since 1945* (London, Taylor & Francis, 1978), pp. 81–7.

Chapter 1: Over a Barrel

1. *New York Times*, 30 January 1977 and 24 March 1974.
2. Henry Kissinger, *Years of Upheaval* (Boston and Toronto, Little, Brown and Company, 1982), pp. 876, 672–3.
3. In 1973, the Organization of Petroleum Exporting Countries (OPEC) also had four non-Arab members: Iran, Venezuela, Indonesia and Nigeria.
4. 'Memorandum of Discussion at the 460th meeting of the National Security Council', 21 September 1960, Foreign Relations of the United States, 1958–1960, Near East Region; Iraq: Iran: Arabian Peninsula, Vol. XII, Document 91, https://history.state.gov/historicaldocuments/frus1969–76v37/d91.
5. Daniel Yergin, *The Prize: The Epic Quest for Oil, Money and Power* (London and New York, Simon & Schuster, 1991), p. 627.
6. *Al Thawra*, 23 May 1975.
7. See Telegram from Beirut Embassy to Foreign and Commonwealth Office, 30 June 1976, British National Archives, Foreign and Commonwealth Office Files, 93/909.
8. Romano Prodi and Alberto Clo, 'Europe', in *The Oil Crisis in Perspective, Daedalus*, 104:4 (1975), pp. 101–2.
9. 'Memorandum of Conversation, Camp David', 28 September 1974, Foreign Relations of the United States, 1969–1976, Energy Crisis, 1974–1980, Vol. XXXVII, Document 9, https://history.state.gov/historicaldocuments/frus1969–76v37/d9.
10. Mohammed Al-Fahim, *From Rags to Riches: A Story of Abu Dhabi* (London, Centre of Arab Studies, 2008), p. 43. See also *New York Times*, 24 March 1974.
11. The Seven Sisters were the Anglo-Persian Oil Company (now British Petroleum); Gulf Oil; Standard Oil of California (SoCal); Texaco (now Chevron); Royal Dutch Shell; Standard oil of New Jersey (Esso); Standard Oil Company of New York (Socony, now ExxonMobil).
12. Cited in Efraim Karsh, *Palestine Betrayed* (London and New Haven, Yale University Press, 2010), p. 87.
13. *The Times*, 1 July 1967.
14. Nadav Safran, 'The War and the Future of the Arab-Israeli Conflict', *Foreign Affairs*, 52:2 (January 1974), p. 221. See also *Daily Telegraph*, 17 August 1967.
15. Jeffrey Robinson, *Yamani: The Inside Story* (New York, Simon & Schuster, 1989), p. 57.
16. Edward Said, 'The Theory and Practice of Banning Books and Ideas', *Al-Hayat*, 4 September 1996.

17. Fawaz Turki, *Exile's Return: The Making of a Palestinian-American* (New York, The Free Press, 1994), p. 189.
18. J. B. Kelly, *Arabia, the Gulf & the West: A Critical View of the Arabs and Their Oil Policy* (New York, Basic Books, 1980), p. 374.
19. See 'Briefing Paper Prepared by the National Security Council Staff', 14 December 1972, Foreign Relations of the United States, 1969–1976, Middle East Region and Arabian Peninsula, 1969–1972, Vol. XXIV, Document 169, https://history.state.gov/historicaldocuments/frus1969-76v24/d169.
20. James E. Atkins, 'The Oil Crisis: This Time the Wolf Is Here', *Foreign Affairs*, 51:3 (April 1973), p. 467; Kelly, *Arabia, the Gulf & the West*, p. 175.
21. See 'Memorandum From the President's Deputy Assistant for National Security Affairs (Haig) to President Nixon', 5 May 1971, Foreign Relations of the United States, 1969–1976, Middle East Region and Arabian Peninsula, 1969–1972, Vol. XXIV, Document 149, https://history.state.gov/historicaldocuments/frus1969-76v24/d149; 'Letter from the Ambassador to Saudi Arabia (Teacher) to the Assistant Secretary of State for Near Eastern and South Asian Affairs (Sisco)', 25 January 1971, Foreign Relations of the United States, 1969–1976, Middle East Region and Arabian Peninsula, 1969–1972, Vol. XXIV, Document 147, https://history.state.gov/historicaldocuments/frus1969-76v24/d147; Richard Nixon, *The Memoirs of Richard Nixon* (London, Sidgwick & Jackson, 1990), p. 1012.
22. Robert D. Kaplan, *The Arabists: The Romance of an American Elite* (New York, The Free Press, 1995), p. 174; Kissinger, *Years of Upheaval*, p. 661; 'Memorandum of Conversation', 12 August 1974, Foreign Relations of the United States, 1969–1976, Arab–Israeli Dispute, 1974–1976, Vol. XXVI, Document 95, https://history.state.gov/historicaldocuments/frus1969-76v26/d95.
23. 'Memorandum of Conversation', 12 August 1974, Foreign Relations of the United States, 1969–1976, Arab–Israeli Dispute, 1974–1976, Vol. XXVI, Document 95, https://history.state.gov/historicaldocuments/frus1969-76v26/d95.
24. *New York Times*, 10 September 1973; *Newsweek*, 17 September 1973.
25. Kissinger, *Years of Upheaval*, p. 663; 'Memorandum from the President's Assistant for National Security Affairs (Kissinger) to President Nixon', undated, 1972, Foreign Relations of the United States, 1969–1976, Middle East Region and Arabian Peninsula, 1969–1972, Vol. XXIV, Document 170, https://history.state.gov/historicaldocuments/frus1969-76v24/d170.
26. *New York Times*, 24 March 1974.
27. 'National Intelligence Estimate', 1 April 1971, Foreign Relations of the United States, 1969–1976, Middle East Region and Arabian Peninsula, 1969–1972, Vol. XXIV, Document 96, https://history.state.gov/historicaldocuments/frus1969-76v24/d96; 'Memorandum of Conversation', 5 June 1970, Foreign Relations of the United States, 1969–1976, Middle East Region and Arabian Peninsula, 1969–1972, Vol. XXIV, Document 23, https://history.state.gov/historicaldocuments/frus1969-76v24/d23; Nixon, *The Memoirs of Richard Nixon*, p. 985.
28. Quoted in Mark Weston, *Prophets and Princes: Saudi Arabia from Muhammed to the Present* (New York, John Wiley & Sons Inc., 2008), p. 217.
29. *New York Times*, 25 August 1973.
30. *New York Times*, 20 October 1976.
31. *New York Times*, 18 December 1976.
32. *New York Times*, 7 October. 1979.
33. Kissinger, *Years of Upheaval*, p. 663.
34. 'Memorandum of Conversation, Camp David', 28 September 1974, Foreign Relations of the United States, 1969–1976, Energy Crisis, 1974–1980, Vol. XXXVII, Document 9, https://history.state.gov/historicaldocuments/frus1969-76v37/d9.
35. Memorandum on the Fourth Arab–Israel War, 7 January 1974, British National Archives, Foreign & Commonwealth Office Files, 93/561.
36. *New York Times*, 30 January 1977; E. A. Kolodziej, 'France and the Arms Trade', *International Affairs*, 56:1 (1980), pp. 58–9; *New York Times*, 28 September 1981.

37. C. C. R. Battiscombe, Kuwait, to A. Ibbott Esq., Foreign Office, 24 September 1967, British National Archives, Foreign & Commonwealth Office Files, 8/615; 'Memorandum of Conversation', 13 October 1969, Foreign Relations of the United States, 1969–1976, Middle East Region and Arabian Peninsula, 1969–1972, Vol. XXIV, Document 131, https://history.state.gov/historicaldocuments/frus1969-76v24/d131.
38. Quoted in Weston, *Prophets and Princes*, p. 229.
39. G. N. Jackson, Kuwait, to R. A. Butler, Foreign Office, 2 January 1964, British National Archives, Foreign & Commonwealth Office Files, 371/174584.
40. Irvine H. Anderson, *Aramco, The United States and Saudi Arabia: A Study in the Dynamics of Foreign Oil Policy, 1933–1950* (Princeton, NJ, Princeton University Press, 1981), p. 13.
41. See 'Briefing Paper Prepared by the National Security Council Staff', 14 December 1972, Foreign Relations of the United States, 1969–1976, Middle East Region and Arabian Peninsula, 1969–1972, Vol. XXIV, Document 169, https://history.state.gov/historicaldocuments/frus1969-76v24/d169.
42. *New York Times*, 24 March 1974.
43. *Middle East International*, February 1976, p. 23.
44. *Middle East International*, October 1977, p. 19.
45. *Middle East International*, November 1974, p. 29.
46. *Al Jazirah*, 22 March 1983.
47. Maurice J. Williams, 'The Aid Programs of the OPEC Countries', *Foreign Affairs*, 54:2 (1975–1976), p. 311.
48. *New York Times*, 24 March 1974.
49. *New York Times*, 17 February 1976.
50. 'Intelligence Memorandum Prepared in the Central Intelligence Agency', n.d. April 1971, Foreign Relations of the United States, 1969–1976, Middle East Region and Arabian Peninsula, 1969–1972, Vol. XXIV, Document 148, https://history.state.gov/historicaldocuments/frus1969-76v24/d148.
51. Sheikh Ahmed Zaki Yamani, 'Oil: Towards a New Producer–Consumer Relationship', text of a lecture given at Chatham House, 17 September 1974, republished in *The World Today*, 30:11 (November 1974), p. 479.
52. *New York Times*, 29 September 1974.
53. 'Memorandum of Conversation, Camp David', 28 September 1974, Foreign Relations of the United States, 1969–1976, Energy Crisis, 1974–1980, Vol. XXXVII, Document 9, https://history.state.gov/historicaldocuments/frus1969-76v37/d9.
54. Interview with secretary of state Henry Kissinger, *US News & World Report*, 16 June 1975.
55. *Middle East International*, November 1978, p. 20; J. B. Kelly, 'Review of Arab Political Memoirs and Other Studies', *International Affairs*, 51: 2 (April 1975), pp. 278–9.
56. James Abourezk, 'Winning America's Ear', *Middle East International*, January 1977, p. 17.
57. *New York Times*, 24 March 1974.
58. *Middle East International*, July 1975, p. 16, and 14 September 1979, p. 10.
59. *Al Ahram*, 18 October 1976.
60. *Middle East International*, February 1978, p. 13.
61. Conclusions of a Meeting of the Cabinet, 22 February 1979, British National Archives, Cabinet Office Files, CAB/128/65/9.
62. Quoted in Weston, *Prophets and Princes*, p. 217.
63. *New York Times*, 19 December 1976; *Middle East International*, July 1975, p. 15.
64. *International Herald Tribune*, 2 July 1979.
65. *Middle East International*, June 1977, p. 5.
66. *Middle East International*, 12 October 1979, p. 3.
67. *Economic and Political Weekly*, 6:6 (February 1971), p. 406.
68. Text of speech by Lord Carrington in House of Lords debate, 9 July 1980, Vol. 411, col. 1192, http://hansard.millbanksystems.com/lords/1980/jul/09/africa-and-the-middle-east#column_1192 .

69. See statement by Foreign Minister Eban in response to the EEC Declaration of 6 November, *Israel Foreign Relations: Selected Documents*, Vol. 2 (Jerusalem, Ministry of Foreign Affairs, 1976), pp. 1066–7; *The Times*, 12 May 1975.
70. *Daily Telegraph*, 17 November 1973.
71. Edward Heath, *The Course of My Life* (London, Hodder & Stoughton, 1988), p. 501.
72. Euro-Arab Dialogue Minutes, 17 and 22 December 1975, British National Archives, Foreign & Commonwealth Office Files, 30/3045.
73. *Middle East International*, 21 December 1979, p. 4.
74. Henry Kissinger, *Years of Renewal* (London, Phoenix Press, 1989), p. 667.
75. Yusif A. Sayigh, 'Arab Oil Policies: Self Interest versus International Responsibility', *Journal of Palestine Studies*, IV:3 (Spring 1975), pp. 59–73.
76. *Middle East International*, 12 October 1979, p. 3.
77. Elizabeth Monroe, 'Faisal: The End of an Era', *Middle East International*, May 1975, p. 11.
78. Kelly, *Arabia, the Gulf & the West*, p. 149.

Chapter 2: Neighbourhood Watch

1. John K. Cooley, 'Iran, the Palestinians, and the Gulf', *Foreign Affairs*, 57:5 (1978–9), p. 1027.
2. *Middle East International*, 2 March 1979, p. 5.
3. *Middle East International*, 5 December 1980, p. 10; Ghazi A. Algosaibi, *The Gulf Crisis: An Attempt to Understand* (London and New York, Routledge, 1993), p. 10.
4. J. B. Kelly, 'The Oil Cringe of the West', *Quadrant*, 24:7 (July 1980), pp. 4–12.
5. *Middle East International*, n.d., 1979.
6. *Middle East International*, January 1972, p. 22.
7. J. B. Kelly, *Arabia, the Gulf & the West: A Critical View of the Arabs and Their Oil Policy* (New York, Basic Books, 1980), p. 315.
8. 'National Intelligence Estimate', 1 April 1971, Foreign Relations of the United States, 1969–1976, Middle East Region and Arabian Peninsula, 1969–1972, Vol. XXIV, Document 96, https://history.state.gov/historicaldocuments/frus1969-76v24/d96.
9. Henry Kissinger, *Years of Renewal* (London, Phoenix Press, 1989), p. 671.
10. 'Memorandum of Conversation', 13 January 1971, Foreign Relations of the United States, 1969–1976, Middle East Region and Arabian Peninsula, 1969–1972, Vol. XXIV, Document 93, https://history.state.gov/historicaldocuments/frus1969-76v24/d93.
11. Gulf News Agency, 22 March 1979; Interview with Foreign Minister, Pars News Agency, 17 July 1979; Ray Takeyh, *Guardians of the Revolution: Iran and the World in the Age of the Ayatollahs* (Oxford, Oxford University Press, 2009), p. 26.
12. Interview in Prince Saud to *As-Siyasah*, reprinted in Kuwait News Agency, 5 February 1979.
13. Defence Attaché, Jedda, Annual Report 1979, British National Archives, Foreign & Commonwealth Office Files, 8/3755.
14. Shaul Bakhash, *The Reign of the Ayatollahs: Iran and the Islamic Revolution* (New York, Basic Books, 1984), p. 53.
15. Ayatollah Ruhollah Khomeini, *Writings and Declarations of Imam Khomeini*, trans. and annotated Hamid Algar (Berkeley, CA, Mizan Press, 1981), p. 286.
16. Quoted in Mark Weston, *Prophets and Princes: Saudi Arabia from Muhammed to the Present* (New York, John Wiley & Sons Inc., 2008), p. 241.
17. Kuwait News Agency, 8 August 1979; Gulf News Agency, 12 September 1979; *Al-Watan*, 4 October 1979.
18. Joseph Kostiner, 'Shi'i Unrest in the Gulf', in Martin Kramer (ed.), *Shi'ism, Resistance, and Revolution* (Boulder, CO, Westview Press, 1987), p. 178; Walker, Bahrain, to Foreign Office, British National Archives, Foreign & Commonwealth Office Files, 8/3307.
19. Gulf News Agency, 26 September 1979.

20. *Daily Report, Middle East & North Africa*, 30 December 1981, FBIS-MEA-81–250; Passmore, Foreign Office, to Bahrain, 8 August 1980, British National Archives, Foreign & Commonwealth Office Files, 8/3489.
21. Conclusions of a meeting of the British Cabinet, 22 February 1979, British National Archives, Cabinet Office Files, CAB/128/65/9.
22. Dale F. Eickelman and M. G. Dennison, 'Arabizing the Omani Intelligence Services: Clash of Cultures?', *International Journal of Intelligence and CounterIntelligence*, 7:1 (1994), p. 20.
23. Haifaa A. Jawad, *Euro-Arab Relations: A Study in Collective Diplomacy* (Reading, Ithaca Press, 1992), p. 146.
24. *New York Times*, 5 October 1980.
25. Abd al-Hadi Khalaf, 'The Elusive Quest for Gulf Security', *Middle East Research and Information Project*, 148 (September–October 1987), http://www.merip.org/mer/mer148/elusive-quest-gulf-security (Accessed 8 February 2015).
26. *Middle East International*, 23 November 1979, p. 10.
27. William Simpson, *The Prince: The Secret Story of the World's Most Intriguing Royal, Prince Bandar Bin Sultan* (New York, Regan, 2006), pp. 177, 181.
28. Takeyh, *Guardians of the Revolution*, p. 130.
29. Ambassador Seyed Hossein Mousavian, 'A Great Partnership: Iran, Iraq and the GCC', Forum for Arab and International Relations, 2012, p. 4; Hassan Ali Al-Ebraheem, *Kuwait and the Gulf: Small States and the International System* (Canberra, Croom Helm, 1983), p. 65; Gerd Nonneman, *Iraq, the Gulf States, & the War: A Changing Relationship 1980–1986 and Beyond* (London, Ithaca, 1986), pp. 22–3.
30. *Al-Anba* (Kuwait), 22 August 1982; *Christian Science Monitor*, 12 November 1981.
31. Interview with Sultan Qaboos of Oman, *Al-Mustaqbal*, 2 May 1981.
32. *Middle East International*, August 1973, p. 18.
33. Transcript of GCC secretary general Bisharah's press conference, 27 May 1981, reprinted in R. K. Ramazani, *The Gulf Cooperation Council: Record and Analysis* (Charlottesville, University of Virginia Press, 1988), p. 31.
34. Abd al-Hadi Khalaf, 'The Elusive Quest for Gulf Security'.
35. *Christian Science Monitor*, 26 May 1981.
36. Abd al-Hadi Khalaf, 'The Elusive Quest for Gulf Security'; Jawid Laiq, 'The Gulf Cooperation Council: Royal Insurance against Pressures from Within and Without', *Economic and Political Weekly*, 21:35 (30 August 1986), p. 1555. See also Emile A. Nakleh, *The Gulf Cooperation Council: Policies, Problems and Prospects* (New York, Praeger, 1986).
37. Takeyh, *Guardians of the Revolution*, p. 189.
38. Hossein Askari, *Collaborative Colonialism: The Political Economy of Oil in the Persian Gulf* (New York, Palgrave Macmillan, 2013), p. 39.
39. Thomas L. McNaugher, *Arms and Oil: US Military Strategy and the Persian Gulf* (Washington, DC, Brookings Institution, 1985), p. 161.
40. Uri Friedman, 'The Ten Biggest American Intelligence Failures', *Foreign Policy*, 3 January 2012, http://foreignpolicy.com/2012/01/03/the-ten-biggest-american-intelligence-failures/ (Accessed 29 May 2014).
41. For a detailed analysis of this doctrine in the wider context of Carter's foreign policy see John Dumbrell, *The Carter Presidency: A Re-Evaluation* (Manchester, Manchester University Press, 1995), pp. 179–209.
42. *Middle East International*, 18 January 1980, p. 3.
43. See 'Briefing Paper Prepared by the National Security Council Staff', 14 December 1972, Foreign Relations of the United States, 1969–1976, Middle East Region and Arabian Peninsula, 1969–1972, Vol. XXIV, Document 169, https://history.state.gov/historicaldocuments/frus1969-76v24/d169.
44. Interview with Crown Prince Fahd, *As-Safir* (Beirut), republished by Qatar News Agency, 9 January 1980.
45. Statement by Clark Clifford, reprinted in *Middle East International*, 15 February 1980, p. 5.

46. Gregory Gause III, *The International Relations of the Persian Gulf* (Cambridge, Cambridge University Press, 2010), p. 127; Telegraph Agency of the Soviet Union, 10 March 1980.
47. *Al-Majallah* (London), 1–7 May 1982, pp. 12–17; Middle East News Agency, 4 April 1985.
48. Ronald Reagan, *An American Life* (New York, Simon & Schuster, 1990), p. 410.
49. *The Economist*, 25 October 1980.
50. Jimmy Carter, *Keeping Faith: Memoirs of a President* (Fayetteville, University of Arkansas Press, 1995), p. 589; Reagan, *An American Life*, p. 411.
51. 'National Intelligence Estimate', 7 April 1970, Foreign Relations of the United States, 1969–1976, Middle East Region and Arabian Peninsula, 1969–1972, Vol. XXIV, Document 140, https://history.state.gov/historicaldocuments/frus1969-76v24/d140; See also *The Economist*, 13 February 1982.
52. GCC Ministerial Meeting: First Extraordinary Meeting Statement, 7 February 1982, reprinted in Ramazani, *The Gulf Cooperation Council*, p. 45.
53. *New York Times*, 1 June 1982; Bakhash, *The Reign of the Ayatollahs*, p. 234.
54. Kuwait News Agency, 16 January 1982; transcript of press conference held by Sheikh Sabah Al-Ahmad Al-Jaber Al-Sabah, Kuwaiti deputy prime minister, foreign and information minister, 24 November 1984, reprinted in Ramazani, *The Gulf Cooperation Council*, p. 168.
55. 'Iran and the Gulf', BBC Summary of World Broadcasts, 11 October 1979, ME/6241/i.
56. *Al Hawadith* (London), 15 June 1984; interview with GCC secretary general Abdallah Bisarah, *Al Tadamun*, 14 December 1985.
57. Interview with interior minister of Kuwait, Sheikh Nawaf Al-Ahmad Al-Jabir Al-Sabah, 27 July 1985, reprinted in Ramazani, *The Gulf Cooperation Council*, p. 45; *New York Times*, 4 October 1987; interview with foreign minister of Bahrain, Sheikh Muhammad Al-Khalifah, *Al-Majallah* (London), 5 March 1986; Associated Press, 26 December 1986.
58. Middle East News Agency, 4 April 1985; *Middle East International*, 15 April 1983, p. 7.
59. Abd al-Hadi Khalaf, 'The Elusive Quest for Gulf Security'.
60. Middle East News Agency, 4 April 1985.
61. Abd al-Hadi Khalaf, 'The Elusive Quest for Gulf Security'.
62. *Radio Peace & Progress* (Moscow), BBC Summary of World Broadcasts, 14 August 1979, part 1, SU/6193/A4/1.
63. *New York Times*, 24 May 1984.
64. *New York Times*, 13 August 1987.
65. President Ronald Reagan, Address to the Nation, 15 June 1987, http://www.reagan.utexas.edu/archives/speeches/1987/061587r.htm (Accessed 19 February 2014).
66. *Christian Science Monitor*, 10 July 1987.
67. See Chookiat Panaspornprasit, *US–Kuwaiti Relations, 1961–1992* (London and New York, Routledge, 2005), p. 104; Tehran Home Service, BBC Summary of World Broadcasts, 23 October 1987 & 26 October 1987, ME/8708/A/1.
68. Abd al-Hadi Khalaf, 'The Elusive Quest for Gulf Security'.
69. *New York Times*, 10 October 1987.
70. *Christian Science Monitor*, 13 October 1987.
71. *New York Times*, 4 May 1988.
72. 'Staying the Course in the Persian Gulf', WikiLeaks, 19 August 1988, 88STATE271057, http://wikileaks.org/cable/1988/08/88STATE271057.html.

Chapter 3: Tax Americana

1. Henry Kissinger, *The White House Years* (Boston and Toronto, Little, Brown and Company, 1979), p. 51.
2. George H. W. Bush, *All the Best: My Life in Letters and Other Writings* (New York, Scribner, 2013), p. 476.

3. *Christian Science Monitor*, 10 August 1990.
4. *Middle East International*, May 1976, p. 24.
5. *New York Times*, 27 December 1981.
6. Middle East News Agency, 4 April 1985.
7. *Al-Watan* (Kuwait), 10 April 1985.
8. *New York Times*, 23 September 1990.
9. *Christian Science Monitor*, 20 November 1981.
10. *The Economist*, 13 February 1982.
11. John Duke Anthony, 'The Gulf Cooperation Council', *International Journal*, 41:2 (Spring 1986), pp. 383–401.
12. Mordechai Abir, *Saudi Arabia: Government, Society and the Gulf Crisis* (London and New York, Routledge, 1993), p. 169.
13. James A. Baker III, *The Politics of Diplomacy: Revolution, War and Peace, 1989–1992* (New York, G. P. Putnam's Sons, 2009), p. 270; Richard K. Herrmann, 'The Middle East and the New World Order – Rethinking US Political Strategy after the Gulf War', *International Security*, 16:2 (1991), p. 52.
14. Ghazi A. Algosaibi, *The Gulf Crisis: An Attempt to Understand* (London and New York, Routledge, 1993), p. 131.
15. William Simpson, *The Prince: The Secret Story of the World's Most Intriguing Royal, Prince Bandar Bin Sultan* (New York, Regan, 2006), p. 196.
16. Pinar Bilgin, *Regional Security in the Middle East: A Critical Perspective* (New York, Routledge, 2011), p. 134.
17. *New York Times*, 23 December 1990.
18. Edward Said, 'The Shattering Effects of Saddam's Invasion', *Arab News*, 5 September 1990.
19. Algosaibi, *The Gulf Crisis: An Attempt to Understand*, p. 69.
20. *Washington Post*, 4 August 1990.
21. Lawrence Freedman and Efraim Karsh, *The Gulf Conflict, 1990–1991: Diplomacy and War in the New World Order* (London and New York, Faber & Faber), 1993, p. 93.
22. Kelly Demarche to Iraq Ambassador, WikiLeaks, 4 August 1990, 90STATE257623, http://wikileaks.org/cable/1990/08/90ST A TE257623.html.
23. Simpson, *The Prince*, p. 203; Baker, *The Politics of Diplomacy*, p. 306.
24. Baker, *The Politics of Diplomacy*, p. 280; Prime Minister Thatcher's interview with PBS Broadcasting for Oral History of Gulf War, http://www.pbs.org/wgbh/pages/frontline/gulf/oral/thatcher/1.html. (Accessed 5 June 2015).
25. *Christian Science Monitor*, 10 August 1990.
26. Robert Fisk, 'Free to Report What We're Told', *The Independent* (London), 6 February 1991.
27. Colin L. Powell (with Joseph E. Persico), *My American Journey* (New York, Random House, 1995), p. 485.
28. James Ridgeway, *The March to War: From Day One to the War's End and Beyond* (New York, Four Walls, Eight Windows, 1991), p. 135.
29. *Al-Watan* (Kuwait), 23 March 1985.
30. Brian Healy and Arthur Stein, 'The Balance of Power in International History: Theory and Reality', *Journal of Conflict Resolution*, 17:1 (1973), pp. 33–61.
31. Freedman and Karsh, *The Gulf Conflict*, p. 67.
32. Prince Khalid bin Sultan, *Desert Warrior* (Beirut, Dar Alsawi, 1995), p. 545.
33. Simpson, *The Prince*, p. 204.
34. Freedman and Karsh, *The Gulf Conflict*, p. 94.
35. *Alsharq Al-Awsat*, 2 January 1991; Freedman and Karsh, *The Gulf Conflict*, p. 241.
36. Dilip Hiro, *Desert Shield to Desert Storm: The Second Gulf War* (New York, Harper Collins, 1993), p. 126.
37. Final Report to Congress: Conduct of the Persian Gulf War, Pursuant to Title V of the Persian Gulf Conflict Supplemental Authorization and Personnel Benefits Act of 1991 (Public Law 102–25), April 1992, Washington, DC.
38. *Al Hawadith* (London), 15 June 1984; *Christian Science Monitor*, 29 November 1984.

39. See Chookiat Panaspornprasit, *US-Kuwaiti Relations, 1961–1992* (London and New York, Routledge, 2005), p. 129.
40. *New York Times*, 21 October 1992.
41. Ellen Laipson, 'Europe's Role in the Middle East: Enduring Ties, Emerging Opportunities', *Middle East Journal*, 44:1 (Winter 1990), p. 7.
42. Louise Fawcett and Robert O'Neill, 'Britain, the Gulf Crisis and European Security', in Nicole Gnesotto and John Roper (eds), *Western Europe and the Gulf: A Study of West European Reactions to the Gulf War* (Brussels, Institute for Security Studies, Western European Union, 1992), p. 142; Charles Krauthammer, 'The Unipolar Moment', *Foreign Affairs*, 70:1 (1991), p. 24.
43. *Glasgow Herald*, 8 February 1980.
44. UAE Foreign Ministry Communiqué announcing the establishment of diplomatic relations between the UAE and USSR, 15 November 1985, reprinted in R. K. Ramazani, *The Gulf Cooperation Council: Record and Analysis* (Charlottesville, University of Virginia Press, 1988), p. 164.
45. *The Economist*, 3 November 1990. See also Hiro, *Desert Shield to Desert Storm*, p. 230.
46. Joe Stork, 'The Middle East Arms Bazaar after the Gulf War', *Middle East Research and Information Project*, 197 (November–December 1995), http://www.merip.org/mer/mer197/middle-east-arms-bazaar-after-gulf-war (Accessed 9 November 2015).
47. *New York Times*, 23 December 1990.
48. Algosaibi, *The Gulf Crisis: An Attempt to Understand*, p. 114.
49. 'Kuwaiti Saudi Relations – A Kuwaiti Perspective', WikiLeaks, 22 November 1990, 90JEDDAH2807, http://wikileaks.org/cable/1990/11/90JEDDAH2807.html; Algosaibi, *The Gulf Crisis: An Attempt to Understand*, p. 72.
50. John Duke Anthony, 'Points, Patterns, Prognosis: the 17th GCC Heads of State Summit and Aftermath: Whither the GCC?', US-GCC Corporate Cooperation Committee Occasional Paper Series, No. 8 (1997) p. 35.
51. Patricia Weitsman, *Waging War: Alliances, Coalitions, and Institutions of Interstate Violence* (Stanford, Stanford University Press, 2013), p. 60, table 3.2.
52. Algosaibi, *The Gulf Crisis: An Attempt to Understand*, p. 109.
53. Rory Miller, *Inglorious Disarray: Europe, Israel and the Palestinians since 1967* (New York, Columbia University Press, 2011), p. 122.
54. *The Economist*, 13 December 1980.
55. *Sawt ash-Sha'b*, 17 February 1991; Fouad Ajami, 'The Summer of Arab Discontent', *Foreign Affairs*, 69:5 (Winter 1990–91), p. 6.
56. Daniel Pipes, 'Heroes and Knaves of the Kuwait Crisis', in Benjamin Frankel (ed.), *A Restless Mind: Essays in Honor of Amos Perlmutter* (London, Routledge, 1996), pp. 175–88.
57. GCC working paper, 26 May 1981, reprinted in Ramazani, *The Gulf Cooperation Council*, p. 29.
58. *New York Times*, 30 December 1990; Freedman and Karsh, *The Gulf Conflict*, p. 216.
59. Herrmann, 'The Middle East and the New World Order', p. 47.
60. *Christian Science Monitor*, 10 September 1990.
61. Algosaibi, *The Gulf Crisis: An Attempt to Understand*, p. 91.
62. Michael Gordon and Bernard Trainor, *The General's War: The Inside Story of the First Gulf War* (London, Atlantic Books, 1995), p. 56.
63. Mark Weston, *Prophets and Princes: Saudi Arabia from Muhammed to the Present* (New York, John Wiley & Sons Inc., 2008), p. 305.
64. Quoted in Mary Ann Tetreault, 'Autonomy, Necessity, and the Small State: Ruling Kuwait in the Twentieth Century', *International Organization*, 45:4 (Autumn 1991), p. 590.

Chapter 4: Thy Brother's Keeper

1. See Michael Scheuer, *Osama bin Laden* (Oxford, Oxford University Press, 2011), p. 83; Michael Scheuer, *Through Our Enemies' Eyes: Osama bin Laden, Radical Islam, and the Future of America* (Washington, DC, Potomac Books, 2006), p. 124.

2. *New York Times*, 6 November 2001; William Simpson, *The Prince: The Secret Story of the World's Most Intriguing Royal, Prince Bandar Bin Sultan* (New York, Regan, 2006), p. 329.
3. Anthony H. Cordesman and Nawaf Obaid, *Al-Qaeda in Saudi Arabia: Asymmetric Threats and Islamist Extremists* (Washington, DC, Center for Strategic and International Studies, 2005), pp. 11–13.
4. *The Guardian*, 18 September 2001.
5. Associated Press, 25 October 2001.
6. Simpson, *The Prince*, p. 178.
7. Mary Buckley and Rick Fawn, *Global Responses to Terrorism: 9/11, Afghanistan and Beyond* (London, Routledge, 2003), pp. 146–7.
8. *New York Times*, 14 October 2011.
9. *Washington Post*, 6 August 2002.
10. *National Review*, 9 August 2002.
11. Over a decade later, in September 2015, a US judge dismissed a long-running lawsuit against Saudi Arabia by families of some of the 9/11 victims, who had alleged that the kingdom had aided Al-Qaeda with financial and material support in the run-up to the attacks. The following year, in May 2016, the US Senate passed a bill that opened the way for family members of victims of 9/11 to sue the government of Saudi Arabia for any involvement it might have had in the attacks.
12. *New York Times*, 16 January 2002.
13. National Commission on Terrorist Attacks, *The 9/11 Commission Report: Final Report of the National Commission on Terrorist Attacks upon the United States*, authorized edition (New York, W. W. Norton & Company, 2004).
14. *Arab News*, 26 July 2003; *Al-Watan*, 26 July 2003.
15. *The Guardian*, 18 September 2001.
16. *New York Times*, 21 October 2001.
17. *The Times*, 12 October 2001.
18. *Denver Post*, 15 October 2001.
19. *Washington Post*, 24 September 2001.
20. *New York Times*, 11 November 2001.
21. Deutsche Presse-Agentur, 1 October 2001.
22. *Gulf News*, 11 October 2001; Agence France-Presse, 10 October 2001.
23. *The Robesonian*, 7 October 1996.
24. *Washington Times*, 12 February 2002.
25. US Newswire, 21 September 2001.
26. *Daily Telegraph*, 13 November 2001.
27. Associated Press, 13 September 2001.
28. *The Prince*, p. 335.
29. *Washington Post*, 26 October 2001; *The Guardian*, 29 October 2001.
30. *New York Times*, 27 September 2001 and 3 October 2001.
31. *The Guardian*, 21 November 2001.
32. *Al-Watan*, 9 November 1997.
33. 7,230 in the West Bank, 8,455 in the Gaza Strip and 662 in Israel proper.
34. Sergey Plekhanov, *A Reformer on the Throne: Sultan Qaboos bin Said Al Said* (Cape Town, Trident Press, 2004), p. 216.
35. Going forward, Qatar's past relations with Israel would be used against it by others in the Arab world. Six years later, for example, during Israel's war with Hezbollah in Lebanon, the state-controlled Saudi media outlet Al-Arabiya, a vocal critic of Qatari foreign policy, claimed that Qatar still had close military and commercial links to Israel. See Mamoun Fandy, *UnCivil War of Words: Media and Politics in the Arab World* (Westport, CT, Praeger, 2007).
36. *Washington Post*, 24 September 2001.
37. *New York Times*, 2 October 2001.
38. *New York Times*, 11 November 2001.
39. *New York Times*, 19 September 2001.
40. *New York Times*, 17 February 2002.

41. *Ha'aretz*, 27 February 2002.
42. Philip H. Gordon, 'Bush's Middle East Vision', *Survival*, 45:1 (Spring 2003), p. 159.
43. *The Guardian*, 26 April 2002.
44. Alfred B. Prados, 'Iraq: Post-War Challenges and U.S. Responses, 1991–1998', Report for Congress, Congressional Research Service (CRS), Washington, DC, 31 March 1999.
45. *The Observer*, 18 February 2001.
46. *New York Times*, 8 October 2002.
47. Agence France-Presse, 11 March 2003.
48. Reuters New Agency, 14 July 2002.
49. Associated Press, 2 March 2003.
50. *Al-bayan*, 5 March 2003.
51. *Al-Rai Al-Aam*, 18 March 2003; *Al-bayan*, 18 March 2003.
52. Associated Press, 2 March 2003.
53. *Washington Times*, 12 February 2002.
54. *New York Times*, 10 June 2002 and 12 December 2002.
55. Raymond W. Copson and Paul Gallis, 'Iraq War? Current Situation and Issues', Report for Congress, Congressional Research Service (CRS), Washington, DC, 4 March 2003.
56. Xinhua General News Service, 18 January 2003.
57. *Al-bayan*, 26 February 2003.
58. CNN, 7 January 2003, http://edition.cnn.com/2003/WORLD/meast/01/03/sprojects.irq.qatar.us/ (Accessed 22 March 2015).
59. See Khalid Al-Mansouri, 'The New Qatar: The Challenges and Opportunities of Small State Diplomacy, State Building and Sustainability, 1995–2010', unpublished PhD thesis, King's College London, 2014, p. 180.
60. *New York Times*, 9 May 2003.
61. Allen James Fromherz, *Qatar: A Modern History* (Reading, I. B. Tauris, 2012), p. 94.
62. *Al-Rai Al-Aam*, 11 May 2003.
63. Report on 9th Annual Emirates Center for Strategic Studies and Research (ECSSR) Conference on Gulf Security, January 2004.
64. *New York Times*, 30 April 2003.
65. *Al-Jazirah*, 22 March 2003.
66. *Al-bayan*, 2 May 2004.
67. Madawi Al-Rasheed, *A History of Saudi Arabia* (Cambridge, Cambridge University Press, 2010), pp. 224–6; Associated Press, 22 May 2003.
68. Cordesman and Obaid, *Al-Qaeda in Saudi Arabia*, p. 12.
69. The Closing Statement of the 25th Session of the GCC Supreme Council, Al-Manama, Kingdom of Bahrain, 21 December 2004, https://www.gcc-sg.org/eng/index46be.html?action=Sec-Show&ID=127 (Accessed 5 June 2015).
70. Ambassador Cofer Black, Coordinator for Counterterrorism, Testimony before the House Committee on International Relations, Subcommittee on the Middle East and Central Asia, Washington, DC, 24 March 2004, http://2001–2009.state.gov/s/ct/rls/rm/2004/30740.htm (Accessed 5 June 2015).
71. Simpson, *The Prince*, p. 331.
72. *Al-Watan*, 23 December 2003.

Chapter 5: Bloc Party

1. *Christian Science Monitor*, 20 November 1981.
2. Ghassan Salameh, 'Hangover in the Gulf', *Middle East Research and Information Project*, 139 (March–April 1986), http://www.merip.org/mer/mer139/hangover-time-gulf (Accessed 8 November 2015).
3. *Middle East International*, 8 September 1995, p. 17.
4. F. Gregory Gause III, 'Saudi Arabia over a Barrel', *Foreign Affairs*, 79:3 (2000), p. 83.
5. *The Economist*, 21 March 2002.
6. Eric Rouleau, 'Trouble in the Kingdom', *Foreign Affairs*, 81:4 (2002), p. 85.

7. Ali Mohammed Khalifa, *The United Arab Emirates: Unity in Fragmentation* (Boulder, CO, Westview Press, 1979), p. 141.
8. *The Economist*, 3 December 2009.
9. 'Memorandum of Conversation', 13 January 1971, Foreign Relations of the United States, 1969–1976, Middle East Region and Arabian Peninsula, 1969–1972, Vol. XXIV, Document 93, https://history.state.gov/historicaldocuments/frus1969-76v24/d93; *Middle East International*, February 1976, p. 23.
10. *The Economist*, 21 March 2002.
11. Ibid.
12. Mike Davis, 'Does the Road to the Future End at Dubai?', *Log*, 6 (Fall 2005), p. 63.
13. Afshin Molavi, 'Dubai Rising', *Brown Journal of World Affairs*, XII:1 (Summer–Fall 2005), p. 108.
14. Christopher Davidson, 'Dubai: Foreclosure of a Dream', *Middle East Research and Information Project*, 251 (Summer 2009), http://www.merip.org/mer/mer251/dubai (Accessed 8 November 2015).
15. *Gulf News*, 2 January 2001.
16. *Gulf News*, 20 February 2005.
17. See Onn Winckler, 'Can the GCC Weather the Economic Meltdown?', *Middle East Quarterly*, 17:3 (Summer 2010), pp. 51–61.
18. *Al-Watan*, 21 December 2003; *Al-Rai Al-Aam*, 20 December 2003; *Al-Seyassah*, 23 December 2003.
19. *Gulf News*, 6 November 2008.
20. Salim Hoss, 'The Gulf Dinar: The Concept and Application', lecture before the Kuwait Chamber of Commerce and Industry, February 1975, reprinted in *The Arab Accounting Dinar* (Kuwait, OPEC, n.d.), pp. 127–53.
21. *The Economist*, 8 July 2008.
22. *Gulf News*, 27 December 2008.
23. Kristian Coates Ulrichsen, 'South–South Cooperation and the Changing Role of the Gulf States', *Brazilian Journal of Strategy & International Relations*, 1:1 (2012), p. 113.
24. *New York Times*, 24 December 2004.
25. *Middle East International*, August 1978, pp. 27–8.
26. *Al-bayan*, 5 June 1979.
27. *Financial Times*, 23 October 2007 and 24 October 2010.
28. *Khaleej Times*, 2 December 2010.
29. *The Economist*, 26 May 2007.
30. *The Economist*, 10 November 2005.
31. *Businessweek*, 6 June 2008; *Gulf News*, 3 April 2008.
32. *Khaleej Times*, 27 May 2008 and 4 May 2005.
33. *The Guardian*, 7 September 2008.
34. Nimrod Raphaeli and Bianca Gersten, 'Sovereign Wealth Funds: Investment Vehicles for the Persian Gulf Countries', *Middle East Quarterly*, 15:2 (Spring 2008), pp. 45–53.
35. *New Yorker*, 26 November 2007.
36. *The Economist*, 7 December 2006; *Financial Times*, 29 July 2007.
37. Nouriel Roubini, 'Bogeymen of Financial Capitalism', Project Syndicate News Service, 3 March 2007.
38. Gawdat Bahgat, *Sovereign Wealth Funds in the Gulf: An Assessment*, research paper, Kuwait Programme on Development, Governance and Globalization in the Gulf States, Centre for the Study of Global Governance, LSE No. 16 (July 2011), http://www.lse.ac.uk/middleEastCentre/kuwait/documents/Bahgat%20paper.pdf.
39. *Asharq Al-Awsat*, 31 August 2007; *Financial Times*, 12 June 2007; *The Economist*, 17 January 2008.
40. *Financial Times*, 14 February 2008.
41. Bloomberg, 10 March 2006; Raphaeli and Gersten, 'Sovereign Wealth Funds', p. 47; *Financial Times*, 22 March 2008.
42. Sven Behrendt, *When Money Talks: Arab Sovereign Wealth Funds in the Global Public Policy Discourse*, Carnegie Papers, No. 12 (October 2008).

43. Rym Ayadi and Salim Gadi, 'EU–GCC Trade and Investment Relations: What Prospect of an FTA between the Two Regions?' Sharaka Research Papers, No. 5 (October 2013).
44. *The Economist*, 7 June 2007.
45. *Financial Times*, 28 January 2009; *The Economist*, 20 September 2008.
46. *Der Spiegel*, 19 May 2008.
47. Rawi Abdelal, 'Sovereign Wealth in Abu Dhabi', *Geopolitics*, 14:2 (2009), p. 320.
48. *The Times*, 22 March 2010.
49. *Financial Times*, 8 February 2008.
50. Behrendt, *When Money Talks*, p. 7.
51. *Financial Times*, 15 March 2010.
52. *The Economist*, 20 September 2008.
53. Reuters, 29 June 2008.
54. Cited in Raphaeli and Gersten, 'Sovereign Wealth Funds', p. 53.
55. *The Times*, 7 May 2010.

Chapter 6: Sheikh Down

1. Reuters, 2 April 2009.
2. Brad Setser and Rachel Ziemba, 'GCC Sovereign Funds Reversal of Fortune', Council on Foreign Relations Working Paper (January 2009); Onn Winckler, 'Can the GCC Weather the Economic Meltdown?', *Middle East Quarterly*, 17:3 (Summer 2010), pp. 51–61.
3. *Gulf News*, 19 January 2008.
4. Robert M. Kimmitt, 'Public Footprints in Private Markets: Sovereign Wealth Funds and the World Economy', *Foreign Affairs*, 87:1 (January-February 2008), pp. 119–30.
5. *Financial Times*, 29 October 2008.
6. *The Economist*, 24 January 2009 and 3 December 2009.
7. *New York Times*, 14 October 2008; Winckler, 'Can the GCC Weather the Economic Meltdown?'; *Gulf News*, 28 October 2008.
8. Sven Behrendt, *When Money Talks: Arab Sovereign Wealth Funds in the Global Public Policy Discourse*, Carnegie Papers, No. 12 (October 2008), p. 4.
9. Reuters, 28 October 2008; *Gulf News*, 30 October 2008.
10. Agence France-Presse, 29 October 2008; BBC News, 1 November 2008.
11. *Daily Telegraph*, 2 November 2008.
12. Kristian Coates Ulrichsen, *The Gulf States and the Rebalancing of Regional and Global Power*, James A. Baker III Institute for Public Policy, Rice University, 2014.
13. *Asharq Al-Awsat*, 4 February 2009.
14. Yusif A. Sayigh, 'Arab Oil Policies: Self Interest versus International Responsibility', *Journal of Palestine Studies*, IV:3 (Spring 1975), pp. 59–73.
15. Ahmad El-Sayed El-Naggar, 'Gulf States: Confronting the International Financial Crisis', Emirates Centre for Strategic Studies, (ECSSR) 16 November 2008; *Daily Star*, 7 October 2009; Reuters, 3 November 2008; *Gulf News*, 13 November 2008; *Al-Waqt*, 18 March 2008.
16. Reuters, 2 November 2008 and 16 November 2008.
17. *Gulf News*, 29 November 2008; *Gulf Times*, 31 May 2009 and 22 November 2008.
18. Reuters, 5 November 2008.
19. *Silicon India News*, 5 November 2008; *The National*, 3 November 2008.
20. *Mahaba.Net News*, 29 October 2008.
21. *Financial Times*, 29 January 2009 and 26 June 2012.
22. *The Economist*, 24 January 2009; Bloomberg, 2 July 2008.
23. *The Times*, 25 August 2012; Reuters, 27 October 2008.
24. Mehran Kamrava, *Qatar: Small State, Big Politics* (Ithaca, Cornell University Press, 2013), p. 99.
25. Saudi Press Agency, 8 November 2008.
26. Agence France-Presse, 29 December 2008.

27. *Gulf News*, 29 November 2008.
28. Reuters, 9 December 2009.
29. *Gulf News*, 11 June 2010.
30. *Gulf News*, 17 August 2009.
31. 'Qatar: 2009 Article IV Consultation', IMF Country Report No. 10/41 (February 2010), http://www.imf.org/external/pubs/ft/scr/2010/cr1041.pdf (Accessed 12 September 2014).
32. Reuters, 6 November 2008; Associated Press, 26 October 2008.
33. Reuters, 21 March 2008.
34. *Gulf News*, 24 September 2008; Reuters, 25 March 2011.
35. *Financial Times*, 19 April 2011.
36. Winckler, 'Can the GCC Weather the Economic Meltdown?'
37. *Gulf News*, 5 December 2006.
38. *The Economist*, 6 January 2013.
39. *The Times*, 9 December 2009.
40. *Financial Times*, 17 March 2009.
41. *Financial Times*, 30 January 2009.
42. *The Economist*, 23 April 2009.
43. *Financial Times*, 23 October 2009.
44. *New York Times*, 29 November 2009.
45. *The Economist*, 3 December 2009.
46. Ian Bremmer, *The End of the Free Market: Who Wins the War between States and Corporations?* (New York, Penguin, 2010), p. 93.
47. Ulrichsen, *The Gulf States and the Rebalancing of Regional and Global Power*, p. 5.
48. *The National*, 25 January 2012.
49. Gawdat Bahgat, *Sovereign Wealth Funds in the Gulf: An Assessment*, research paper, Kuwait Programme on Development, Governance and Globalization in the Gulf States, Centre for the Study of Global Governance, LSE No. 16 (July 2011), p. 16, http://www.lse.ac.uk/middleEastCentre/kuwait/documents/Bahgat%20paper.pdf.
50. Philippe Gugler and Julien Chaisse, 'Sovereign Wealth Funds in the European Union: General Trust despite Concerns', Swiss National Centre of Competence in Research, working paper No. 2009/4 (January 2009), p. 23, http://phase1.nccr-trade.org/ip-3/index.php%3Foption%3Dcom_content%26task%3Dview%26id%3D1428%26Itemid%3D215.html; Silvia Colombo, 'The Gulf and the EU: Partners or Competitors?', in Sieglinde Gstöhl and Erwan Lannon (eds), *The Neighbours of the European Union's Neighbours: Diplomatic and Geopolitical Dimensions beyond the European Neighbourhood Policy* (London, Routledge, 2015), pp. 99–122.
51. Jørgen Ørstrøm Møller, *The Global Economy in Transition: Debt and Resource Scarcities* (Singapore, World Scientific, 2013).
52. *Gulf News*, 15 January 2008.
53. *Gulf News*, 28 October 2008; Reuters, 2 November 2008.
54. *The Times*, 2 February 2012; *Gulf News*, 29 June 2010.
55. *The Guardian*, 15 June 2010.
56. *Financial Times*, 25 October 2010; *Daily Mail*, 13 March 2012; *The Independent* (London), 21 June 2013.
57. *Financial Times*, 10 May 2010.
58. *The Guardian*, 26 October 2010.
59. *Financial Times*, 14 March 2013 and 17 April 2013; *The Guardian*, 5 July 2010; *Gulf News*, 21 February 2012.
60. *The Times*, 25 March 2009; *Financial Times*, 23 March 2009; *Der Spiegel*, 23 March 2009.
61. *Financial Times*, 22 May 2009.
62. *Al-Monitor*, 27 December 2012.
63. *Der Spiegel*, 14 March 2012, pp.1–5; *Financial Times*, 2 July 2012.
64. *Financial Times*, 4 December 2014.
65. *Gulf News*, 10 March 2010 and 24 September 2008.
66. Agence France-Presse, 18 August 2009.
67. *Financial Times*, 29 April 2008.

68. Statement by the Hon. Yousef Hussain Kamal, Governor's Statement No.7, International Monetary Fund & World Bank Group 2012 Annual Meeting, 12 October 2012, https://www.imf.org/external/am/2012/speeches/pr07e.pdf.
69. *Financial Times*, 4 December 2014.

Chapter 7: Self-Defence

1. *The Guardian*, 11 February 2011; Reuters, 11 February 2011.
2. *Al-Jazeera*, 21 October 2011.
3. GCC secretary general Abdullah Bisharah, lecture before GCC diplomats, Saudi Foreign Ministry, Riyadh, 24 January 1986, reprinted in R. K. Ramazani, *The Gulf Cooperation Council: Record and Analysis* (Charlottesville, University of Virginia Press, 1988), p. 164.
4. *The Economist*, 27 January 1979.
5. GCC secretary general Bisharah's press conference, 27 May 1981, reprinted in Ramazani, *The Gulf Cooperation Council*, p. 32.
6. Ghassan Salameh, 'Hangover in the Gulf', *Middle East Research and Information Project*, 139 (March–April 1986), p. 44, http://www.merip.org/mer/mer139/hangover-time-gulf (Accessed 8 November 2015).
7. 'Memorandum of Conversation', 29 September 1972, Foreign Relations of the United States, 1969–1976, Middle East Region and Arabian Peninsula, 1969–1972, Vol. XXIV, Document 164, https://history.state.gov/historicaldocuments/frus1969-76v24/d164.
8. *Christian Science Monitor*, 13 December 1982.
9. See Khalid Al-Mansouri, 'The New Qatar: The Challenges and Opportunities of Small State Diplomacy, State Building and Sustainability, 1995–2010', unpublished PhD thesis, King's College London, 2014. For a wide-ranging discussion on Qatar's regional diplomacy during and following the time of the Arab Spring, see Kristian Coates Ulrichsen, *Qatar and the Arab Spring* (Oxford and New York, Oxford University Press, 2014).
10. Abdullah Baabood, 'Dynamics and Determinants of the GCC States' Foreign Policy, with Special Reference to the EU', in Gerd Nonneman (ed.), *Analyzing Middle East Foreign Policies and the Relationship with Europe* (London and New York, Routledge, 2005), p. 159.
11. See Norbert Wildermuth, 'Defining the "Al-Jazeera Effect": American Public Diplomacy at a Crossroad', *Media Res*, 1:2 (February 2005).
12. Tarek Cherkaoui, 'Al Jazeera's Changing Editorial Perspectives and the Saudi–Qatari Relationship', *Political Economy of Communication*, 2:1 (2014), pp. 17–32.
13. 'The Rise of the Gulf States', WikiLeaks, 14 April 2009, 09DOHA252, http://wikileaks.org/cable/2009/04/09DOHA252.html.
14. Quoted in Kristian Coates Ulrichsen, 'Qatar and the Arab Spring', *OpenDemocracy*, 12 April 2011, https://www.opendemocracy.net/kristian-coates-ulrichsen/qatar-and-arab-spring (Accessed 5 July 2015).
15. Hugh Eakin, 'The Strange Power of Qatar', *New York Review of Books*, 27 October 2011.
16. For a wide-ranging analysis of China's response to the Arab Spring see Rory Miller and Kun-Chin Lin, ' "Lessons Learnt: Adapting to the Arab Spring": Chinese Economic Statecraft and the Quest for Stability in the Contemporary Middle East', History of British Intelligence and Security Research Project, London, Arts & Humanities Research Council (2012), http://www.ahrc.ac.uk/What-We-Do/Extend-engagement/Inform-public-policy/Documents/Arab_Spring.pdf (Accessed 5 January 2016).
17. *The Guardian*, 1 December 2005.
18. *The National*, 24 June 2011.
19. See Al-Mansouri, 'The New Qatar', Chapter 6. For a detailed examination of the role of Qatar in Egypt, Tunisia and Libya during the Arab Spring see also Kristian Coates Ulrichsen, *Qatar and the Arab Spring* (London, Hurst, 2014).
20. Hugh Miles, 'The Al Jazeera Effect', *Foreign Policy*, 8 February 2011, http://foreignpolicy.com/2011/02/09/the-al-jazeera-effect-2/(Accessed 16 July 2015).
21. *Al-Majallah* (London), 1–7 May 1982, pp. 12–17.

22. René Rieger, 'In Search of Stability: Saudi Arabia and the Arab Spring', GRM Papers, Gulf Research Centre (2014), p. 5.
23. Jack A. Goldstone, 'Understanding the Revolutions of 2011', *Foreign Affairs*, 90:3 (May–June 2011), p. 14.
24. Rieger, 'In Search of Stability', p. 3.
25. F. Gregory Gause III, *Kings for All Seasons: How the Middle East's Monarchies Survived the Arab Spring*, Brookings Doha Centre Analysis Paper, No. 8 (September 2013), pp. 13–14.
26. Reuters, 12 December 2012.
27. Amnesty International 'Years of Rebellion: The State of Human Rights in the Middle East and North Africa', (London, 2012), pp. 32–7.
28. 'Qatar Country Summary', *Human Rights Watch*, January 2012, p. 1; *Gulf News*, 2 June 2011 and 25 October 2011.
29. Rieger, 'In Search of Stability', p. 2.
30. Justin Gengler, 'Qatar's Ambivalent Democratization', *Foreign Policy*, 1 November 2011, http://foreignpolicy.com/2011/11/01/qatars-ambivalent-democratization/ (Accessed 16 August 2015).
31. Ibid.
32. *Middle East International*, 8 September 1995, p. 17; *Gulf News*, 31 December 2000.
33. 'Memorandum of Conversation', 13 January 1971, Foreign Relations of the United States, 1969–1976, Middle East Region and Arabian Peninsula, 1969–1972, Vol. XXIV, Document 93, https://history.state.gov/historicaldocuments/frus1969-76v24/d93
34. Kristian Coates Ulrichsen, 'Gulf States: Studious Silence Falls on Arab Spring', *OpenDemocracy*, 25 April 2011, https://www.opendemocracy.net/kristian-coates-ulrichsen/gulf-states-studious-silence-falls-on-arab-spring (Accessed 16 July 2014).
35. *The Economist*, 16 October 2011.
36. *Asharq Al-Awsat*, 6 April 2011.
37. Ibid.
38. *Time* magazine, 18 February 2011.
39. Ibid., 24 February 2011.
40. Amnesty International 'The Arab Spring: Five Years On', https://www.amnesty.org/en/latest/campaigns/2016/01/arab-spring-five-years-on/ (Accessed 12 March 2016).
41. Jack A. Goldstone, 'Understanding the Revolutions of 2011', p. 8.
42. GUNA News Agency, 20 December 1981.
43. Ulrichsen, 'Gulf States: Studious Silence Falls on Arab Spring'.
44. Ali Alfoneh, 'Mixed Response in Iran', *Middle East Quarterly*, 18:3 (Summer 2011), p. 36.
45. Ulrichsen, 'Gulf States: Studious Silence Falls on Arab Spring'.
46. *Asharq Al-Awsat*, 15 March 2011.
47. 'Years of Rebellion: The State of Human Rights in the Middle East and North Africa', pp. 32–7.
48. Speech of King Abdullah of Saudi Arabia before the *Majlis al-Shura*, 25 September 2011.

Chapter 8: Oil Change

1. *Middle East International*, 17 February 1995, p. 8.
2. *Financial Times*, 23 October 2009.
3. *Gulf Times*, 21 March 2007.
4. *The Economist*, 21 January 1967.
5. *Middle East International*, 8 September 1995, p. 17.
6. Gal Luft, 'To Drill or Not to Drill', *Foreign Policy*, 27 May 2013, http://foreignpolicy.com/2013/05/27/to-drill-or-not-to-drill/ (Accessed 15 September 2015).
7. 'MENAP Oil-Exporting Countries', REO Update (May 2015), International Monetary Fund, Middle East and Central Asia Department, p. 5.

8. Steffen Hertog, 'A Comparative Assessment of Labor Market Nationalization Policies in the GCC', in Steffen Hertog (ed.), *National Employment and Education in the GCC* (Berlin, Gerlach Press, 2012), p. 1.
9. *Financial Times*, 3 December 2015.
10. Onn Winckler, 'Can the GCC Weather the Economic Meltdown?', *Middle East Quarterly* 17:3 (Summer 2010), pp. 51–61.
11. *Middle East International*, 11 December 1981, p. 12.
12. *Khaleej Times*, 2 December 2010.
13. Steffen Hertog, 'Arab Gulf States: An Assessment of Nationalisation Policies', Gulf Labor Markets and Migration (GLMM) research paper, 2014/1, Migration Policy Centre (2014).
14. *Middle East*, October 2013, p. 36.
15. *New York Times*, 16 February 2016.
16. *Khaleej Times*, 15 February 2007.
17. *Middle East International*, November 1978, p. 20.
18. *Middle East International*, July 1978, p. 19.
19. *Middle East International*, December 1981, p. 12.
20. Foud Ajami, 'The Saudi Boom's Paradox', *New York Times*, 20 July 1978.
21. *The Economist*, 19 November 2008; *Middle East*, October 2013, p. 33.
22. *The Times*, 16 December 1970.
23. *Gulf News*, 14 March 2001.
24. *Al-Watan* (Doha), 14 May 2010.
25. Abdulkhaleq Abdullah, 'The Challenge of Human Capital Investment in the GCC', in *Human Resources and Development in the Arabian Gulf* (Emirates Center for Strategic Studies and Research, Abu Dhabi, 2009), p. 51.
26. Speech of King Abdullah of Saudi Arabia before the *Majlis al-Shura*, 25 September 2011.
27. Abdulkhaleq Abdullah, 'The Challenge of Human Capital Investment in the GCC', p. 54.
28. Maria Saab and Joshua Haber, 'The Slow Pace of Female Empowerment in the Gulf', *OpenDemocracy*, 18 March 2014, https://www.opendemocracy.net/arab-awakening/maria-saab-joshua-haber/slow-pace-of-female-empowerment-in-gulf (Accessed 23 November 2014).
29. Ghassan Salameh, 'Hangover in the Gulf', *Middle East Research and Information Project*, 139 (March–April 1986), http://www.merip.org/mer/mer139/hangover-time-gulf (Accessed 8 November 2015).
30. *Financial Times*, 13 August 2009.
31. *Arabian Business*, 21 March 2016.
32. Reuters, 30 January 2013.
33. CNBC, 22 May 2015, http://video.cnbc.com/gallery/?video=3000382178 (Accessed 15 October 2015).
34. 'The Quest for Diversity', sponsored special report, *Foreign Policy* (September–October 2015), p. 3.
35. *Financial Times*, 23 October 2009.

Chapter 9: Divided We Stand

1. *Wall Street Journal*, 22 November 2013; Associated Press, 10 May 2015.
2. US National Security Strategy, 1 May 2010, https://www.whitehouse.gov/sites/default/files/rss_viewer/national_security_strategy.pdf.
3. Silvia Colombo, 'The GCC Countries and the Arab Spring: Between Outreach, Patronage and Repression', Istituto Affari Internazionali (IAI) Working Papers 12/09 (March 2012), p. 13.
4. F. Gregory Gause III, *Kings for All Seasons: How the Middle East's Monarchies Survived the Arab Spring*, Brookings Doha Analysis Paper, No. 8 (September 2013), pp. 18–19.

5. Jacob Høigilt, *Islamist Rhetoric: Language and Culture in Contemporary Egypt* (London and New York, Routledge, 2011), p. 66.
6. *Al-Arabiya*, 13 March 2015.
7. *Al-Monitor*, 22 February 2015.
8. Marc Lynch, 'Money to Meddle: Can the Wealthy Powerbrokers of the Persian Gulf Create the Egypt they Want?', *Foreign Policy*, 11 July 2013, http://foreignpolicy.com/2013/07/11/money-to-meddle/ (Accessed 15 September 2015).
9. *Financial Times*, 17 December 2011.
10. *Al-Monitor*, 24 February 2012.
11. *The Economist*, 30 May 2015.
12. 'NATO and the Gulf Cooperation Council Discuss Middle East Security', 30 January 2012, http://www.nato.int/cps/en/natohq/news_83848.htm?selectedLocale=en.(Accessed 22 November 2015).
13. The Rt Hon Lord Howell of Guilford, 'UK Relations with the GCC Region: A Broadening Partnership', GCC and the City Conference, 20 June 2012, https://www.gov.uk/government/speeches/uk-relations-with-the-gcc-region-a-broadening-partnership (Accessed 22 November 2015).
14. Reuters, 15 January 2013.
15. Manama Supreme Council Summit: Press Conference held by Bahraini Foreign Minister Muhammad Ibn Mubarak Al-Khalifah, reprinted in R. K. Ramazani, *The Gulf Cooperation Council: Record and Analysis* (Charlottesville, University of Virginia Press, 1988), p. 150; Saudi King Fahd comments on Fifth GCC Summit, 29 November 1984, reprinted in Ramazani, *The Gulf Cooperation Council*, p. 164.
16. Agence France-Presse, 19 April 2015.
17. 'Interview with Turki Al-Faisal on Syria and Hezbollah', *Der Spiegel*, 17 June 2013.
18. *Gulf News*, 11 January 2013.
19. Speech of King Abdullah of Saudi Arabia before the *Majlis al-Shura*, 25 September 2011.
20. David Andrew Weinberg, 'Kuwait's Espionage Revelations Could Disrupt Rapprochement with Iran', and 'Bahrain and Iran Expel Each Other's Diplomats', Foundation for the Defense of Democracies Policy Briefs, 8 September and 5 October 2015, http://www.defenddemocracy.org/ (Accessed 16 November 2015).
21. Ray Takeyh, *Guardians of the Revolution: Iran and the World in the Age of the Ayatollahs* (Oxford, Oxford University Press, 2009), pp. 129–30.
22. *Gulf News*, 23 March 2013.
23. Statement of Kenneth Katzman, Specialist in Middle Eastern Affairs, Foreign Affairs, Defense and Trade Division of Congressional Research Service before the Subcommittee on the Middle East and North Africa House Committee on Foreign Affairs, House of Representatives, Hearing on 'The Gulf Cooperation Council Camp David Summit: Any Results?', 9 July 2015, http://foreignaffairs.house.gov/hearing/subcommittee-hearing-gulf-cooperation-council-camp-david-summit-any-results (Accessed 16 November 2015).
24. *World Post*, 9 October 2015.
25. *The Guardian*, 23 October 2015.
26. *The National*, 11 April 2015.
27. *Al-Jazeera*, 20 May 2015.
28. David Pollock, 'New Saudi Poll', Fikra Forum, 22 October 2015, http://fikraforum.org/?p=7907#.Vlqe6WQrKX0 and 'New Kuwaiti Survey Reveals Sectarian Divide, Concerns about Iran', Fikra Forum, 28 October 2015, http://fikraforum.org/?p=7967#.VlqfAGQrKX0 (Accessed 16 November 2015).
29. Ana Echagüe, 'Change or Continuity? US Policy towards the Middle East and Its Implications for EU Policy', working paper 95, FRIDE (March 2010), p. 5.
30. Ibid., p. 6.
31. *Wall Street Journal*, 16 February 2010.
32. Frank A. Rose, deputy assistant secretary, Bureau of Arms Control, Verification and Compliance, Peter Huessy Breakfast Series, Capitol Hill Club, Washington, DC,

14 May 2014, http://www.state.gov/t/avc/rls/2014/226073.htm (Accessed 16 November 2015).

33. See Marcus Weisgerber, 'The Middle East Has Four Minutes to Act if Iran Fires a Missile', *Defense One*, 13 May 2015, http://www.defenseone.com/threats/2015/05/middle-east-has-four-minutes-act-if-iran-fires-missile/112720/(Accessed 16 November 2015).
34. *New York Times*, 18 March 2011.
35. Jeffrey Goldberg, 'The Obama Doctrine', *The Atlantic*, April 2016, http://www.theatlantic.com/magazine/archive/2016/04/the-obama-doctrine/471525/.
36. Thomas Lippman, 'Obama's Legacy in the Gulf: Despite Disgruntlement US Remains Indispensable', Middle East Institute, Washington, DC, 19 November 2014, http://www.mei.edu/content/article/obama's-legacy-gulf-despite-disgruntlement-us-remains-indispensable (Accessed 16 November 2015).
37. Ali Alfoneh, 'Mixed Response in Iran', *Middle East Quarterly*, 18:3 (Summer 2011), p. 39.
38. 'Interview with Turki Al-Faisal on Syria and Hezbollah', *Der Spiegel*, 17 June 2013.
39. *Washington Post*, 14 May 2015; *New York Times*, 15 August 2015; Joint Statement released by the U.S.–GCC Foreign Ministers Meeting in Doha, State of Qatar on 3 August 2015, http://www.state.gov/r/pa/prs/ps/2015/08/245619.htm (Accessed 16 November 2015).
40. Goldberg, 'The Obama Doctrine'.
41. Remarks by Saudi Arabian foreign minister Saud Al-Faisal, Riyadh, Saudi Arabia, 3 March 2013.
42. BBC News, 21 October 2015.
43. BBC News, 14 January 2012.
44. US–Gulf Cooperation Council Camp David Joint Statement, White House, 14 May 2015, https://www.whitehouse.gov/the-press-office/2015/05/14/us-gulf-cooperation-council-camp-david-joint-statement (Accessed 16 November 2015).
45. Agence France-Presse, 30 November 2015.
46. Reuters, 15 December 2015.
47. Kuwait News Agency, 25 November 2014.
48. Statement by J. Matthew McInnis, Resident Fellow, American Enterprise Institute, before the Subcommittee on the Middle East and North Africa House Committee on Foreign Affairs, House of Representatives, Hearing on 'Iran's Strategy towards the Gulf Cooperation Council: A Look after the Camp David Summit', 9 July 2015, http://foreignaffairs.house.gov/hearing/subcommittee-hearing-gulf-cooperation-council-camp-david-summit-any-results (Accessed 16 November 2015); *The Guardian*, 23 October 2015.
49. *The Guardian*, 23 October 2015.
50. Agence France-Presse, 30 November 2015.
51. *Oman Times*, 2 February 2015; David Held and Kristian Coates Ulrichsen, 'The Arab Spring and the Changing Balance of Power', *OpenDemocracy*, 26 February 2014, https://www.opendemocracy.net/arab-awakening/david-held-kristian-coates-ulrichsen/arab-spring-and-changing-balance-of-global-power (Accessed 16 November 2015).
52. 'Change Is the Only Constant – Prince Turki', 2 January 2012, Saudi-US Relations Information Service, http://susris.com/2012/01/02/change-is-the-only-constant-prince-turki/ (Accessed 16 November 2015).
53. Kuwait News Agency, 25 November 2014; *Gulf Daily News*, 8 December 2013.
54. *Al-Arabiya*, 11 December 2013.
55. Agence France-Presse, 8 December 2013.
56. Kuwait News Agency, 25 November 2014.
57. *Gulf News*, 6 May 2010.
58. See, for example, *Arab Times*, 7 December 2015.
59. *China Daily*, 4 June 2014; *gbtimes*, 4 November 2014.
60. *Al-Majallah* (London), 9–15 April 1986.
61. *Gulf News*, 16 May 2011.

62. *Financial Times*, 2 June 2011.
63. *Al Arabiya*, 10 April 2016.

Chapter 10: The Hub

1. William O. Beeman, 'Gulf Society: An Anthropological View of the Khalijis – Their Evolution and Way of Life', in Lawrence G. Potter (ed.), *The Persian Gulf in Modern Times: People, Ports and History* (New York, Palgrave Macmillan, 2014), p. 148.
2. John W. Fox, Nada Mourtada-Sabbah and Mohammed Al-Mutawa, 'The Arab Gulf Region', in Fox, Mourtada-Sabbah and Al-Mutawa (eds), *Globalization and the Gulf* (London and New York, Routledge, 2006), p. 4.
3. Rodney Wilson, 'The Development of Islamic Finance in the GCC', working paper, Kuwait Programme on Development, Governance and Globalisation in the Gulf States, Centre for the Study of Global Governance, LSE (May 2009), p. 27.
4. *The Economist*, 13 December 2006.
5. Wilson, 'The Development of Islamic Finance', p. 3.
6. *Murabaha* is an acceptable form of credit sale under Islamic religious law that is not an interest-bearing loan and *ijara* is an exchange transaction in which a known benefit arising from a specified asset is made available in return for a payment, but where ownership of the asset itself is not transferred.
7. Abd al-Hadi Khalaf, 'The Elusive Quest for Gulf Security', *Middle East Research and Information Project*, 17:148 (September–October 1987), http://www.merip.org/mer/mer148/elusive-quest-gulf-security (Accessed 8 February 2015).
8. *Al-Majallah* (London), 9–15 April 1986.
9. Sheikh Tamim bin Hamad al-Thani, 'The Next Step', *The Business Year*: 2014, https://www.thebusinessyear.com/qatar-2014/the-next-step/inside-perspective.
10. Report on conference hosted by Canadian Security and Intelligence Service (CSIS) on 'Competing Visions of the State: Political and Security Trends in the Arab World and the Middle East', Ottawa, 19–20 January 2012, p. 24.
11. *Al-Arabiya*, 5 August 2013.
12. *Al-Arabiya*, 6 May 2013.
13. IMF, *Regional Economic Outlook: Middle East and Central Asia* (Washington, DC, October 2014), p. 37.
14. Reuters, 30 January 2013.
15. *The National*, 17 May 2010.
16. Quoted in Gawdat Bahgat, *Sovereign Wealth Funds in the Gulf: An Assessment*, research paper, Kuwait Programme on Development, Governance and Globalization in the Gulf States, Centre for the Study of Global Governance, LSE No. 16 (July 2011), p. 31, http://www.lse.ac.uk/middleEastCentre/kuwait/documents/Bahgat%20paper.pdf.
17. *Financial Times*, 17 April 2012 and 26 June 2012.
18. Reuters, 5 November 2008.
19. *Gulf News*, 26 May 2009.
20. *Indian Express*, 3 November 2008.
21. *The National*, 21 January 2016.
22. Kadira Pethiyagoda, 'Dealing with Delhi: How Culture Shapes India's Middle East Policy', Brookings Doha Center, policy briefing, December 2015, p. 10.
23. *Gulf News*, 9 November 2008.
24. *The Hindu*, 6 January 2012.
25. Reuters, 7 June 2012.
26. *Economic Times*, 18 August 2015.
27. Cited in Sarah Bazoonbandi, *Political Economy of Government Wealth Funds* (London and New York, Routledge, 2012), p. 46.
28. *Gulf News*, 11 April 2012.
29. *Financial Times*, 15 May 2012.
30. *The Economist*, 19 November 2008; *Financial Times*, 25 October 2010.
31. Reuters, 25 January 2009.

32. *Financial Times*, 1 October 2012.
33. *Financial Times*, 10 July 2009.
34. *Financial Times*, 19 November 2009.
35. *Gulf News*, 10 July 2009.
36. Kristian Coates Ulrichsen, *The Gulf States in International Political Economy* (London and New York, Palgrave Macmillan, 2016), p. 143.
37. Kristian Coates Ulrichsen, 'South-South Cooperation and the Changing Role of the Gulf States', *Brazilian Journal of Strategy & International Relations*, 1:1 (2012), p. 113.
38. Ibid. p.113; *The Guardian*, 6 March 2010.
39. *PR Newswire*, 21 June 2012.
40. *The Peninsula*, 12 May 2009.
41. *The Economist*, 10 January 2015.
42. McKinsey & Company, 'Global Flows in a Digital Age', http://www.mckinsey.com/business-functions/strategy-and-corporate-finance/our-insights/global-flows-in-a-digital-age (Accessed 16 February 2016).
43. *Financial Times*, 28 June 2015.
44. Quoted in *Doha News*, 13 October 2015.
45. *Otago Daily Times*, 26 November–27 December 2007, p. 12.
46. 'Sports Tourism – UAE: Abu Dhabi, Economic News Update', Oxford Business Group, 22 July 2010, http://www.oxfordbusinessgroup.com/news/sport-tourism (Accessed 6 January 2016).
47. See 'Qatar's Sports Strategy, 2011–2016', http://www.aspire.qa/Document/Sports_sector_strategy_final-English.pdf (Accessed 5 March 2016).
48. Kristian Coates Ulrichsen, 'Small States with a Big Role: Qatar and the United Arab Emirates in the Wake of the Arab Spring', No. 3 (October 2012), HH Sheikh Nasser Al-Mohammad Al-Sabah Publication Series, pp. 11–12.
49. 'Qatar Wins World Cup: Qatar? Really?', CBSnews.com, 2 December 2010, http://www.cbsnews.com/news/qatar-wins-world-cup-qatar-really/ (Accessed 3 February 2016).
50. Art.intern.net, 8 February 2012, http://en.artintern.net/index.php/news/main/html/1/1866 (Accessed 4 February 2016).
51. *The Guardian*, 16 April 2012.
52. *Financial Times*, 24 August 2007.
53. *Kuwait Times*, 4 December 2010.
54. Human Rights Watch, 'Building a Better World Cup: Protecting Migrant Workers in Qatar Ahead of FIFA 2022', 12 June 2012, p. 5.
55. *The Observer*, 21 September 2013; *Handelsblatt*, 19 March 2014.
56. Human Rights Watch World 2016: Events of 2015, pp. 462, https://www.hrw.org/sites/default/files/world_report_download/wr2016_web.pdf (Accessed 5 April 2016).
57. The UAE is at number 12; Bahrain is at 27; Saudi Arabia is at 37; Qatar is at 39; Oman is at 44; Kuwait is at 45.

Conclusion: (In) Capacitated

1. *The Economist*, 10 January 2015.
2. See 'There Will Be Pandemonium: The End of the Old Oil Order Has Already Begun', *Salon*, 29 April 2016, http://www.salon.com/2016/04/29/there_will_be_pandemonium_partner/ (Accessed 5 May 2016).
3. Shale oil and gas are extracted by pumping water, sand and chemicals into the ground at high pressure to crack open rocks, a process known as fracking.
4. *Nasdaq*, 23 June 2015.
5. Fred Halliday, *The Middle East in International Relations: Power, Politics and Ideology* (Cambridge, Cambridge University Press, 2005), p. 200.
6. Jeffrey Goldberg, 'The Obama Doctrine', *The Atlantic*, April 2016, http://www.theatlantic.com/magazine/archive/2016/04/the-obama-doctrine/471525/
7. Christopher M. Davidson, *After the Sheikhs* (London, Hurst & Co., 2012), p. 2.

8. Nafeez Ahmed, 'The collapse of Saudi Arabia is inevitable', *Middle East Eye*, 28 September 2015, http://www.middleeasteye.net/columns/collapse-saudi-arabia-inevitable-1895380679 (Accessed 2 April 2016); Sarah Chayes, 'Start Preparing for the Collapse of the Saudi Kingdom', *Defense One*, 16 February 2016, http://www.defenseone.com/ideas/2016/02/de-waal-and-chayes-saudi-arabia/125953/ (Accessed 2 April 2016).
9. *Financial Times*, 30 December 2015.
10. *New York Times*, 25 November 2015.
11. *Financial Times*, 10 June 2009.

BIBLIOGRAPHY

Aarts, Paul and Gerd Nonneman, *Saudi Arabia in the Balance: Political Economy, Society, Foreign Affairs*, New York, New York University Press, 2006.

Aarts, Paul and Carolien Roelants, *Saudi Arabia: A Kingdom in Peril*, London, Hurst & Co., 2015.

Abir, Mordechai, *Saudi Arabia: Government, Society and the Gulf Crisis*, London and New York, Routledge, 1993.

Abu-Lughod, Janet, 'Urbanization and Social Change in the Arab World', *Ekisitcs*, 50:300 (1983).

Albaharna, Husain M., *The Legal Status of the Arabian Gulf States: A Study of Their Treaty Relations and International Relations*, Manchester, Manchester University Press, 1968.

Algosaibi, Ghazi A., *The Gulf Crisis: An Attempt to Understand*, London and New York, Routledge, 1993.

Al-Alkim, Hassan Hamdan, *The GCC States in an Unstable World: Foreign Policy Dilemmas of Small States,* London, Saqi Books, 1994.

Al-Fahim, Mohammed, *From Rags to Riches: A Story of Abu Dhabi*, London, Centre of Arab Studies, 2008.

Al-Kilani, Kamal, *Progress of a Nation: A Biography of King Fahd bin Abdul-Aziz*, London and New York, Namara Publications, 1985.

Al-Rasheed, Madawi, *A History of Saudi Arabia*, Cambridge, Cambridge University Press, 2010.

Al-Sabah, Meshal, *Gender and Politics in Kuwait: Women and Political Participation in the Gulf*, Reading, I. B. Tauris, 2013.

Anderson, Irvine H., *Aramco, The United States and Saudi Arabia: A Study in the Dynamics of Foreign Oil Policy, 1933–1950*, Princeton, NJ, Princeton University Press, 1981.

Anthony, John Duke, 'The Gulf Cooperation Council', *International Journal*, 41:2 (Spring 1986).

——, 'Points, Patterns, Prognosis: the 17th GCC Heads of State Summit and Aftermath: Whither the GCC?', US-GCC Corporate Cooperation Committee Occasional Paper Series, No. 8 (1997).

Askari, Hossein, *Collaborative Colonialism: The Political Economy of Oil in the Persian Gulf*, London and New York, Palgrave Macmillan, 2013.

Atkins, James E., 'The Oil Crisis: This Time the Wolf Is Here', *Foreign Affairs*, 51:3 (April 1973).

Ayadi, Rym and Salim Gadi, 'EU–GCC Trade and Investment Relations: What Prospect of an FTA between the Two Regions?' Sharaka Research Papers, No. 5 (October 2013).

Bahgat, Gawdat, *Sovereign Wealth Funds in the Gulf: An Assessment*, research paper, Kuwait Programme on Development, Governance and Globalization in the Gulf States, Centre for the Study of Global Governance, LSE, No. 16 (July 2011).

Baker III, James A., *The Politics of Diplomacy: Revolution, War and Peace, 1989–1992*, New York, G. P. Putnam's Sons, 2009.

Beblawi, Hazem and Giacomo Luciani, *The Rentier State*, London, Croom Helm, 1987.

Behrendt, Sven, *When Money Talks: Arab Sovereign Wealth Funds in the Global Public Policy Discourse*, Carnegie Papers, No. 12 (October 2008).

Bilgin, Pinar, *Regional Security in the Middle East: A Critical Perspective*, New York, Routledge, 2011.

Bin Sultan, Khalid, *Desert Warrior*, Beirut, Dar Alsawi, 1995.

Buckley, Mary and Rick Fawn, *Global Responses to Terrorism: 9/11, Afghanistan and Beyond*, London, Routledge, 2003.

Byman, Daniel, *Al Qaeda, the Islamic State, and the Global Jihadist Movement: What Everyone Needs to Know*, New York, Oxford University Press, 2015.

Cherkaoui, Tarek, 'Al Jazeera's Changing Editorial Perspectives and the Saudi–Qatari Relationship', *Political Economy of Communication*, 2:1 (2014).

Colombo, Silvia, 'The GCC Countries and the Arab Spring: Between Outreach, Patronage and Repression', Istituto Affari Internazionali (IAI) Working Papers 12/09 (March 2012).

Cooke, Miriam, *Tribal Modern: Branding New Nations in the Arab Gulf*, Berkeley and Los Angeles, University of California Press, 2014.

Cooper, Andrew F., R. A. Higgott and K. R. Nossal, 'Bound to Follow? Leadership and Followership in the Gulf Conflict', *Political Science Quarterly*, 106:3 (1991).

Copson, Raymond W. and Paul Gallis, 'Iraq War? Current Situation and Issues', Report for Congress, Congressional Research Service, Washington, DC, 4 March 2003.

Cordesman, Anthony H., *Bahrain, Qatar, Oman and the UAE: Challenges of Security*, Boulder, CO, Westview Press, 1997.

——, *Saudi Arabia Enters the Twenty-first Century: The Political, Foreign Policy, Economic, and Energy Dimensions*, Westport, CT, Praeger, 2003.

Cordesman, Anthony H. and Nawaf Obaid, *Al-Qaeda in Saudi Arabia: Asymmetric Threats and Islamist Extremists*, Washington, DC, Center for Strategic and International Studies, 2005.

Crystal, Jill, 'Coalitions in Oil Monarchies: Kuwait and Qatar', *Comparative Politics*, 21:4 (July 1989).

——, *Oil and Politics in the Gulf: Rulers and Merchants in Kuwait and Qatar*, Cambridge, Cambridge University Press, 1990.

Davidson, Christopher, 'Dubai: Foreclosure of a Dream', *Middle East Research and Information Project*, 251 (Summer 2009).

——, *After the Sheikhs*, London, Hurst & Co., 2012.

——, *Power and Politics in the Persian Gulf Monarchies*, London, Hurst & Co., 2012.

Echagüe, Ana, 'Change or Continuity? US Policy towards the Middle East and Its Implications for EU Policy', working paper, 95, FRIDE (March 2010).

Ehteshami, Anoush, *Dynamics of Change in the Persian Gulf: Political Economy, War and Revolution*, London and New York, Routledge, 2013.

Ehteshami, Anoush and Steven Wright, 'Political Change in the Arab Oil Monarchies: From Liberalization to Enfranchisement', *International Affairs*, 83:5 (2007).

—— (eds), *Reform in the Middle East Oil Monarchies*, Reading, Ithaca Press, 2008.

Emirates Center for Strategic Studies and Research, *Human Resources and Development in the Arabian Gulf*, ECSSR, Abu Dhabi, 2009.

——, *The Arabian Gulf: Between Conservatism and Change*, ECSSR, Abu Dhabi, 2009.

Fandy, Mamoun, *UnCivil War of Words: Media and Politics in the Arab World*, Westport, CT, Praeger, 2007.

Fawcett, Louise (ed.), *International Relations of the Middle East*, Oxford, Oxford University Press, 2013.

Field, Michael, *A Hundred Million Dollars A Day: Inside the World of Middle East Money*, New York, Praeger Publishers, 1976.

Fox, John W., Nada Mourtada-Sabbah and Mohammed Al-Mutawa (eds), *Globalization and the Gulf*, London and New York, Routledge, 2006.

Freedman, Lawrence, *A Choice of Enemies: America Confronts the Middle East*, London, Phoenix, 2009.

Freedman, Lawrence and Efraim Karsh, *The Gulf Conflict, 1990–1991: Diplomacy and War in the New World Order*, London and New York, Faber & Faber, 1993.

FRIDE, *The Gulf in the New World Order: A Forgotten Emerging Power*, FRIDE Working Paper 101 (September 2010).

Fromherz, Allen James, *Qatar: A Modern History*, Reading, I. B. Tauris, 2012.

Gause III, F. Gregory, 'Saudi Arabia over a Barrel', *Foreign Affairs*, 79:3 (2000).

——, *The International Relations of the Persian Gulf*, Cambridge, Cambridge University Press, 2010.

——, *Kings for All Seasons: How the Middle East's Monarchies Survived the Arab Spring*, Brookings Doha Centre Analysis Paper, No. 8 (September 2013).

Gnesotto, Nicole and John Roper (eds), *Western Europe and the Gulf: A Study of West European Reactions to the Gulf War*, Brussels, Institute for Security Studies, Western European Union, 1992.

Gordon, Michael and Bernard Trainor, *The General's War: The Inside Story of the First Gulf War*, London, Atlantic Books, 1995.

Gordon, Philip H., 'Bush's Middle East Vision', *Survival*, 45:1 (Spring 2003).

Gugler, Philippe and Julien Chaisse, 'Sovereign Wealth Funds in the European Union: General Trust despite Concerns', Swiss National Centre of Competence in Research, working paper No. 2009/4 (January 2009).

Halliday, Fred, *The Middle East in International Relations: Power, Politics and Ideology*, Cambridge, Cambridge University Press, 2005.

Haykel, Bernard, Thomas Hegghammer and *Stéphane* Lacroix (eds), *Saudi Arabia in Transition: Insights on Social, Political, Economic and Religious Change*, Cambridge, Cambridge University Press, 2015.

Held, David and Coates Ulrichsen, Kristian (eds), *The Transformation of the Gulf: Politics, Economics and the Global Order*, London and New York, Routledge, 2011.

Herb, Michael', 'Emirs and Parliaments in the Gulf', *Journal of Democracy*, 13:4 (October 2002).

Herrmann, Richard K., 'The Middle East and the New World Order – Rethinking US Political Strategy after the Gulf War', *International Security*, 16:2 (1991).

Hertog, Steffen (ed.), *National Employment and Education in the GCC*, Berlin, Gerlach Press, 2012.

——, 'Arab Gulf States: An Assessment of Nationalisation Policies', Gulf Labor Markets and Migration (GLMM) research paper, 2014/1, Migration Policy Centre (2014).

Hiro, Dilip, *Desert Shield to Desert Storm: The Second Gulf War*, New York, HarperCollins, 1993.

Kaplan, Robert D., *The Arabists: The Romance of an American Elite*, New York, The Free Press, 1995.

Kechichian, Joseph A., 'The Gulf Cooperation Council: Search for Security', *Third World Quarterly*, 7:4 (October 1985).

Kelly, J. B., *Arabia, the Gulf & the West: A Critical View of the Arabs and Their Oil Policy*, New York, Basic Books, 1980.

Khalaf, Abd Al-Hadi, 'The Elusive Quest for Gulf Security', *Middle East Research and Information Project*, 148 (September–October 1987).

Khalifa, Ali Mohammed, *The United Arab Emirates: Unity in Fragmentation*, Boulder, CO, Westview Press, 1979.

Khomeini, Ruhollah, *Writings and Declarations of Imam Khomeini*, trans. and annotated Hamid Algar, Berkeley, CA, Mizan Press, 1981.

Kimmitt, Robert M., 'Public Footprints in Private Markets: Sovereign Wealth Funds and the World Economy', *Foreign Affairs*, 87:1 (January-February 2008).

Kinninmont, Jane, *Future Trends in the Gulf*, London, Chatham House, 2015.

Kissinger, Henry, *The White House Years*, Boston and Toronto, Little, Brown and Company, 1979.
——, *Years of Upheaval*, Boston and Toronto, Little, Brown and Company, 1982.
——, *Years of Renewal*, London, Phoenix Press, 1989.
Koch, Christian and David E. Long (eds), *Gulf Security in the Twenty-first Century*, London, I. B. Tauris, 1997.
Krauthammer, Charles, 'The Unipolar Moment', *Foreign Affairs*, 70:1 (1991).
Laiq, Jawid, 'The Gulf Cooperation Council: Royal Insurance against Pressures from Within and Without', *Economic and Political Weekly*, 21:35 (30 August 1986).
Legrenzi, Matteo, *The GCC and the International Relations of the Gulf: Diplomacy, Security and Economic Coordination in a Changing Middle East*, London and New York, I. B. Tauris, 2011.
Lynch, Marc, *The Arab Uprisings Explained: New Contentious Politics in the Middle East*, New York, Columbia University Press, 2014.
Mabon, Simon, *Saudi Arabia and Iran: Power and Rivalry in the Middle East*, Reading, I. B. Tauris, 2015.
Matthiesen, Toby, *Sectarian Gulf: Bahrain, Saudi Arabia, and the Arab Spring That Wasn't*, Stanford, Stanford University Press, 2013.
McNaugher, Thomas L., *Arms and Oil: US Military Strategy and the Persian Gulf*, Washington, DC, Brookings Institution, 1985.
Miller, Rory and Kun-Chin Lin, '"Lessons Learnt: Adapting to the Arab Spring": Chinese Economic Statecraft and the Quest for Stability in the Contemporary Middle East', History of British Intelligence and Security Research Project, London, Arts & Humanities Research Council (2012).
Molavi, Afshin, 'Dubai Rising', *Brown Journal of World Affairs*, XII:1 (Summer–Fall 2005).
Nakleh, Emile A., *The Gulf Cooperation Council: Policies, Problems and Prospects*, New York, Praeger, 1986.
National Commission on Terrorist Attacks, *The 9/11 Commission Report: Final Report of the National Commission on Terrorist Attacks upon the United States*, authorized edition, New York, W. W. Norton & Company, 2004.
Nonneman, Gerd (ed.), *Analyzing Middle East Foreign Policies and the Relationship with Europe*, London and New York, Routledge, 2005.
Onley, James, *The Arabian Frontier of the Raj: Merchants, Rulers and the British in the Nineteenth Century Gulf*, Oxford and New York, Oxford University Press, 2007.
Ottaway, David, 'The King and US: U.S.–Saudi Relations in the Wake of 9/11', *Foreign Affairs*, 88:3 (2009).
Panaspornprasit, Chookiat, *US–Kuwaiti Relations, 1961–1992*, London and New York, Routledge, 2005.
Petersen, Tore T., *The Decline of the Anglo-American Middle East 1961–1969: A Willing Retreat*, Portland, OR, Sussex Academic Press, 2006.
Peterson, J. E., 'Qatar and the World: Branding for a Micro-state', *Middle East Journal*, 60:4 (Autumn 2006).
Plekhanov, Sergey, *A Reformer on the Throne: Sultan Qaboos bin Said Al Said*, Cape Town, Trident Press, 2004.
Potter, Lawrence G. (ed.), *The Persian Gulf in Modern Times: People, Ports and History*, New York, Palgrave Macmillan, 2014.
Prados, Alfred B., 'Iraq: Post-war Challenges and U.S. Responses, 1991–1998', Congressional Research Service (CRS), Washington, DC, 31 March 1999.
Prodi, Romano and Alberto Clo, 'Europe', in *The Oil Crisis in Perspective*, *Daedalus*, 104:4 (1975).
Ramazani, R. K., *The Gulf Cooperation Council: Record and Analysis*, Charlottesville, University of Virginia Press, 1988.
Raphaeli, Nimrod and Bianca Gersten, 'Sovereign Wealth Funds: Investment Vehicles for the Persian Gulf Countries', *Middle East Quarterly*, 15:2 (Spring 2008).

Ridgeway, James, *The March to War: From Day One to the War's End and Beyond*, New York, Four Walls, Eight Windows, 1991.

Rieger, René, 'In Search of Stability: Saudi Arabia and the Arab Spring', GRM Papers, Gulf Research Centre (2014).

Robinson, Jeffrey, *Yamani: The Inside Story*, New York, Simon & Schuster, 1989.

Rouleau, Eric, 'Trouble in the Kingdom', *Foreign Affairs*, 81:4 (2002).

Saab, Maria and Joshua Haber, 'The Slow Pace of Female Empowerment in the Gulf', *Open Democracy*, 18 March 2014.

Salameh, Ghassan, 'Hangover in the Gulf', *Middle East Research and Information Project*, 139 (March–April 1986).

Sayigh, Yusif A., 'Arab Oil Policies: Self Interest versus International Responsibility', *Journal of Palestine Studies*, IV:3 (Spring 1975).

——, *The Economies of the Arab World: Development since 1945*, London, Taylor & Francis, 1978.

Scheuer, Michael, *Osama bin Laden*, Oxford, Oxford University Press, 2011.

Setser, Brad W. and Rachel Ziemba, 'Understanding the New Financial Superpower: The Management of the GCC Official Foreign Assets', New York, Council on Foreign Relations (December 2007).

——, 'GCC Sovereign Funds Reversal of Fortune', New York, Council on Foreign Relations Working Paper (January 2009).

Simpson, William, *The Prince: The Secret Story of the World's Most Intriguing Royal, Prince Bandar Bin Sultan*, New York, Regan, 2006.

Stork, Joe, 'The Middle East Arms Bazaar after the Gulf War', *Middle East Research and Information Project*, 197 (November–December 1995).

Tarzi, Amin, James Zogby, Leon Hadar and Jon Alterman, 'The United States in Middle Eastern Eyes: A Reliable Security Partner or a Problem to be Managed?', *Middle East Policy*, 17:4 (Winter 2010).

Telhami, Shibley and Fiona Hill, 'Does Saudi Arabia Still Matter?', *Foreign Affairs*, 81:6 (2002).

Tetreault, Mary Ann, 'Autonomy, Necessity, and the Small State: Ruling Kuwait in the Twentieth Century', *International Organization*, 45:4 (Autumn 1991).

Ulrichsen, Kristian Coates, 'Small States with a Big Role: Qatar and the United Arab Emirates in the Wake of the Arab Spring', No. 3, HH Sheikh Nasser Al-Mohammad Al-Sabah Publication Series, Durham University (October 2012).

——, *The Gulf States and the Rebalancing of Regional and Global Power*, James A. Baker III Institute for Public Policy, Rice University (2014).

——, *Insecure Gulf: The End of Certainty and the Transition to the Post-oil Era*, Oxford and New York, Oxford University Press, 2015.

——, *The Gulf States in International Political Economy*, London and New York, Palgrave Macmillan, 2016.

Victor, David G. and Linda Yueh, 'The New Energy Order: Managing Insecurities in the Twenty-first Century', *Foreign Affairs*, 89:1 (2010).

Wehrey, Frederic, *Sectarian Politics in the Gulf: From the Iraq War to the Arab Uprisings*, New York, Columbia University Press, 2014.

Weitsman, Patricia, *Waging War: Alliances, Coalitions, and Institutions of Interstate Violence*, Stanford, Stanford University Press, 2013.

Weston, Mark, *Prophets and Princes: Saudi Arabia from Muhammed to the Present*, New York, John Wiley & Sons Inc., 2008.

Williams, Maurice J., 'The Aid Programs of the OPEC Countries', *Foreign Affairs*, 54:2 (1975–1976).

Wilson, Rodney, 'The Development of Islamic Finance in the GCC', working paper, Kuwait Programme on Development, Governance and Globalisation in the Gulf States, Centre for the Study of Global Governance, LSE (May 2009).

Winckler, Onn, 'Can the GCC Weather the Economic Meltdown?', *Middle East Quarterly*, 17:3 (Summer 2010).

Yamani, Ahmed Zaki, 'Oil: Towards a New Producer–Consumer Relationship', *World Today*, 30:11 (November 1974).

Yergin, Daniel, *The Prize: The Epic Quest for Oil, Money and Power*, London and New York, Simon & Schuster, 1991.

Yodfat, Aryeh Y. *The Soviet Union and the Arabian Peninsula: Soviet Policy towards the Persian Gulf and Arabia*, New York, St Martin's Press, 1983.

Zahlan, Rosemary Said, *The Origins of the United Arab Emirates: A Political and Social History of the Trucial States*, London, Macmillan, 1978.

——, *The Making of the Modern Gulf States: Kuwait, Bahrain, Qatar, United Arab Emirates and Oman*, Reading, Ithaca Press, 1989.

ILLUSTRATION CREDITS

All pictures are licensed from Alamy, with credits to the following copyright holders:

1. Ahmad Faizal Yahya. 2. World History Archive. 3. Keystone Pictures USA. 4. Keystone Pictures USA. 5. Art Directors & TRIP. 6. Keystone Pictures USA. 7. Richard Ellis. 8. Jason Moore. 9. DoD Photo. 10. DoD Photo. 11. Al-Jazeera/Zuma Press, Inc. 12. Boitano Photography. 13. Mark Reinstein. 14. National Geographic Creative. 15. Gavin Hellier. 16. Rainer Jensen/dpa picture alliance archive. 17. Justin Kase zninez. 18. Hussain Albahrani/Pacific Press. 19. Barry Iverson. 20. dpa picture alliance. 21. DoD photo by Senior Master Sgt. Adrian Cadiz (released)/military first collection. 22. Planetpix. 23. Egyptian Presidency Handout Photo/Barry Iverson/Pool Photo. 24. iDubai. 25. Rolf Richardson.

INDEX